Key Elements of Social Theory Revolutionized by Marx

Studies in Critical Social Sciences Book Series

Haymarket Books is proud to be working with Brill Academic Publishers (www.brill.nl) to republish the *Studies in Critical Social Sciences* book series in paperback editions. This peer-reviewed book series offers insights into our current reality by exploring the content and consequences of power relationships under capitalism, and by considering the spaces of opposition and resistance to these changes that have been defining our new age. Our full catalog of *SCSS* volumes can be viewed at https://www.haymarketbooks.org/series_collections/4-studies-in-critical-social-sciences.

Series Editor
David Fasenfest (Wayne State University)

Editorial Board
Eduardo Bonilla-Silva (Duke University)
Chris Chase-Dunn (University of California–Riverside)
William Carroll (University of Victoria)
Raewyn Connell (University of Sydney)
Kimberlé W. Crenshaw (University of California–LA and Columbia University)
Heidi Gottfried (Wayne State University)
Karin Gottschall (University of Bremen)
Alfredo Saad Filho (King's College London)
Chizuko Ueno (University of Tokyo)
Sylvia Walby (Lancaster University)
Raju Das (York University)

Key Elements of Social Theory Revolutionized by Marx

Paul Zarembka

Haymarket Books
Chicago, IL

First published in 2020 by Brill Academic Publishers, The Netherlands
© 2020 Koninklijke Brill NV, Leiden, The Netherlands

Published in paperback in 2021 by
Haymarket Books
P.O. Box 180165
Chicago, IL 60618
773-583-7884
www.haymarketbooks.org

ISBN: 978-1-64259-610-6

Distributed to the trade in the US through Consortium Book Sales and Distribution (www.cbsd.com) and internationally through Ingram Publisher Services International (www.ingramcontent.com).

This book was published with the generous support of Lannan Foundation and Wallace Action Fund.

Special discounts are available for bulk purchases by organizations and institutions. Please call 773-583-7884 or email info@haymarketbooks.org for more information.

Cover design by Jamie Kerry and Ragina Johnson.

Printed in the United States.

10 9 8 7 6 5 4 3 2 1

Library of Congress Cataloging-in-Publication data is available.

To Nina and Beata, and in memory of my parents, with love

Contents

List of Tables XII
Abbreviations XIII
Note on the Citing of *Capital, Volume I* XIV

Introduction 1

PART 1
The Atrophy of Philosophy

1 The Problem of Hegel 9
   1 Hegel and *Capital, Volume I*, 1st German Edition 10
   2 2nd German and French Editions of *Volume I* 11
   3 Sieber on Marx and Criticizing His Use of Hegel; Marx's Reaction 13
      3.1 *Sieber's 1871 Book* 13
      3.2 *Sieber, Mikhaylovsky and Marx, 1874–1877* 14
      3.3 *1881: Marx's Comment on Sieber and Reply to Zasulich* 16
   4 After Marx's 1883 Death, Sieber's Decline and Plekhanov's Influence 18
   5 Lenin's Evolution toward Dialectical Materialism 21
   6 Conclusion: Moving Forward 23

PART 2
Key Elements of Political Economy

2 Marx's Evolution and Revolution with the Concept of Value: Abstract Labor and Labor Power 27
   1 *Poverty of Philosophy* (1847): Economic Concepts Historically Conditioned 28
   2 *Contribution* (1859): Abstract Labor as the Substance of Value 29
   3 *Capital, Volume I* (1867): Labor Power 33
   4 Other Additions in *Volume I* 39
      4.1 *Socially Necessary Labor Time* 39
      4.2 *Form of Value* 39
      4.3 *Labor Time Embodied in Constant Capital* 43
   5 Marx's Retrospective on Value 44

3 Not Engels, but Marx's Final Edition of *Capital, Volume I* (1882) 47
  1 Marx's Parts I–VI 49
  2 The Structural Divisions Desired by Marx, Contrasted to Engels' Editions 52
  3 Marx's Parts VII and VIII (1882) Compared with Engels' 3rd German Edition (1883) 55

4 Text: "The General Law of Capitalist Accumulation", Sections 1–4, as Desired by Marx (1882) 64
  1 Section 1: the Increased Demand for Labour-Power that Accompanies Accumulation, the Composition of Capital Remaining the Same 65
  2 Section 2: Changes in the Composition of Capital with the Progress of Accumulation and Relative Diminution of that Part of Capital that is Exchanged against Labor Power 65
  3 Section 3: Progressive Production of a Relative Surplus-Population or Industrial Reserve Army 73
  4 Section 4: Different Forms of the Relative Surplus-Population. The General Law of Capitalist Accumulation 83
  5 Section 5: Illustrations of the General Law of Capitalist Accumulation 84

5 Marx on Primitive Accumulation Contrasted to Engels' Handling of the Topic 85
  1 Why, for Marx, Primitive Accumulation became a New Part VIII 86
  2 Engels' Disparate Handling of the English (1887) and 4th German (1890) Editions of *Volume I*; Danielson's 2nd Russian edition (1898) 89
  3 Engels' Continuing Failure to Recognize Marx's Advances 95
  4 Postscript: Marx's Primitive Accumulation Conflated with Modern Dispossessions/Enclosures 98

6 Marxist Accumulation of Capital? 102
  1 Accumulation of Capital in *Capital, Volume I* 108
  2 Schemes of Reproduction in *Capital, Volume II* 113
  3 Ambiguity 114
  4 "Marxist Accumulation of Capital" 117
  5 An Algebraic Model of Marxist Accumulation with Fixed Constant Capital Included 119

7   Three Troubling Issues   124
    1   Conundrum: Value under Marxist Accumulation of Capital   124
    2   Sieber's Query of Value in Marx   128
    3   Prejudices of Marx and Engels   130

8   The Composition of Capital Clarified Theoretically, Empirically   133
    1   Materialized Composition of Capital and the Rate of Profit   135
    2   Luxemburg's Recognition of the Materialized Composition, Considering It to be Rising   140
    3   Marx's and Engels' Estimations for Cotton Spinning   141
    4   Estimates of the Composition of Capital, Post-World War II   145
    5   Updated Estimation for the United States   151
        5.1   *Introduction by Shaikh of a Revised Methodology for Capital Stock Measurement*   153
        5.2   *Quality Adjustment in Capital Stock Measurement*   157
        5.3   *Paitaridis and Tsoulfidis' Implementation of Shaikh's Methodology*   160
        5.4   *Sector Estimates*   161
    6   Limitations of the Current Discussion   164

9   Luxemburg's *Accumulation of Capital* and Consideration of the Evidence   165
    1   The Issue Luxemburg Addressed   167
    2   Luxemburg's Critique of Marx on Accumulation and Her Response to Bauer's Criticism   170
        2.1   *Bauer's Critique and Luxemburg's Reply*   177
    3   Criticism of Luxemburg's *Accumulation* after her Death: Bukharin to Shaikh   182
    4   Luxemburg Gets Assists from Robinson and Kowalik   189
    5   Historical Accumulation and Fraction of Surplus Value Required   191

PART 3
Considering Nationalism and State Machiavellianism

10 Luxemburg's "The National Question and Antonomy" and Lenin's Criticism   197
    by Narihiko Ito
    1   The Features of Luxemburg's Theory on the National Question   198

	2	The Polish Question and Marx and Engels 201
	3	Luxemburg's "The National Question and Autonomy" 203
		3.1 *Negation of the Right of National Self-determination* 203
		3.2 *Abolition of the Nation-State* 205
		3.3 *Centralization or Local Autonomy* 207
		3.4 *Conditions of "National Autonomy"* 210
		3.5 *The Domain of "Polish Autonomy"* 212
		3.6 *Is "The National Question and Autonomy" an Unfinished Work?* 215
	4	Criticism and Evaluation of "The National Question and Autonomy" 216
		4.1 *Lenin's Criticism* 216
		4.2 *Nation-State vs. Autonomy* 218
		4.3 *Theoretical Differences between Lenin and Luxemburg and Historical Reality* 221
		4.4 *Luxemburg's Theory on the National Question* 223
	5	Epilogue 225
11	**Marxism, Machiavellianism, and Conspiracy Theory** 226	
	1	Conspiracies and Marxist Theory of the Nation State 227
	2	Marx on Louis Bonaparte's Conspiratorial Coup 228
	3	Were Wars Initiated by Provocations, Prevarications, or False-Flags? Some Background 231
		3.1 *"Spotty Lincoln" and the Mexican-American War* 231
		3.2 *The Explosion of the USS Maine and the Spanish-American War* 232
		3.3 *Assassination of Archduke Ferdinand* 233
		3.4 *Mukden or Manchurian Incident* 233
		3.5 *Reichstag Burning and the Gleiwitz Incident* 233
		3.6 *The Second Gulf of Tonkin Incident before Escalation in Vietnam* 236
	4	"Conspiracy Theory" Becomes a Weapon of the State after the Assassination of John F. Kennedy 236
	5	Dismissing a Jury Trial Conviction of State Conspiracy in the Assassination of Martin Luther King, Jr. 238
	6	Utilization of the "Conspiracy Theory" Weapon: the World Trade Center and the Pentagon in 2001 240
		6.1 *Alleged Muslim Hijackers* 241
		6.2 *Falling Skyscrapers* 242
		6.3 *The Pentagon* 243

6.4 *Calls from Planes?* 243
  6.5 *Insider Trading* 244
  6.6 *September 11th and Conspiracy Theory* 245
  6.7 *Conclusion* 245

References 247
Index 265

Tables

1. Growth rates of output values and labor hours for alternative α, s/ν, and β   123
2. Methodologies used for estimates of constant capital   147
3. Estimates of C/v and of materialized composition of capital, $C/(v+s)$: productive sectors in the United States   148
4. Cost ratios   150
5. Measures of materialized compositions of capital, with Shaikh's data   155
6. Sector estimates of materialized composition of capital in U.S., $C/(v+s)$ 162

Abbreviations

c.w.   Karl Marx and Frederick Engels, *Collected Works* (50 volumes) London: Lawrence & Wishart, 1975–2005.

MEGA²   Karl Marx and Frederick Engels, *Gesamtausgabe*, Berlin: Dietz/Akademie Verlag, 1975-.

Note on the Citing of *Capital, Volume I*

In his lifetime, Marx's work had two German editions and one French edition, and thereafter edited by Engels, there were two more German editions and one English edition. I use the 1867 date of the first edition in citations, although I am utilizing the English edition as later amended to include changes by Engels for his 4th German edition. The cited version was published by Lawrence and Wishart, as indicated. I prefer this English edition over the Penguin translation by Ben Fowkes as it was translated and edited by people who knew Marx personally and remains within the historical record that plays an important role in my Chapters 3 though 5.

I use this occasion to note my belief that the Appendix to the Fowkes' edition, "Results of the Immediate Process of Production" should have been published separately from *Volume I*, since Marx did not include it and including can be misinterpreted. Formal and real subsumption of labor to capital, for example, is included therein, but Marx had deleted all references to those concepts by the time of his French edition (see p. 51 below).

Introduction

Karl Marx's legacy is so broad that different people are able to be attracted to the aspects most useful to them, not only scholars but, more importantly, working people. I am drawn especially to his concept of "labor power" which took Marx a couple of decades to produce within his theory. It is as applicable today as when Marx came to clearly formulate it two years before his decisive book *Capital, Volume 1*, first published in 1867 in German. I believe it deserves an initial introduction given its significance.

For capitalist enterprises in Brazil, China, Egypt, India, Mexico, Russia, South Africa, Switzerland, United States or anywhere, labor power reflects the reality that workers sell their labor hours to capitalists and they are told what to do without any democratic input from them. Workers do not need to care what they produce: they need the money. Capitalists do not care either: they want profit. Workers only receive as compensation the equivalent, in some currency, of the laboring time needed to produce somewhere in the world the commodities they can get for whatever subsistence that they can get. The remainder in laboring hours that the capitalist keeps is "surplus value", the fundamental concept for Marx that Frederick Engels assessed as important as the discovery of oxygen by Lavoisier.

The actual lives of people around the world differ greatly. Some do better, some do worse, and a fraction may find some satisfaction in their work. But almost all products we consume anywhere, within our deep capitalism, have been produced by workers who are merely hired hands. Marx's work mentions workers being thereby "alienated", and this has been chosen by some for an emphasis although it leaves open the question of alienation from "what" and, to me, is less satisfactory than focusing upon buying and selling of "labor power". Marx also develops concepts to explain how capitalists are able to appropriate ever more surplus value. He explains the motivation for technology changes experienced much more in capitalism than in prior societies. He describes the forces around the accumulation of capital, and the division of surplus value into industrial profits, rent and interest. He provides analyses for financial expansion. He even addresses environmental issues appropriate to his time so that we can find those insights useful today. He analyzed the U.S. Civil War as it was developing, albeit missing interface with the Indigenous (Nelson, 2020).

Marx describes what workers actually did when they had power in Paris in 1871. But he also describes the ferocity of the subsequent opposition by capitalists, namely, a bloodbath. He would not be surprised at all by the Chilean coup in 1973 nor the U.S. hostility to the Chinese or Cuban revolutions. He would not be surprised that May Day with origins in the 1886 event in Haymarket, Chicago, is not celebrated by the government of its country of origin.

Still, Marx should be treated at starting point of social theory, not in any way an end. In any case, and this is important, great intellectuals can be misused. They can be objects of misuse precisely because of their penetrating insights. When Marx exposes capitalism in the raw for workers, some can refer to his insights for their own purposes, purposes that have nothing do with the emancipation of workers, even as they might so suggest. This problem is not a simple one and to better address it we have to understand more correctly what motivated him and what he stood for at its deepest level.

This book focuses attention on three dimensions of Marx's evolving work, the relations to philosophy, to the class nature of the economy, and to some political factors that deserve critical attention. Part 1, "The Atrophy of Philosophy", argues that whatever Marx's attraction to Hegel earlier in life, it diminished to the point that we should not be focusing on Hegel or his philosophy if we want to stay with the most mature of Marx's work. Actually, it difficult to find anything about Hegel in Marx after 1868, i.e., the last decade and a half of his life, but the issue cannot be so simply dispatched.

Part 2, "Key Elements of Political Economy" is the most intensely addressed in this book, both for the subject matters and the number of chapters. I would think that some familiarity with Marx's *Capital* will be needed to grasp many of the issues at stake. The first issue is the sharp distinction in Marx between labor and "labor power", the new concept. As I said, his understanding was crystalized only a couple of years before *Volume I* and came about because the concept of labor (a single word by itself) in classical political economy did not capture the capitalist social relations of production. A lot of water went under the bridge before he crossed over to this concept of "labor power", and the chapter reports the process by which Marx came to it, under the rubric of value.

Chapters 3, 4 and 5 address the fact the Engels' editions of *Capital* failed to follow Marx's instructions left when Marx struggled with his health and succumbed. The failure focused on the part of *Volume I* on accumulation of capital including primitive accumulation. It comprises the fact that Marx wanted primitive accumulation as a distinct part of his work, rather than being integrated with accumulation of capital proper. Engels' failure meant that non-English readers are almost always reading a book of seven "Parts", with text suggesting a broader sweep of history than Marx had had in his French edition and had wanted for his 3rd German edition. Furthermore, Marx's discussion of accumulation of capital proper had major changes focusing around issues of employment of workers that Engels simply left the same as in the 2nd German edition. I argue that Marx's research on Russia were very important in his own evolving understandings, while Engels had no interest in even trying to appreciate what Marx might be learning from it. Via the Bolshevik Revolution of 1917, an interpretation of Marx's social theory became deeply embedded within the dialogue about Marxist theory that might have been quite different if Engels had followed instructions precisely.

Marx's discussion of accumulation of capital proper is fairly clear, but not without ambiguities. It is far too easy to slide into a thought that he meant accumulation of more means of production, as bourgeois economics promotes that conception. But if we think of *capital* as anything close to the idea of more means of production, we promote an annoyance of class relations that are decisively important in everything Marx wanted us to understand. Unlike the concept of "labor power" against the concept of "labor", Marx did not introduce a new concept against "accumulation of capital". I argue in Chapter 6 that a reformulation is embedded in his work and propose the concept "Marxist accumulation of capital" as a distinction from bourgeois economics. As an exercise, I offer how Marx's schemes of reproduction could be correspondingly modified and the implication for analyzing the development of capitalism.

Chapter 7 addresses three troubling issues. The first is that Marx's "value" had been defined in a context of a fully developed capitalist formation. However, Marxist accumulation of capital is not consistent with such a context in a longer historical time of drawing in more workers to produce more value and surplus value. It thus leaves us with an outstanding theoretical question. Second, Nikolai Sieber's work was very much respected by Marx, but he argued that value needed to focus not only upon production but also consumption. Marx did not indicate objection to such consideration: perhaps he thought it to be a non-starter, but we do not know. Given Marx's respect of Sieber, I feel more consideration needs to be given to Sieber's work. A third issue that should not be avoided is that Marx and Engels had prejudices. This needs to be accepted so I provide some introduction to this issue.

Chapter 8 on the composition of capital is the most technical. Marx brought it up to the fore in his French edition and Engels so included in his editions after Marx's death and it needs to be dealt with. The chapter argues that Marxist political economy needs to get away from using the phrase "organic composition of capital" and supports using instead the "materialized composition of capital" for empirical work. It surveys empirical work by Marx and by Engels using this concept and addresses evidence for the United States using the concept. There are many outstanding issues, however, and so the chapter hopes to advance consideration of many factors behind such research, without pretending to offer something attempting to be definitive.

Luxemburg's *Accumulation of Capital* truly deserves every respect. This work of hers has faced a lot of criticisms. There is something wrong thereby. I restate my understanding of what she said was a deficiency in Marx, a critique within the highest respect of Marx. It seemed to be too much for others to take. I survey some of the opposition to Luxemburg's work and a few who did seem to understand the main issue. However, I conclude the chapter with a brief empirical exercise leading to the question whether accumulation of capital has not been overestimated as the main use of surplus value. If so, it would seem to have major implications for the development of political economy.

Addressing social theory arising from Marx would not be complete without some consideration of the political dimension. Part 3, "Considering Nationalism and State Machiavellianism" addresses nationalism and state manipulation of society for achieving an end. It is widely known that within Marxism that Lenin and Luxemburg had very different views on the national question. In fact, it is rather impossible to avoid their controversy, as it is so well known, at least in popular renditions of their respective positions. In 2010 the *Research in Political Economy* published Narihiko Ito's deep discussion of the controversy in a long article. Never have I seen a more careful work on it than this one and it needs exposure. Also, that version was too long for most readers and had some errors and syntax issues (Ito, since deceased, was not fluent in English and I had tried to help him as the volume's editor). This chapter is a condensed and corrected version. Luxemburg was promoting "national autonomy", rather than "the right of national-state for self-determination", because national cultures deserved every respect (as she respected Polish culture) while the state is, after all, a repressive apparatus. Yet she was writing in a context mostly concerned with Poland, and not making an overall statement. Lenin did not react at the time she was writing, a time when their personal relationship was decent, but rather four years later when they had sharp differences. Ito's chapter also includes the background on this question in Marx and Engels.

I have been surprised how many Marxists do not wish to discuss anything that would be a conspiracy by the state. Of course, it is a difficult topic precisely because it would be below the surface of society. But conspiracy does happen and a 1999 trial and conviction in the United States for state conspiracy in the murder of Martin Luther King, Jr., should be enough to eliminate objection to such considerations. Yet it has not had that effect. Rather it is not cited at all, perhaps even unknown to too many. I myself do not fully understand the hesitation. In any case, I attempt in the last chapter "Marxism, Machiavellianism, and Conspiracy Theory" to help sustain serious consideration of such issues, having myself been involved considerably with research into September 11th in the United States.

•••

Perhaps the single most important message from Marx is that another world other than capitalism is possible and absolutely necessary. Possible, because we have had other worlds before. And necessary, as we have no choice but for another and better world, given the truth about the disastrous implications of capitalism!

This book is focused on evolving issues in Marx's revolution in social theory, both in his lifetime and, where related, to issues after his 1883 death. I am not at all claiming these as the only issues and am well aware of profound work by others on such issues as gender, race, ethnicity, and sexual orientations, and divisions within the working classes and divisions internationally. I am also aware of the absence of addressing the issues of the environment, organizing for socialism, and consideration of principles and practices of socialism.

It is not good enough to say that Marx wanted a society free of exploiting classes. The very next question would be how to get there. In fact, "how" is perhaps far more important and difficult. We must respect people, but we also must respect the power of those against the people, and that power is much greater now than in Marx's time. As an illustration, the U.S. government used nuclear weapons openly, and proudly, twice for mass extermination.[1] If push comes to shove – and that was not even the case for Hiroshima and Nagasaki – Marx's understanding would tell us that there are no limits. I repeat: no limits. Marx is giving us a message. And we are obligated to take account of it if we are to be really for the people.

---

1 As a matter of record and of warning, during the Cuban missile crisis when out of communication for several days while deep in an Atlantic submarine, one individual Vice Admiral Vasily Arkhipov refused to authorize a nuclear missile launch against the United States that two other officers had authorized.

PART 1

The Atrophy of Philosophy

∴

CHAPTER 1

The Problem of Hegel

No one contests the early influence of Hegel on Marx.[1] Yet, some Marxists believe Hegel remained important for Marx himself even as his thinking matured. And, at a popular level, certain renderings use a simplistic caricature of Hegel, such as the thesis-antithesis-synthesis formulary, and take that to be Marx's as well, and then attack Marx through the caricature. Meanwhile, the question is infrequently posed whether Hegel's influence persisted for Marx and if, as his work deepened, he defended the necessity of Hegel's philosophy for his political economy. We shall demonstrate, with considerable evidence from Marx himself, the declining need for Hegelian philosophy in Marx's evolving understanding of political economy.

One piece of evidence we shall develop is Marx's appreciation of a book by Nikolai Sieber published in 1871, an appreciation well-known as a simple fact, while not understanding that Sieber expressed a clear aversion to Hegel. Actually, it is nothing less than astonishing that Sieber's discussion of Marx had not appeared in any translation until 2001, i.e., 130 years after the fact. The long-term absence of a translation appears to be a political decision with deep roots in the intellectual history of Marxism, thus a history of a particular suppression, perhaps partly unconscious. The early history intertwines with major issues in Marxism in the late 19th and early 20th century, leading in this chapter to inclusion of discussion of Plekhanov, Lenin, and Luxemburg.

Louis Althusser (1969a, p. 90) argued that Marx was driven "irresistibly to the *radical* abandonment of every shade of Hegelian influence" (emphasis in original). *Capital*, says Althusser, still included traces of Hegelian influence – in his vocabulary of use-value and value while describing two entirely different things, in a reference to "negation of the negation", and in the theory of fetishism. Only in 1875 in his *Critique of the Gotha Program* and thereafter is Marx's intellectual process regarding Hegel completed. Althusser has been sharply criticized by some, even for Stalinism. We will not pursue Althusser's argumentation here.

James White (1996) takes a quite different approach by very carefully examining intellectual history. I am referring to his *Karl Marx and the Intellectual Origins of Dialectical Materialism*. White addresses wide-ranging German and Russian sources in circumstances for which "it is essential to verify everything, wherever possible, with first-hand materials" (p. 19). In my opinion, White's

---

[1] This chapter is a more concise version of Zarembka (2014).

book is too little known and appreciated. The present author reviewed it positively (Zarembka, 2001), responding to a negative review by Sean Sayer. The journal involved, namely *Historical Materialism*, gave Sayer space to rebut my support of White's work, but no space was provided to White as the book's author, even after a request.

I proceed to survey the development of Marx's political economy from 1867 onward in order to reach a conclusion, and then turn to the early history after Marx's death.

1 Hegel and *Capital, Volume I*, 1st German Edition

The first edition of Marx's *Capital, Volume I* was of course published in 1867, itself a result of a long, intense project. Although it can be argued that it was less influenced by Hegel than earlier work, this first edition had certain Hegelian formulations, and there were considerable references to Hegel, particularly in the first part. As described by White (1996, pp. 20–23), that edition contained references to major philosophical concepts flowing from Kant and Hegel (often even italicized), concepts such as universal and particular. A draft outline written by Marx a decade earlier for his overall project, published in the 20th century in the *Grundrisse*, was even organized around the concepts of the universal and the particular, as well as of individuality (White, p. 161).

During proofs for the first edition of *Capital*, Marx was cautioned about the difficulty of use of Hegelian language and he responded by including a simplification in an Appendix on the "value form". Still, when published, Marx received criticisms for Hegelianism. Perhaps as a defensive reaction to these criticisms, Marx mentioned in a letter to Joseph Dietzgen in May, 1868, that he wanted to write on dialectics. This has been erroneously reported by some as Marx's intention eight years later (1876), i.e., to help to sustain an interpretation of Marx's continuity with Hegel past completion of his French edition.[2] In 1868, Marx also added a note concerning Hegel into his drafting of *Volume II* which has also been both mistranslated and misdated.[3] It seems that in 1868

---

2   K. Marx and F. Engel's, *Sochineniia Vol. 32*, Politizdat, Moscow, 1964, p. 456. In 1876 Dietzgen was to report this letter of Marx, leading some to say it had been written that year. Hall (2003, p. 114) cites Marx's letter using that year, in turn citing page 61 of Sidney Hook's *From Hegel to Marx* who had erroneously given 1876 as the year of the letter.

3   When E.E. Dühring's review commented critically on the Hegelian language of the first edition, Marx added a footnote to his 1868 draft of *Volume II* criticizing that review for missing the point of his book (MEGA², II/11, p. 32, fn. 10). Claiming Marx as a devotee of Hegel, Dunayevskaya (1982, p. 149) was to provide an English rendition of Marx by following Rubel's

Marx initially wanted to explain himself, a desire that was not to be implemented and likely for reasons that I am developing.

In 1868 Marx moved away from the British context that had underlain *Capital* and moved toward a study of Germany and then Russia. For Germany Marx read Georg Maurer's works, writing to Engels that his books are "extraordinarily important". From Maurer Marx learned that communal organization in agriculture had been important in early Germanic history and even that aspects persisted. Marx came to the view that force was needed to destroy it (White, pp. 206–207). Thus, for Marx, the British case was becoming ... only the British case, rather than some kind of universal. His turning shortly thereafter toward Russia, including learning its language and history, only reinforced this intellectual development. These researches of Marx were significant background as Marx corrected and began publishing, in serial, the first French edition, and the second German edition, of *Capital*.

2   2nd German and French Editions of *Volume I*

The French edition prepared under Marx's direct supervision was published in serial form starting from March 18, 1872 until April 28, 1875. Many of the changes from the 1st German, but not all, were concomitant with changes in the 1872 2nd German edition; indeed, Marx's "Afterword" to the French edition describes the relation: "Having once undertaken this work of revision [of the French translation in draft], I was led to apply it also to the basic original text (the second German edition)...". However, the full German 2nd edition came out well before the last parts of the French, giving Marx time to make further changes for those.

Besides White (1996), there seems to be too little consideration for the changes made by Marx. White himself argues that Marx ran into a theoretical problem when relying upon Hegel as a basis for understanding of historical development and so had Hegelian language removed and fifteen references to Hegel in the first edition halved in later editions. Thus, the changes made by Marx were now driven rather by his increasing depth of research. Abandoning Hegelian concepts,

---

1968 mistranslation into French of Marx's German: Hegel as Marx's "lehrer" ("teacher") became Marx as a "disciple" of Hegel; Dühring's description of Marx's relation to Hegel as "treue anhänglichkeit" ("faithful adherent") became a "zealous devotion". Hudis (2012, p. 5, fn. 7) has this portion of Dunayevskaya's wording, even as he cites the German. He further claims the year of Marx's drafted note for *Volume II* to be 1875, not the actual 1868.

Marx never employed the terms Universality, Particularity or Individuality again in his writings, and henceforth he turned his attention increasingly to the study of agrarian communities, especially those in Russia. ... In this edition [the 2nd German], the first chapter was substantially altered in such a way as to reduce drastically the occurrence of philosophical terminology and render what remained inessential to the argument. (White, p. 207)

For the editions of *Capital* after the 1st German, the prior appendix on the "value form" was brought up to replace the prior first chapter and was also rewritten. An important change in the serialized French edition as I discuss in Chapters 3 and 5 here was the elimination by Marx of the reference to "classic form" – which suggests universality – in discussing primitive accumulation in Part VIII, and in substituting language referring only to Western Europe. Unfortunately, Engels failed to incorporate this important change in the third and fourth German editions, even as other changes from the French were often included. Anderson (1983, pp. 76–77) sees this failure by Engels as "perhaps most important of all", and it persists in all modern translations using Engels' 4th edition (to the best of my knowledge). White concludes that

> Marx rewrote several sections and took the opportunity to bring to a logical conclusion the changes he had made in the second German edition. Thus, in the French version any trace which remained of philosophical vocabulary performed a purely stylistic function.... The second German edition and the French translation of *Capital Volume I* continued a process that had begun in the preparation of the first edition, that of eliminating the philosophical structure which had been built up in earlier drafts. (White, 1996, pp. 208, and 209–210)

A Russian translation of Marx's *Volume I* appeared in 1872 based upon the first German edition with its Hegelian philosophical language. This edition was the first non-German full edition of *Capital*, was quite popular, and set the stage for decades of Russians who wished to read *Capital*. Not until 1898 did the next Russian language translation based on a later edition appear (mentioned in Resis, 1970, p. 223). Thus, we know what was actually being read in Russia when Vera Zasulich (in Shanin, 1983, p. 98) wrote Marx in early 1881,

> You are not unaware that your *Capital* enjoys great popularity in Russia. Although the edition has been confiscated, the few remaining copies are

read and re-read by the mass of more or less educated in our country; serious men are studying it.

The importance of the 1st edition, the 1867 edition of *Capital* being the basis for the Russian translation will become apparent below.

3 Sieber on Marx and Criticizing His Use of Hegel; Marx's Reaction

3.1 Sieber's 1871 Book

In 1871 Nikolai Sieber in Kiev published in Russian his Master's dissertation entitled *David Ricardo's Theory of Value and Capital in Connection with the Latest Contributions and Interpretations*. He discussed Marx extensively, particularly Marx's early chapters with their more Hegelian language, based of course upon consideration of Marx's 1st edition of *Capital*. In Russia, Sieber's work was the first introduction to Marx's *Capital* and will have considerable importance.

While noting "the peculiar language and the quite laconic manner of expression" in Marx's *Volume 1*, Sieber wrote that "as far as the *theory* itself is concerned, Marx's method is the deductive method of the whole English school, and both its faults and its merits are those shared by the best of the theoretical economists" (Sieber, 2001, p. 30, emphasis in original). Marx had been interested enough in Russia to proceed to learn its language in 1870. He used that knowledge to good effect in reading Sieber's book in December 1872–January 1873, a timing that is *after* the beginning of the serial publication of the French edition and *after* the completed second German edition was ready. Marx's "Afterword" to the 2nd German edition, dated January 24, 1873, includes this passage about Sieber's work:

> As early as 1871, N. Sieber, Professor of Political Economy in the University of Kiev, in his work *David Ricardo's Theory of Value and of Capital*, referred to my theory of value, of money and of capital, as in its fundamentals a necessary sequel to the teaching of Smith and Ricardo. That which astonishes the Western European in the reading of this excellent work, is the author's consistent and firm grasp of the purely theoretical position.

Even though Sieber focused upon describing Marx's Part 1 on commodities with its Hegelian use of language and exhibited no support for Hegel nor for those philosophical concepts included in the first edition, Marx offered no objection whatsoever to its absence. Indeed, Sieber's book is a support for comprehending that Marx felt he could be understood quite well *without Hegelian language*. This fits with Marx's own changes in the 2nd edition. Still, Marx did affirm in this same "Afterword" that he had a dialectical method adequately described in an 1872 article in the *European Messenger,* published in St. Petersburg. He translated the description and noted that his method was the direct opposite of Hegel's. He clarified his position by saying that his 1st edition of *Capital* in the chapter on value had "coquetted with the modes of expression peculiar to [Hegel]".[4]

3.2   *Sieber, Mikhaylovsky and Marx, 1874–1877*

In 1874 Sieber published in the Russian journal *Znanie* an article on "Marx's Economic Theory". Referring to Marx's reception in Russia upon reading in translation of the 1st German edition, Sieber reported that some

> are put off by the unaccustomed complexity of the subject and the ponderous argumentation encased in the impenetrable armor of Hegelian contradictions.... In order to render Marx's most important theoretical tenets ... more understandable for the Russian public, we are taking on ourselves the task of writing some essays.... The objectives will be: (1) to explain Marx's significance as an original economist; (2) to present his theories of value, money, and capital in a form freed from metaphysical subtleties, so that they will no longer cause the reader difficulty. (Sieber, 1874, pp. 156–157)

Sieber's desire to reformulate Marx without Hegel is, therefore, absolutely clear.

Sieber's critique of Marx's theory is also not trivial. After expositing on Marx's work for ten pages, Sieber writes,

---

4 Appropriate for mentioning here, Carchedi (2010) offers an original view of dialectics, arguing his own as a crystallization of Marx's and not obtainable when reading Marx through a Hegelian lens. He offers his interpretation as the deeper meaning of Marx's passages we have just discussed. Hegel's universality, particularity, and individuality do not appear in Carchedi's argumentation.

If formal logic were to be the alternative, Carchedi offers a challenge when he writes that "acceptance of formal logic as *the* method of social analysis excludes the analysis of social change. The banning of dialectics cannot but result in a static and thus conservative view". (p. 42, emphasis in original). Formal logic, for him, does retain importance as an auxiliary method, but not as primary (p. 43).

> Hitherto we have agreed completely with Marx; but here, or rather, somewhat further on, we shall in part disagree with him, and not so much on the essence of the matter, as on the form, the methods and approaches by which he conducts his investigations. First of all we would inquire of Marx why he has to begin his study of capital with the examination of the most complex forms of human economy – which capitalist production is – and moreover with the abstractions of value and utility, rather than with the real relations, which underlie these abstractions, than with the simpler forms or the forms of all-human economy?... Moreover, the entire corpus of Marx's investigations clearly shows that real relations, in his opinion, precede abstract ones, and act as the root and the raison d'être of the latter. But in the given case, he leaves reality aside, and although he returns to it later, the reader nevertheless is unable to free himself from the idea that for Marx it is the abstractions of use-value and exchange-value, and not the phenomena, of which they are more or less successful labels that are the real point.... In any event, the investigation of real relations ought to have *preceded* the analysis of abstractions, and not *followed* it. (pp. 164–165)

Sieber used no Hegelian language in his exposition of Marx's value theory and is somewhat critical of the approach Marx makes to his subject matter. And Sieber notes that, "Marx himself in the aforementioned postscript to the second edition of *Capital* rebuts the accusation that he has made use of the Hegelian method" (p. 164). Sieber also goes on to propose an addition to Marx's value theory claiming that Marx "wrongly attributes in the whole doctrine of the forms of value too great a weight to the concept of labor alone, leaving out consumption" (p. 187). Since Sieber's proposal has been unknown apart from a few Russian readers, no one has subsequently even considered Sieber's proposal for an evaluation, as far as I know, and it is discussed again in Chapter 7 below.

Marx read this article by Sieber, yet only objected to a separate matter, i.e., a matter distinct from the issues of Hegel or on consumption needing consideration. (White, 1996, p. 234)

In 1877 Sieber published a significant reply to a position taken by the Russian Y.G. Zhukovsky. The latter thought that Marx was much influenced by Hegel, while arguing that capitalism was not, in fact, a necessary historical stage in human development, but was fortuitous. Sieber replied that the necessity of capitalism was universal, a position within Marx's 1st and 2nd German editions (but not his French). Given Sieber's work on Marx's *Capital* and Marx's known approval, Sieber's position could be considered by Russians – at least for a time – to be also Marx's own, more so given the wording of the available Russian version of *Capital* based as it was upon the 1st German edition. Another Russian, N.K. Mikhaylovsky also commented on Zhukovsky, applying a similar understanding of Marx for the necessity of a capitalist stage as Sieber had and criticized belief in such a necessity. (White, 2019a, pp. 27–30)

Marx received all of this and in November 1877 prepared a reply to Mikhaylovsky with his own concern. Marx complained of metamorphose of his "historical sketch of the genesis of capitalism in Western Europe into a historico-philosophical theory of the universal path (*marché général*) every people is fated to tread" and elaborated his objection, including noting the expropriated Roman peasants did not become wage laborers (White, 2019a, p. 32). Marx's changed perspective had already been incorporated into the French edition of *Capital*. Apparently upon advice of others, Marx did not send it in for publication. The effect was that Zhukovsky's and Mikhaylovsky's opinions were not challenged publicly by Marx in his lifetime. Marx's reply to Mikhaylovsky did appear in Russian translation but only in 1886 and 1888 (in German in New York in 1887 and in the original French in 1902). The delay meant that the *universal need for a capitalist stage could persist for a time as Marx's own, even after Marx had drafted a denial*. After its publication, populists in Russia would cite Marx's reply (Walicki, 1979, p. 408, fn.6), but notably Plekhanov chose *not* to publish Marx's reply although Engels sent it to him in 1884.

3.3   *1881: Marx's Comment on Sieber and Reply to Zasulich*

In a private 1881 letter, Marx commented on a book by Adolf Wagner that

> Mr. Wagner could have familiarized himself with the difference between me and Ricardo both from *Capital* and from *Sieber's work* (if he knew Russian). Ricardo did indeed concern himself with labor solely as a *measure of the magnitude of value*, and was therefore unable to find any link between his theory of value and the nature of money. (Marx, 1881, emphasis in original)

Note that the concern is with Marx's Part I. As with the 1873 "Afterword", this ought not to be interpreted as an endorsement by Marx of Sieber's overall understanding of *Capital*, but rather that Sieber's explicitly non-Hegelian reading accomplishes the understanding needed for Part I. On the other hand, the concept of labor power is a vital distinction by Marx from Ricardo's labor: while Sieber does mention labor power he does not discuss Marx's chapter on "The

Buying and Selling of Labor Power", a reflection of the fact that this concept is not understood by Sieber in the decisive sense Marx meant.

From 1873 to 1881, Marx continued to credit Sieber's non-Hegelian reading of *Volume I*, Part I, with having understood him. Surely, it could help answer criticisms being made of a claimed dependence of Marx upon Hegel – answer an oppositional strategy of defeating Marx's work in political economy by defeating Hegel. Unfortunately, Marx's remarks were very rarely known, at least outside Russia. While Marx had not explicitly delimited what aspect of Sieber he appreciated and outside Russia Sieber was not read, inside Russia Sieber was read.[5] Allisson (2015) has developed an argument that Sieber paved the way for the re-introduction of Ricardo into a Russian environment where Marx was getting much more attention and led, decades later, to a "Russian synthesis". His argument seems to connect to my argument in Zarembka (2003) of Lenin's backward step toward Ricardo.

In February 1881 Vera Zasulich wrote Marx from Geneva asking his opinion about the future of the Russian commune, an opinion she wished to publish. After several drafts (see Wada in Shanin, 1983, pp. 64–69, and White, 1996, pp. 273–280), Marx replied in March, although not for publication. In the case of the Russian peasants, in contrast to the Western case, he wrote her that

> *their communal property would have to be transformed into private property.*
>
> The analysis in *Capital* therefore provides no reasons either for or against the vitality of the rural commune. But the special study I have made of it, including a search for original source-material, has convinced me that the commune is the fulcrum for social regeneration in Russia. But in order that it might function as such, the harmful influences assailing it on all sides must first be eliminated, and it must then be assured the normal conditions for spontaneous development. (Wada in Shanin, p. 124, emphasis in original)

---

5 Of incidental interest, Sieber did begin to show interest in Hegel, but an elementary one: According to Mikhaylovsky who met Sieber in early 1878, "An outstanding specialist in his field, Sieber struck me as a complete novice in philosophy, in which he was attracted to Hegel via Marx and Engels.... As a novice in Hegelianism he was relentless..." (cited in White, 1996, p. 338). We have no record whether Marx knew of this claim, but Mikhaylovsky's text does reaffirm his own perception of Marx's connection to Hegel.

Incidentally, Marx and Sieber met in London in January, 1881, but their discussion is not known.

While Marx's reply to Zasulich was known privately to persons such as Plekhanov, then also in Geneva, it was not published until 1924.[6] Strangely, both Plekhanov and Zasulich denied to many, including in 1911 to David Ryazanov, even the existence of any reply whatsoever from Marx (Wada and Ryazanov, in Shanin, pp. 41 and 127).

Marx died in March 1883. White argues that

> [A]t the end of his life Marx was still in the process of learning about the evolution of society and its relation to economics. Yet the more he relied on empirical studies like Kovalevsky's or Morgan's the less applicable his original theoretical framework became. But, at the same time, one had to assume that every empirical study would be supplanted by another and so *ad infinitum*. One encountered the limitations of knowledge based on experience that the German philosophical tradition had tried to overcome. (White, 1996, p. 280)

While it is not difficult to make a case that Marx *had* thought of capitalism as a universal stage of human societies, there is enough evidence of Marx changing his mind after 1868, arguably reinforcing the argument that a Hegelian conception was leading nowhere for him.

4 After Marx's 1883 Death, Sieber's Decline and Plekhanov's Influence

For what was to be his last work, in 1885 Sieber published *David Ricardo and Karl Marx in their Socio-Economic Investigations*. Although starting from his 1871 book, it had more material on Marx's work, including the material that Marx had been sent from 1872 onward, especially the article from 1874 discussed above that initiated a series. This book did have a couple of references to Hegel, but did not include a discussion of Hegelian philosophy or of dialectics. At that time, Sieber should be considered the most important presenter in Russia of Marx's work, i.e., apart from the Russian edition of *Capital*. As it happened, Sieber died in 1888 at age 44 of a debilitating illness. His death facilitated his subsequent downgrading as a scholar of Marx's work by those so interested. And Russians had Marx's *Volume I* only in its 1st edition with its

---

6 Bergman (1983, pp. 76–77, fn. *), citing a 1959 Russian source, improbably asserts that Marx "wrote the letter only with the prior stipulation that Zasulich agreed beforehand not to publish it".

Hegelian language until a new Russian edition appeared in 1898. These facts are important for the Russian context. As it happened, Russia became a crucial context for the development of Marxist thought.

White (2001a, p. 11) reports that, "it was from Sieber that Plekhanov, Lenin and much of the revolutionary generation in Russia learnt their Marxism".[7] In the year of Marx's death in 1883, in Geneva exile, Plekhanov (born 1856) established, with others including Zasulich, the first Russian Marxist group, "Emancipation of Labor". At Marx's death, Lenin and Luxemburg were aged twelve (Lenin close to thirteen, Luxemburg just turning twelve), both native Russian speakers with Luxemburg of course being from Russian-occupied Poland. Plekhanov's first reading of *Capital* could have been from the first Russian translation or possibly from the French edition (he had arrived in Geneva already in 1880), but his knowledge of German was not very good at the beginning of 1882 (White, 1996, p. 308). Whatever the case, he had to have been aware of the Russian readership using the translation of the first German edition, the one with most Hegelian language. Lenin read *Volume I* in late 1888 (White, 2001b, p. 30), and his wife would report that by 1893:

> *Lenin had a wonderful knowledge of Marx.* In 1893, when he came to St. Petersburg, he astonished all of us who were Marxists at the time with his tremendous knowledge of the works of Marx and Engels.
>
> In the nineties, when Marxist circles began to be formed, it was chiefly the first volume of "Capital" which was studied. It was possible to obtain "Capital", although with great difficulties. But matters were extremely bad with regard to the other works of Marx. Most of the members of the circles had not even read the "Communist Manifesto".
>
> Lenin understood foreign languages, and he did his best to dig out everything that he could by Marx and Engels in German and French. Anna Ilyinishna tells how he read "The Poverty of Philosophy" in French together with his sister, Olga. He had to read most in German. (Krupskaya, 1933)

Basically, Lenin was fluent in all the languages that were relevant, and he used that skill to great advantage. Nevertheless, I can only find it strange that his

---

7 On the other hand, Luxemburg did read Sieber but was unimpressed: "I'm also working on the theory of value. I have already read carefully through Ziber. He has given me little, and all in all, I'm disappointed in him. I can use him only as a reference book when I have to look up some economist or another". – letter to Jogiches, December 12, 1898, in (Laschitza, et al., 2011, p. 98).

Development of Capitalism in Russia cited the 1st German edition of Marx's *Capital*, even though all German editions, as well as the French, the English, even the 2nd Russian were published by 1899. Indeed, Lenin was only turning three years old when the 2nd German edition appeared. Recall that the 1st German edition was the most Hegelian and, with regard to accumulation of capital, the least developed. The subsequent changes were significant. But Lenin did not seem to be interested.

Luxemburg almost certainly did not read *Capital* in the *Russian* translation (according to a private message to this author from the co-editor of her letters, Annelies Laschitza, March 6, 2012). Luxemburg had already become knowledgeable of German while still in Poland and we only need to recall Marx's 2nd German edition of 1872.

Plekhanov is well known to have influenced Lenin and, at least initially, also Luxemburg. She even wrote in 1891 from Switzerland to a friend that Plekhanov "knows everything better than I do" (Ettinger, 1986, p. 45). Nevertheless, within a year Plekhanov was no longer held in high regard by Luxemburg (nor by Leo Jogiches, her lover, who became particularly hostile).

Plekhanov's political agenda after 1882 would find that Hegel could be useful. That agenda asserted that revolution had to come from the workers rather than peasants, yet the conditions were not ripe for anything but the establishment of capitalism in Russia. Hegel's concept of motion could thus prove useful in justifying patience or explaining the futility of an overthrown of the Russian state in the then existing conditions of extreme capitalist underdevelopment. In 1891 Plekhanov published an article in *Neue Zeit* using for the first time the term "dialectical materialism", tying Marx to Hegel more so than Marx himself had done (Plekhanov, 1891). An 1896 comment even referred to Marx as "the father of present-day dialectical materialism" (Plekhanov, 1896, p. 136). Although Lenin was not yet in Switzerland, Luxemburg was and likely heard of the phrase "dialectical materialism" directly from Plekhanov. How much of Hegel's work did Plekhanov know at the time of that article?

> The main Hegelian work that Plekhanov refers to in this article is the *Philosophy of History* which he thinks is reminiscent of Marx's scheme in *Contribution to the Critique of Political Economy*. In other words, Plekhanov has very little idea of what Hegel is about, but he gets away with it because nobody else has much idea either. (White, private message to this author, January 24, 2012)

Plekhanov did have the important support of Engels.

Plekhanov's views on the importance of Hegel for Marxism were later summarized in his 1908 pamphlet "Fundamental Problems of Marxism" (Plekhanov, 1908). His indebtedness to Engels, rather than Marx, is clear. While mentioning some of Marx's early work, Plekhanov only cites Marx's 2nd edition "Afterword" and "the numerous remarks made *en passant* in the same volume" concerning Hegel (p. 119, emphasis in original). The accuracy of the remark would seem more correct for the 1st edition of *Capital* and the first Russian translation, and seems to reflect Plekhanov's lack of attention to changes Marx had made in later editions. Yet, while Hegel was still useful for the same agenda Plekhanov had had back in the 1880s and 1890s, in 1908 "dialectical materialism" only appears in one early footnote.

5   Lenin's Evolution toward Dialectical Materialism

Lenin came to Marxism around 1889 and in 1892 adopted Plekhanov's position against what they labeled "Narodism" (Russian populism), albeit with different argumentation. In 1894, Lenin wrote and circulated *What the "Friends of the People" Are*, which, in a dozen pages (pp. 163–174), deals with the difference between Marx's and Hegel's dialectic, not, however, from reading Hegel, rather from reading Marx's "Afterword" and Engels' *Anti-Dühring* and *Feuerbach and the End of Classical German Philosophy*. Lenin is not too concerned with Hegel and says that critics

> fastened on Marx's manner of expression and attacked the origin of the theory, thinking thereby to undermine its essence.... [I]nsistence on dialectics, the selection of examples to demonstrate the correction of the [Hegelian] triad, is nothing but a relic of the Hegelianism out of which scientific socialism has grown, a relic of its manner of expression. (Lenin, 1894, pp. 163–164; see also, Louis Althusser, 1969b, p. 107)

While Lenin does make a reference to "dialectical materialism", it appears casually. It can therefore be concluded that for Lenin at this time Hegel was unnecessary for understanding Marx – an interpretation that would be consistent with Sieber's publications.

After Engels' death in 1895, Karl Kautsky in Germany (born 1854) and Plekhanov in Russian exile (two years younger) were the acknowledged leaders of Marxism. Kautsky had not followed Plekhanov on "dialectical materialism" and, initially, Lenin had not either. Lenin was to meet Plekhanov for the first time in 1895, while visiting Geneva.

In 1909, having broken with Plekanov but still not having read Hegel, Lenin published a long work, *Materialism and Empirio-Criticism*, an attack on Bogdanov who was contesting Lenin's party leadership. Relying upon Engels but now upgrading the importance of dialectics, Lenin (1909, p. 20) refers negatively to those who undertake a "complete renunciation of dialectical materialism, i.e., of Marxism".[8] What had now changed for Lenin that was not at stake for him in 1894? He had a choice of staying with his 1894 position of some indifference to "dialectical materialism" or defending it as such. He chose the latter in his struggle against Bogdanov. Then, in 1914, Lenin finally read Hegel and made extensive notes on Hegel's *Science of Logic*. Lenin now claims that it is "impossible completely to understand Marx's *Capital*, and especially its first chapter, without having thoroughly studied and understood the *whole* of Hegel's *Logic*" (Lenin, 1914, p. 180, emphasis in original). While Lenin's position in 1894 had seemed consistent enough with Sieber's opinion and with his interpretation of Marx, clearly, something was now a stake for Lenin.

I would argue that it was politically useful for Lenin to support the complete connection of Engels to Marx, as Plekhanov had done, rather than allow a certain separation or distinction in their thoughts. To allow some separation would open the door to wider interpretations of Marx, just as was happening with those persons (such as Bogdanov) chosen to be the objects of criticism in Lenin's *Materialism and Empirio-Criticism*. It was a kind of all-or-nothing strategy of intellectual conquest: "I know the Marxist truth". In the 1890s, Lenin had been utilizing a similar strategy of conquest, then centered upon political economy. Lenin had emphasized his claim that his economics is *the* Marxist theory. Lenin is now using a similar strategy of conquest for philosophical questions, that his philosophy is also *the* Marxist one. Did subsequent Marxist thought inherit from Lenin and from Soviet Marxist culture the claim of absolute necessity of Hegel for Marxism? Can this be said even of the value-form approach to Marxism arising from Soviet work of Rubin (1928), in which there would be no alternative offered for the penetration of appearances, whether labeled empiricist or economistic, except via Hegel using a form-content

---

8   The editor's note to the title of the 1972 Progress edition claims that this work by Lenin "enabled the philosophical ideas of Marxism to spread widely among the mass of party members and helped the party activists and progressive workers to master dialectical and historical materialism". In truth, the work is so complicated that it is beyond the reach of virtually everyone.

dichotomy. Or, later, in the promotion of Marx's *Grundrisse* arising from work of the Ukrainian Roman Rosdolsky (a supporter of Trotsky).

6 Conclusion: Moving Forward

In Luxemburg's work, support for the importance of Hegel for Marx is not deep or long lasting, although Göçmen (2007) makes an attempt that I address in Zarembka (2014, pp. 72–75). By 1917 on the very day of the beginning of the February Revolution in Russia, i.e., March 8, she wrote to Hans Diefenbach,

> In theoretical work as in art, I value only the simple, the tranquil and the bold. This is why, for example, the famous first volume of Marx's *Capital*, with its profuse rococo ornamentation in the Hegelian style, now seems an abomination to me (for which, from the Party standpoint, I must get 5 years' hard labor and 10 years' loss of civil rights….). (Bronner, 1978, p. 185)

Many political economists have been instrumental in simply ignoring Hegel and getting on with their class analyses. In the 1930s Michał Kalecki (born 1899 in Russian-occupied Poland) was one example of those early independent thinkers, influenced in his case by Luxemburg (Kowalik, 2009). Paul Sweezy (born 1910 in the United States) was another example. The works of Louis Althusser and of those associated with him were a flag for rethinking the Hegelian issue. One expression of Marxist political economists ignoring Hegel can be seen in *The Elgar Companion to Marxist Economics* (Fine and Saad-Filho, 2012).[9] Of course, ignoring Hegel does not solve anything, but only opens doors for further development of Marxism, an example being White's concern that Marx faced a major theoretical problem in connecting *Capital, Volume II* to *Volume I*, a problem that Hegelian thought could not help solve. In any case, the main issue at hand should be deepening the theory of social development originating from Marx, with clear knowledge of Marx's own theoretical evolution.

---

9 An exception is an entry on the "Value-form approach".

PART 2

Key Elements of Political Economy

CHAPTER 2

Marx's Evolution and Revolution with the Concept of Value: Abstract Labor and Labor Power

The conception of value is the foundation of Marx's understanding of the capitalist mode of production; it is the theoretical heart of *Capital*.[1] Therefore, the intellectual development of Marx's understanding of what constitutes value is reconstructed here. Fundamentally, Marx does not hold the same theory at age 23 (the time of his doctoral dissertation) or three years later (*1844 Manuscripts*, unpublished by him), as by age 54 (*Capital*, 2nd edition). As Marx matures, his emphasis changes and the fulcrum of his thought moves as well. Against a claim of "the profound continuity of his writings from his doctoral dissertation onwards" (Baronian, 2013, p. 6), or a more limited assertion by Engels late in his life that Marx "completed his criticism of political economy … toward the end of the fifties" (Engels, 1891, p. 21), I argue the necessity to comprehend that the rupture regarding value was only concluded in *Capital, Volume I*.

Conceptions of classical political economists appear quite unchallenged in Marx's early work. Within his unpublished *Economic and Philosophical Manuscripts of 1844*, "capital, accumulation, competition, division of labour, wages, profit, etc … are concepts of Classical Political Economy, which Marx borrows *just as* he finds them there, without changing them one iota, without adding to them any new concept, and without modifying anything at all of their theoretical organization" (Althusser, 1974, p. 109, fn. 4, emphasis in original). One year later, however, Marx begins to introduce new conceptions: mode of production, relations of production, and productive forces. Further development of his conceptual categories would continue over two decades, and even more, and constitutes more than a mere elaboration of his understanding from 1844. Rather it represents a shift of focus that initially culminates in *Volume I* of *Capital*, but continues to develop further even after this.

Works that were published by Marx himself, rather than those he did not publish (notably, the *1844 Manuscripts* and *Grundrisse*), are the emphasis here, although some of his correspondence is mentioned. A survey of Marx's evolving understanding of value is undertaken from *Poverty of Philosophy*, to *A Contribution to a Critique of Political Economy*, to the 1st edition of *Capital* introducing "labor power", and then the next edition of *Capital*, and beyond.

---

1 This chapter is a more concise and corrected version of Zarembka (2016).

1 *Poverty of Philosophy* (1847): Economic Concepts Historically Conditioned

Marx's intellectual project truly begins in 1847 when he publishes *The Poverty of Philosophy* as a critique of Proudhon. In this work there is no direct criticism of the classical economist he most respected, David Ricardo, except for a remark on the tendency to eternalize economic concepts ahistorically. Ricardo's value theory is the "scientific interpretation of actual economic life" (1847, p. 124), in contrast to Proudhon's utopianism. Twelve years later, Marx continues to cite the importance of his 1847 work: "The salient points of our conception were first outlined in an academic, although polemical, form in my *Poverty of Philosophy*" Marx (1859, p. 264). Only later does he refer to Ricardo's scientific "inadequacy" when drafting *Theories of Surplus Value* (Marx 1905b, p. 164)[2] and, still later at the end of the first chapter in *Capital, Volume I*, when elaborating his concerns with Ricardo, along with classical political economy more generally, in three long footnotes (the second appearing for the first time in the 2nd German and French editions, Marx, 1867, pp. 84–86).

The most important distinction in *Poverty* is the recognition by Marx that economists eternalize the categories they use, that is to say, concepts are applied analytically to all modes of production: "Economists express the relations of bourgeois production, the division of labour, credit, money, etc., as fixed, immutable, eternal categories.... Economists explain how production takes place in the above-mentioned relations, but what they do not explain is how these relations themselves are produced, that is, the historical moment which gave them birth". Furthermore, they miss the origins of their concepts. "Economic categories are only the theoretical expressions, the abstractions of the social relations of production". Economists such as Smith and Ricardo "have no other mission than that of showing how wealth is acquired in bourgeois production relations, of formulating these relations into categories, into laws, and of showing" their superiority to those of feudal society. All the economists "represent the bourgeois relations of production as eternal categories" (Marx, 1847, pp. 162, 165, 176, 202). This weakness of classical economists proves fundamental to all of Marx's subsequent reconsiderations of political economy.

---

2 In the same work, Marx thought that "the entire Ricardian contribution is contained in the first two chapters" of Ricardo's *Principles*, but that he forced "science to get out of the rut ... and in general, to examine how matters stand with the contradiction between the apparent and actual movement of the system" (Marx, 1905b, pp. 169 and 166). Still, Ricardo must be reproached "for regarding the phenomenal form as *immediate and direct* proof or exposition of the general laws, and for failing to *interpret* it" (p. 106, emphasis in original).

In the following, I follow Marx as he develops his new understanding of value – an understanding that ultimately does not correspond to those of the classical economists.[3]

2   *Contribution* (1859): Abstract Labor as the Substance of Value

After years of work and hints in his 1857–58 *Grundrisse,* the crucial new concept of "abstract labour" is finally introduced by Marx in *A Contribution to the Critique of Political Economy.* The phrase is often expanded to three words as "abstract universal labour". An example in the *Contribution* of Marx's use is the following:

> ...the labour which posits exchange value is a specific social form of labour. For example, tailoring if one considers its physical aspect as a distinct productive activity produces a coat, but not the exchange value of the coat. The exchange value is produced by it not as tailoring as such but as *abstract universal labour,* and this belongs to a social framework not devised by the tailor. Women in ancient domestic industry, for instance, produced coats without producing the exchange value of coats. Labour

---

[3] Oishi (2001) claims that *Poverty of Philosophy* is fundamental to understand Marx's critique of political economy and implicitly targeting Ricardo, in addition to the obvious target of Proudhon. Marx had witnessed the development of private property through litigation surrounding theft of wood from what had been common land. So, according to Oishi, Marx focused thereafter on the essence of private property leading to the importance of estranged labor in his earlier *1844 Manuscripts.* In *Poverty* Marx understands Proudhon as eternalizing economic categories in the same way as the classical economists (albeit via a detour), and, for Marx, this represents a contradiction to the actual historical emergence of private property in the then recent times. Having witnessed the emergence of private property in Germany, Marx breaks with such an eternalization, and thereby with the analytical method used by the classical economists.

Oishi's primary theme is the continuity and unity of Marx's thought centered upon the principle of estranged or alienated labor. For Oishi, the importance of alienated labor had been negated by Soviet Marxists and Western followers when, for him, there was no rupture or break in Marx's own thought as he matures. White (1996), like Oishi, sees little change in Marx's basic scheme after the emphasis on alienated labor and private property in the *1844 Manuscripts*; the later "abstract labour" is little more than a substitution for alienated labor, and "surplus value" a substitution for private property (pp. 146–147; see also p. 199). Unlike Oishi, however, White sees a major shift in Marx's late thought away from the importance of Hegel, as I indicated in the previous chapter. And I argue major conceptual changes by Marx as his thought evolves.

A final comment concerning Oishi: On p. 135, he equates alienated labor to labor under the control of others. How capitalism would be distinguished from slavery is not made clear.

as source of material wealth was well known both to Moses, the law-giver, and to Adam Smith, the customs official. (Marx, 1859, p. 278, emphasis is ours)

Rubin (1927) argued for the importance of the "abstract labour" concept and, furthermore, considered Marx's use of "universal" in the *Contribution* to be an essential component and, for him, a relevant carryover from Hegelian language. However, Rubin (p. 119) recognizes that most of the Hegelian language disappears from *Capital* in Marx's second edition. As discussed in Chapter 1 here, such a point is driven home by White (1996, Chapter 4) who describes, among other changes, the dropping of the word "universal" throughout much of Marx's text, including from the above phrase "abstract universal labour". In an otherwise informative article, Reuten (2019, p. 133) writes that abstract arrives for the first time in *Capital, Volume 1*, but this is incorrect.

Without Hegelian language, Marx's meaning can be described as follows: Commodities have all kinds of use-values, that is, useful qualities. Abstracting "from the material constituents and forms which make it a use value [a commodity is] no longer a table, a house, yarn, or any other useful thing. All its sensuous characteristics are extinguished. Nor is it any longer the product of the labour of the joiner, the mason, the spinner, or of any other particular kind of productive labour" (Marx, 1867, pp. 45–46). Although Marx himself did not make the analogy, it is rather like in physics: objects of all different shapes, sizes and colors are pulled towards a heavier mass and Newton abstracted from those differing qualities to arrive at "gravity" as the commonality to describe this pull, a fact we all still learn in school today. In Marx's case, a commodity has value "only because human labour in the abstract has been embodied or materialized in it". Labor in the abstract is essential to the capital–wage-labor relation. Value is the *objectification of abstract labor, which itself is a product of capitalism*. In Cleaver's words,

> to make abstraction from [any commodity's] use-values is to make abstraction from their particular attributes. That, in turn, is to make abstraction from the special characteristics of the human labour which created those attributes and made them different from other commodities.... In abstraction from their material reality as use-values and as products of particular forms of useful labour, these commodities emerge as only products of human labour in abstraction from any particularity. This human labour that is common to them Marx calls abstract labour. As products of abstract human labour they are qualitatively equivalent and

> as such he calls them *values*.... [Abstract labour is] meaningful because capital itself, in its continual struggle with labour to create and maintain the division of labour which is the basis for commodity production, exchange, and social control, tries to continually make labour more malleable to its needs. (Cleaver 1979, pp. 110–112, emphasis in original, paragraphing not indicated; also, Mohun, 1991b, and Milios, et al. 2002, pp. 17–21)

Value, based upon abstract labor within capitalism is a concept only applicable to the capitalist mode of production and is not trans-historical. Like Cleaver, Postone (1993) says that the "*essential* difference between Marx's critique of political economy and classical political economy is precisely the treatment of labour" and that "a trans-historical conception of value-constituting labour ... hinders an adequate analysis of the capitalist social formation". (pp. 54–55, emphasis in original)

Turning to another aspect of the *Contribution*, Marx surveyed the history of political economy for the problems other economists had with the classical (especially Ricardian) determination of exchange-value by labour time. Suggesting where he himself fits in, the relevant portion begins:

> *David Ricardo*, unlike Adam Smith, neatly sets forth the determination of the value of commodities by labour time, and demonstrates that this law governs even those bourgeois relations of production which apparently contradict it most decisively. Ricardo's investigations are concerned exclusively with the *magnitude of value*, and regarding this he is at least aware that the operation of the law depends on definite historical preconditions. He says that the determination of value by labour time applies to "such commodities only as can be increased in quantity by the exertion of human industry, and on the production of which competition operates without restraint".
>
> This in fact means that the full development of the law of value presupposes a society in which large-scale industrial production and free competition obtain, in other words, modern bourgeois society. For the rest, the bourgeois form of labour is regarded by Ricardo as the eternal natural form of social labour. (Marx, 1859, p. 300, emphasis in original, the quotation corrected to Ricardo's actual words, rather than the re-translation back from Marx's German)

Marx then offered four points of comparison of which the following problem is most relevant:

> If the exchange value of a product equals the labour time contained in the product, then the exchange value of a working day is equal to the product it yields, in other words, wages must be equal to the product of labour. But in fact the opposite is true. *Ergo*, this objection amounts to the problem, – how does production on the basis of exchange value solely determined by labour time lead to the result that the exchange value of labour is less than the exchange value of its product? This problem is solved in our analysis of capital. (Marx, 1859, pp. 301–302)

Marx promises an analysis to solve the problem of the origin of surplus value, having achieved confidence from his personal clarifications written in notes, published after his death as the *Grundrisse*. The *Grundrisse* is, in fact, where Marx originally develops many of the new theoretical concepts which would appear in the first volume of *Capital*. Even so, the concept of labor power is not even hinted at.

Baronian (2013) addresses "living labour" in Marx and relates somewhat to our argument. He says that political economy is based upon "phenomena arising in the sphere of circulation, in which economic agents relate to each other only as possessors of commodities" (p. 8). Marx realized that Hegel had incorrectly conceived labor "in the same way as political economy, as alienated labour or commodity producing labour" (p. 4) and overcame that conception by instead focusing on living labour:

> ...Although political economy always grasps the commodity in its two-fold nature, i.e. as use value and exchange value, it conceives living labour itself just as labour that creates use values. ... Had the economists defined the living labour both as concrete labour and abstract labour, the exchange of products as commodities would have immediately appeared to them as a very particular way under which society coordinates and exchanges producers' various activities. (Baronian, 2013, p. 7)

However, when Baronian then gives attention to the transition to capitalism and includes discussion of well-known works by Sweezy, Dobb, Hilton, Wood, and Brenner (siding with Dobb and Hilton), he, unfortunately, fails to show explicitly how living labor is evident in some of these authors and missing in others. A similar problem occurs in later chapters on the Cambridge controversy regarding Ricardian versus neoclassical capital theory, the transformation problem, the process of abstraction of labor (including Taylorism and cognitive labor), surplus population and the claim of working-class immiseration, circuits of capital and Keynesian monetary theory, as well as the role of constant capital in crisis (the topic which concludes his book).

3   *Capital, Volume I* (1867): Labor Power

> Suddenly the voice of the labourer, which had been stifled in the storm and stress of the process of production, rises: The commodity that I have sold to you [my beloved employer] differs from the crowd of other commodities, in that its use creates value, and a value greater than its own. That is why you bought it.
>
> Marx (1867, p. 224)

Contemporary Marxists often take the concept of "labor power" for granted and consider it easily grasped. Yet this important theoretical concept was developed late and after Marx's *Contribution*. To illustrate its great importance, when presenting a copy of his earlier *Poverty of Philosophy* to Natalia Utina in 1876, Marx pens only four corrections, the first of which adds the word "power" after "labour" in the following: "Labour, inasmuch as it is bought and sold, is a commodity like any other commodity, and has, in consequence, an exchange value" (Marx, 1847, p. 130).

Oakley (1984, p. 173) had claimed that a first reference to labor power can be found in the *Grundrisse* drafted by Marx in 1857–58 (Marx, 1939–41a, pp. 282–283), although adding that Marx "had yet to grasp its analytical significance more fully". A later translation of the *Grundrisse*, unavailable to Oakley, pointed out that the original German refers on rare occasions to *Arbeitsvermögen*, or labor capacity, but not to *Arbeitskraft*, labor power as used throughout *Capital* (Marx, 1939b–41b, p. 212 and 554, fn. 85). While labor power had not emerged, other concepts emerged in the *Grundrisse* such as constant and variable capital and absolute and relative surplus value (Marx, 1939–41a, p. 389 and 407–408; see also Oakley, p. 180). A theoretical project was in progress, yet incomplete.

In the Ricardian understanding of political economy, the labor time required for a commodity's production determines its value (and thus exchange value).[4] Yet, asks Marx, were the worker selling labor directly to the capitalist

---

4   For determining value, Ricardo does not actually refer to *labor time*, but rather to time *and* labor: "the value of [hunted] animals would be regulated, not solely by the time and labour necessary to their destruction, but also by the time and labour necessary for providing the

which is itself labor time (value), how could surplus value (profit) be created at all? If "the value of a commodity is determined by the labour-time required for its production; how does it happen that this law of value does not hold good in the greatest of all exchanges, which forms the foundation of capitalist production, the exchange between capitalist and labourer? Why is the quantity of materialized labour received by the worker as wages not equal to the quantity of immediate labour which he gives in exchange for his wages?" (Marx, 1910, p. 89, written about 1863 commenting on James Mill). Marx was in the process of realizing fully that *labor itself is not produced nor sold*. Rather, what is produced and becomes an expense for capitalists is the *cost* of workers' subsistence needs.

Previously alluding to "labor capacity" (*Arbeitsvermögen*), by 1865 Marx settled upon a new theoretical concept: *labor power*. The capitalist purchases *labor power* at its exchange-value, the labor time required to produce the worker's subsistence needs. The capitalist confronts the laborer on the market – a living human being with material needs (which must in turn be produced): "That which comes directly face to face with the possessor of money on the market, is in fact not labour, but the labourer. What the latter sells is his labour power. As soon as his labour actually begins, it has already ceased to belong to him; it can therefore no longer be sold by him" (Marx, 1867, p. 503). Marx's new concept *Arbeitskraft* was well known within German working-class culture (Biernacki, 1995, pp. 42–43, 272–74). In English, Marx lectured workers using it (Marx, 1865), becoming then incorporated in *Volume I*. Editions of other draft volumes were to be corrected posthumously (e.g., see Marx, 2015, p. 94, fn. 17).

Does the addition of "power" to "labor", when appropriate, contain the solution to the problem? By purchasing labor power, the capitalist obtains a very specific, and unique, use-value: the workers' ability to produce value. While the use-value of a light bulb is to provide light, the use-value to the capitalist purchasing labor power is the value the worker produces (not specific items like light bulbs, toothpaste, and cars, which are of no interest to the capitalist).

> In order to be able to extract value from the consumption of a commodity, our friend, Moneybags, must be so lucky as to find, within the sphere of circulation, in the market, a commodity, whose use-value possesses

hunter's capital, the weapon" (Ricardo 1821, p. 23). A few pages earlier Ricardo nevertheless cites Smith favorably, for whom labor time is clearly indicated: "what is usually the produce of two days', or two hours' labour, should be worth double of what is usually the produce of one day's, or one hour's labour" (p. 13). Smith, it might be noted, neglected the weapon mentioned by Ricardo.

the peculiar property of being a source of value, whose actual consumption, therefore, is itself an embodiment of labour, and, consequently a creation of value. (Marx, 1867, p. 164)

Luckily for the money-owner, the use-value of labor power is precisely its ability to produce value.[5] Furthermore, the value produced is above cost.

For the use-value of labour-power to the capitalist as a capitalist does not consist in its *actual* use value, in the usefulness of this particular concrete labour – that it is spinning labour, weaving labour, and so on. He is as little concerned with this as with the use value of the product of this labour as such, since for the capitalist the product is a commodity (even before its first metamorphosis), not an article of consumption.... [T]he use-value of the labour is, for him, that he gets back a greater quantity of labour-time than he has paid out in the form of wages. (Marx, 1905a, p. 156, emphasis in original)

For it [capital], the use-value of labour-power is precisely the excess of the quantity of labour which it performs over the quantity of labour which is materialized in the labour-power itself and hence is required to reproduce it.... [The] concrete character, which is what enables it to take the form of a commodity, is not its *specific use-value* for capital. Its specific use-value for capital consists in its quantity as labour in general, and in the difference, the excess, of the quantity of labour which it performs

---

5 Foley (1983) notes that labor power "requires the separation of the direct producers from means of production so that they cannot produce and sell the product of their own labour". The use value of labor power is "its capacity to produce value" (p. 296). Contrast this to (Sinha 1996, p. 207) who writes that the "use-value of labor-power happens to be the working activity itself", or to (Hunt 2002, p. 217) who says that the use-value of labor power is "simply the performance of work – the actualizing of the potential labor". If working activity or the performance of work occurs in all modes of production, there is no recognition in these sentences by Sinha and Hunt for labor in the abstract as a property of the capitalist relations of production.

While a formulation such as Sinha's or Hunt's could be thought to find a support in Marx when citing "the use-value supplied by the labourer to the capitalist is not, in fact, his labour-power, but its function, some definite useful labour, the work of tailoring, shoemaking, spinning, etc.", it would be more easily swallowed if its following sentence is ignored: "That this same labour is, on the other hand, the universal value-creating element, and thus possesses a property by which it differs from all other commodities, is beyond the cognisance of the ordinary mind" (Marx 1867, p. 506).

> *over* the quantity of labour which it costs. (Marx, 1905a, p. 400, emphasis in original)[6]

Marx is now able to show the weakness of Ricardo's system. Ricardo can only demonstrate that the value of "labor" depends upon the means of subsistence, which depends, in turn, upon supply and demand.

> Instead of *labour*, Ricardo should have discussed labour-*power*. But had he done so, *capital* would also have been revealed as the material conditions of labour, confronting the labourer as power that had acquired an independent existence and capital would at once have been revealed as a *definite social relationship*. Ricardo thus only distinguishes capital as "accumulated labour" from "immediate labour". And it is something purely physical, only an element in the *labour-process*, from which the relation between labour and capital, wages and profits, could never be developed. (Marx, 1905b, p. 400, emphasis in original)

In other words, by referring to the sale of "labor", Ricardo skips over the fact that workers work with means of production they do not own or control. Ricardo's conception ignores that the workers do *not* have labor to sell, which would require means of production to be able to produce. Instead, as Marx described in a draft chapter for *Volume I*, the worker sells only the *capacity for labor*:

> [T]he worker is compelled to sell not a commodity but his own labour-power as a commodity. This is because he finds on the other side, opposed to him and confronting him as alien property, all the means of production, all the material conditions of work together with all the means of subsistence, money, and means of production. and means of subsistence as alien property... [T]he *conditions of his labour confront* him as *alien property*. (Marx, 1933, p. 1003, emphasis in original)

---

6   Also, a couple of remarks in Marx (1910):
   [T]he specific feature of this commodity [labour-power] is that its use-value is itself a factor of exchange-value, its use therefore creates a greater exchange-value than it itself contained. (p. 90)
   The use-value of labour-power is *labour*, the element which produces exchange-value.... [T]he value which the capitalist receives from the worker in exchange [for labour-power] is greater than the price he pays for this labour. (p. 178, emphasis in original)

In sum, the class character of capitalism and the social relations of production of capitalism cannot be theorized adequately without clearly distinguishing between labor and labor power, as we would otherwise limit ourselves to the terrain of commodity transactions. Marx further notes:

> The insufficiency of Ricardo's analysis of the magnitude of value, and his analysis is by far the best, will appear from the 3rd and 4th books of this work. As regards value in general, it is the weak point of the classical school of Political Economy that it nowhere expressly and with full consciousness, distinguishes between labour, as it appears in the value of a product, and the same labour, as it appears in the use value of that product. ... [I]t has not the least idea, that when the difference between various kinds of labour is treated as purely quantitative, their qualitative unity or equality, and therefore their reduction to abstract human labour, is implied.
> Marx (1867, p. 84, fn. 1)

Political economists after Ricardo struggled with the problem of what it is that workers sell. This problem, however, could not be solved without distinguishing labor power from labor. It took someone like Marx, with his intellectual powers and commitment to working-class struggle, to do so. Other economists either did not share his commitment to the working-class, or were explicitly committed to the capitalist class.[7]

Engels recognized the great significance of the concept of labor power, even as he seems to have failed to realize when Marx came to the concept. Following Marx's death, Engels in his Preface to the second volume of *Capital* compared Marx's discovery of labor power to Lavoisier's discovery of "oxygen". Posing the

---

7 An interesting comment by Hunt (2002, p. 282) suggests that the classical labor theory of value itself originated from the struggle of the industrial capitalist against landlords and merchants, not from within the class character of capitalism itself: Commodity prices are determined by quantity of labor (setting aside scarce or one-of-a-kind commodities – Ricardo 1821, p. 12). Distinguishing then between productive and unproductive labor within the labor theory thus became a weapon of the industrial capitalists against the landlords (indeed, even manufacturing capitalists of the time often undertook labor). As capitalism developed in the 19th century, such a theory was no longer very useful for bourgeois interests as the struggle against workers rose in importance. So, bourgeois interests found their own solution: dump labor as the creator of the value of commodities. In its place came marginalism with its inaccurate individualism (pp. 283–284) and an abandonment of a class-based political economy. Ricardo's theory had fulfilled its mission for capital. To drive political economy forward required a transformation of the object of political economy to the interests of the working class, the aim of Marx's political economy.

question of what separates Marx from classical economists, Engels recalls the theoretical revolution Lavoisier triggered in chemistry through the discovery of a new chemical element, oxygen. While the phlogistic theorists Priestley and Scheele had discovered the *fact* of oxygen without recognizing what an innovation it was, Lavoisier created a new category, that is, discovered the new element, and thereby placed "all chemistry, which in its phlogistic form had stood on its head, squarely on its feet". Engels then says that Marx stands in the same revolutionary relationship to his predecessors in classical economics. Although the existence of surplus value was known long before him (albeit under different names), Marx, says Engels, understood that he had to *explain* this fact, explain what value was, and critique Ricardian theory: "By substituting labour-power, the value-producing property, for labour he solved with one stroke one of the difficulties which brought about the downfall of the Ricardian school, viz., the impossibility of harmonizing the mutual exchange of capital and labour with the Ricardian law that value is determined by labour" (Marx, 1885, pp. 16–17).[8] This clear exposition by Engels, however, leads to a clear problem with the comment by Engels (1891, p. 21) six years later that

---

8 Althusser (1965) has pointed out the significance of this passage, since Engels is describing how Marx revolutionized the theoretical object of classical economics by recognizing the *relations of production* as a concept. That is, Marx's distinction "does not lie in his having claimed or even demonstrated the primacy of production (Ricardo had already done this is his own way), but in his having transformed the *concept of production* by assigning to it an object radically different from the object designated by the old concept" (Althusser, p. 170, emphasis in original). Marx saw the importance of the material conditions of production belonging to the concept of production – hence he "attributed much more importance to *the category of use-value*" than his predecessors. Where Smith reduced wealth exclusively to labor, Marx broke "with this idealism of labour by thinking the concept of the material conditions of every labour process and by providing the concept of the *economic forms of existence* of these material conditions: in the capitalist mode of production, the decisive distinctions between constant and variable capital on the one hand, and between Department I and Department II on the other" (p. 172, emphasis in original). In turn, this understanding leads to the recognition that the social relations of production must include the material elements of the production process.

Labor power as a concept has been subject to counter-attack. Steedman has a six-page discussion stating that no problem is solved by introducing the concept. However, his position amounts to no more than an assertion, not a demonstration (Steedman, 1982, p. 149): Workers are like land, a fixed resource utilized in production. Although workers are reproduced when obtaining their subsistence needs, thereby permitting them to stay alive and work (for capitalists), Steedman apparently does not consider that their reproduction (survival) requires any production at all. He is followed later by Sinha (1996, pp. 210–213) who refers explicitly to a fixed resource and argues that "*the market for labor-power does not exist*" (p. 213, emphasis in original).

Marx's criticisms of political economy were completed by 1859 – the concept of labor power came thereafter!

4 Other Additions in *Volume I*

4.1 *Socially Necessary Labor Time*

By *Volume I* of *Capital*, Marx is able to emphasize *socially necessary labor time* as the commonality between commodities exchanged on the market, and that this is not the same as the *actual* labor time contained in the production of a specific commodity being sold. Sieber saw its importance early on:

> The introduction into science of this concept [of socially necessary labour time] once and for all eliminates any possibility of discussing the question of value within those narrow, atomistic, confines in which very many economists speak of it: once and for all the ground is cut from under the feet of those objections to Ricardo's theory (Walras, Bastiat, Macleod, etc.), who try to show its falsity in specific instances of exchange.... The value of a specific product is aligned here with the average value.... A product may cost less, but until this relative cheapness of production has become social the owner of the product enjoys on the market a certain advantage, which also does not infringe the law of the average, social value, because it is a special, individual phenomenon. (Sieber, 2001, pp. 32–33)

Relative cheapness by a single capitalist does push other capitalists to innovate, such as by developing technological improvements in production – an insight that Marx incorporates into his concept of the production of relative surplus value.

4.2 *Form of Value*

Also emerging in *Capital* is the concept of "value-form" – including "relative" and "equivalent" forms.[9] Upon the advice of both Engels and Kugelmann who

---

9 Marx's chapter "Disintegration of the Ricardian School" in *Theories of Surplus Value* cannot be said to introduce this concept of the value form, as there is but one use of it within the text: "The point of departure in the process of the production and circulation of capital, is the independent *form of value* which maintains itself, increases, measures the increase against the original amount..." (Marx, 1910, p. 131, emphasis is ours).

warned of the Hegelian language in the text, a special appendix entitled "The Value-Form" was added while Marx worked on proofs for the first edition (Marx and Engels, 1948, p. 105). Marx must have been sufficiently satisfied with his new "non-dialectical" language, as he used much of the language from this appendix in the body of the next edition (also removing most of the remaining Hegelian language from *Capital* – White, 1996, Chapter 4, and Chapter 1 above). The third section of Chapter I in later editions then becomes "The Form of Value or Exchange-Value".[10] In that second edition, Marx says that if, like the classical economists, "we treat this mode of production as one eternally fixed by Nature for every state of society, we necessarily overlook that which is the differentia specifica of the value form, and consequently of the commodity

---

10 Ranganayakamma (1999, Part I, Chapter 3) provides a straightforward understanding of the value-form, describing it with examples such as the "value of the cloth, that did not appear before the exchange [with a coat], appears in the form of a coat" (p. 81; N.B., the coat, not a value of the coat). Thus, the 1867 Appendix to his first edition gives an example of linen exchanging for a coat; the "linen is the commodity *which expresses its value in the body of a commodity different from it*, the coat" (1867, cited as Marx, 1978, p. 134, emphasis in original). The linen's value is expressed in a coat, the linen's value is seen in the coat (while value itself is not seen). In later editions we find that a commodity's function, in consideration of the relative form of value, "is merely to serve as the material in which the value of the first commodity is expressed" (1867, p. 55). And when a material such as gold monopolizes a position as universal equivalent, the money-form becomes the general form of value. This reading of the value-form is sustained in Arthur's (2004) work.

Interpretations of the value-form include works by the Uno school in Japan, specifically, Itoh and Sekine, as well as elsewhere in works by Arthur, Lapavitsas, Reuten, Smith, and Williams. Discussing their works would take us afield with little use for present purposes, except to say that a critique by Weeks (1990) appears consistent with the understanding of the present author: "the law of value must derive from the insight that capitalism is primarily a commodity *producing* society, and only secondarily a commodity *exchanging* society" (p. 18, emphasis in original). Kliman's (2000) article, following upon Rubin and Dunayevskaya, relates to the value-form, but with a subtle change. Standing upon a phrase "intrinsic value" used only once by Marx, Kliman says that value is the "third thing" present in each commodity exchanged. Thus, "*living* labour *creates* value, is the 'value-forming substance', while the commodity considered as the container of this labour in objective form, *dead* labour, *is* value". It is not trans-historical but "an alienated and fetishistic relation between subject and object" (pp. 106–107, emphasis in original). By distinguishing value from exchange-value in this manner, Kliman asserts that a domination of dead labor over living labor is thereby expressed – value is contained in dead objects (commodities), having been previously created by living labor. Similar argumentation appears in Dunayevskaya's conceptual discussion of the organic composition of capital. Her argumentation centers wholly upon her one point: Marx's concept of alienation "broke through all criticism" of bourgeois society (see Zarembka 2002b, p. 35). Marx's discussion of the value-form is not closely followed by her, and "intrinsic value" in Kliman seems to be offered as a substitute concept.

form, and of its further developments, money form, capital form, &c" (1867, p. 85, fn. 1).

In the 1859 *Contribution*, Marx had not distinguished value from exchange-value:

> The labour time objectified in the use-values of commodities is both the substance that turns them into exchange values and therefore into commodities, and the standard by which the precise magnitude of their value is measured. ... [A]ll use-values are equivalents when taken in proportions which contain the same amount of expended, objectified labour time. Regarded as exchange-values all commodities are merely definite quantities of *congealed labour time*. (Marx, 1859, p. 272, emphasis in original)

That is to say, there is no way to separate exchange-value from value itself. By August 1862, Marx began to address the problem of how values are translated into prices (e.g., Marx's letter to Engels, Marx and Engels, 1948, pp. 74–78). The distinction between value and exchange-value could not be easily ignored. This translation problem was later to become a tool of Marx's bourgeois critics, partly originating in errors in Engels' editorship of the third volume of *Capital* and in Bortkiewicz's alteration of textual evidence for his own purposes (see Ramos, 1998–99).

Volume I is interspersed with such comments as "we assume that the capitalist sells at their value the commodities he has produced, without concerning ourselves either about the new forms that capital assumes while in the sphere of circulation, or about the concrete conditions of reproduction hidden under these forms" (Marx, 1867, pp. 529–530).[11] To make it absolutely clear, Marx adds in his 2nd edition,

> The calculations given in the text are intended merely as illustrations. We have in fact assumed that prices = values. We shall, however, see, in

---

11 Marx has the following in his first chapter, first edition, fn. 9: "when we employ the word value with no other additional determination, we refer always to exchange value". As this footnote is absent in later editions of *Volume 1*, Dussel (2001, p. 19, citing himself in 1990) claims that Marx "at the very earliest, in 1872, distinguished between 'value' and 'exchange-value'". Yet, how then does Dussel understand Marx's earlier work on the transformation problem? And was not the footnoted sentence left out merely because the Appendix to the first edition was used as the basis for the re-write of the first chapter for the next edition?

Book III, that even in the case of average prices the assumption cannot be made in this very simple manner. (p. 212, fn.1)

There is an obsession with this issue of the relationship between labor time in production and the pricing of commodities.[12] Sinha's (2010) wide-ranging criticism of Marx includes a focus on this concern (pp. 181–188, 205–213, 222–258) and follows a path led by Böhm-Bawerk whose well-known 1896 critique of Marx, according to Sinha, "is among the best and most forceful to date" (p. 205). This issue can even be argued to be an important conceptual argument against Marx taken up by Keynes after reading a book by McCracken. McCracken (1933, pp. 53–54) had considered the introduction of the concept of socially necessary labor time to be one of Marx's three weaknesses, albeit a necessary

---

[12]   I avoid considering in the text Milios et al. (2002) who have argued that Marx's value concept (and, thus, surplus value) is a *monetary* one, determined in exchange. Value, for them, is only indirectly measurable through its monetary form, through its appearance therein, so that value itself, they say, is *conceptually non-measurable*: "In Marx's system, value does not belong to the world of empirically detectable (and measurable) quantities; only money does... Exchange value is the sole *objective materialisation* (form of appearance) of value" (p. viii and 21, emphasis in original). That exchange-value is the sole appearance of value does, indeed, appear very early in *Capital*: "The progress of our investigation will show that exchange-value is the only form in which the value of commodities can manifest itself or be expressed" (Marx, 1867, p. 46). But it is quickly followed as to the measurement of value:
>   How, then, is the magnitude of this value to be measured? Plainly, by the quantity of the value-creating substance, the labour, contained in the article. The quantity of labour, however, is measured by its duration, and the labour-time in its turn finds its standard in weeks, days, and hours. (p. 46)

Similar reference by Marx to value being connected with labor time is frequent, even past all of Part I of *Capital*. While Milios et al. (p. 17) find that the first half-dozen pages of *Capital, Volume I* (i.e., Section 1 of Chapter I) are thoroughly Ricardian and that the next hundred-plus pages of *Volume I* after Section 1 "*theoretically recast*" (emphasis in original) those first pages, is not the measurability of value sustained throughout *Capital*? Part II says that the value of labor power "is determined, as in the case of every other commodity, by the labour time necessary for the production, and consequently also the reproduction, of this special article" (p. 167). This passage goes on to illustrate a calculation of the value of labor power, and repeats that "the value of every commodity is determined by the labour-time requisite to turn it out so as of normal quality" (p. 169). In Part III, reference is made to "determining the value of the yarn, or the labour-time required for its production" (p. 182). In Part IV, we find "the value of labour-power, i.e., the labour-time requisite to produce labour-power" (p. 297), and the "law of the determination of value by labour-time" (p. 302). In Part V, "the value in which a day's labour is embodied, increases with the length of that day" (p. 493). Therefore, I cannot follow Milios et al. in claiming value's non-measurability for Marx.

one if goods are to be exchanged at value. McCracken refers the reader to Böhm-Bawerk's "admirable" treatment of the question. Keynes was to write to McCracken saying, "I have found it [the book] of much interest, particularly perhaps the passages relating to Karl Marx, with which I have never been so familiar as I ought to have been" (Kates, 2010, p. 44).

Assuming that prices reflects value for individual commodities, as he does in *Volume I* of *Capital*, was Marx's way of dispensing with the issue for the sake of arriving at his fundamental analysis of the capitalist mode of production.[13]

4.3   *Labor Time Embodied in Constant Capital*

Luxemburg's remarks on value in her *Accumulation of Capital* usefully centered upon discussion of Marx's correction of Adam Smith to include that the value of commodities must include not only living labor but also the dead labor time embodied in constant capital. She based it upon the extended remarks in Marx's *Theories of Surplus Value*. Despite his other theoretical advances, Smith saw the price of individual commodities as $v+s$ (in Marx's expression), so that "the total annual production of commodities by society could also be divided without remainder in terms of their total value into these two parts: wages and surplus value. Here the category of capital has suddenly completely disappeared: society produces nothing but revenue, nothing but articles of consumption, which are also completely consumed by society" (1913, p. 32). However, Luxemburg elaborates:

> That this posed an extremely difficult theoretical problem is demonstrated by the extent to which Marx himself burrowed deep into the matter without at first making any progress or finding a way out; these attempts can be retraced in *Theories of Surplus Value*. However, he did finally manage to provide a brilliant solution, and this came precisely on the basis of his theory of value. Smith was perfectly right: the value of each individual commodity, and of the total production of commodities, represents

---

[13] Keeping somewhat within such methodology, although not within Marx's own attempt to do so in *Volume III*, could not one limit analysis to a collection of commodities regularly consumed by workers? The total price of the collection of these commodities could correspond to their values. Such an approach may address some of the technical concerns that have been raised regarding individual commodity pricing, including the difficult problem of "joint production". With this approach we would find surplus value to be the difference between the overall value that workers produce compared to the value of their labor power. One could suspect that some room would still be left for further criticism of Marx.

nothing other than labor. Furthermore, he was right when he stated that, from the capitalist point of view, all labor can be divided into paid labor (which replaces wages) and unpaid labor (which accrues to the various classes of owners of the means of production). However, he forgot (or rather he overlooked) the fact that labor, alongside its characteristic of creating new value, has also the attribute of transferring the old value contained in the means of production to the commodities newly produced with the latter. (Luxemburg, 1913, p. 34)

Marx's solution was to point out that living labor is not only newly created value, but also the source for transferring past labor (having been engaged in creating means of production) into the value of current commodities, that is, an amalgamation of old, transferred value and newly created value. Thus, where Smith had neglected to incorporate the means of production into commodity values, Marx did not. And, it becomes "of decisive importance for the use of the commodity whether it is itself a means of production or a means of consumption" (Luxemburg, p. 40), a distinction that in turn underpins, for her, the importance of Marx's schemes of reproduction in *Volume II* in which production of the means of production is separated from production of the means of consumption.

5 Marx's Retrospective on Value

A critical comment against the first edition of *Volume I* in an 1868 publication in Leipzig led Marx to write privately a sharp defense of the concept of value to his friend Louis Kugelmann:

> ...if there had been no chapter at all on "Value" in my book, then the analysis of the real relations which I provide would contain the proof and evidence of the real relation of value. All the gossip about the necessity of proving the concept of value is based only on the most complete ignorance, as much of the problem under discussion as of the scientific method. Every child knows that any nation which stopped work – I will not say for one year – but just for a couple of weeks, would die. And every child knows that the volume of products corresponding to the various needs calls for various and quantitatively determined amounts of total social labour. (Marx and Engels, 1948, p. 148)

Value is not to be "proven"; attempting to do so misses the point. And,

> Science consists precisely in working out *how* the law of value asserts itself. So if one wishes to "explain" all the phenomena which appear to contradict the law from the very start, then one would have to provide the science *before* the science. This is exactly Ricardo's mistake.... (p. 148, emphasis in original)

(If one were to study the rate of acceleration of a falling object near the surface of the earth, one does not explain the effect of air resistance *before* establishing the law of acceleration as being 32 feet per second per second.) As late as 1880 Marx writes, "the connection between 'value' and 'production price' ... does not belong at all to the theory of value as such" (Marx and Engels, 1948, p. 198, writing to Domela-Nieuwenhuis).

Marx's 2nd edition of *Capital* in German was completed in 1872, although not published until 1873. The main change was that the text in the Appendix of the 1st edition was brought up to the main text in the 2nd edition, having as a consequence reducing Hegelian-type language (addressed in the previous chapter here). Also, Marx had not had much discussion of commodity fetishism in the 1st edition (only a limited amount in the Appendix) but it became a full section of a dozen pages at the end of his Chapter 1 in the 2nd edition. When he later prepared the 3rd edition in 1882 Marx was sufficiently satisfied with the 2nd that only a change in Chapter 3 on the circulation of money was indicated. Nevertheless, as I have already indicated, the fact that the 1st edition was used for the Russian translation until 1898 must have had some influence regarding how early Russian readers were to understand his work, including the fact that commodity fetishism only had its extended discussion in the 2nd edition.

In 1881 Marx wrote notes on Adolph Wagner's *Lehrbuch der Politischen Ökonomie*. The notes are, of course, reactions to Wagner's writings, but also reaffirm Marx's conclusions about value. The duality of any commodity is "the dual *character* of the *labour* whose product it is: of *useful* labour, i.e. the concrete modes of the labours which create use-values, and of abstract *labour*, of *labour as expenditure of labour power*, regardless of the 'useful' way in which it is expended" (Marx, 1930, p. 546, emphasis in original). In other words, he reaffirms the importance of recognizing and understanding abstract labor in the capitalist mode of production. Once again, he also addresses value, in that "exchange-value is merely a '*form* of expression', an independent way of presenting the *value* contained in the commodity... [Thus,] the *concrete social form* of the product of labour, the '*commodity*', is on the one hand, use-value and on the other, 'value', not exchange value, since the mere *form* of expression is not its own *content*". (pp. 544–545, emphasis in original)[14]

---

14 Kristjanson-Gural (2005) asks whether, for individual commodities, value is solely defined in production prior to exchange, or whether exchange has a role in the determination of value. But his question seems inconsistent with Marx's conception of value insofar as exchange is a form of value, not a determination thereof.

CHAPTER 3

Not Engels, but Marx's Final Edition of *Capital, Volume I* (1882)

> [Douai] must without fail, when translating, compare the 2nd German edition with the *French edition* in which I have included a good deal of new matter and greatly improved my presentation of much else. Re: There are two things I shall be sending you *in the course of this week*:
> 1. *A copy of the French edition for Douai.*
> 2. A list of places where *the French edition* shouldn't be *compared with the German*, but the French text be used as the only basis.
>
> Marx to Sorge, September 27, 1877, of possible English translation (*c.w.*, Volume 45, pp. 276–277, emphasis in original)

> In regard to the second [Russian] edition of the *Capital*, I beg to remark:
> 1. I wish the *divisions into chapters* – and the same holds good for the *subdivisions* – be made according to the French edition.
> 2. That the translator compares always carefully the second German edition with the French one, since the latter contains many important changes and additions…
>
> Marx to Danielson, November 15, 1878 (Marx and Engels, 1948, p. 190, emphasis in original)

Before proceeding to my discussion of accumulation of capital, Marx's intellectual history with *Capital, Volume I* is needed. He published his 1st edition in 1867 in German. He prepared a 2nd edition in 1872 (albeit not in print until 1873) and this edition had considerable changes from the 1st edition. From 1872 to 1875 Marx prepared a French edition sequentially, extensively editing his translator Roy. The French has considerable distinctions from the 2nd German edition. The 3rd German edition of *Volume I,* arose in 1882 because supplies at the publisher for the 2nd edition were running low. Marx had been informed by his publisher Meissner that a new 3rd edition would be necessary, with Marx expressing in December 1881 to his daughter Jenny disappointment that a new edition would interrupt his work on *Volume II* (*c.w.*, Vol. 46, p. 158). He must have felt sufficient dissatisfaction with the 2nd to know that he did not want a mere reprinting of the 2nd edition, although he reports to Jenny in late March 1882 that, for the moment, any work on *Volume I* is impossible (p. 225, probably for health reasons as well as being in Algiers). By October-November, however, Engels asks Bernstein for information that Marx needs for the 3rd edition, demonstrating that Marx was now working on it (pp. 347 and 359). On January 9, 1883, Marx wrote his daughter Eleanor that Meissner had written that

> he is rapidly running out of copies of Capital. Naturally he is getting impatient about the revised sheets. It is an unconscionable time since he heard from me on the subject. Now he will get some definite news. (p. 423; "sheets" refers to text)

The next day Marx also wrote Engels, "I have up till now been scarcely capable of pressing on with the revision. But I believe that, given patience and rigorous self-discipline, I shall soon get back onto the rails again". (p. 425). Patience, however, did not reward Marx's legacy as he died in March.

The changes that Marx had accumulated for the 3rd edition of *Volume I* up to the time of his death are listed in MEGA², II/8, pp. 7–20. Of course, we do not know exactly what the published version would have been, but we know fully his intentions up to his death. Compared to the 2nd German edition, the changes for Parts I–VI are listed in five pages (pp. 7–11, albeit very little for Parts I and II). The changes for the remainder are listed in nine pages (pp. 12–20) including the division of the German Part VII, Chapter 24, into seven chapters instead of seven sections, and the titling of a new "Part VIII", both of which had already occurred in the French edition. The indicated changes for Part VII in the German 2nd were considerably more than for the earlier parts, with whole blocks of text to be drawn from the French edition. Engels himself points this out (Marx, 1867, p. 32). Those nine pages of instructions represented far more page changes in the actual text. If Marx had lived somewhat longer, we would have had his own 3rd edition. I refer to Marx's changes up to his death as his "1882" edition, reflecting accumulating changes that were intended, while also distinguishing it from Engels' 1883 edition of Marx's work.

Until the MEGA² project of reproducing the entirety of Marx and Engels papers into separate volumes regarding *Capital*, we could not, without great difficulty, analyze Engels' activity when he provided his 3rd and his later 4th German editions of *Volume I*, nor his editions of *Volumes II* and *III*. All of those MEGA² volumes are now published, and also are available online[1] and are

---

[1] Available online at http://telota.bbaw.de/mega or https://thecharnelhouse.org/2016/02/05/mega-marx-engels-gesamtausgabe-on-mega.

summarized by van der Linden and Hubmann (2018). With regard to *Volume I*, in this chapter I provide the results of my analysis of Marx's intended 3rd edition, knowing that Engels' editions were not fully what Marx explicitly instructed; in fact, omissions are serious as one gets into Part VII on the accumulation of capital.

While Marx's instructions draw considerably from the French edition, these are not exclusively the case. Other authors have made a contrast between the French edition and the later German editions edited by Engels, but my take appears to be distinct. Because MEGA², II/8, provides the exact instructions by Marx for a 3rd German edition up to the time of his death, *we can produce Marx's 3rd and final German edition, i.e., in order to obtain a definitive final edition.* We do not need to discuss that Engels' did not particularly like the French edition (Roth, 2018, p. 34), nor whether one language or another is preferable for rendering Marx's own understanding, as we would have the Marx's own German edition which would be the standard and the basis for proper translations.

Comparing the 3rd or 4th German edition by Engels to the French edition is not particularly meaningful because neither the 3rd or 4th are what they should have been. We can do better. The co-editor of MEGA² misses the standard I am proposing and simply makes some comparisons between the French to the German editions by Engels, as if Engels' rendering of Marx's instructions were not itself problematic (Roth, pp. 32–36). Actually, since Engels' 4th edition only added a few additional changes to his 3rd, Engels' 3rd edition represented his standard for editing. The difference between what Marx wanted and what Engels' passed down to us is considerable and not acceptable once we arrive at Part VII.

I offer in this chapter a catalog of changes Marx made ready for his own 3rd edition of *Capital, Volume I*. For those passages of his new edition deemed particularly significant, I provide a translation into English, either in this chapter or the next. The reader should, therefore, be able to have a clear understanding of Marx's own final edition. After this exegesis, we will be better prepared to further discuss his work.

1   Marx's Parts I–VI

For the 3rd German edition of *Volume I* relative to the 2nd German edition, Marx had only one textual change within all of Parts I and II. This change was for a few sentences in Chapter 3, Part I, and were incorporated by Engels. Part I of the 2nd German and the French had been prepared more or less simultaneously (Marx and Engels, 1948, pp. 172–173, letters from Marx dated May 28 and June 21, 1872; also, Lefebvre, 1983, p. XIX).

Part II in his German 3rd was only to be divided into three chapters, as had been the case in the French edition, rather than have Part II be three sections of one chapter. Of some significance, the buying and selling of labor power would be presented in its own chapter. Chapter numbering would change as a result. Engels did not follow this instruction. Nevertheless, as a textual matter, Marx must have been satisfied with the presentation in Parts I and II when planning his 3rd German edition: his major changes had already occurred with his editing of the 2nd German relative to the 1st.

Parts III through VI had some changes to be made, often drawing from the portions of the serial continued publications of the French that post-dated Marx's preparation of the 2nd German (this portion of the serial was continuing through 1873). Marx wanted the first chapter of *Part III* on the labor process to be divided into subsections; Engels did so, and at least here pointing to Engels' attention to the instructions with regard to sectioning. Marx wanted three minor changes of about four pages in the second section and then two minor changes in a later paragraph; Engels included all those. There were also small changes in two footnotes in the chapter on the "The Working-Day", both included by Engels, and another small change near the beginning of the chapter on "Rate and Mass of Surplus Value" that ends Part III (but I do not understand this particular one by Marx).

For Part IV, "Production of Relative Surplus-Value", in the title of its Section 3, third chapter, Engels incorporated "Serial" replacing "Organic". The next change Marx wanted was some seventy-five pages later for the next chapter on "Machinery and Modern Industry", Section 4, and it was a small addition incorporated by Engels, although another small footnote change at the end of the section was not. In Section 5, Marx wanted a change in a second paragraph to have footnoted material integrated into the text, but Engels omitted it. Toward the end of this section, utilizing the French, a table, a paragraph, and an additional passage were to be inserted and Engels so included. In the next section on compensation theory, Marx had indicated four changes, utilizing the French, the first being one paragraph modified by Engels (but with less provocative language[2]), while the next three were included. In Section 7 there was

---

2 Compared to Marx (1867, pp. 413–414), Marx (1872–75, p. 190 left, first paragraph) reads, in translation from French:
>   Also, this is nothing that the doctrines of compensation are riding on. For them, the great matter is the subsistence of the dismissed workers. By releasing our fifty workers from their £1500 salary, the machine releases £1500 of subsistence from their consumption. This is the fact in its sad reality! Cutting off the food supply to the worker, the full-bellies

a small addition incorporated by Engels. Finally, in Section 9 on factory legislation, Marx planned an additional five pages from the French; Engels did not comply in his 3rd edition, but did so in his 4th.

In Part v, within its first chapter "Absolute and Relative Surplus-Value" and *against Marx's instructions, Engels left in subjection* (subsumption in the Penguin edition). Specifically, Marx instructed use of the French edition for the first four pages, yet Engels did so only for the first two pages, but not thereafter and thus leaving in mention of formal and real subjection of labor (*Subsumtion* in German) in his revised wording. This meant that Marx's discussion in the 1st and 2nd German editions that had mentioned subjection/subsumption was to be completely eliminated, yet it was not in Engels' edition. The implication is that what Marx had drafted concerning subjection/subsumption for his unpublished "Results of the Immediate Process of Production" (Marx, 1933, pp. 943–1084), would no longer have even a brief mention in his 3rd German, it being already removed in the French. Attention came to be drawn to the concept when "Results" later became published as if it might still belong in *Volume 1* (see Penguin edition of Marx, 1867, p. 645, fn. *, citing its pp. 1019–1038 on subsumption in spite Marx's decision to eliminate any mention).

The issue of eliminating any mention of subjection (subsumption) was discussed by White (1996) as part of Marx's intellectual progress, although without pointing to its mention being completely eliminated only in the French edition. An example of the misleading result of Engels' editing error is Das' (2012) recent article treating subsumption as part of *Capital*, perhaps unaware of Marx's instruction to eliminate all mention. Two other changes in this chapter, both utilizing the French, were included by Engels, one of which was a few sentences and the second being two full pages at the end.

The next chapter within Part v included five small changes in Section 1, four of which Engels included. Three paragraphs at the end of the section were indicated by Marx to be changed according to the French text: Engels retained two paragraphs from the 2nd German while moving the first to the end, expanded according to the French. Much of the first paragraph of Section 2 was to be replaced from the French, but Engels did not do so (and I think he was correct to leave it as before). A short Section 3 was to be fully replaced from the French text and Engels incorporated the change.

---

call it making food *available* to the worker as a new fund for employment in another industry. As you can see, it all depends on how you express yourself. *Nominibus mollire licet mala.*

For Part VI, "Wages", only the last chapter was indicated by Marx for changing – by adding considerable material – and was incorporated into the 3rd by Engels.

∴

Pulling together the changes noted above, *excepting the two pages of Part V that included subjection (subsumption),*[3] *up to the end of Part VI, the German text after its 4th edition is an accurate representation of Marx's instructions* (or the German 3rd if adding the five-page addition within Section 9 of "Machinery and Modern Industry" incorporated into the 4th).

The changes instructed by Marx for Part VII, "The Accumulation of Capital", intended for the 3rd German edition, and including division into Part VII and Part VIII, are extensive. They utilize the last of the serial French edition, completed only in 1875. As to be seen, these changes were not appropriately followed by Engels in his editions. The timing gap between the 1872–73 portions of the French serial and the 1875 dating of the last serial allowed Marx to make important adjustments in his theoretical conceptions of accumulation of capital relative to prior conceptions contained in the 2nd German edition. They were supposed to be included in the 3rd German edition.

2 The Structural Divisions Desired by Marx, Contrasted to Engels

> *The division into chapters* should be done as in the *French edition* (*better than in the German*).
>
> Marx's instruction for an American edition, 1877 (MEGA², II/8, p. 21, emphasis in original)

> The sections of the German edition, chapter twenty-four (The So-called Primitive Accumulation) are to be referred to as chapters, as in the French edition.
>
> Marx's instruction Engels had in hand (MEGA², II/8, p. 17)

The 1st German edition (1867) of *Capital, Volume I*, was divided into six "Chapters". In the 2nd edition (1872), "Chapters" became "Parts" and included

---

3 Of lesser importance are two paragraphs later in Part V and some minor changes.

twenty-five chapters within seven Parts, the material on wages having been in the fifth "chapter" now placed and expanded in a new Part VI, "Wages". The French edition of 1872–75 had thirty-three chapters and eight Parts. A new Part VIII, "L'accumulation primitive", consisted of eight chapters, drawn from seven sections of first chapter of Part VII in the 2nd German edition as well as the last chapter on colonialism. In the French, as I already indicated, Part II was broken into three chapters, which explains thirty-three chapters total count.

The French edition for the last Parts VII and VIII had been edited by Marx in early 1875 (unlike the prior Parts of the French). These two Parts of the French had had more than two years to allow Marx to reconsider his presentation of the accumulation-of-capital subject matter. The time interval led to significant changes. By contrast, Parts I–VI of the French had been published in serial form already in 1872–73, the first serial even before the 2nd German edition, delayed until its appearance in May 1873 due to difficulties at the publisher (a fact allowing the well-known Afterword by Marx).

In November 1878, as an expression of importance of the structural changes, Marx wrote Danielson, who had prepared the first Russian translation in 1872, that he wanted the next Russian edition to follow the French chapter divisions (Marx and Engels, 1948, p. 190). Danielson would prepare a 2nd Russian edition, but that would await 1898 and thus later in our story. In connection with a possible translation into English, Marx had previously stated in 1877 that the chapter divisions in the French are better than in the German (MEGA², II/8, p. 21). And Engels knew of Marx's desire to use the structure of the French edition for future editions. Specifically, Engels had Marx's preparatory notes to use for the upcoming 3rd German edition which, among many other changes to be incorporated, directly pointed to incorporation of the French structural division. Marx explicitly referenced both the existing 2nd German edition to be changed and the French edition, and Engels does report that he had consulted Marx's notes for the 3rd German edition (Marx, 1867, p. 32). In fact, Engels did follow Marx's desire with regard to one minor structural matter, confirming any doubt whether he was paying close attention.[4] Nevertheless, in 1883, when

---

4 As I indicated before in this chapter, in the 2nd German edition, the first chapter in Part III on production of absolute surplus value is undivided as to sections, but is indicated by Marx for the 3rd edition to be divided into the two sections as in the French (MEGA², II/8, p. 7, compared to II/6, Inhalt). This small change is indeed followed by Engels. On the other hand, Engels did *not* follow the division of Part II into three chapters, nor the division of Part VII of five chapters into two Parts VII and VIII of eleven chapters, with the latter having eight

Engels put out his 3rd German edition of *Volume I* he retained the earlier German division into twenty-five chapters and seven parts. (And he continued to retain that division later in his 4th edition, as I address later.) Of particular significance, the material on primitive accumulation was left without its analysis being separated within a new Part VIII, as in the French. *To this day, anyone reading the German edition of* Capital, *Volume I, edited by Engels reads from a different structure than the English reader,* or French readers reading Marx's French edition. (Most strangely, a new French translation appeared a century later that even reverted, without explanation, to the German structure.)

We know that Marx had carefully corrected before publication Roy's translation into French of *Volume I* and that he had found innumerable problems (see Lefebvre, 1983, pp. xi-xxix). We know that Engels put in a lot of work after Marx's death toward getting the 3rd edition ready (Marx and Engels, 1948, p. 218, i.e., letters from Engels dated June 29 and August 30, 1883). We also know that Engels had a rather unfavorable opinion of the French edition ("the French translation is partly a dulled version of the German, and Marx would never have written the German like that" – the June 29 letter). Still, why did Engels' edition retain in the 3rd German edition, the divisions of 2nd German edition, in spite of Marx's desire? Translation as such cannot the explanation.

A few years later and published in 1887, Engels was to supervise the first English edition, translated by Samuel Moore and Edward Aveling, with significant assistance from Marx's daughter Eleanor Aveling regarding English language citations therein. *This English edition did have the divisions of the French, not of the 3rd German.* In Chapter 5, I address this distinction when also addressing that the 4th German edition still retained the 2nd German division.

Although supportive of the French edition's importance, discussion by Anderson (1983) neglected to mention this difference in divisions. Later, Anderson (2010, p. 174) does so refer. Arthur (1996, pp. 176–178) usefully addresses confused explanations by others as to why the English has a different division than the German and simply concludes that too little attention is being paid to the distinct French edition.

The issue of differing part and chapter divisions between the German and the French is not unimportant and *translation issues as such are irrelevant* for comprehending this. Understanding the substantive issues at stake requires examination of inclusions and exclusions between what Marx wanted and what Engels did or did not incorporate. They are significant. I will offer in

---

chapters, as the case for the French and indicated by Marx for the next German edition (MEGA², II/8, pp. 7 and 17).

Chapter 5 some explanations as to Marx's motivation for his changes in structure and in substance.

3   Marx's Parts VII and VIII (1882) Compared with Engels' 3rd German Edition (1883)

> [W]hatever the literary defects of this French edition may be, it possesses a scientific value independent of the original and should be consulted even by readers familiar with the German.
>   Marx (1867, p. 31, dated April 28, 1875).

> But now that I am suddenly expected to take Marx's place in matters of theory and play first fiddle, there will inevitably be blunders and no one is more aware of that than I.
>   Engels (Marx and Engels, c.w., Vol. 47, p. 202, October 15, 1884)

Substantive differences between Part VII of the 2nd German edition and Parts VII and VIII of the French have been brought to some attention by Anderson (1983 and 2010) and Arthur (1996). Anderson (pp. 73–74) pointed to several paragraphs in the Section 3 of the French chapter "The General Law of Capitalist Accumulation" missing altogether in later German editions. He calls particular attention to the issue of crises and unemployment addressed in the French not incorporated into the Engels' 3rd or 4th German editions.[5] However, he erroneously refers (pp. 72–73) to Marx's 1875 Afterword to the French in order to suggest that Marx had changes in the French that had not yet been included even in the 2nd German edition. In fact, those were already incorporated in the 2nd German, particularly, on accumulation and on fetishism of commodities. The French Afterword is actually referring to the 2nd German Afterword of 1873 that was reporting changes compared to the 1st German. In any case, Anderson's 1983 article was a leading work calling attention to the basic problem, and his comments on Marx's preference for the French edition (p. 176) remain important. Unfortunately, Anderson (2010, pp. 173–180) still does not give full attention to the extent of differences in the French edition compared to Engels' editions and does not refer to Marx's instructions.

For the 3rd German edition, Marx wanted the entire short introduction to Part VII, "The Accumulation of Capital" to use the French edition. For the

---

5 Anderson (pp. 75–76) also focused on the French text in a section on "The Factory", for which Marx had *not* indicated use of the French in his planned 3rd German.

chapter "Conversion of Surplus Value in Capital", he wanted incorporated from the French all six pages of Section 1, three pages within Section 4, and another three pages representing most of Section 5. Even more significantly, for the next chapter "The General Law of Capitalist Accumulation", he wanted most of Sections 2, 3 and 4 changed, comprising 27 pages in the 2nd German. Of those 27 pages in three sections, fully 19 pages are indicated by Marx for use in full from the French into the 3rd German, namely all of Sections 2 and 4 and a major part of Section 3. And the text was often to be expanded. There are other scattered changes indicated. The entire "The Secret of Primitive Accumulation" (a section in the 2nd German, being a chapter in the French) was also instructed to be replaced using the French.

For Marx's material on accumulation of capital, I now turn to more detailed attention to differences between Marx's intentions for the 3rd edition and resulting publication under Engels' editorship. Engels' 4th German edition of 1890 is addressed in Chapter 5 where some additional inclusions do appear, but the standard of Engels' editing was with the 3rd.

> *Part VII*: Introduction and first two chapters "Simple Reproduction" and "Conversion of Surplus Value into Capital"

For the introduction to Part VII, for the most part, Engels's 3rd edition complied with Marx's changes, although adding two sentences in the fourth paragraph and a first sentence into the next, last paragraph.

For the "Simple Reproduction" chapter, from the French Marx instructed an additional paragraph to be inserted, an additional footnote citing Adam Smith, two short substitutions, a rather long substitution almost a page, and finally a one paragraph substitution. Marx also mentioned to two minor changes. All were incorporated by Engels.

For the chapter "Conversion of Surplus Value into Capital", and given the incorporations that were to take place later in the 4th German edition Engels edited, the result can be accepted in a qualified manner: That is, for Section 1, the entire six pages were to be replaced using the French edition which would entail some expansion. The first four pages were incorporated by Engels into his 3rd through "The more the capitalist has accumulated, the more is he able to accumulate" (Marx, 1867, p. 546). The following long paragraph in the 3rd German was Engels' rewording of the remainder of the 2nd edition while none of the next three pages of the French were included into the 3rd (they were simply left out altogether). In the 4th edition, Engels incorporates the remaining pages – pp. 548–551, yet he leaves in what he written for the 3rd edition. If a reader would delete the long paragraph beginning, "In so far as the surplus-value…" (p. 546) to the bottom of the next page, the French edition would then be fully incorporated as instructed by Marx.

Regarding Sections 2 and 3, Marx indicated a number of small changes and a longer one; they were included by Engels in the 3rd edition. Section 4 had somewhat more changes, usually drawing from the French edition. While Engels included them, there are passages (pp. 566–567) that rather seem to be Engels' reformulation of the French. For Section 5, "The So-called Labour-Fund", Marx wanted the text up to his citing Fawcett (i.e., p. 570 up to p. 572) to be replaced from the French in order to permit an elaboration (three footnotes being retained). Engels, however, left the 2nd German language.

I would like to note the fact that two pages into the "Conversion" chapter, the 3rd edition appropriately included an important footnote that had appeared for the first time in the French reading, "In order to examine the object of our investigation in its integrity, free from all disturbing subsidiary circumstances, we must treat the whole world as one nation, and assume that capitalist production is established everywhere and has taken possession of every branch of industry" (1867, p. 545, fn. 1). When Marx also separated out primitive accumulation in the French into a new Part VIII, he mirrored this delimitation since the "General Law" chapter is no longer to be interfaced with primitive accumulation, as had been the case in the inclusive Part VII of the 2nd German. Consideration of primitive accumulation becoming a distinct subject matter is addressed in my Chapter 5 below.

N.B.: Up to the chapter "The General Law of Capitalist Accumulation", after Engels' 4th German edition, the text is acceptable since almost all changes (not all, the most important being the needed elimination of subjection/subsumption) that Marx had instructed for his 3rd edition were by then included by Engels. However, serious troubles begin thereafter. The corrected "General Law" chapter is presented in my next chapter (up to its last section).

...

Part VII: Chapter on "The General Law of Capitalist Accumulation"

The text of Section 1 in the 3rd edition mostly follows Marx's desires for change from the 2nd German, except a couple of additional paragraphs from the French near the beginning that Engels reduced to a shorter addition. The most important change by Marx is to begin the entire chapter by defining, from the French, three versions of the composition of capital. This had not been included in the second 2nd German, Marx remarking that it was "missing" (apparently meaning that it should already have been included in the 2nd). In Chapter 8 below, I address the issues raised. While the German title for the section, "The Increased Demand for Labour-Power that Accompanies Accumulation, the Composition of Capital Remaining the Same" was retained by Engels, and, in the French, the title reads, "As the Composition of Capital remains the Same, the Progress of Accumulation tends to raise the Wage Rate", Marx did not mention a title change.

Section 2 contains significant omissions on the part of Engels; all six pages were supposed to be entirely substituted from the French. The 2nd German had been titled "Relative Diminution of the Variable Part of Capital Simultaneously with the Progress of Accumulation and of the Concentration that Accompanies It". In the French reference in the title to concentration is deleted and Marx re-phrased the title to "Successive Changes in the Composition of Capital with the Progress of Accumulation and Relative Diminution of that Part of Capital that is exchanged against Labor Power". Engels retained the 2nd German titling. Comparing the differences between 2nd and 3rd German editions, the first two short paragraphs are appropriately changed by Engels. The third paragraph of one-half page in the 2nd was to have been replaced from the French comprising some two pages explaining the forces behind changes in the technical composition of capital, Engels retained the 2nd German in his 3rd edition (Marx, 1867, p. 581, as per 2nd). An English translation of the intended French text is provided in Chapter 4 here. The next four paragraphs beginning "This change in the technical composition of capital" are included by Engels, but the following paragraphs beginning "In Part v..." (pp. 583–584) was to be substituted using the French, adding considerable explanation, yet not adopted by Engels. The language of the French in translation is provided in the next chapter, after the paragraphs Engels did incorporate. While including one paragraph on centralization, Engels did not incorporate the last three-plus pages in the French in which "concentration" is distinguished, for the first time, from "centralization" (Marx, 1867, pp. 585–589).

Section 3 has further deficiencies. While its title, "Progressive Production of a Relative Surplus Population or Industrial Reserve Army", was left to be unchanged from the 2nd German, Marx had wanted the first eight pages of the French text to substitute for the first four pages of the German 2nd. The beginning two pages (even including a further change by Marx made subsequent to the French edition language) were to elaborate *Marx's changed focus toward employment* and followed by his illustrative discussion. Engels failed to include the changes. The considerably change of focus is obvious just from reading the beginning paragraphs:

French (Marx, 1872–1875, p. 276–277, in English translation, present author):

The absolute demand for labour caused by a capital is not because of its absolute size, but because of its variable part, which alone is exchanged for labour power. The relative labour demand that a capital generates, i.e. the proportion between its own size and the amount of labour it absorbs, is determined by the proportional size of its variable fraction. We have just shown that the accumulation that increases social capital simultaneously reduces the proportional size of its variable component and thus reduces the relative demand for labour. Now, what is the effect of this movement on the fate of the working class?

To solve this problem, it is clear that it is first necessary to examine how the reduction suffered by the variable part of an accumulating capital affects the absolute size of this part, and as a consequent, how does a decrease in the relative demand for labour react to the absolute or actual demand for labour?

German 2nd, retained in Engels' 3rd and 4th (Marx, 1867, p. 589):

The accumulation of capital, though originally appearing as its quantitative extension only, is effected, as we have seen, under a progressive qualitative change in its composition, under a constant increase of its constant, at the expense of its variable component.

The specifically capitalist mode of production, the development of the productive power of labour corresponding to it, and the change thence resulting in the organic composition of capital, do not merely keep pace with the advance of accumulation, or with the growth of social wealth. They develop at a much quicker rate, because mere accumulation, the absolute increase of the total social capital, is accompanied by the centralisation of the individual capitals of which that total is made up; and because the change in the technological composition of the additional capital goes hand in hand with a similar change in the technological composition of the original capital. With the advance of accumulation, therefore, the proportion of constant to variable capital changes....

Only when coming to refer to Merivale – about four pages into the 2nd German – is there a return, desired by Marx, for one paragraph of the 2nd German text. After this "Merivale" paragraph, possible rising unemployment (growing reserve army) is highlighted in the French[6] to replace the 2nd German, but was

---

6 If it were conjectured that Engels may have felt that later economic developments after 1873 no longer warranted the change in focus that Marx had included in the French edition and had also desired for the 3rd German, then, I would point to a comment in Engels' letter of

not incorporated by Engels.[7] Graßmann (2018, pp. 151–154) discusses the importance of this omission and an earlier one in the section. All of the text in question is in translation in the next chapter.

Section 4 of seven pages was to be replaced in full using the French edition. These changes are rather in details, however, and some passages were already in the 2nd German. In the third paragraph, where capital is stated to want "larger numbers of youthful labourers, a smaller number of adults" (Marx, 1867, p. 600), Marx's desired change for the 3rd German indicated a gender issue presented in the French – "greater proportion of women, children, adolescents, young people, than men are needed" (Marx, 1872–1875, p. 283). Engels did not include this change.

As for Section 5, it contains sixty pages of illustrations of the preceding material with scattered, small changes noted by Marx.

I conclude that the changes Marx wanted in this chapter clearly should have been incorporated by Engels as they do reflect a changed emphasis toward employment and analyzing the effects upon laborers of the consequences of the production of relative surplus value. Anderson was correct in this regard. But is the glass three-quarters full or a quarter empty? The next contributes to a more complete judgement.

French, Part VIII, "Primitive Accumulation", Chapter 26, "The Secret of Primitive Accumulation"

German 2nd and Engel's 3rd and 4th, Part VII, "The Accumulation of Capital", within Chapter 24, "The So-Called Primitive Accumulation", first section "The Secret of Primitive Accumulation"

May 10–11, 1883, in which he refers to increasing crises of overproduction (*c.w.*, Vol. 47, p. 25), a comment that would not sustain such a conjecture.

7 German 2nd, and retained in Engels' 3rd and 4th German (Marx, 1867, pp. 594–595):

Capitalist production can by no means content itself with the quantity of disposable labour power which the natural increase of population yields. It requires for its free play an industrial reserve army independent of these natural limits.

Up to this point it has been assumed that the increase or diminution of the variable capital corresponds rigidly with the increase or diminution of the number of labourers employed.

The number of labourers commanded by capital may remain the same, or even fall, while the variable capital increases. This is the case if the individual labourer yields more labour.... Increase of variable capital, in this case, becomes an index of more labour, but not of more labourers employed....

In the French, Chapter 26 begins a new Part VIII and was so desired by Marx for the 3rd German. As already noted, Engels did not accept this. While Engels made most of the textual changes up to the last paragraph (with exceptions noted in MEGA² II/10 Apparat, pp. 777–778), *a very significant issue for revision into the 3rd German is the last paragraph of the French chapter that Engels did not include*:

French (Marx, 1872–1875, p. 315, in English translation):

> In the history of primitive accumulation, all revolutions are epoch-making that act as levers for the capitalist class in course of formation, above all, those moments when great masses of men are suddenly and forcibly torn from their means of production and traditional existence, and hurled impromptu on the labor-market. But the basis of this whole evolution is the expropriation of the cultivators.
>
> So far, it has been carried out in a radical manner only in England; this country will therefore necessarily play the leading role in our sketch. But all the countries in Western Europe are going through the same process, although in accordance with the particular environment it changes its local color, or confines itself to a narrower sphere, or shows a less pronounced character, or follows a different order of succession.

German 2nd, and retained in Engels' 3rd and 4th (Marx, 1867, pp. 669–670):

> In the history of primitive accumulation, all revolutions are epoch-making that act as levers for the capitalist class in course of formation; but, above all, those moments when great masses of men are suddenly and forcibly torn from their means of subsistence, and hurled as free and "unattached" proletarians on the labour-market. The expropriation of the agricultural producer, of the peasant, from the soil, is the basis of the whole process. The history of this expropriation, in different countries, assumes different aspects, and runs through its various phases in different orders of succession, and at different periods. In England alone, which we take as our example, has the classic form.

Do not miss the difference! In his revision, *Marx delimits discussion only to Western Europe and also circumscribes it with "local character", "narrower sphere", and "less pronounced character".* Russia, India, China and rest of the world are not to be included. Anderson (2010, pp. 178–180) also points this out. While Engels incorporated most of preceding changes for this introduction from the French compared to the 2nd German, he *stops* at making this last change! In my judgement, this failure by Engels cannot be defended. Furthermore, he retained this material as one *section* of seven *within a single chapter* on primitive accumulation, all still within Part VII.

Engels' editing here was significant and had to be intentional. Likewise, so was Marx's in deciding to leave out Russia and the rest of the world, besides Western Europe, when addressing primitive accumulation and in his placing this subject matter within a new Part VIII of *Volume 1*. Engels' double failures – indeed, rejections of Marx's corrections – seems connected. Chapter 5 here further discusses these issues.

> *German 2nd and Engel's 3rd and 4th, Part VII,* "The Accumulation of Capital", Chapter 24, "The So-Called Primitive Accumulation", second through seventh sections

> *French Part VIII,* "The So-Called Primitive Accumulation", Chapters 27 to 32

The first page in the French of the chapter, "Expropriation of the Agriculture Population from the Land", changed "Europe" to "Western Europe", although the MEGA² does not have indication from Marx for its incorporation into his 3rd German, perhaps simply his oversight. There were, otherwise, many changes in these pages instructed by Marx, sometimes independent of the French and sometimes drawing upon the French, but none of much length.

> *German 2nd and Engel's 3rd and 4th, Part VII,* "The Accumulation of Capital", Chapter 25, "The Modern Theory of Colonialism"

> *French Part VIII,* "The So-Called Primitive Accumulation", Chapter 33, "The Modern Theory of Colonialism"

A significant change for the final chapter on colonialism occurs in the French, although Marx had not pointed it out for specific inclusion in the 3rd German. That is, in the 1st German edition expropriation had been described as being "accomplished" (*vollbrach*) without qualifier. In the 2nd German (retained by Engels in later editions), expropriation was described as "more or less" accomplished (*mehr oder minder vollbrach*). In the 1875 French edition, Marx delimits it further to its being accomplished only "in part" (*en partie*). This sequence exhibits a changing perception on the Marx's part. I footnote the three texts.[8]

---

8 German 1st: Im Westen von Europa, dem Heimathsland der politischen Oekonomie, ist der Proceß der ursprünglichen Akkumulation vollbracht.

Marx's instructions indicated a change immediately after the above: capitalist regime (*das kapitalistische Regiment*) replaces the capitalist mode of production (*die kapitalistische Produktionsweise*), seemingly representing a lessening focus on the economy. This was incorporated by Engels. There were a number of other scattered changes in this last chapter I do not survey.

German 2nd, retained in Engels' 3rd and 4th: Im Westen von Europa, dem Heimathsland der politischen Oekonomie, ist der Proceß der ursprünglichen Akkumulation mehr oder minder vollbracht.

French: Dans l'Europe occidentale, mère-patrie de l'économie politique, l'accumulation primitive, c'est-à-dire, l'expropriation des travailleurs, est en partie consommé...

CHAPTER 4

Text: "The General Law of Capitalist Accumulation", Sections 1–4, as Desired by Marx (1882)

The standard 4th German edition of *Capital, Volume 1*, edited by Engels has considerable shortcomings, even errors, compared to Marx's intentions for *his* next German edition after the 2nd. Engels' edition became almost universally the reference point, not least for translations in most other languages. Deficiencies have been cited occasionally, but corrections have not been incorporated into the representation of Marx's last desired presentation. To help remedy this problem for the main sections of the "General Law of Capitalist Accumulation", the first four of five, I provide Marx's desired language for *his* 3rd edition.[1] This supplements analysis in the previous chapter of Marx's intentions, which concluded that the main problem within Engels' 4th edition before arriving at this "General Law" chapter was in retaining subjection/subsumption that should have been removed.

Note:

- For Marx's intended inclusions into *his* 3rd German, translations into English from the French edition, otherwise absent, are by the present author.
- Sections 2 and 3 below provide both those passages appropriately included by Engels (using the Moore/Aveling translation for which Engels was editor) and those not included (where I provide translation).
- Page references are to Marx (1867, the Moore/Aveling edition as amended after Engels' 4th German). Footnotes not otherwise included are marked with *; these simply cite sources.
- A detailed comparison between the 4th German edition and the French edition is available at MEGA² II/10, Apparat, i.e., pp. 762–776 for first four sections, and pp. 776–783 for the last section not addressed here. *However*, since I address only those changes specifically instructed by Marx for his next German edition (as provided in MEGA² II/8, pp. 7–20), *only* these changes are taken to be warranted. Thus, I am not giving any priority to the French edition as such.

---

[1] I thank Hagar Hafez for her assistance with these translations.

1   Section 1: the Increased Demand for Labour-Power that Accompanies Accumulation, the Composition of Capital Remaining the Same

> (*Three textual changes were intended by Marx for Section 1. They were **incorporated by Engels** (pp. 574–582), with some changes in wording (p. 575) where the French begins with "After these preliminary remarks [on the composition of capital], let us return to capitalist accumulation". It continues with "Growth of capital…" See also Chapter 6 here, p. 112, fn. 5. The text is not reproduced here.*)

2   Section 2: Changes in the Composition of Capital with the Progress of Accumulation and Relative Diminution of that Part of Capital that is Exchanged against Labor Power

> (*Full substitution from the French text for Section 2 was intended by Marx. The titling in French was **not incorporated by Engels**, but the initial text substitution was **incorporated by Engels for first two paragraphs** (pp. 582–583) and follows.*)

According to the economists themselves, it is neither the actual extent of social wealth, nor the magnitude of the capital already functioning, that lead to a rise of wages, but only the constant growth of accumulation and the degree of rapidity of that growth. (Adam Smith, Book I, Chapter 8) So far, we have only considered one special phase of this process, that in which the increase of capital occurs along with a constant technical composition of capital. But the process goes beyond this phase.

Once given the general basis of the capitalistic system, then, in the course of accumulation, a point is reached at which the development of the productivity of social labour becomes the most powerful lever of accumulation. "The same cause", says Adam Smith, "which raises the wages of labour, the increase of stock, tends to increase its productive powers, and to make a smaller quantity of labour produce a greater quantity of work".

> (*Long substitution intended by Marx from the French text was **not incorporated by Engels** for the third paragraph: "Apart from…" (p. 583 per 2nd ed.), Translation from the French text follows.*)

But how is this result achieved? Through a series of changes in the manner of producing that puts a given labour force in a position to move an ever-increasing mass of means of production. With this increase, compared to the labour force employed, the means of production play a dual role. Some of them, such as machines, buildings, furnaces, drainage devices, mineral fertilizers, etc., are increased in number, extent, mass and efficiency to make work more productive, while others, raw and auxiliary materials, are increased because work that has become more productive consumes more in a given time.

At the birth of large industry, a method was discovered in England to convert molten iron into wrought iron using coke. This process, called *puddling*, which consists of refining the iron in specially constructed furnaces, resulted in a huge expansion of the blast furnaces, the use of hot bellows apparatuses, etc., and such an increase in the tools and materials used by the same amount of work that the iron was soon delivered in sufficient quantities and at a price low enough to drive stone and wood workers from a host of jobs. Since iron and coal are the main levers of modern industry, the importance of this innovation cannot be overstated.

However, the puddler, the worker engaged in refining the smelting, carries out a manual operation in such a manner that the size of the batches he is able to handle remains limited by his personal abilities, and it is this limit that now stops the wonderful growth that the metallurgical industry has enjoyed since 1780, the date of the invention of puddling.

"The fact is", exclaims *The Engineering*, one of the organs of English engineers, "that the old process of hand-puddling is little better than a barbarism.... The current trend in our industry is to operate different levels of manufacturing with an wide range of methods. Thus, almost every year, larger blast furnaces, heavier steam hammers, more powerful rolling mills, and more gigantic instruments applied to the many branches of metal manufacturing are produced. In the middle of this general increase – an increase in the means of production compared to the work employed – the puddling process has remained almost stationary and today puts unbearable obstacles in the development of the industry.... Also, it is being supplemented in all major factories by furnaces with automatic revolutions and capable of colossal batches completely beyond the reach of manual labour". (*The Engineering*, 12 June 1874)

Thus, after having revolutionized the iron industry and caused a great extension of the tools and mass of materials used by a certain amount of work, puddling has become, in the course of accumulation, an economic obstacle which is being eliminated by new processes capable of pushing back the limits it is still setting to the increase in the material resources of production in relation to the work employed. This is the story of all the discoveries and inventions that occur as a result of accumulation, as we have proved by tracing the course of modern production from its origin to our time (see Part IV of this book).

In the progress of accumulation, there is therefore not only a quantitative and simultaneous increase in the various real elements of capital. The development of the productive powers of social work that this progress brings is also manifested by qualitative changes, by gradual changes in the technical composition of capital, whose objective factor gradually gains in proportion to the subjective factor, i.e., the mass of tools and materials increases more and more in comparison with the sum of the labour force required to implement them. As capital increases making labour more productive, it reduces the demand for it relative to its own size.

*(Four paragraph substitution by Marx from the French text was **incorporated by Engels** (pp. 583–584) as follows.)*

This change in the technical composition of capital, this growth in the mass of means of production, as compared with the mass of the labour-power that vivifies them, is reflected again in its value-composition, by the increase of the constant constituent of capital at the expense of its variable constituent. There may be, *e.g.*, originally 50 per cent of a capital laid out in means of production, and 50 per cent in labour-power; later on, with the development of the productivity of labour, 80 per cent in means of production, 20 per cent in labour-power, and so on. Of course, it is not the capital as a whole, but only its variable part, which is exchanged for labor power and forms the fund to be distributed among the employees [this sentence in the French is absent from Engels' edition. P.Z.]. This law of the progressive increase in constant capital, in proportion to the variable, is confirmed at every step (as already shown) by the comparative analysis of the prices of commodities, whether we compare different economic epochs or different nations in the same epoch. The relative magnitude of the element of price, which represents the value of the means of production only, or the constant part of capital consumed, is in direct proportion; the relative magnitude of the other element of price that pays labour (the variable part of capital) is in inverse proportion to the advance of accumulation.

This diminution in the variable part of capital as compared with the constant, or the altered value-composition of the capital, however, only shows approximately the change in the composition of its material constituents. If, *e.g.*, the capital-value employed today in spinning is 7/8 constant and 1/8 variable, whilst at the beginning of the 18th century it was 1/2 constant and 1/2 variable, on the other hand, the mass of raw material, instruments of labour, etc., that a certain quantity of spinning labour consumes productively to-day, is many hundred times greater than at the beginning of the 18th century. The reason is simply that, with the increasing productivity of labour, not only does the mass of the means of production consumed by it increase, but their value compared with their mass diminishes. Their value therefore rises absolutely, but not in proportion to their mass. The increase of the difference between constant and variable capital is, therefore, much less than that of the difference between the mass of the means of production into which the constant, and the mass of the labour-power into which the variable, capital is converted. The former difference increases with the latter, but in a smaller degree.

To avoid errors, it should be noted that the progress of accumulation, by decreasing the relative size of variable capital, does not exclude its absolute growth [this sentence in the French is absent from Engels' edition. P.Z.]. But, if the progress of accumulation lessens the relative magnitude of the variable part of capital, it by no means, in doing this, excludes the possibility of a rise in its absolute magnitude. Suppose that a capital-value at first is divided into 50 per cent. of constant and 50 per cent. of variable capital; later into 80 per cent. of constant and 20 per cent. of variable. If in the meantime the original capital, say £6,000, has increased to £18,000, its variable constituent has also increased. It was £3,000, it is now £3,600. But whereas formerly an increase of capital by 20 per cent. would have sufficed to raise the demand for labour 20 per cent, now this latter rise requires a tripling of the original capital.

(*Substitution by Marx from the French text was **not incorporated** by Engels, for the long paragraph "In Part IV..." (pp. 584–585 per 2nd ed.). Translation from the French text follows.*)

Cooperation, division of manufacturing, machinery, etc., in a word, the methods likely to give rise to the powers of collective labour, can only be introduced where production is already carried out on a fairly large scale. As it expands, these methods develop. Based upon the employed, the scale of operations depends primarily on the size of the capital accumulated in the hands of private entrepreneurs. Thus, a certain "previous accumulation",[2] the genesis of which we will later examine, becomes the starting point of modern industry, the set of social combinations and technical processes that we have named the specific mode of capitalist production, capitalist production properly labelled. But all the methods it uses to fertilize labour are methods to increase the surplus value or net proceeds, to feed the source of accumulation, to produce capital by means of capital. If, therefore, accumulation must have reached a

---

2 "Accumulation of stock is previously necessary for carrying on this great improvement in the productive powers of labour" (A. Smith, Book II).

certain degree of magnitude for the specific mode of capitalist production to be established, it accelerates the build-up of further progress which, by allowing the scale of enterprises to be further expanded, influences again the development of capitalist production, etc. These two economic factors, because of the reciprocal impulse they give to each other, provoke changes in the technical composition of capital that gradually reduce the variable part of it compared to the constant part.

> (*Substitution from the French intended by Marx was **not incorporated by Engels**, beginning with "Every individual capital..." (pp. 585–586, being a two paragraph mixing of 2nd, 3rd and 4th eds.). Translation from the French text follows.*)

Each of the individual capitals composing the social capital represents at first sight a certain *concentration*, in the hands of a capitalist, of means of production and of means of maintaining labour. To the extent it accumulates, concentration becomes extended. By increasing the reproductive elements of wealth, accumulation thus causes at the same time an increasing concentration in the hands of private entrepreneurs. This kind of concentration, which is the necessary corollary of accumulation, moves, nevertheless, between more or less narrow limits.

Social capital, distributed among the different spheres of production, takes the form of a multitude of individual capitals which, side by side, follow their movements of accumulation, i.e., of reproduction on a progressive scale. The movement first produces the surplus of the constituent elements of wealth, which it then aggregates to their groups having already been combined and acting as capital. In proportion to its already acquired size and degree of its reproductive power, each of these groups, each capital, is enriched by these additional elements, thus enlarging its own vitality, and maintaining by enlarging, its distinct existence and limiting the sphere of action of others. The movement of concentration is therefore dispersed not only on as many points as the accumulation, but the splitting of social capital into a multitude of capitals independent of each other is consolidated precisely because all individual capital functions as a *focus of relative concentration*.

Since the summation of those increments whose accumulation increase individual capital will increase social capital by the same amount, the relative concentration that all of these capitals represent *on average* cannot increase without a simultaneous increase in social capital – social wealth dedicated to reproduction. This is a first limit of concentration which is the corollary of accumulation.

That's not all. The accumulation of social capital results not only from the gradual expansion of individual capital, but also from the increase in its number, either because dormant values are converted into capital, or because cuttings of old capital are detached and take root independently. Finally, large, slowly accumulated assets are at one point split into several separate assets, for example, when an estate is divided among capitalist families. Concentration is thus affected by both the formation of new capital and the division of old capital.

The movement of social accumulation, on the one hand, therefore presents an increasing concentration in the hands of private entrepreneurs, of the reproductive elements of wealth, and, on the other, the dispersion and multiplication of the centers of relative accumulation and concentration which mutually repel each other from their particular orbits.

At some point in economic progress, this fragmentation of social capital into a multitude of individual capitals, or the repulsive movement of its constituent parts, comes to be thwarted by the opposite movement of their mutual attraction. It is no longer concentration that is confused with accumulation, but rather a fundamentally distinct process, an attraction that brings together different centers of accumulation and of concentration, a concentration of capital already formed, a fusion of a greater number of capitals into a smaller number, in a word, *centralization* properly stated.

(*Substitution by Marx from the French text was **incorporated by Engels** (pp. 586–587) and follows.*)

The laws of this centralisation of capitals, or of the attraction of capital by capital, cannot be developed here. A brief hint at a few facts must suffice. The battle of competition is fought by cheapening of commodities. The cheapness of commodities depends, *cæteris paribus*, on the productiveness of labour, and this again on the scale of production. Therefore, the larger capitals beat the smaller. It will further be remembered that, with the development of the capitalist mode of production, there is an increase in the minimum amount of individual capital necessary to carry on a business under its normal conditions. The smaller capitals, therefore, crowd into spheres of production which Modern Industry has only sporadically or incompletely got hold of. Here competition rages in direct proportion to the number, and in inverse proportion to the magnitudes, of the antagonistic capitals. It always ends in the ruin of many small capitalists, whose capitals partly pass into the hand of their conquerors, partly vanish. Apart from this, with capitalist production an altogether new force comes into play – the credit system,[3] not only itself becoming a new powerful weapon in the competitive battle, but through invisible threads pulls together larger or more smaller masses of fragmented funds into the hands of more individual or associated capitalists, and turns into a machinery for the centralization the capital.

> (*Remaining substitution for Section 2 by Marx from the French was **not incorporated by Engels**, beginning "Every individual capital..." (pp. 587–589, this being a mixing of 2nd, 3rd and 4th eds.). Translation from the French text follows.*)

As capitalist accumulation and production flourishes, competition and credit, the most powerful agents of centralization, take off. Likewise, the progress of accumulation increases the matter to be centralized – individual capitals – and the development of the capitalist mode of production creates, with social need, also the technical facilities of these vast enterprises whose implementation requires a prior centralization of capital. In our time, the attractive force between individual capitals and the tendency towards centralization prevails therefore more than in any previous period. But, although the relative scope and energy of the centralizing movement is to some extent determined by the acquired size of capitalist wealth and the superiority of its economic mechanism, the progress of centralization does not depend on a positive increase in social capital. This is what distinguishes it above all from concentration, which is only the corollary of reproduction on a progressive scale. Centralization requires only a change in the distribution of the capital present, only a modification in the quantitative arrangement of the integral parts of social capital.

The capital will be able to grow here by large masses because elsewhere it will have escaped in large number. In a particular industry, centralization would only have reached its last limit when all the capital committed to it would become a single individual capital. And, in a given society it would only have reached its last limit at the moment the entire national capital would become a single capital in the hands of a single capitalist or a single company of capitalists.

Centralization only supplements the work of accumulation by enabling manufacturers to expand the scale of their operations. Whether this result is due to accumulation or centralization, whether it is done by the violent process of

---

[3] From here, the 4th German edition to the end of the paragraph differs somewhat from the 3rd. [P.Z.]

annexation – some capitals becoming centers of gravity so powerful towards other capitals, destroying their individual cohesion and enriching themselves with their disintegrated elements –, or whether the fusion of a host of capitals is already formed or in the process of formation, accomplished by the more painful process of corporations, etc., – the economic effect will not be less. The extended scale of companies will always be the starting point for a broader organization of collective work, for a broader development of its material springs, in a word, for the progressive transformation of fragmented and routine production processes into socially combined and scientifically ordered production processes.

But it is obvious that accumulation, the gradual increase of capital by means of linear spiral reproduction, is only a slow process compared to that of centralization, which in the first place only changes the quantitative grouping of the integral parts of social capital. The world would still be without the railway system, for example, if it had to wait until individual capital was enlarged enough by accumulation to be able to do such a task. The centralization of capital, through joint stock companies, has done so, so to speak, in a jiffy. By increasing, thus accelerating the effects of accumulation, centralization extends and precipitates changes in the technical composition of capital, changes that increase its constant part at the expense of its variable part or cause a decrease in the relative demand for labour.

Large capital, improvised by centralization, reproduces itself like others, but faster than others, and thus becomes in turn powerful agents of social accumulation. It is in this sense that, by talking about the progress of the latter, we are justified in citing the effects produced by centralization.

The additional capital (see Part VII, Chapter 24, of this work) provided by accumulation, is preferably suitable as a vehicle for new inventions, discoveries, etc., in a word, industrial improvements, but the old capital, as soon as it has reached its period of complete renewal, also reproduces itself in the perfected technical form, where a lesser quantity of labour force is sufficient to implement a greater mass of tools and materials. The absolute decrease in demand for labour brought about by this technical metamorphosis must become all the more significant as the capital that passes through it has already been increased by the centralizing movement.

On the one hand, the additional capital that is formed in the course of accumulation reinforced by centralization attracts a number of workers proportionally to its size. On the other hand, the technical metamorphoses and corresponding changes in the value composition that former capital periodically undergoes make it repel an ever-increasing number of workers who were once attracted to it.

3   Section 3: Progressive Production of a Relative Surplus-Population or Industrial Reserve Army

(*Up to the last four pages of Section 3, almost full substitution from French was intended by Marx, although revised titling was not mentioned. There is considerable textual substitution, not incorporated by Engels, for first four pages (pp. 589–593 per 2nd ed.). Translation follows of the French text.*)

The absolute demand for labour caused by a capital is not because of its absolute size, but because of its variable part, which alone is exchanged for the labour force. The relative labour demand that a capital generates, i.e. the proportion between its own size and the amount of labour it absorbs, is determined by the proportional size of its variable fraction. We have just shown that the accumulation that increases social capital simultaneously reduces the proportional size of its variable component and thus reduces the relative demand for labour. Now, what is the effect of this movement on the fate of the working class?

To solve this problem, it is clear that it is first necessary to examine how the reduction suffered by the variable part of an accumulating capital affects the absolute size of this part, and as a consequent, how does a decrease in the relative demand for labour react on the absolute or actual demand for labour?

As long as a capital does not change its size, any proportional decrease in its variable part is at the same time an absolute decrease. For this to be otherwise, the proportional decrease must be offset by an increase in the total sum of the capital value advanced. The variable part that functions as a salary fund therefore decreases due directly to the decrease in its proportional size and inversely to the simultaneous increase in the entire capital.

[The next paragraph and the following first sentence is Marx's improved wording for his 3rd German edition, rather than his earlier wording in the French; thereafter, he returns to the French text. P.Z.]

For a capital of same size, any proportional decrease of its variable component shall include its absolute decrease, unless the latter is offset by a simultaneous increase in the total capital advanced. On the other hand, as the size of a capital increases, its variable component also increases, unless there are circumstances to the contrary. The variable part, which functions as a wage fund, is thus reduced in direct proportion to the decrease in its proportional size and in inverse proportion to the simultaneous growth of the total capital. We therefore obtain the following combination:

First: If the proportional size of the variable part of the capital decreases in inverse proportion to the growth of total capital, the absolute size of the salary fund remains unchanged. It will still amount, for example, to 400 francs, whether it forms two-fifths of a capital of 1000 francs or one-fifth of a capital of 2000 francs.

Second: If the proportional size of variable capital decreases greater than the increase in the total capital, the wage fund suffers an absolute decrease, despite the absolute increase in the value of the advanced capital.

Third: If the proportional size of the variable capital decreases less than the increase of the entire capital, the wage fund undergoes an absolute increase, despite the decrease of its proportional magnitude.

From the point of view of social accumulation, these different combinations affect the form, as well as successive phases of social capital distributed among the different spheres of production one upon another, often in different directions, and many different conditions simultaneously presented by different spheres of production. In the chapter on large industry we considered these two aspects of the movement.

We remember, for example, factories where the same number of workers is sufficient to implement an increasing amount of materials and tools. There, the increase of the capital resulting only from the extension of its constant part reduces the proportional magnitude of its variable part or the proportional mass of the exploited labour force, without altering its absolute magnitude.

As examples of an absolute decrease in the number of workers employed in some major branches of industry and its simultaneous increase in others, although all of them were also marked by an increase in the capital employed and an increase in their productivity, we should mention here that in England, from 1851 to 1861, the number of personnel employed in agriculture fell from 2,011,447 individuals to 1,924,110; those engaged in the manufacture of long wool from 102,714 to 79,249; those engaged in the manufacture of silk from 111,940 to 101,678, while in the same period the personnel engaged in spinning and cotton weaving rose from 371,777 individuals to 456,646, and those engaged in ironworks from 68,053 to 125,711*.

Finally, as for the other side of social accumulation, which shows its progress in the same branch of industry alternately by an increase, decrease or steady state in the number of workers, the history of the cotton industry's vicissitudes has provided us with the most striking example of this.

Looking at a period of several years, for example, a ten-year period, we will generally find that with the progress of social accumulation the number of exploited workers has also increased, although the different years taken separately contribute in very different degrees to this result or some do not even contribute at all. It is therefore necessary that the stationary state or decrease of the absolute number of the employed working population, which is ultimately found in some industries, be alongside other industries for which a considerable increase in the capital employed and an increase in the employed labour force definitively outweighed any movement in the opposite direction. But this result can only be achieved in the midst of tremors and under conditions that are increasingly difficult to be fulfilled.

The proportional decrease in size that the variable part of capital undergoes in the course of accumulation and the simultaneous extension of powers of labour is progressive. For example, if the ratio between constant capital and variable capital was originally 1:1, and it will become 2:1, 3:1, 5:1, 6:1, etc., so that it moves from degree to degree through 2/3, 3/4, 5/6, 6/7, etc., of the total capital value advanced in terms of means of production, then it moves through 1/3, 1/4, 1/6, 1/7, etc., only for the labor force. If the total amount of capital were to be tripled, quadrupled, sixfold, sevenfold, etc., this would not be enough to increase the number of workers employed. To produce this effect, the exponent for the increase in the mass of share capital must be greater than the exponent for the proportional decrease in the wage fund.

So, the lower its proportional figure has already fallen, the faster must be the progression in which social capital increases. Yet, this very progression becomes the source of new technical changes that further reduce the relative demand for labour. The game must therefore be restarted.

In the chapter on large industry, we have addressed at length the causes that, despite trends to the contrary, lead the ranks of the employees to grow with the progress of accumulation. We will recall here in a few words what is immediately relevant to our subject.

The same development of productive labour powers which causes a decrease, not only relatively but often absolutely, in the number of workers employed in certain major branches of industry, allows them to deliver an ever-increasing mass of cheap products. They thus stimulate other industries, those to which they provide means of production, or those from which they derive their materials, instruments, etc.; they cause those to expand. The impact on the labour market of these industries will be very significant, if manual work predominates. "The increase in the number of workers", says the official editor of the 1861 Census of the English Peoples, "generally reaches its maximum in branches of industry where machines have not yet been successfully introduced".* But we have seen elsewhere that all these industries in turn go through the technological metamorphosis that adapts them to the modern production model.

The new branches of production which economic progress gives rise provide additional opportunities for work. At their origin they took the form of trade, of manufacturing, or finally of large industry. In the first two cases, they will have to go through mechanical transformation, in the last the centralization of the capital allows them to build huge industrial armies that surprise the eye and seem to come out of the ground. But, however vast the labour force thus hired may seem, its proportional figure, initially low compared to the mass of capital committed, decreases as soon as these industries have taken root.

Finally, there are intervals where technical upheavals are less noticeable, where accumulation is more of a quantitative expansion movement on the new technical basis once acquired. So, whatever the current composition of capital, the law according to which the demand for labour increases in the same proportion as the capital more or less restartes to operate. But, at the same time as the number of workers attracted by capital reaches its maximum, the products become so overabundant that with the least obstacle to their flow the social mechanism seems to stop; the repulsion of labour by capital suddenly operates, on the largest scale and in the most violent way; the disarray even imposes on capitalists supreme efforts to save on labour. Gradually accumulated improvements in detail are then concentrated under this high pressure. They are embodied in technical changes that revolutionize the composition of capital throughout the periphery of large spheres of production. Thus, the American civil war pushed English spinners to populate their more powerful machine shops and depopulate them of workers. Finally, the duration of these intervals where accumulation most favors labour demand is gradually shortening.

As soon as the mechanical industry gains the upper hand, the progress of accumulation doubles the energy of the forces that tend to decrease the proportional magnitude of variable capital and so weakens those that tend to increase its absolute magnitude. It increases with the social capital of which it is a part, but it increases in decreasing proportion.[4]

Since the demand for effective labour is regulated not only by the size of the variable capital already engaged but also by the average of its continued

---

4 A striking example of this increase due to a decreasing trend is provided by the movement of the painted cotton canvas factory. Let us compare some figures: In England this industry exported in 1851 577, 867,229 yards (a yard equals 0.914 meters) with a value of £10, 295,621, but in 1861 828,873,922 yards with a value of £14,211,572. The number of employed persons, which in 1851 was 12,098, was in 1861 only 12,556, which is an increase of 458 individuals, or, for the whole ten-year period, an increase of about 4 per cent.

increase, the labour supply remains normal as long as it follows this movement. But, when the variable capital falls to a lower average increase, the same labour supply that was hitherto normal is now becoming abnormal, i.e., overabundant, so that a more or less considerable fraction of the working class, having ceased to be necessary for the development of capital and having lost its raison d'être, has now become superfluous, supernumerary. As this game continues to be repeated with the upward march of accumulation, it leads to increasing overpopulation.

The law of the proportional decrease in variable capital, and the corresponding decrease in relative labour demand, therefore has as a corollary the absolute increase in variable capital and the absolute increase in labour demand in a decreasing proportion, and finally as a complement: the production of a relative overpopulation. We call it "relative" because it does not come from a positive increase in the working population that would exceed the limits of wealth being accumulated, but, on the contrary, from an accelerated increase in social capital that allows it to do without a more or less considerable part of its labourers. As this overpopulation exists only in relation to the momentary needs of capitalist exploitation, it can suddenly swell and tighten.

By producing the accumulation of capital, and as it succeeds, the working class thus produces itself the instruments of its retirement or metamorphosis into relative overpopulation. This is the *law of population* that distinguishes the capitalist era and corresponds to its particular mode of production. Indeed, each of the historical modes of social production also has its own population law, a law that applies only to it, that passes with it, and therefore has only historical value. An abstract and unchanging population law exists only for plants and animals, and only as long as they are not influenced by humanity.

(*The following paragraph of citations was within Marx's intended 3rd edition, although included by Engels as a footnote in his 4th edition within the passage otherwise retaining the 2nd German edition text – Marx (1867, pp. 591–592, fn. 2).*)

The law of progressive diminution of the relative magnitude of variable capital and its effect on the condition of the class of wage workers is conjectured rather than understood by some prominent economists of the classical school. The greatest service was rendered here by John Barton, although he confounds constant capital with fixed capital and variable capital with circulating capital. In his *Observations on the Circumstances which influence the Condition of the Labouring Classes of Society*, he says:

> The demand for labour depends on the increase of circulating, and not of fixed capital. Were it true that the proportion between these two sorts of capital is the same at all times, and in all circumstances, then, indeed, it follows that the number of labourers employed is in proportion to the wealth of the state. But such a proposition has not the semblance of probability. As arts are cultivated, and civilisation is extended, fixed capital bears a larger and larger proportion to circulating capital. The amount of fixed capital employed in the production of a piece of British muslin is at least a hundred, probably a thousand times greater than that employed in a similar piece of Indian muslin. And the proportion of circulating capital is a hundred or thousand times less ... the whole of the annual savings, added to the fixed capital, would have no effect in increasing the demand for labour.

Ricardo, while agreeing with Barton's general views, makes the following remark about the quoted passage: "It is not easy, I think, to conceive that under any circumstance, an increase in capital should not be followed by an increased demand for labour; the most that can be said is that the demand will be in a diminishing ratio".* Elsewhere he says that "the fund, from which landlords and capitalists derive their revenue, may increase, while the other, that upon which the labouring class mainly depend, may diminish, and therefore it follows, if I am right, that the same cause which may increase the net revenue of the country, may at the same time render the population redundant, and deteriorate the condition of the labourer".[5] Richard Jones states: "Demand [for labour] will rise ... not in proportion to the accumulation of the general capital.... Every augmentation, therefore, in the national stock destined for reproduction, comes, in the progress of society, to have less and less influence upon the condition of the labourer".* Let us again quote *Ramsay*: "The demand for labour is ... not in proportion to the general capital. As society progresses, any increase in the national fund for reproduction will have less and less influence on the fate of the worker".*

If accumulation, the progress of wealth on the capitalist basis, therefore necessarily produces workers overpopulation, this in turn becomes the most powerful lever of accumulation, a condition of existence of capitalist

---

5 Engels does not correctly follow Marx's two citations of Ricardo when he has instead, "The same cause which may increase the net revenue of the country may at the same time render the population redundant, and deteriorate the condition of the labourer". (Ricardo, l. c., p. 469.) With increase of capital, "the demand [for labour] will be in a diminishing ratio". (Ibid., p. 480, Note.) [P.Z.].

production in its state of integral development. It forms an *industrial reserve army* that belongs to capital as absolutely as if it had raised and disciplined it at its own expense. It provides its needs of floating valorisation and, regardless of natural population growth, the human material that is always exploitable and always available.

The presence of this industrial reserve, its partial or general re-entry into active service, then its reconstitution on a larger scale, all this is at the heart of the rugged life that modern industry is going through, with its almost regular ten-year cycle – apart from other irregular tremors – of periods of ordinary activity, of high pressure production, of crisis and of stagnation.

This singular march of industry, that we do not encounter in any previous epoch of humanity, was also impossible in the infancy of capitalist production. Then, as technological progress was slow and becoming more widespread, changes in the composition of social capital were barely felt. At the same time, the extension of the recently created colonial market, the corresponding multiplication of needs and means of satisfying them, the emergence of new branches of industry, activated, with accumulation, the demand for labour. Although not very fast from the point of view of our time, the progress of accumulation came up against the natural limits of the population, and we will see later on that these limits were only pushed back by coups d'état. It is only under the regime of large industry that the production of a superfluous population becomes a regular springboard for the production of wealth.

If this regime endows social capital with a sudden force of expansion, a wonderful elasticity, it is because, under the spur of favorable opportunities, credit brings new capital to the production of the extraordinary masses of growing social wealth, of new capitals whose owners are eager to assert them, constantly waiting for the right moment; it is, on the other hand, the technical springs of large industry making it possible and converting suddenly a huge increase in products into additional means of production, and of transporting goods more quickly from one part of the world to another. While the low prices of these commodities first open up new markets and expand old ones, their oversupply is gradually tightening the general market to the point where they are suddenly rejected. Commercial vicissitudes thus manage to combine with the alternative movements of social capital which, in the course of its accumulation, sometimes undergoes revolutions in its composition, sometimes increases on the technical basis once acquired. All these influences contribute to the expansion and sudden contractions in the scale of production.

The expansion of production by jerky movements is the primary cause of its sudden contraction; this, it is true, in turn causes it, but would the exorbitant expansion of production, which forms the starting point, be possible without a reserve army under the orders of capital, without an increase in the number of workers independent of the natural increase of the population? This is achieved through a very simple process and which every day throws workers on the pavement, namely the application of methods that make work more productive and reduce the demand for it. The ever-renewed conversion of part of the working class into as many half-employed or completely idle hands thus gives the movement of modern industry its typical form.

As the celestial bodies once thrown into their orbits for an indefinite time, so does social production once thrown into this alternative movement of expansion and contraction repeats by a mechanical necessity. Effects in turn become causes, and events, initially irregular and apparently accidental, increasingly affect the form of a normal periodicity. But it is only at a time when the mechanical industry, having had fairly deep roots, exerts a major influence on all national production; when, thanks to it, foreign trade began to take precedence over domestic trade; when the universal market successively annexed vast areas in the New World, in Asia, and in Australia; when finally the industrial nations entering the race have become quite numerous, it is only from this period that the reviving cycles date, whose successive phases embrace years and which always lead to a general crisis, the end of one cycle and the starting point of another. Until now, the periodic duration of these cycles is ten or eleven years, but there is no reason to consider this figure as constant. On the contrary, we must infer from the laws of capitalist production, as we have just developed them, that it is variable and that the period of cycles will gradually shorten.

When the periodicity of industrial vicissitudes became apparent to everyone, there were also economists ready to admit that capital could not do without its reserve army, formed by *infima plebs* of the supernumeraries.

(*The following paragraph was retained by Marx from his 2nd ed. (pp. 593–594) and retained by Engels.*)

"Suppose", says H. Merivale, formerly Professor of Political Economy at Oxford, subsequently employed in the English Colonial Office, "suppose that, on the occasion of some of these crises, the nation were to rouse itself to the effort of getting rid by emigration of some hundreds of thousands of superfluous hands, what would be the consequence? That, at the first returning demand for labour, there would be a deficiency. However rapid reproduction may be, it takes, at all events, the space of a generation to replace the loss of adult labour. Now, the profits of our manufacturers depend mainly on the power of making use of the prosperous moment when demand is brisk, and thus compensating themselves for the interval during which it is slack. This power is secured to them only by the command of machinery and of manual labor. They must have hands ready by them, they must be able to increase the activity of their operations when required, and to slacken it again, according to the state of the market, or they cannot possibly maintain that pre-eminence in the race of competition on which the wealth of the country is founded".* Even *Malthus* recognizes overpopulation as a necessity of modern industry, though, after his narrow fashion, he explains it by the absolute over-growth of the laboring population, not by their becoming relatively supernumerary. He says: "Prudential habits with regard to marriage, carried to a considerable extent among the laboring class of a country mainly depending upon manufactures and commerce, might injure it.... From the nature of a population, an increase of labourers cannot be brought into market in consequence of a particular demand till after the lapse of 16 or 18 years, and the conversion of revenue into capital, by saving, may take place much more rapidly: a country is always liable to an increase in the quantity of the funds for the maintenance of labour faster than the increase of population".* After Political Economy has thus demonstrated the constant production of a relative surplus-population of labourers to be a necessity of capitalistic accumulation, she very aptly, in the guise of an old maid, puts in the mouth of her "beau ideal" of a capitalist the following words addressed to those supernumeraries thrown on the streets by their own creation of additional capital: – "We manufacturers do what we can for you, whilst we are increasing that capital on which you must subsist, and you must do the rest by accommodating your numbers to the means of subsistence".*

> (*Marx's intended substitution from French was **not incorporated by Engels** for "Capitalist production ... dictates of capital" (p. 594 bottom to p. 595 bottom per 2nd ed.), except partially footnoted later. Translation from the French text follows.*)

Industrial progress, which follows the course of accumulation, not only reduces more and more the number of workers needed to implement a growing mass of means of production, it also increases the amount of work that the individual worker must provide. As it develops the productive powers of labour and thus produces more products from less labour, the capitalist system also develops the means to extract more labour from the wage earner, either by extending his day or by making his labour more intense, or by apparently increasing the number of workers employed by replacing a higher and more expensive force with several lower and cheap forces, man by woman, adult by teenager and child, one Yankee by three Chinese. These are all methods to reduce the demand for labour and make it overabundant, in a word, to manufacture supernumeraries.

The excess work imposed on the portion of the employee class in active service increases the ranks of the reserve, and by increasing the pressure that the latter's competition exerts on the former, forces it to more obediently submit to orders of capital. In this respect it is very instructive to compare the admonitions of English manufacturers in the last century, on the eve of the mechanical revolution, with those of English factory workers in the middle of the nineteenth century. The spokesman for the former, appreciating very well the effect that a reserve of supernumeraries has on those in active service, exclaims: "another cause of idleness, in this kingdom, is the want of a sufficient number of labouring hands.... Whenever, from an extraordinary demand for manufacturers, labour grows scarce, the labourers feel their own consequence, and will make their masters feel it likewise: it is amazing; but so depraved are the dispositions of these people, that, in such cases, a set of workers have combined to distress their employer, by idling a whole day together",[6] that is, these "depraved" people imagine that the price of goods is regulated by the "holy" law of supply and demand.

Today things have changed a lot, thanks to the development of the mechanical industry. No one would dare claim, in this good kingdom of England, that the lack of hands makes workers idle! In the midst of the cotton shortage, when the English factories had thrown most of their hard-working men on the pavement and the rest were only busy for four or six hours a day, some Bolton manufacturers tried to impose extra working time on their spinners, which according to the Factory Act, could only hit adult men. The workers replied with a pamphlet from which we extract the following passage: "The adult operatives employed at this mill had been asked to work from 12 to 13 hours per day, while there are hundreds who are compelled to be idle who would willingly work partial time, in order to maintain their families and save their brethren from a premature grave through being overworked.... We would ask if the practice of working overtime by a number of hands, while others are unwillingly idle, is likely to create a good feeling and establish confidence between masters and servants. Those who are working overtime feel the injustice equally with those who are condemned to forced idleness. There is in the district almost sufficient work to give to all partial employment, if fairly distributed. We feel that we are only asking what is right in requesting the masters generally to pursue a system

---

6   The citation is to *Essay on Trade and Commerce*, London, 1770, pp. 27–28, and I am applying the English original. The full paragraph here was also translated from French by Graßmann (2018, p. 153), without use of the English original. [P.Z.]

of shorts hours, particularly until a better state of things begin to dawn upon us, rather than to work a portion of the hands overtime, while others, for want of work, are compelled to exist on charity".[7]

(Remaining pages of Section 3 were retained by Marx and then Engels from 2nd ed. (p. 595 bottom "The condemnation...", to p. 600), except Marx adding one paragraph from the French into the middle of the last long paragraph that Engels rephrased.)[8]

The condemnation of one part of the working class to enforced idleness by the overwork of the other part, and the converse, becomes a means of enriching the individual capitalists,[9] and accelerates at the same time the production of the industrial reserve army on a scale corresponding with the advance of social accumulation....

4   Section 4: Different Forms of the Relative Surplus-Population. The General Law of Capitalist Accumulation

(Full substitution from French was intended by Marx and was largely incorporated by Engels (pp. 600–606), although Marx's opening paragraph in French is more nuanced and is translated here for reference. Some cited

---

7 The citation is to *Reports of Insp. of Factories*, 31 Oct. 1863, p. 8, and I am applying the English original [P.Z.].
8 Rendered rather differently by Engels, a translation follows of the paragraph to be inserted from the French into Marx (1867, p. 599, middle of page):
   The workers affected by a partial conversion of funds for wages instead for machines belong to various categories. First are those who have been made redundant, then their regular replacements, and finally those absorbed by an industry in its ordinary state of expansion. They are all available now, and any additional capital about to be put into service can be used. Whether it attracts them or others, its effect on the general demand for labor will always remain nil if this capital is just enough to take as many hands off the market as the machines have thrown into the market. If it withdraws less, the supernumerary figure ultimately increases, and if it withdraws more, the general demand for labor will only increase by the excess of the hands it "engages" over those "released" by the machine. The impetus that any additional capital in the process of being invested would otherwise have given to the general demand for hands is, in any case, thus neutralized by the amount of hands thrown by the machines onto the labor market. [P.Z.]
9 At this point, a footnote is placed in the English edition that cites the factory reports that Marx had within his French text. The footnote also cites the passage from the 1770 *Essay on Trade and Commerce* offered in the previous paragraph in the French. [P.Z.]

passages became footnotes with Engels, but nothing besides the first paragraph is provided here.)

Apart from major periodic changes which, as soon as the industrial cycle moves from one phase to another, generally occur, relative overpopulation always presents infinitely varied nuances. However, one can soon distinguish a few broad categories, a few strongly pronounced differences – the floating, latent and stagnant forms.

...

5   Section 5: Illustrations of the General Law of Capitalist Accumulation

(*Corrections of details were intended by Marx and are listed in MEGA² II/8, pp. 16–20, but not addressed here.*)

CHAPTER 5

Marx on Primitive Accumulation Contrasted to Engels' Handling of the Topic

The next edition of *Volume I* after the French edition edited by Marx and Engels' 3rd edition of 1883 was in Polish in 1884 by a collective inclusive of Ludwik Krzywicki. It was based upon the French edition, with Engels giving copyright permission for publication. The new edition in 1889 relied, however, upon Engels' 3rd edition (http://karlmarx.lu/Kapitalpol.htm, accessed December 29, 2018). The first full Italian edition was translated and published in 1886 by Gerolamo Boccardo from the French edition, including its divisions. Engels was not aware of it until much later. As it happened, that translation was the only Italian translation until after World War II, its quality being contested (Favilli, 1996, p. 208). The first Spanish translation also was in 1886 and also based on the French edition (Correa y Zafrilla, 1985). Both of latter are Romance languages for which translating from French would not be a surprise. A Danish translation occurred around the same time, published in 1887, and had the seven parts, twenty-five chapters of the Engels' 3rd German (http://arbejderen.dk/artikel/2008-12-23/allerede-i-1887-kom-kapitalen-p-dansk, accessed November 15, 2019). To an overwhelming extent, the movement away from the French edition continued, trusting that Engels was a faithful executor of Marx's desires. It is difficult at this stage, but necessary, to unwind this history.

As stated in Chapter 3, a 3rd German edition came about because supplies of the 2nd edition were running low. Marx had explicit instructions for the new edition, but died before completion and sending it to the publisher. We had assumed Engels followed all instructions, yet, his neglects are not accidental, but seem driven by a certain unwillingness to accept Marx's evolution after the 2nd German, mostly represented in the 1875 last serial of the French edition. In Chapter 3 within the context of citing Marx's changes for Part VII, I have offered certain suggestions about the changes. In Chapter 4, I offer a reconstruction of Marx's chapter on "The General Law of Capitalist Accumulation". In this chapter, I offer further considerations, focused upon Marx's Part VIII on primitive accumulation.

1 Why, for Marx, Primitive Accumulation became a New Part VIII

> [T]he accumulation of capital pre-supposes surplus-value; surplus-value pre-supposes capitalist production the pre-existence of considerable masses of capital and of labour power in the hands of producers of commodities. The whole movement seems to turn in a vicious circle, out of which we can only get by supposing a primitive accumulation (previous accumulation of Adam Smith) preceding capitalistic accumulation; an accumulation not the result of the capitalistic mode of production, but its starting point. (Marx, 1867, p. 667)

Within the entire Part VII, "The Accumulation of Capital", primitive accumulation is mentioned only twice, in the chapter "Simple Reproduction"[1] and in "The General Law of Capitalist Accumulation", second section. In the French edition and the English, the reader then comes to a new Part VIII on "Primitive Accumulation", no longer embedded within the prior subject matter "The Accumulation of Capital". This division was initiated by Marx in the process of carefully editing the last parts of French edition of *Capital* and he wanted this new division incorporated for the 3rd German edition he was preparing before he died. To this day, other than the English, most editions of *Volume I*, including German editions, exhibit no such separation of primitive accumulation into a separate Part VIII, the responsibility for which begins with Engels. The French edition had "labor power" added in the opening paragraph on primitive accumulation, as well as mentioning that the "whole movement seems to turn in a vicious circle"; both were included by Engels in his later German editions (extracted above).

I believe Marx's research on Russia advanced his understanding of the complexity of getting the engine of capitalist started, so to speak. More recent research would sustain Marx. Blaming the commune's existence as a major factor in the 19th-century Russian agrarian crisis, Watters (1968) reported data showing for European Russia in 1892 that three-quarters of male peasants were working communally owned land. Even by 1905 less than 5% of peasants worked individually owned private land while, on allotment land, communal tenure applied to some 80%. Taking into account peasant-association-owned

---

[1] The Moore-Aveling translation happens to leave out the "primitive" adjective that had appeared in the German and French: "it therefore seems likely that the capitalist, once upon a time, became possessed of money, by some [primitive] accumulation that took place independently of the unpaid labor of others" (Marx, 1867, p. 534).

private land, communally-owned private land, and leased land, Watters concluded that about 43% of all cultivable land was communally controlled, worked by a larger, unspecified, percentage of the peasantry (pp. 147–151).

Mironov (1990) looks closely at the actual functioning of communes. While there could be many aspects to discuss, such as the democratic assembly (pp. 15–17, noting it excluded women) and the commune as a group reference exceeding the importance of the family (p. 18), crucial was the commune's resistance to class differentiation. Peasants supported the commune when a movement for land reform developed in the late 1870s, so much that statistical analysis within European Russia found that some 89% of peasant households were in communes whether examining 1877 or 1905 (pp. 29–39). Indeed, says Mironov, "the commune was not compatible with an intensive market economy, with significant differentiation in property, culture, and social status; with formal rationality; with a clearly expressed individualism; with a constitutional state…" (p. 32).

Where Watters blames the commune for Russian agrarian backwardness and Mironov explains the commune, Lenin (1899b) had simply ignored it. White (2001b, p. 43 and 2019b, p. 27) concludes that Lenin writes out the existence of peasant community by "[c]lassifying the commune as a social or ethnographic phenomenon [so that] the commune, its dynamics, or how communal life influenced the economic situation of the peasantry in the post-Reform era, is not discussed". In spite of the post-1905 Stolypin reforms undertaken by a terrorist state with thousands of dissidents executed, success was still not overwhelming in breaking up the communes. Marx had been correct to have taken the Russian commune seriously.

Luxemburg understood that primitive accumulation concerns the historical question of the rise of capital out of feudalism:

> During original [primitive] accumulation, i.e. during the historical emergence of capitalism in Europe at the end of the Middle Ages, the dispossession of the peasants in the U.K. and on the continent represented the most tremendous means for transformation the means of production and labor power into capital on a massive scale.
>
> Since then, however, and to the present day, this same task has been accomplished under the rule of capital through an equally tremendous, although completely different, means: modern colonial policy.… This is no longer a question of original [primitive] accumulation: this is a process that continues to this day. (Luxemburg, 1913, pp. 266–267)

Althusser states that Part VIII of *Capital* contains the second, after "surplus value", of Marx's greatest discoveries:

The first was the discovery of 'surplus value'. The second is the discovery of the incredible means used to achieve the 'primitive accumulation' thanks to which capitalism was 'born' and grew in Western societies, helped also by the existence of a mass of 'free labourers' (i.e. labourers stripped of means of labour) and technological discoveries. This means was the most brutal violence: the thefts and massacres which cleared capitalism's royal road into human history.... Capitalism has always used and, in the 'margins' of its metropolitan existence – i.e. in the colonial and ex-colonial countries – is still using well into the twentieth century, *the most brutally violent means*. (Althusser, 1969b, p. 85, emphasis in original)

In his last writings, Althusser (2006) elaborates that the early encounters leading to the capitalist mode of production were not fated, but rather "took hold", were "aleatory" (pp. 197–198). Turchetto (2000, pp. 368–369) notes Marx's emphasis for 18th-century England on coercive, non-economic methods predominating in the formation of wage labor, and that the history of merchant capital was bloody: primitive accumulation in *Volume I* is "a long way from classical economics, and especially from Smith's idea of the evolution of society through the progressive development of the division of labor and the consequent expansion of trade". Patriquin (2004) addresses earlier English agrarian history.

In my view, primitive accumulation as a concept focuses attention on the need to understand transition to the capitalist mode of production and not be taken for granted or inevitable, merely because history happened that way. "In the history of primitive accumulation, all revolutions are epoch-making that act as levers for the capitalist class in course of formation" (Marx, 1867, p. 669). The French edition delimited Marx's presentation to "Western Europe", in my view, as a result of his researches on Russia leading him to realize that he should not make broad claims beyond evidence he was encountering. I can add that, compared to the period of primitive accumulation with its contention for capitalist hegemony against an alternative dominant class with its own victims and resistances, the current domination by capital does not face another dominant class to contend with, and so the character of class struggles in the period of primitive accumulation differs manifestly from the present.

Frank (1977, pp. 88–89, and 1978, particularly Chapter 7) distinguishes "primary accumulation" from the primitive, with "primary" referring only to modern capitalist undermining of non-capitalist forms of production. Primitive accumulation thus retains Marx's usage as the "original" separation of labor from means of production in the initial transition to capitalist mode of production, particularly in the United Kingdom. In spite of this advance in clarity, accumulation of capital proper otherwise retains a widespread ambiguity I address in the next chapter.

A related incident worth mentioning exposes the frailty of opinions taken too strongly. Dunayevskaya claimed that Part VIII of *Capital* was *integrated* by Marx into Part VII *after* the first two German editions. She claimed the integration to be significant.[2] As we have seen, the text on primitive accumulation was, however, always within one Part VII in *all four* German editions. Parts VII and VIII became *separated* in the French edition and were instructed by Marx to be also separated into Parts VII and VIII for the 3rd German edition. Dunayevskaya's logic turns against her opinion when the facts of the matter are corrected.

2   Engels' Disparate Handling of the English (1887) and 4th German (1890) Editions of *Volume I*; Danielson's 2nd Russian edition (1898)

In 1887 Engels edited and published the first English edition from a translation based upon the 3rd German he had prepared. Undertaken initially by Samuel Moore beginning in June 1883, Engels thought him easily the best choice for translator (*C.W.*, Vol. 47, p. 31), being a long-time friend of Marx and himself, very conversant in Marx's work, and having translated the *Communist Manifesto* into English. While Marx may have wanted the English to be based directly from the French (claimed by Foner, cited by Anderson, 2010, p. 176, in turn citing a person who received in 1880 the French edition from Marx himself), the choice of Moore was quite reasonable. Yet, if neither Moore, nor Aveling as eventual co-translator from the German, were fluent in French, they would not be in a position to seriously address the French edition.

The Moore's translation was about half done by the end of 1884 (*C.W.*, Vol. 47, p. 245), and Aveling was slowly added when Moore's other commitments burdened him. But Aveling, by 1884 Eleanor Marx's partner, was not as proficient in German (*C.W.*, Vol. 47, pp. 127, 245 and 401–402). While Eleanor, born

---

2   Marx, says Dunayevskaya, "far from considering Part 8 [separate from Part 7] as 'justifiable', held that the real logic of 'so-called Primitive Accumulation' was that it was not merely the historic origin, but the logical continuation of the process of capitalist accumulation – which is why he left no doubt in anyone's mind that Part 8 was integral to Part 7" (Dunayevskaya, 1982, p. 139, fn. *). And she adds, "Marx had included it [Part 8], ever since the French edition, as a separate chapter under Part 7, 'The General Law of Capitalist Accumulation'" (p. 148, fn. 21) and she went on to put a blame on Ernest Mandel as the editor of the Fowkes' edition.

in England and proficient in German and in French,[3] could have been the co-translator, she was otherwise directly involved with the English edition, being charged with the time-consuming task of restoring the original English textual material that had appeared in German. Probably she was simply too busy to be a co-translator. By February 1886, Moore and Aveling's work was handed over to Engels for editing (Marx and Engels, *c.w.*, Vol. 47, p. 400).

The English edition has the same structural division as the French. Why did the English edition not correspond to the Engels' 3rd German edition if Engels was again the editor and had at hand his own earlier decision for the 3rd German? Possibly, Marx's daughter Eleanor knew directly from her father his preference; in fact, she was literary co-executor with Engels for Marx's works (Marx and Engels, 1948, p. 217, i.e., letter of April 11, 1883). Possibly, Eleanor had paid careful attention to the French-edition divisions and pointed this out to Aveling, the translator for Chapter 25, "General Law of Capitalist Accumulation" and the whole of Part VIII "The So-Called Primitive Accumulation" (Marx, 1867, p. 13). Another possibility: Correspondence was occurring between Engels and Nikolai Danielson – to whom Marx had directly expressed his wish for the 2nd Russian to follow the French. Danielson had received from Engels in April 1884 the 3rd German edition (*c.w.*, Vol. 47, p. 129), it neglecting the French edition divisions desired by Marx. In November 1885, Engels acknowledged receiving and reading from Danielson copies of several letters Marx had written Danielson. That delivery, according to the publisher's note, included the letter of November 15, 1878, in which Marx stated to Danielson his desire that the French edition's division be used by Danielson in the next Russian edition (Marx and Engels, *c.w.*, Vol. 47, p. 348 and note 470). This letter could have influenced Engels' editing of the English translation that he received a few months later, i.e., the following February. We do know that Engels did a lot of work editing the English edition translation (*c.w.*, Vol. 47, pp. 436, 506 and 522).

Whatever the explanation, for the English edition, the resulting part and chapter division is the same as the French. Even the modern English translation retains the French division, perhaps unwilling to challenge Engels even in this respect in order to conform to the German editions (unlike the leading modern French translation by Lefebvre that adopts the German division without explanation and, remarkably enough, against Marx's own French division).

---

3 She undertook in this period the first translation Flaubert's *Madame Bovary* into English as well as having other activities (Holmes, 2014, p. 249).

Engels sent the English edition to Danielson in February 1887 (*C.W.*, Vol. 48, p. 26), who would have at least noticed that the English edition now had divisions corresponding to what Marx had told Danielson he wanted for the 2nd Russian edition. But, the *text* of the English edition is still based on Engels' 3rd German (later modified to correspond to the 4th edition), as I have addressed in the previous two chapters.

When supplies of the 3rd German edition were running low a decision was made by Engels to put out a 4th German edition, rather than reprinting the 3rd. For this and most other issues of comparison to the French, the die had been cast already with the 3rd German edition. Engels did include a few additional changes from the French and this new edition appeared in 1890. In his Preface, Engels listed the changes here and there totaling about ten pages. He added five pages to the Part IV chapter "Machinery and Modern Industry", Section 9, compared to the 3rd German (three of which he had already added to English edition, namely, Marx, 1867, pp. 462–465). He added almost four pages into the Part VII chapter "The Conversion of Surplus Value into Capital", Section 1, and two pages for "General Law" chapter added at the end of Section 2, and a changed first footnote in Section 3 (on the census in England and Wales). Still, even though Engels had in front of him the English edition he himself edited with its differing divisions from the 3rd German, nevertheless, Engels did not make corresponding changes in the divisions for the 4th German edition, changes that would be quite simple and were instructed by Marx. Why? Why did not Engels come to accept the division in the French, as desired by Marx, even if he had not yet done so for the 3rd German? Was it only reluctance to admit a prior mistake? Was it because he already knew of the 1887 Dutch edition and the new 1889 Polish being based upon the 3rd German, but did not know of the Italian and Spanish editions using the French? Yet, he was personally closest to the English translation that did have the division of the French, for whatever is the explanation.

The 2nd Russian edition by Danielson had to wait to 1898. In his Preface Danielson says he took some account of all published editions, including the 3rd and 4th German editions, the French and the English. Nevertheless, he did not follow, nor even mention, the difference in the chapter divisions between the French or English edition compared to the German, even though he himself had received from Marx a letter that the French divisions were preferred for a 2nd Russian edition. He only updated part and chapter divisions of the 1st Russian edition to correspond to the 2nd German, but otherwise followed Engels in retaining the division in the 2nd. Danielson was surely unaware of Marx's own instructions for the 3rd, and would likely have expected Engels to have been as near as anyone to Marx's wishes. Such a presumption would be perfectly understandable ... only that Engels failed to follow Marx instructions!

The "Preface" by Danielson to his 2nd Russian edition of *Volume I* is informative about his perceptions.[4] The last paragraph is particularly significant in its connection with Marx wanting a separate Part VIII. It reads as follows, while a translation of the preceding portion is footnoted:[5]

---

4   Shortly afterwards, a different Russian translation directly based on the 4th German edition would be published.
5   The Preface by Danielson to his 2nd Russian edition of *Capital, Volume I*, dated January, 1898, was obtained from archives in Russia by François Allisson and translated by James B. White, excluding Danielson's long discussion of "stoimost" as the appropriate translation into Russian of "value". I thank them both for making this rare 2nd Russian edition of *Volume I* known and Danielson's "Preface", pp. XIII, XVII–XIX, and XXI, available for consideration. Emphasis is in the original.

   Preface

   To the Second Russian Edition

   The 1st Russian edition of *Volume I* of "Capital" appeared more than 25 years ago. In this time three new editions in the original came out, a French translation, reviewed and revised by the author himself, and an English translation, which appeared after the death of the author and was revised by Engels.

   Thus, with the 2nd edition of the Russian translation it appeared necessary, as a preliminary, to compare it with the latest edition of the original, because a great part of the book has been more or less rewritten by the author, since in some parts one cannot limit oneself simply to correcting the existing translation, but has to do it anew. Thus, a great part of the first section – "The commodity and money" has been freshly translated, just as have many places of the four following sections. Comparatively fewer changes have been made by the author in the middle part of the book, beginning with the second section, approximately a third of the whole. But even here there is not a page where more or less significant corrections and additions have not been made. In general there are so many corrections that perhaps it would have been better to translate the whole volume afresh...

   As a basis for such corrections and additions the 4th German edition has been taken. But a comparison was made simultaneously with the French and English translations. With the French, because the author himself, in the Postface "To the Reader" of the French translation, says that "the French edition possesses a scientific value, independent of the original, and should be consulted even by readers familiar with German"; because "for the translation", the author explains, "I revised the whole text of the original, in some cases I simplified, in others I completed my arguments, gave additional historical or statistical material, added critical remarks etc". (p. 348). Then, with the publication of the 2nd German edition, the author writes: "One should compare both editions (the French and the 2nd German) because I added something and changed something in the French edition ... some places I was obliged to write anew ... to make them fully accessible to a French public". All this forces one to compare the original with the French translation and make use of the one that seems to have a more accessible exposition.

   Comparison with the English translation is necessary for another reason. The author constantly refers to data of English economic life, citing English authors and including extracts from the Blue Books, from the accounts of factory inspectors and from various

English official sources, translating them of course into German, if they appear in his text. When an English edition of "Capital" was proposed, it was necessary either to translate all these English quotes from German back into English, or to take them directly from the original. But in the latter case there was an enormous job of tracking down all the references made by the author, of finding all the quotes from countless publications. The editor preferred the latter approach; Marx's daughter Eleanor took on the task of carrying out this enormous work. So that for the Russian translation one had to compare all these quotations from various English authors and publications with the extracts from the originals which are quoted in the English edition of "Capital". In some cases in the English edition these extracts are somewhat extended. This applies to the data taken from the Blue Books and the reports of the different parliamentary commissions. Some of these additions also were included in the Russian translation of the present edition, but some details which did not add anything new were not included, just as they were not included in the German original; for example many details from the testimony of the miners, namely the coal miners, given by them to the parliamentary commission on the coal industry (in the extensive extract on pp. 433–439 of the present edition).

Unfortunately, in the 26 years that have passed since the publication of the 1st Russian edition there have been no reactions to the translation itself which could be used for the present edition. All we have heard are reproaches for the allegedly unsuccessful translation of the term to express Wert, value, valeur, which is rendered as "stoimost"; in Russian...

Marx's economic theory, in so far as it is reflected in his work "Capital", has to date not been critically evaluated. Apart from Sieber's book: *The Theory of Value of David Ricardo*, which appeared in 1871, the short note of Mr I.I. K[aufman] in *Vestnik Evropy* in May 1872, and a few other more or less fleeting remarks, in Russian economic literature you won't find any books or articles worth the mention, and which would critically approach this theory knowledgeably and in good faith. Moreover, a critical analysis of this work is very desirable.

Marx's theory demands not only a dispassionate critical analysis – like any other scholarly research – it also demands further development, testing it by factual verification, that is, a verification by the facts of socio-economic life. This is all the more necessary since new economic factors are constantly appearing and old ones, which were only in embryo when Marx wrote his work, have undergone significant development. In the world market there is a group of countries in which the capitalist mode of production has become consolidated. This mode has begun to penetrate into countries which until now have been the main markets for the countries of old capitalist culture. Such penetration of new conditions of production cannot but be reflected on the whole social structure of such countries and cannot but shake the very bases of that order, calling forth many phenomena whose explanation has still to be investigated.

Although in terms of completion and refinement the first volume of "Capital" is the most perfected of the three volumes, the author himself was not satisfied with it in its present form, and did not give up his intention to rework it completely, to develop its basic principles, illustrate it with new data, which were accumulating in extraordinary quantity. In particular, he was interested in data from the U.S.A., on the one hand, as a country without any kind of traditions, consequently, one in which capitalist conditions of production could develop without any more or less significant obstacles. But free development would be possible only with the abolition of slavery, and this development was

...Marx definitely rejects the idea that the laws of economic life have a universal validity, and are uniformly applicable to both the present and the past. *For him there are no such things as abstract laws.* The same phenomenon is definitely subject to different laws if the constitution of the whole social organism is different, if its individual organs change, if the conditions in which it functions alter. (Cf. The Author's Preface to the 2nd edition of *Capital, Volume 1*) Especially emphatically he insists on this in his famous letter, where he categorically protests against attempts "to transform my sketch of the origin of capitalism in Western Europe into a historico-philosophical theory of the general course of development that

> just beginning at the time when the book was already written. On the other hand he was no less interested in Russia, as a country, that after the liberation of the peasantry, had only just embarked on the road of development of capitalist production, having behind it a history of many centuries of the development of economic relations and conditions completely different from those coming into being. And in this case, at the time that he was writing his book, the antagonism of the old and new conditions of production still had not had time to appear.
>
> In view of all this, when, a year and a half before his death, the German publisher told him that a new, third, edition of the first volume of "Capital" was needed, he wrote: "This news comes at a very bad time for me. Firstly, I have to regain my health, and secondly, I want to finish the second volume as soon as possible (understanding by this the whole of the theoretical part, i.e. the second and third).... However that may be, I will arrange with my publisher that I shall make for the 3rd edition only the fewest possible alterations and additions, but, on the other hand, that this time he should publish no more than a thousand copies instead of the three thousand he wanted. When these thousand copies of the 3rd edition are sold, I shall then be in a position to rewrite the book in the way I would do at the present time, if the circumstances were different". This intention was not destined to be fulfilled ... Even the 3rd edition came out after the death of the author, under the editorship of Engels. The enormous significance Marx gave to these new phenomena which arose under completely peculiar, exceptional conditions, one can judge, firstly, from the fact that as far back as the 1870s he kept postponing the reworking of both the first and the following volumes in order to utilise the statistical and other materials that should have appeared in the USA, and which would have illustrated the conditions of economic life that had recently emerged there. Secondly, and to an even greater degree, from the enormous labour which he expended in studying the phenomena of Russian economic life, and for which he did not balk even at learning the Russian language for the purpose.
>
> Thus, the further development of Marx's doctrine demands the factual study of the phenomena of economic life without any preconceptions. Anyone who takes up the study of "Capital" not as an inspiration to further the development of science, but as "in the middle ages they looked upon the works of Aristotle, Ptolemy and Hippocrates and other ancient thinkers, i.e. as on an authority the bounds of whose doctrine any attempt to go beyond would be futile and even sacrilegious", such a person would be in direct contradiction both with Marx's doctrine itself and with the method that he followed. Needless to say, such an approach would only hinder the attainment of the truth....

all peoples are destined to follow, whatever the historical circumstances in which they find themselves, in order that finally they arrive at that economic order which ensures the greatest expansion of productive powers of social labour and the most complete development of man". He then shows, using the example of the fate of the plebeians of ancient Rome, that "events strikingly analogous, but taking place in different historical surroundings, lead to completely different results". From this he concludes that: "by studying each of these forms of evolution separately, and then comparing them, one can easily find the key to these phenomena, but one will never arrive at an understanding of them by using a *passe par tout* historico-philoshical theory, the supreme virtue of which consists in being super-historical (*'supra historique'*)". [Danielson is citing Marx's 1878 draft letter to the editorial board of *Otechestvennye zapiski* that was first published in translation into Russian in 1888 by Danielson from the French original – see White (1996, p. 242). P.Z.].

3 Engels' Continuing Failure to Recognize Marx's Advances

In 1884, Engels moved to prepare for publication a first edition of *Volume II* and he had to decide what to include and what to exclude. It did not take him long to exclude all of Marx's work on Russia. This decision upset some in Russia, including Kovalevsky writing to Lavrov in July 1884 and Chuprov writing to Danielson in January 1886 (White, 2019a, p. 48). It also upset Danielson who had been in enough communication with Marx to be taken seriously by Engels. Danielson tried to encourage Engels. And when material on Russia didn't appear in *Volume II* he hoped it would be in *Volume III*. That did not happen. Engels felt that he was too old to get into the large volume of Marx's work on Russia, and even donated Marx's entire library on Russia to Lavrov already in 1884 (Marx and Engels, *c.w.*, Vol. 47, p. 88). Engels simply did not understand what concerned Marx as a result of his Russian research, nor seemed to care to find out. Danielson was quite disappointed and reflected on it twenty-five years after Marx's death, i.e., in 1908:

> It is a very great pity that all these hopes were dashed. The whole of Marx's enormous labours in studying the materials on Russian economic life were lost to science. The second and third volumes of "Capital" appeared just as they had been written in the 1860s. The Russian material of the 1870s remained unused... (Danielson, cited by White, 2019b, p. 16)

The consequences are being lived to this day as far as understanding Marx's development of his theory and indeed how Marxist political economy is understood.

Rather than with Danielson, Engels was more in tune with Georgi Plekhanov, who had formed with a few other Russians the Emancipation of Labor emigre group in Geneva in 1883, the same year Marx died. We met him in Chapter 1 in connection with Hegel. Plekhanov had been a populist, moving to Marxism in the early 1880s, including translating the *Communist Manifesto* into Russian in 1882 with a foreword by Marx and Engels. In 1885, he published *Our Differences* which was mainly an attack on the position that capitalism is impossible in Russia because it impoverishes the rural population and thus undermines its own need for markets. Plekhanov countered this line of argument with an empirical analysis of Russia and other historical examples. The work is not one of theoretical abstraction, although he did study and use the work by Sieber (1871).[6] From the late 1880s Plekhanov had contact with Engels, until the latter's death in 1895. In subsequent years Plekhanov occupied an authoritative role within Marxism, second only to Karl Kautsky. Plekhanov was to promote the concept "dialectical materialism", and he had a decisive influence on Lenin. Writing to Engels a few months before Engels' death, Plekhanov wrote, "As for Danielson, I fear there is nothing to be done with him" (Marx and Engels, 1948, p. 285). Plekhanov had pejoratively labeled Danielson a "Narodnik" and Engels hadn't called him on that characterization. Further discussion of Plekhanov is included in my first chapter, while for more context the reader can consult White (2019a, Chapter 4, and 2019b) who argues that Danielson and Vorontsov have a better claim for continuing Marx's theoretical heritage than Plekhanov, in spite of Engels. One could ask, "if Danielson were a 'Narodnik', why not Marx?"

In 1891, Engels wrote an "Introduction" to a new edition of Marx's *Wage-Labour and Capital*. He writes that the Marx's criticism of political economy had already been completed "toward the end of the fifties" (sic!). I find this astonishing. It asserts that, for Engels, Marx's theoretical work after 1859 was nothing more than elaboration, filling in details, that sort of thing. It says that Marx learning Russian and studying Russian developments had no particular importance. It says that there was no impact on Engels' understanding of his friend when the latter wrote him in 1870 that the most important work published since Engels' own *Condition of the Working Class in England* was Flerovsky's *Condition of the Working [Peasant] Class in Russia* (Marx, 1948,

---

6 See Sieber (2001). *Volume II* of *Capital* would appear in the next year 1885 (*Volume III* in 1894) and Plekhanov, in any case, never showed great interest in abstract political economy.

p. 165). It says that Marx assembling a whole library of more than a hundred books on Russia was of no particular importance for Marx's continuing study of political economy. And this is only about Russia, not all the other studies undertaken by Marx. It would even say that *Volumes II* and *III* of *Capital*, both being written after 1859, were not very consequential elaborations of earlier work, even with Engels' personal time and energy in publishing his editions of these two volumes.

The 1891 remark is astonishing in a further respect. Engels actually says that his own principal alteration of Marx's 1949 *Wage-Labour and Capital* centers around one point: "According to the original reading, the worker sells his labour for wages, which he receives from the capitalist; according to the present text, he sells his labour-power". Engels expends most of his remarks on clarifying this change he makes. Yet, as I pointed out in Chapter 2, Marx did not come to develop and apply "labor power" as a *concept* until sometime *after* 1859, in fact, around 1865, i.e., the timing of "Value, Price and Profit" (which actually used "laboring power"). That is, the concept was not in Marx's 1859 *Contribution to a Critique of Political Economy* and was one of many theoretical investigations and developments Marx made *after* 1859 up to the end of his life. Engels is contradicting himself.

Given Engels' 1891 statement, it can be more clearly understood, but not accepted, why slippages occurred between what Marx wrote in the French version of *Volume I* and what Engels decided to include or not include from explicit Marx's instructions for the German 3rd edition. Yes, Engels included much, with a lot of work on his part. But the exclusions also matter and they have had too much influence on subsequent Marxist thought, indeed more than recognized. Engels' 3rd German edition of *Volume I*, and then his 4th, arrested a development in political economy that Marx had started and was continuing. If any other person had done so, the contrast with Marx's instructions, when published, would have been noticed, analyzed, dissected, and challenged, given the explicit instructions left for the 3rd edition. But the instructions were not published in excess of a hundred years.

On Marx's part, Engels' role was in no way unreasonable. When you die, you are out of control and a choice is well to be made beforehand. Who else could have been given the task? Nevertheless, Engels' editions was making a statement and the authority of Engels is demonstrated later in so many ways: (1) while the 1884 Polish edition used the French version for the initial translation, it was later converted to Engels' editions, (2) No 2nd Russian edition ever adopted the division change Marx wanted, (3) German editions ever followed Engels closely without mentioning problems (although a new German edition of *Volume I* by T. Kuczynski, 2017, moves in the correct direction), (4) most translators into other languages utilize Engels' 4th German, (5) even the

Lefebvre 1983 French edition followed Engels' desire, and (6) the Fowkes' English edition stayed with the division that Marx actually wanted, simply because Engels had once authorized that (are we so afraid to challenge Engels?).

4 Postscript: Marx's Primitive Accumulation Conflated with Modern Dispossessions/ Enclosures

Many apply the concept of primitive accumulation equally in the present period as with the origins of capital's dominance. However, I think "primitive accumulation" is used too casually.

Perelman's (2000) presented primitive accumulation as Perelman understands it, and then turns to examining the writings of classical political economists in their historical context. Perelman appears to be uncomfortable that Marx, even late in life, diminished "the importance of primitive accumulation by relegating it to a distant past" (p. 27). The material on primitive accumulation in *Volume I*, he says, "does not appear to be qualitatively different" from Marx's discussion of accumulation proper, and suggests Marx's willingness to include force and violence for both (pp. 28–29). Perelman cites the passage from *Volume I* that "accumulation of capital is … multiplication of the proletariat" and explicitly claims that this is about primitive accumulation (p. 36). He fails to mention that this important passage appears in "The General Law of Capitalist Accumulation" but nothing is said about primitive accumulation in the entire chapter other than describing it as an historical issue (Marx, 1867, p. 585). After citing a passage from *Volume III*,[7] he goes on to provide his own examples of separation from means of production continuing in the present: "primitive accumulation remains a key concept for understanding capitalism – and not just the particular phase of capitalism associated with the transition from feudalism, but capitalism proper. Primitive accumulation is a process that continues to this day". (p. 37) In sum, Perelman takes separation as synonymous with primitive accumulation. An explanation offered for Marx's own downgrading of the continuing importance of separation from means of production is that such a focus on the violence of separation would have tended to undermine another important message: the brutality of market forces itself.

---

7 He quotes the *Volume III* passage discussing falling profits referring to "expropriating the final residue of direct producers who still have something left to expropriate", saying that the passage is important because "it indicates that Marx realized the ongoing nature of primitive accumulation" (p. 31).

A discussion began in 2001 with the on-line publication *The Commoner* which devoted an issue to "Enclosures", the process of separation of laborers from any means of production so that they become free wage-laborers for the purposes of capitalist exploitation, often resulting in violent confrontations continuing to this day. A debate ensued. The issue of *The Commoner* began by reprinting Perelman's chapter "The Enduring Importance of Primitive Accumulation" that had introduced his book. *The Commoner* offered other contributions. The book by Bonefeld (2008) provided revised versions of a number of the earlier contributions within the debate, including those by De Angelis, himself, and myself (Chapters 2, 3, 4, respectively), as well another by himself (Chapter 5).

De Angelis developed an argument that "primitive accumulation is necessarily present in 'mature' capitalist systems and, given the conflicting nature of capitalist relations, assumes a 'continuous' character" (p. 28). He proposes that the "core of Marx's approach is the concept of *separation between producers and means of production*" and that the "difference between accumulation and primitive accumulation, not being a substantive one, is a difference in the conditions and forms in which this *separation* is implemented" (pp. 31 and 33, emphasis in original). He suggests that primitive accumulation is *ex novo* separation, while accumulation proper is separation "on a greater scale" (p. 35).

> By rationalizing the working day, restructuring the work process and dismissing the work force, the introduction of machinery aims at bypassing that "social barrier" that was erected and therefore re-creates the *separation* between forces of production and producers at a greater scale. In so doing it intensifies labour to the extent that "the denser hour of the 10-hour working day contains more labour, i.e. expended labour power, than the more porous hour of the 12-hour working day" (Marx, 1867, p. 534). It goes without saying that any attempt to repeal the law that sets the extension of the working day would be instead an act of *ex novo* production of that separation, an act of primitive accumulation. (De Angelis, pp. 43–44, emphasis in original and the citation to Marx being to the Fowkes' edition)

More intense hours of work – through the introduction of facilitating machinery in this illustration – is seemingly greater separation, i.e., accumulation proper. On the other hand, forcing *more* work hours – repealing working-day laws – is additional separation, his primitive accumulation. An historical period does not seem to be involved in the distinction.

Bonefeld's own chapter unequivocally asserts incorporation of primitive accumulation into accumulation proper. "Primitive accumulation is a constantly reproduced accumulation, be it in terms of the renewed separate of new populations from the means of production and subsistence, or in terms of the reproduction of the wage relation in the 'established' relations of capital". Claiming "formidable political consequences" for his perspective, revolution against capital "cannot be achieved through a politics on behalf of the working class [which] leads to the acceptance of programs and tickets whose common basis is the everyday religion of bourgeois society: commodity fetishism". Such a politics needs to be "negated". (2008, p. 61). If Bonefeld's perspective were accepted and no distinction between accumulation proper and primitive accumulation even attempted, the question arises whether bother at all with any concept of primitive accumulation, a concept that, in fact, became a whole Part VIII of *Capital, Volume I* in the French edition.[8]

De Angelis and Bonefeld are quite correct to emphasize separation from means of production. But never do they cite a place in Marx where Marx himself refers to primitive accumulation other than in the historical process of movement from feudalism to capitalism. And they avoid certain passages in Marx where he is quite clear with his own context being historical for usage of primitive accumulation. Thus, neither one cites the first paragraph of Marx's "The So-called Primitive Accumulation" in which Marx notes that accumulation of capital presupposes surplus-value and surplus-value presupposes capitalist production and, therefore, everything "seems to turn in a vicious circle, out of which we can only get by supposing a primitive accumulation ... preceding capitalistic accumulation; an accumulation not the result of the capitalistic mode of production, but its starting point" (Marx, 1867, p. 667 – presented as such for the first time in French edition). Primitive accumulation "appears as primitive, because it forms the pre-historic stage of capital and of the mode of production corresponding with it" (p. 668). De Angelis and Bonefeld would need to confront these passages. But they would also have to deal satisfactorily with many other similar, less well-known passages elsewhere in Marx, which I have tallied (Zarembka, in Bonefeld, 2008, pp. 71–72).

---

8 Bonefeld (p. 52) makes a reference to Luxemburg while trying to read her being consistent with his position. Luxemburg did recognize dispossession as included within accumulation proper as "a process that takes place between capital and non-capitalist forms of production. [...] Here violence, fraud, oppression, and plunder are displayed quite openly, without any attempt to disguise them, and it requires a lot of effort to uncover the strict laws governing the economic process beneath this turmoil of political violence and trials of strength". Luxemburg (1913, p. 329). But, she gives no space to giving up on primitive accumulation being the historical subject matter of the transition of the feudal to capitalist mode of production.

Bonefeld provided an answer to the above concern, leaning upon a translation problem from German and upon Hegel. He cites his earlier phrasing in *The Commoner* that "primitive accumulation is suspended (*Aufhebung*) in capitalist accumulation as its secret history of constitution" (2008, p. 79), but in 2008 he clarifies that his use of "suspended" as the translation of *Aufhebung* was unfortunate and inconsistent with a Hegelian dialectical process: In the context "*Aufhebung* means that the historical form of primitive accumulation is raised to a new level" in accumulation proper (p. 81). However, Marx himself does not describe accumulation proper in this manner. Bonefeld's is merely an interpretation.

Staying with Marx's own definition of primitive accumulation and then probing more deeply Marx's concept of accumulation of capital is needed. This is addressed in the next chapter. Luxemburg's *The Accumulation of Capital* is consistent with this concern, but she did not address the conception of accumulation of capital as such.

In a new interpretation, Pradella (2015, p. 158) argues that Marx's primitive accumulation "does not represent a 'historical' part separate from the 'economic', but examines the role of the state in the genesis and the expanded reproduction of capital". However, she does not even try to explain why Marx offered a separate concept of primitive accumulation, separate from accumulation proper – he even going so far as introducing the separate Part VIII, beginning with the French edition. Nor does she mention that Marx's introduction of the topic clearly refers to the *historical* process of the consolidation of the capitalist mode of production.

CHAPTER 6

Marxist Accumulation of Capital?

> Accumulate, accumulate! That is Moses and the prophets! ... Accumulation for accumulation's sake, production for production's sake: by this formula classical economy expressed the historical mission of the bourgeoisie ... Political Economy takes the historical function of the capitalist in bitter earnest.
> Marx (1867, p. 558)

> ...reproduction on a progressive scale, i.e. accumulation, reproduces the capital-relation on a progressive scale, more capitalists or larger capitalists at this pole, more wage-workers at that.... Accumulation of capital is, therefore, increase of the proletariat.
> Marx (1867, pp. 575–576)

I invite the reader[1] to re-reread an important writing of his or her choice that relies on the concept "accumulation of capital" and ask what it means for *that author*. If you try, in most cases you would either have to *project* its meaning for the author, perhaps incorrectly, or else you would realize a vague, generalized usage (as in a word like "capitalism"). Sometimes, though, the authors are clear, at least implicitly, and I give just one example. Following upon earlier work of both, Thompson (1998) and Laibman (1998) vigorously debated the movement of the rate of profit. Without explicitly defining accumulation of capital, for both it is clearly nothing but more constant capital (more "K"), a conception that has roots in Smith, Ricardo, and incorporated into neoclassical economics. I do not accept such a definition within Marxism, but, in any case, vagueness in usage of the concept is the typical case.

Before beginning, it is perhaps important to recall that Marx was concerned with definitions, that definitions of concepts mattered. One of Smith's greatest scientific achievements, says Marx, was that Smith defines "productive labour as labour *which is directly exchanged with capital;* that is, he defines it by the exchange through which the conditions of production of labour, and value in general, whether money or commodity, are first transformed into capital (and labour into wage-labour in its scientific meaning)" (Marx, 1905a, p. 157, emphasis in original). Unproductive labor is directly exchanged against revenue, whether wages or profit (or interest or rent). Marx proceeds to note that "these

---

1 The first three sections of this chapter are a more concise version of Zarembka (2000), pp. 183–198), while the fourth draws upon pp. 222–225.

definitions are therefore not derived from the material characteristics of labour ... but from the definite social form, the social relations of production, within which the labour is realised". And Richard Jones "quite correctly reduces Smith's productive and non-productive labour to its essence – capitalist and non-capitalist labour" (Marx, 1910, p. 431–432). Furthermore, Marx was concerned about his own definition of productive labor, saying that the laborer is only productive "who produces surplus-value for the capitalist, and thus works for the self-expansion of capital", going on to mention a teaching factory owned by a school proprietor (Marx, 1867, pp. 476–477).

On the subject of constant and variable capital, Marx refers to that part of capital "which is represented by the means of production ... [and] does not, in the process of production, undergo any quantitative alteration of value", as the "constant part of capital, or, more shortly, *constant capital*. On the other hand, that part of capital, represented by labour-power, does, in the process of production, undergo an alteration of value [since it] both reproduces the equivalent of its own value, and also produces an excess, a surplus value.... I therefore call it the variable part of capital, or, shortly, *variable capital*". (Marx, 1867, p. 202, emphasis in original) In the following paragraphs Marx then elaborates on the "definition" of constant capital. In short, definitions mattered for Marx.

Accumulation of capital for Marx did not receive a lot of specific attention before Tugan-Baranovsky. Sieber (1871, Chapter 6) discussed it somewhat in the contest of his work on classical economists. Kautsky's (1887) summarized and popularized Marx, with many later editions, and gave some attention to accumulation. He started from Marx's statement that "[e]mploying surplus-value as capital, reconverting it into capital, is called accumulation of capital". He then concluded with a focus on labor that I have not seen cited in recent works: "accumulation of surplus-value means the appropriation of unpaid labour for the purpose of extending the appropriation of unpaid labour" (p. 207). A decade later, in a section "Accumulation in Capitalist Society", Lenin (1897) would discuss accumulation in his critique of Sismondi (1819): "The 'day labourers' who are pushed out of agriculture by the conversion of the 'peasants' into 'farmers' provide labour-power for capital, and the farmers are purchasers of the products of industry, not only of articles of consumption ..., but also of instruments of production" (pp. 139–140). He concluded that accumulation "opens a new market *for means of production without correspondingly expanding the market for articles of consumption, and even contracting this market*" (p. 159, emphasis in original).[2] Lenin's emphasis is on constant capital.

---

2 Lenin made subtle changes in his positions over time with regard to the role of consumption and the meaning of Marx's schemes of reproduction in *Volume II*. The last instance was a

Discussing accumulation of capital became important with Tugan-Baranovsky's intervention. In 1898 Tugan expressed concern about a passage in Marx's *Volume III*. Tugan was disturbed by passage in Marx that the conditions of realization are limited both by

> the proportional relation of the various branches of production and the consumer power of society. But this last-named is not determined either by the absolute productive power, or by the absolute consumer power, but by the consumer power based on antagonistic conditions of distribution, which reduce the consumption of the bulk of society to a minimum varying within more or less narrow limits. It is furthermore restricted by the tendency to accumulate.... This internal contradiction seeks to resolve itself through expansion of the outlying field of production. But the more productiveness develops, the more it finds itself at variance with the narrow basis on which the conditions of consumption rest. (Marx, 1894, pp. 244–245)

For Tugan, the passage seems to say that products "may not find a market even if the distribution of production is proportional" (Tugan, "Capitalism and the Market", *Mir Bozhy*, 1898, No. 6, p. 122, as cited by Lenin, 1899a, p. 58). Tugan (1901, German edition) then *objects* to Marx's splitting of the causes of crises into two elements, as Tugan wants to promote uniquely a disproportionality interpretation of crises that is close to Say's Law that he does support (as had Ricardo): "given a proportional distribution of social production, supply and demand must coincide", there being no other concern (Tugan, p. 80, n. 3). Tugan shifts attention to the schemes of reproduction in Marx's *Volume II*, with an unfortunate consequence that simple mathematical details often became the attention. He did understand Marx insofar as accumulation involved both constant capital and variable capital – accumulation is "carried out by the

---

reply to an article by P. Nezhdanov. There, Lenin's discussion of the role of consumption appears longer and more complete than ever before, saying that the disparity between production and consumption "is expressed (as Marx has demonstrated clearly in his Schemes) by the fact that the production of the means of production can and must outstrip the production of articles of consumption" (1899c, p. 162). His claim is in spite of the fact that the schemes of *Volume II* actually hold constant the composition of capital. He goes on to say that "consumption must, in the final analysis, follow production, and, if the productive forces are driving towards an unlimited growth of production, while consumption is restricted by the proletarian condition of the masses of the people, there is undoubtedly a contradiction present" (p. 164). Lenin clearly feels the pressure of a need for more exact explanation of his position.

transformation of profit into means of production and wage goods" (p. 72). He also understood the distinctive character of capitalism relative to slavery and feudalism – the "laws of capitalism competition categorically force him [the capitalist] to expand production and to capitalize a large part of profit. In slave and feudal economy, the production was aimed directly to consumption, namely, to the consumption of the ruling social class". (p. 73)

Kautsky (1902, p. 211) had a long review of Tugan's book. It argued that "human labor ultimately always remains the value-producing factor, and the expansion of *human* consumption is ultimately also decisive for the expansion of production. Production is and remains production for human consumption". (Emphasis in original) Plekhanov, in his turn, became worried about the similarity of Lenin's theoretical position to Tugan's:

> I have never been a supporter of the theory of markets in general or that of crises in particular, a theory which spread like the plague in our legal literature on Marxism in the nineties. According to this theory whose main propagator was Mr. Tugan-Baranovsky, *overproduction* is impossible and crises are explained by the simple disproportion in the distribution of the means of production. This theory is very gladdening for the bourgeoisie, to whom it brings the pleasant conviction that the productive forces of capitalist society will never outgrow the production relations peculiar to capitalism.... The real father of this by no means new doctrine was *Jean Baptiste Say*.... Besides Mr. Tugan-Baranovsky, Mr. Vladimir Ilyin [Lenin] also professed the theory of J.B. Say in "Notes on the Theory of Markets" (*Scientific Review*, January 1899) and *The Development of Capitalism in Russia*. (Plekhanov, 1885, in note added to the 1905 2nd edition, p. 237, emphasis in original)

Kindersley's (1962, pp. 146–154) study of these issues concluded that, other than debating points, the differences among Lenin, Tugan-Baranovsky, as well as Bulgakov and Struve (whom I discuss in Zarembka, 2003), were not great nor very revealing. Hilferding (1910) discusses accumulation of capital mostly in the context of the schemes of reproduction, appearing in his Chapters 16, "The General Conditions of Crises" and Chapter 19, "Money Capital and Productive Capital during the Depression". Never does he say that accumulation refers to increased employment of labor power, other than implied by variable capital growing within a scheme of accumulation.

Luxemburg (1913) met Tugan's challenge on its terms, but she soon became quite aware of a consequence of Tugan's focus on mathematical formula, noting later that her critics' considerable attention to formula "is linked very closely to their points of view on the subject. Yet the problem of accumulation is itself purely economic and social; it does not have anything to do with mathematical formulas, and one can demonstrate and comprehend the problem without them". (Luxemburg, 1921, p. 348) As to Sismondi, her opinion was similar to Marx's:

> [Sismondi's] theory of reproduction suffers from the fundamental error he took over from Smith, namely, the conception that the total annual product is accounted for entirely by personal consumption, without leaving any portion of value over for the replacement of constant capital, and likewise that accumulation consists exclusively of the transformation of capitalized surplus value into additional variable capital. Yet, when later critics of Sismondi (such as, for example, the Russian Marxist [V.I.] Lenin) believed, with an air of condescension, that they could dismiss his entire theory of accumulation as invalid, as "nonsense", by referring to this fundamental error in the value-analysis of the total product, they merely demonstrated that they themselves had failed to notice the actual problem with which Sismondi was concerned. (Luxemburg, 1913, pp. 131–132)

Regarding Sismondi, Marx (1910, p. 56) had written that he "is particularly aware of the fundamental contradiction: on the one hand, unrestricted development of the productive forces and wealth which, at the same time, consists of commodities and must be turned into cash; on the other hand, the system is based on the fact that the mass or producers is restricted to the necessaries".

Lenin (1915) was to claim that accumulation for Marx is the "transformation of a part of surplus value into capital, and its use, not for satisfying the personal needs or whims of the capitalist, but for new production ... divided into *means of production* and variable capital" (pp. 63–64, emphasis in original). Yet, accumulation focused on new production cannot be found in Marx and so Lenin's interpretation in this as well as in other respects represented a step backwards from Marx toward Ricardo (see Zarembka, 2003).[3] If Marxist political

---

3 "Time after time, Lenin offers an interpretation of Marxist political economy that connects in one way or another to issues of production, and is not dissimilar to Ricardo's emphasis on production even when the bourgeoisie could be at the short end of his stick. Marx had said, regarding Ricardo, that where 'the bourgeois comes into conflict with [production or the productive development of human labor], he is just as *ruthless* towards it as he is at other times towards the proletariat and the aristocracy'" (Zarembka, 2003, p. 298, and citing Marx, 1905b, p. 118, emphasis therein). I continued: "Was Lenin's attack on the Narodniks and Sismondi, his criticism of Luxemburg's political economy, his support of Taylorism, his emphasis

economy had worked from Kautsky's conception we would have been better off. Alas.

Let us go back before Marx for a moment and consider "capital". Adam Smith (1776, pp. 262–263) considered it to be that portion of "stock" possessed by individuals that yields a revenue or profit over time, while another portion of stock would be for immediate consumption. Such capital can be circulating, as for wages, material costs, and purchasing/reselling goods; or it can be fixed, as for land improvements and machinery and equipment. Accumulation of capital is then the increase in these elements of the stock. Smith did not analyze *how* capital accumulates, or its effects. Ricardo (1821) did not contest Smith's definition of capital, and was more precise. "Capital is that part of the wealth of a country which is employed in production, and consists of food, clothing, tools, raw materials, machinery, etc. necessary to give effect to labour" (p. 95). The reference to food and clothing needed to give effect to labor in production refers, of course, to subsistence needs of workers that must be advanced as the production process goes forward, and not restricted to an agricultural setting. Later, neoclassical economics will restrict "capital" to the tools, machinery, and structures and Clark (1899) went so far as to consider them "malleable" to motivate a definition of "real capital" ... as if it were a definable factor of production (my own views on the neoclassical interpretation have been expressed in Zarembka, 1976).

Surely, Marx would not accept either the classical or the neoclassical approach for understanding accumulation of capital. In a capitalist environment, Marx's *Capital* refers to constant capital as the labor time required for producing raw materials, tools, and machinery, and variable capital as the labor time required for producing subsistence for workers. Marx's earlier writings had not focused on the definition of accumulation of capital, using it in a manner little distinguished from the classical economists, but by *Capital*, Marx fundamentally used the word "capital" to refer to the relationship of the capitalist class and wage-laboring class. The last chapter on colonization of *Volume I* even has a passage stating that means of production are not necessarily capital at all and classical political economists are admonished for arguing otherwise:

> We know that the means of production and subsistence, while they remain the property of the immediate producer, are not capital. They

---

upon accounting and control and upon electrification, not a reflection of his political economy?" I might add that in order to enforce accounting and control, Lenin (1918, p. 414) exposed his own ruthless attitude when saying that one method (of five) for ensuring accounting and control could be that "one out of ten idlers will be shot on the spot".

become capital, only under circumstances in which they serve at the same time as means of exploitation and subjection of the labourer. But this capitalist soul of theirs is so intimately wedded, in the head of the political economists, to their material substance, that he christens them capital under all circumstances, even when they are the exact opposite. (Marx, 1867, pp. 717–718)

The subtitle of *Capital* is *A Critique of Political Economy* and implies a critique of the whole structure of bourgeois political economy. If Marx redefined "capital" to refer to a class relation, surely, it would also apply in the case of discussing the "accumulation" of that class relation. His chapters on "Simple Reproduction" and "Conversion of Surplus-Value into Capital" are summarized in the following chapter by writing that accumulation "reproduces the capitalrelation on a progressive scale, more capitalists or larger capitalists at this pole, more wage-workers at that" and so is "increase of the proletariat" (pp. 575–576).

Nevertheless, I argue in this chapter that the concept retains an ambiguity in Marx. In Chapter 2, I said that late in his theoretical development Marx introduced "labor power" in order to distinguish it from "labor", from classical political economy, from common usage. So too he might have reconsidered "accumulation of capital". The theoretical space left unsettled has been unconsciously refilled, in part, with classical conceptions by many writing in the Marxist tradition. This chapter makes the case that Marx's definition of accumulation of capital is sufficiently ambiguous to lead to troublesome conceptions after his death. Therefore, a definition is offered that would enforce the highlighting of the class issues and will be labeled "Marxist accumulation of capital".

1 Accumulation of Capital in *Capital, Volume 1*

Early work by Marx did not contest the use by classical economists of accumulation of capital. The *1844 Manuscripts* has a nine-page section "The Accumulation of Capital and the Competition among the Capitalists" with six of its pages being quotations from the classical economists and focusing on competition versus concentration of capitals. The only passage and a short one that could be considered outside such purview would be the following: "Whilst the division of labor raises the productive powers of labor and increases the wealth and refinement of society, it impoverishes the worker and reduces him to a machine. Whilst labor brings about the accumulation of capital and with this the increasing prosperity of society, it renders the worker ever more dependent on the capitalist, leads him into competition of a new intensity, and drives him into the headlong rush of over-production, with its subsequent corresponding slump" (1932, pp. 70–71).

The first evidence that Marx considered prior use of accumulation to be problematic is found in the *Grundrisse* (putting aside references to primitive accumulation). In English this is conflated with a translation issue. The Progress Publishers' edition includes a note written by Marx, when examining the connection between workers and capital, reading, "we shall have to look more closely at this concept of *accumulation* later" (Marx, 1939–41b, p. 430, emphasis in original as with next citation). The Nicolaus' edition, however, notes the German context as *Aufhäufung* (rather than *Akkumulation*) and renders the translation, "we shall have to examine this notion of *stockpiling* still more closely later on" (Marx, 1939–41a, p. 506). Each text stays with its rendering in then pointing to agglomeration of laborers and instrument of production under capital. The significance of the translation issue is of course a judgment as to whether, in the context, *Aufhäufung* is close enough to *Akkumulation* for "accumulation" to be the better translation; by using "stockpiling" instead, the Nicolaus' edition suggests not. In either case, this is evidence that Marx was beginning in 1858 to consider or reconsider the meaning of accumulation of capital. Yet, it was not undertaken.

Beginning in 1861 Marx's work had the topics of the transformation of money into capital, absolute surplus value, and relative surplus value, and then turning for all of 1862 to reviewing the classical economists. Corresponding notebooks became *Theories of Surplus Value* and include only a few passages relevant for discussing accumulation (Oakley, 1985, pp. 2–3). Any notebook that may have dealt explicitly with accumulation is unpublished (as far as I know), and perhaps was unwritten. The most significant discussion of accumulation of capital in Marx is therefore in *Capital, Volume I*, Part VII, "The Accumulation of Capital", and supplemented later in *Volume II*, Part III, "The Production and Circulation of the Aggregate Social Capital" (its last chapter, in particular). *Volume I* was published in Marx's lifetime and his legacy is naturally weightier than for works left in draft form. For interested readers, results of a "search" by this author for "accumulation" in much of Marx's writings are available at my web link www.buffalo.edu/~zarembka/accumula.htm, albeit without consideration of MEGA².

Accumulation of capital is defined in *Volume I*, Chapter 24, "Conversion of Surplus Value into Capital", and represents a significant departure from the classical economists. This chapter begins immediately at the main point: "Hitherto we have investigated how surplus-value emanates from capital; we have now to see how capital arises from surplus-value. Employing surplus-value as capital, reconverting it into capital, is called accumulation of capital". (p. 543) Reading simply enough, Marx goes on directly with a numerical example for an individual capitalist that captures a conception Marx uses throughout most of his work: accumulation of capital entails increases in *both* the value of the means of production used in production processes *and* in the value of the expenditure on labor power, i.e., increases in both constant capital and variable capital. Marx continues:

> To accumulate it is necessary to convert a portion of the surplus-product into capital. But we cannot, except by a miracle, convert into capital anything but such articles as can be employed in the labour-process (i.e. means of production), and such further articles as are suitable for the sustenance of the labourer (i.e. means of subsistence). Consequently, a part of the annual surplus-labour must have been applied to the production of additional means of production and subsistence, over and above the quantity of these things required to replace the capital advanced. In one word, surplus-value is convertible into capital solely because the surplus-product, whose value it is, already comprises the material elements of new capital.
>
> Now in order to allow of these elements actually functioning as capital, the capitalist class requires additional labour. If the exploitation of the labourers already employed does not increase, either extensively or intensively, then additional labour-power must be found. For this the mechanism of capitalist production provides beforehand, by converting the working-class into a class dependent on wages, a class whose ordinary wages suffice, not only for its maintenance, but also for its increase. It is only necessary for capital to incorporate this additional labour-power, annually supplied by the working-class in the shape of labourers of all ages, with the surplus means of production comprised in the annual produce, and the conversion of surplus-value into capital is complete. From a concrete point of view, accumulation resolves itself into the reproduction of capital on a progressively increasing scale. The circle in which simple reproduction moves, alters its form, and, to use Sismondi's expression, changes into a spiral. (Marx, 1867, pp. 544–545)

The image is consistent with a capitalist, and indeed the capitalist class as a whole, having ten factories with a thousand workers each, and accumulating capital by building an eleventh factory and employing another thousand workers who must be paid their variable capital (their subsistence). No account is taken of technological changes that could cheapen the cost to capital of goods consumed by workers with their wages, that is, cheapen the exchange value of labor power so as to employ the same workers for less variable capital. In other words, no account of the production of relative surplus value, discussed in an earlier Part of *Capital,* is included. There is also no account in this example of the new factory adopting a technology that would change the number of workers employed and, of course, there is also no account of the new factory being produced with a technology that conserves the labor power for its production. Furthermore, *increases in production* resulting from accumulation *are not mentioned* either in Marx's initial definition or in the elaboration through example.

At the end of the first of two paragraphs cited above, as I already mentioned in Chapter 3, Marx adds the significant footnote to the 1875 French serial edition, saying (after excluding foreign trade from consideration) that "in order to examine the object of our investigation in its integrity, free from all disturbing subsidiary circumstances, we must treat the whole world as one nation, and assume that capitalist production is everywhere established and has possessed itself of every branch of industry" (p. 545, fn. 1). Earlier German editions had not invoked this delimitation. Luxemburg (1913, p. 236–238) points to similar statements in *Volume II* (drafted by Marx, it should be recalled, after 1875) to remove doubt concerning Marx's delimitation. For example, "there are here only two classes: the working-class disposing only of its labor-power, and the capitalist class, which has a monopoly of the social means of production and the money" (Marx, 1885, p. 425). Capitalism is assumed to have completely occupied the space of theoretical discussion.

The next chapter "The General Law of Capitalist Accumulation", after offering three definitions of the composition of capital (a new development in the French edition, addressed more in Chapter 8 below), summarizes what had been learned from the prior chapter. The language is concise and not really subject to much ambiguity. I quote the passage of immediate interest, placing in ellipses in two separate portions discussed in footnotes.

> Growth of capital involves growth of its variable constituent or of the part invested in labour power. A part of the surplus-value turned into additional capital must always be re-transformed into variable capital, or additional labour-fund. If we suppose that, all other circumstances remaining the same, the composition of capital also remains constant ...., then the demand for labour and the subsistence-fund of the labourers clearly increase in the same proportion as the capital, and the more

rapidly, the more rapidly the capital increases....[4] As simple reproduction constantly reproduces the capital-relation itself, i.e. the relation of capitalists on the one hand, and wage-workers on the other, so reproduction on a progressive scale, i.e. accumulation, reproduces the capital-relation on a progressive scale, more capitalists or larger capitalists at this pole, more wage-workers at that....[5] Accumulation of capital is, therefore, increase of the proletariat. (pp. 575–576)

The text is quite clear that *the essential factor of accumulation of capital is the increase in wage-labor,* not an increase in constant capital. Note the reference to either "more capitalists" or "larger capitalists", but when the issue comes to labor it is simply "more wage-workers" – only the number is important. More means of production, although seemingly required, are not mentioned.

Material prepared by Marx for *Capital* but not included makes a similar point, although here increasing means of production ("conditions of labour") are cited. "Results of the Immediate Process of Production" reads that accumulation:

> entails the *new creation of wage-labourers,* of the means of realize and increase the available amount of capital. It does this either by extending its rule to sections of the population not previously subject to itself, such as women or children; or else it subjugates a section of the labouring masses that has accrued through the natural growth of population.... [Capital] produces a growing mass of men, the material through which alone it can function as additional capital. Therefore, it is not only true to say that labour produces on a constantly increasing scale the conditions of labour in opposition to itself in the *form of capital,* but equally, capital produces on a steadily increasing scale the productive wage-labourers it requires. (Marx, 1933, p. 1061, emphasis in original)

---

[4] The text continues and further recognizes the implications of what is being described as the accumulation of capital. The increasing "demand" for labor power over time can put pressure on its "supply".

[5] The French text here is shortened from the 2nd German edition to be: "The reproduction of capital includes its great instrument of development, the labour power" ("La reproduction du capital renferme celle de son grand instrument de mise en valeur, la force de travail", Marx, 1872–1875, p. 270). The French text is more consistent with the context than was Engels' rendition into German.

2   Schemes of Reproduction in *Capital, Volume II*

While Part III of *Volume II*, "The Reproduction and Circulation of the Aggregate Social Capital", is 173 pages long, only 35 of its pages are devoted to the chapter "Accumulation and Reproduction on an Extended Scale", the bulk being focused on simple reproduction. The explanation for this disparity is Marx's belief in the necessity to first elaborate simple reproduction since no economist of any persuasion (excepting, in a partial sense, the Physiocrat Quesnay) had worked on what would now be called a "two-sector" model. Marx was in new territory. Marx was led there after having demonstrated the critical importance of the distinction between production of means of production versus production of consumption goods. He had noted in *Volume I* the major error of Smith and Ricardo in which they had supposed that all surplus value used for accumulation were used for only variable capital, the purchase of labor power, when, in fact, accumulated surplus value is also used for constant capital:

> Adam Smith has made it the fashion, to represent accumulation as nothing more than consumption of surplus-products by productive laborers, which amounts to saying that the capitalizing of surplus-value consists in merely turning surplus-value into labour-power.... There can be no greater error than that which Ricardo and all subsequent economists repeat after A. Smith, viz., that "the part of revenue, of which it is said, it has been added to capital, is consumed by productive labourers". According to this, all surplus-value that is changed into capital becomes variable capital. So far from this being the case, the surplus value, like the original capital, divides itself into constant capital and variable capital, into means of production and labour-power. (Marx, 1867, pp. 552–553)

This error is connected to another error of the classical economists mentioned in Chapter 2 above when dividing the value of a commodity into only variable capital and surplus value, ignoring the constant capital in the value of a newly produced commodity (see, e.g., *Theories of Surplus Value, Part I* – Marx, 1905b, p. 491). In *Part II* of *Theories,* Marx notes similar propositions scattered throughout Ricardo's work, and says that it leads "to a wrong approach to the whole question of accumulation" (1905b, pp. 470; also 470 ff and pp. 535–536). The distinction underpins the importance of Marx's schemes of reproduction in which production of means of production are separated from production of means of consumption.

At the beginning of the *Volume II* chapter on accumulation in which the models/schemes are developed, Marx indicates a distinction between his material on accumulation in *Volume I* and the discussion undertaken in *Volume II*: the former deals with the individual capitalist while the discussion in *Volume II* deals with reproduction as a whole. However, *Volume I* clearly deals with some global consequences of accumulation of capital that could not be addressed outside of the total context, e.g., on the overall "demand" for labor power relative to "supply" and the consequent effect on wages (see in Chapter 4 above, Sections 2 and 3 of Chapter 25 of the French edition, considerably neglected in Engels' editions, although intended by Marx for his 3rd edition. Note that Marx does not make an argument that the very meaning of accumulation of capital would be affected by whether the individual capitalist or the capitalist economy as a whole is being discussed.

A remarkable aspect of the schemes of *Volume II*, drafted after the French edition of *Volume I* with its elaboration of the composition of capital, is that Marx always holds both the rate of surplus value as well as the ratio of constant to variable capital fixed. Constant capital c and variable capital v are both displayed in an unchanging relationship (the ratio is not referred to as an "organic" composition of capital, perhaps because of his increased clarity of expression coming with the 1875 French edition of *Volume I* – a topic I will elaborate below in Chapter 8). Both s/v and c/v appear fixed in spite of the fact that technological improvements might be expected to be associated with accumulation of capital and such improvements could be expected to raise the rate of surplus value, as the cost of variable capital decreases, perhaps also changing the relation of constant capital to variable capital. On the one hand, Marx is engaging in simple arithmetical examples in preparing a book never completed. On the other hand (and to the best of my knowledge this has not been pointed out before), the schemes in this last chapter of *Volume II* fully correspond to that opening of the chapter on "The General Law of Capitalist Accumulation", *Volume I*, discussed above. Any over-emphasis by him on the rate of surplus value would forget that the *mass of surplus value* "depends not only on the rate of surplus value but on the number of workers simultaneously employed" (Marx, 1905b, p. 542).

3 Ambiguity

Returning to *Volume I*, and going further into "The General Law of Capitalist Accumulation", as I explained above in Chapter 3, Marx wanted the titling of Section 2 to follow the French in focusing on employment and leaving out mention of concentration. Engels did not comply. Thereafter, this error in editing by Engels was to give Hilferding (1910) more space for his well-known work that focused on concentration of capital and cartels, not employment of labor.

The French text had rather more discussion in Section 2 of a rising composition of capital as accumulation progresses, although it added, "to avoid errors, it should be noted that the progress of accumulation, by decreasing the relative size of variable capital, does not exclude its absolute growth" (Marx, 1872–1875, p. 274; absent from Engels' editions). In Section 3, Marx says that, compared to the earlier period of capitalism, modern industrial expansion also depends "upon the constant transformation of a part of the labouring population into unemployed or half-employed hands" (Marx, 1867, p. 593[6]). Section 4 has Marx's remark that "the demand for an agricultural labouring population falls absolutely, while the accumulation of the capital employed in agriculture advances, without this repulsion being, as in non-agricultural industries, compensated by a greater attraction" (p. 601). In other words, such a case in agriculture still represents an accumulation of capital with lesser agricultural workers; nevertheless, there could be more workers overall under capitalist domination (rather than just agricultural). Compared to beginning of the chapter, the definition of accumulation of capital seems reopened. If *Theories of Surplus Value* were examined for Marx's earlier thinking (but carrying an element of contingency), his discussion of Richard Jones regarding increasing technical knowledge of production has Marx saying "accumulation does not have to set new labor in motion, it may simply direct the labor previously employed in new channels" (Marx, 1910, p. 441).

It has been a virtual dogma within Marxism that, as accumulation takes place, the ratio of constant capital to variable capital rises, i.e., the value composition of capital c/v rises. The dogma arises out of the second (and third) sections of the "General Law" and will be addressed in Chapter 8 here. Yet Marx's prior chapter that forms his basis for the discussion of accumulation of capital actually indicates that the opposite can occur, that *constant capital may not rise at all* – or anyway less than variable capital – as accumulation occurs. Marx has a long exposition examining the three basic sectors, factories, extractive industries, and agriculture, in succession. In factories, "additional labour, begotten of the greater tension of labour-power, can augment surplus-product and surplus-value (i.e. the subject-matter of accumulation), without corresponding augmentation in the constant part of capital". In extractive industries, due "to the elasticity of labour-power, the domain of accumulation has extended without any previous enlargement of constant capital". In agriculture, it is "once again the direct action of man on Nature which becomes an immediate source of greater accumulation, without the intervention of any

---

6   French edition in translation: "The ever-renewed conversion of part of the working class into as many half-employed or completely idle hands thus gives the movement of modern industry its typical form" (Marx, 1872–1875, p. 280).

new capital". (pp. 564–565) Defining accumulation of capital would thus also seem to include circumstances in which constant capital is not growing, not even absolutely, and certainly not relative to variable capital.

As we have been progressing, Marx first seems to define accumulation to necessarily include an increase in the number of workers under the domination of capital, as both constant capital and variable capital increase. Then, accumulation seems to include a case where the number of workers stays the same or even declines. Yet another passage suggests that accumulation could take place without a change in constant capital. So, what is accumulation of capital for Marx? Could accumulation of capital be any increase in variable capital and/or constant capital, with both at the same time being the most typical case? In other words, could accumulation of capital be simply $c + v$ increasing with the proportions between c and v unimportant for the definition?[7] Is this broad range of possibilities a way out, or is it a way of saying so much that we wind up saying very little or nothing at all? Most importantly, is it consistent with the very concept of "capital" in Marx? These questions are unresolved in Marx's writing and become an ambiguity embedded in Marxism up to the present.

Perhaps we should not be surprised. Marx himself found the issue of accumulation of capital very difficult (even apart from the well-known issues concerning crises). During his work on final editing of the French translation of *Volume I*, Marx noted (to Lavrov in February 1875) that the "most important changes contained in the French edition, however, are in the sections that have not yet been published, that is, the chapters on accumulation" (Marx and Engels, 1948, p. 178). As I have shown in Chapter 3, Marx marked off sections of the "General Law" chapter of the French edition for inclusion into other editions, particularly for his 3rd German edition. *Volume I* was a work constantly in development, not least with regard to accumulation of capital.

As to *Volume III*, drafted before *Volume I* was published and not reconsidered later, it does contain some scattered references to accumulation of capital. For one example, while discussing internal contradictions in the law of the

---

7 Marx's (1865, p. 54), a couple of years before *Volume I*, is suggestive of this interpretation, regardless of whether c/v is believed to be increasing: "If the proportion of these two elements of capital was originally one to one, it will, in the progress of industry, become five to one, and so forth. If of a total capital of 600, 300 is laid out in instruments, raw materials, and so forth, and 300 in wages, the total capital wants only to be doubled to create a demand for 600 working men instead of for 300. But if of a capital of 600, 500 is laid out in machinery, materials, and so forth and 100 only in wages, the same capital must increase from 600 to 3,600 in order to create a demand for 600 workmen instead of 300. In the progress of industry the demand for labor keeps, therefore, no pace with the accumulation of capital. It will still increase, but increase in a constantly diminishing ratio as compared with the increase of capital".

falling tendency of the rate of profit, Marx writes that it is the separation of the conditions of production (the means of production) from the producers (the workers) that "forms the conception of capital. It begins with primitive accumulation, appears as a permanent process in the accumulation and concentration of capital…". (Marx, 1894, p. 246) This suggests that separation of labor from means of production is a part of accumulation of capital proper, a process that "begins" with primitive accumulation. Another example is several pages later that could be connected to the agricultural case I cited above where "the decrease of the element of living labor may be absolute…. At any rate, it is but a requirement of the capitalist mode of production that the number of wage-workers should increase absolutely, in spite of its relative decrease". (Marx, 1894, p. 263; see also p. 218) Nevertheless, it is difficult to use these two short passages from *Volume III*, written before the first edition of *Volume I*, to be more assertive of Marx's intentions. *Volume III* was less ready for publication than *Volume II*, and Marx never got around to reconsidering any of what Engels was to make of *Volume III*.

In summary, Marx leaves us with an ambiguity as to his meaning of accumulation of capital. There does seem to be a greater emphasis on the importance of increasing labor power than any other factor in defining and using accumulation of capital. But ambiguity nevertheless remains. A contrasting recent work illustrates the conceptual problem: "Accumulation of capital or the self-expansion of value that is the keynote of the capitalist mode takes places when profits in the form of money capital are repeatedly reinvested back into productive capital, i.e. land, tools, machines, which makes possible the production of yet more commodities for sale and their realization as more money profit" (Heller, 2019, p. 14). I am saying, no, it is not defined in this manner by Marx since value, and more value, does not arise out of machines and more machines (constant capital and more constant capital), but rather living labor power, and more living labor power. Nevertheless, clarity in the definition is required.

4 "Marxist Accumulation of Capital"

As I have already said, it was only a few years before the 1st edition of *Volume I* that Marx generated the decisively important distinction between labor of the classical economists and his own separation of labor from labor power. Marx could have spelled out this difference without ever offering a new two-word theoretical concept, but he would have burdened everyone afterwards with constant clarifications, over and over, when instead a new concept was able to summarize the major break of classical conceptions. Marx's revisions as he addresses accumulation of capital suggest a definition allowing a focus on social relations of production, and rather than upon constant capital. Consider once more the beginning of Marx's "General Law" chapter, a summary of the prior chapter on converting surplus value into more capital as representative of the main point: "Reproduction on a progressive scale, i.e. accumulation, reproduces the capital-relation on a progressive scale, more capitalists or larger capitalists at this pole, more wage-workers at that.... Accumulation of capital is, therefore, increase of the proletariat".

I define: *Marxist accumulation of capital as that increase of wage-labor which is productive of surplus value with the associated constant capital.* This accumulation will generally include additional constant capital. It refers to the productive sectors, not unproductive ones, and if related to the production of relative surplus value (technological improvements) as is often the case, it would be discussed as such. Whether the composition of capital also increases is not directly germane; if there is no increase in productive wage-labor, there is no accumulation under this definition.

Increased employment of wage-labor is available from
- relative surplus population (the reserve army of labor) and longer work hours,
- population increase, and
- proletarianizations concomitant with creation of home markets and markets abroad, including drawing in of new sections of the population such as women and children.

When discussing Ricardo's theory of accumulation, Marx (1905b, p. 477) explicitly mentions much of these in drafting *Theories of Surplus Value*. Regarding the possibility of increased work hours, though, Marx adds that it "cannot be regarded as a method of accumulation which can be continuously used". Increasing population forms the basis, as far as Marx is concerned, for accumulation on a steady, continuous process. As to the third, Marx is not as inclusive but does say that the laboring population can increase "when previously unproductive laborers are turned into productive ones, or sections of the population who did not work previously, such as women and children, or paupers, are drawn into the production process". Luxemburg (1913) who I discuss in Chapter 9 below regarded the third case as of decisive importance theoretically and went quite a bit beyond Marx. Thus, she wrote

> Given its mercurial capacity for expansion, the accumulation of capital can no more afford to wait for the natural increase in the working population than it can be content to bide its time during the naturally long process of disintegration of noncapitalist forms and their transition to commodity-economy. Capital knows no other solution to the problem

than violence, which has been a constant method of capitalist accumulation as a historical process, not merely at its emergence, but also to the present day. (p. 267)

The definition of accumulation offered here – Marxist accumulation of capital – does lead to deeper issues of Marxist thought: the relations and struggles between and among social classes, not delimited to capital versus wage-labor in a purely capitalist environment. "To accumulate, is to conquer the world of social wealth, to increase the mass of human beings exploited by him, and thus to extend both the direct and the indirect sway of the capitalist" (Marx, 1867, p. 555). It focuses the question to the class issues and away from production or from productivity, away from claims such as "the object of accumulation is productivity increase" (Fine, 1991, p. 3). It calls for a tighter theoretical structure that would prohibit using accumulation of capital so loosely as to be almost synonymous with the word capitalism. It calls forth the question, if accumulation is to increase the mass of humans to be exploited by capital, how far has accumulation come and how much more room does it have. And what is surplus value used for, if not for accumulation?

5 An Algebraic Model of Marxist Accumulation with Fixed Constant Capital Included[8]

Marx's schemes of reproduction in *Volume II* represent one of his final efforts in political economy, worked on a dozen years or more after his drafting attempt at *Volume III*. It certainly moved into new territory (the complete texts of Marx's drafts are provided in MEGA², II/13). I do not share Roth's (2018, pp. 36–37) apparent view that the schemes under extended reproduction should not be taken very seriously. Instead, I update Marx's schemes so as to include fixed capital, while understanding the schemes as an intended long-term perspective, not as any attempt toward modeling of crisis. Marx's neglect of the cost of fixed capital within his model of accumulation is quite serious. An algebraic model, rather than a numerical example as Marx presented, is utilized, it becoming rather complicated even under certain simplifications. A rough long-term empirical estimation follows at the end of Chapter 9.

The *stock* of fixed constant capital is quite distinct from the *consumption* of constant capital, and Marx is quite clear at the beginning of his discussion of

---

[8] With certain modifications, this section draws from and condenses work in Zarembka (2010, pp. 156–165).

schemes of simple reproduction. While side-stepping depreciation, he writes clearly:

> *Constant Capital.* This is the value of all the means of production employed for productive purposes in this branch. These, again, are divided into *fixed* capital, such as machines, instruments of labour, buildings, labouring animals, etc., and *circulating* constant capital, such as materials of production: raw and auxiliary materials, semi-finished products, etc....
>
> Portion c of the value, representing the constant capital *consumed* in production, does not coincide with the value of the constant capital *employed* in production. True, the materials of production are entirely consumed and their values completely transferred to the product. But only a portion of the employed *fixed* capital is wholly consumed and its value thus transferred to the product. Another part of the fixed capital, such as machines, buildings, etc., continues to exist and function the same as before, though depreciated to the extent of the annual wear and tear.... At this point in the study of the total social product and of its value, however, we are compelled, at least for the present, to leave out of account that portion of value which is transferred from the fixed capital to the annual product by wear and tear, unless fixed capital is replaced in kind during the year. (Marx, 1885, p. 400, emphasis in original)

As he goes on into his discussion of simple reproduction he has a long discussion of the "Replacement of the Fixed Capital" (pp. 453–473). Nevertheless, when he comes to his schemes of extended reproduction in the next chapter, he ignores the significant outlay for *additional* fixed constant capital represented in machinery and equipment. Hilferding (1910, pp. 244–246 and 251–252) is aware of the problem, but doesn't attempt to solve it within the schemes. Luxemburg (1913) did not mention the problem.

A model is developed here that incorporates the need for the production of new fixed constant capital C in order to implement an accumulation of capital.[9] This model follows the long-run nature of Marx's exposition. It applies a stable $C/(v+s)$ – a stable materialized composition of capital – that is suggested to be approximately the case for the United States (see Chapter 8). $C/(v+s)$ abstracts from the rate of surplus value s/v in describing the

---

9 Although fixed capital has been included in empirical work regarding constant capital, the problems of identifying it are rarely described in the conceptual detail that is in the work of Swanson (1986). Shaikh and Tonak (1994) devoted little attention to the issue; Shaikh (2016, particularly Chapter 6) offers quite a bit more but with scarcely any attention to "constant capital".

composition of capital, where the value composition of capital, i.e., C/v, would be influenced by the behavior of s/v. When taking the rate of surplus value as a constant at unit value in his schemes, Marx implicitly also took the materialized composition as stable, although he did not even refer at all to a "composition of capital", only to constant and variable capitals with their symbols. My model permits discussion of alternative rates of surplus value.

The more general model than Marx's schemes has the following characteristics:

- The rate of surplus value s/v is unchanging, but not necessarily unity (as in Marx schemes).
- Allocation of surplus value between capitalist accumulation and consumption is parameterized, with α representing the proportion of surplus value devoted to accumulation and $1-\alpha$ the proportion consumed by capitalists. Therefore, $\alpha \cdot s$ is the level of accumulation. If k represents the level of capitalist consumption, then $k=(1-\alpha)s$.
- Circulating constant capital c is a constant fraction β of new value created, that is, $c=\beta(v+s)$. For example, using the data in Chapter 9 of Marx's *Volume I* – discussed in Chapter 8 below – β would be calculated as £378/£132 = 2.86, noting the denominator $v+s$ being £52 + £80.
- Fixed constant capital C relative to new value created, $C/(v+s)$, is 2 and unchanged.
- Turnover of circulating constant capital is four (4) times yearly.

The last two roughly correspond to empirical estimates presented in Chapter 8, but of course, alternatives could be examined. While production of relative surplus value is omitted from direct consideration, my main purpose is offering a model more general than Marx's and including fixed capital.

Accumulation $\alpha \cdot s$ requires investment in new fixed constant capital, new circulating constant capital, and new variable capital. For convenience, the gestation of new fixed capital is the full year, i.e., it takes a year to construct and put into place the new fixed capital. New circulating constant capital in new intermediate goods and new variable capital are taken to require one turnover period, the last quarter, given turnover to be quarterly. Variable capital v represents yearly flow, as does circulating constant capital c. Therefore, accumulation, in each department, is the *additional* $C+c/4+v/4$. Dividing by v, we obtain the additional constant capital relative to variable capital as

$C/v + ¼\, c/v + ¼$.

With the empirical approximation that $C/(v+s)=2$, then the first term $C/v=2(1+s/v)$. Since $c=\beta(v+s)$, then the term $c/v=\beta(1+s/v)$. Thus, the expression in either department for additional constant capital, fixed and circulating, relative to variable capital, i.e., the value composition of capital, D, is

$D = 2(1+s/v) + ¼\,\beta(1+s/v) + ¼ = (2+¼\beta)(1+s/v) + ¼$.

This value composition of capital, applicable to either department, rises when the rate of surplus value rises.

Both fixed capital and circulating constant capital come from Department I. Compared to the total of both constant and variable capital, the proportion of new capital needs coming from Department I is therefore $(2 + \frac{1}{4}\beta)(1 + s/v) \div D$ and the proportion coming from Department II is $\frac{1}{4} \div D$.

A Model of Accumulation can now be presented, with the rate of surplus value = s/v, capital accumulation = $\alpha \cdot s$ and capitalist consumption $k = (1-\alpha)s$, $C/(v+s) = 2$, and $c/(v+s) = \beta$. The calculations required for the model are offered in footnotes. Balance between the departments requires that the ratio of the value of Department II output *relative to* Department I output be given by[10]

$$\{1 + s/v[1 - \alpha(2 + \frac{1}{4}\beta)(1 + s/v)]/D\} \div \{\beta(1 + s/v) + \frac{1}{4}\alpha s/v/D\}.$$

---

10   In order to demonstrate this relationship, first note that the flows between Department I and Department II must match. The value of production in either department can be reformulated as follows:

$$c + v + s = c + c/(c/v) + (s/v)c/(c/v)$$

Since $c/(v+s) = 2$ with the approximate empirical finding being adopted, then $c/v = 2(1 + s/v)$ and we have

$$c + c/(2(1 + s/v)) + (s/v)c/(2(1 + s/v)),$$

an expression applicable for both departments. In order to ascertain the portion available for sale to the other department, from this sum the amount being retained within either department must be subtracted. For Department I, this subtraction is the consumed constant capital c needing to be replaced, along with the proportion of surplus value – i.e., $(s/v)c/(2(1 + s/v))$ – used for accumulation, i.e., α, along with the proportion of accumulation allocated to Department I, i.e., $(2 + \frac{1}{4}\beta)(1 + s/v)/D$. Recall the definition of D from the text. The latter subtraction is, therefore,

$$\alpha(s/v)[c/(2(1 + s/v))](2 + \frac{1}{4}\beta)(1 + s/v)/D.$$

Department I therefore sells its net output of means of production as follows:

$$c + c/(2(1 + s/v)) + (s/v)c/(2(1 + s/v)) - c - \alpha(s/v)[c/(2(1 + s/v))] \cdot (2 + \frac{1}{4}\beta)(1 + s/v)/D$$

After simple algebra and now adding the departmental subscript, Department I sells,

$$[c_I/(2(1 + s/v))] \cdot \{1 + s/v[1 - \alpha(2 + \frac{1}{4}\beta)(1 + s/v)]/D\}.$$

For Department II consumption goods, we similarly obtain

$$[c_{II}/(2(1 + s/v))] \cdot \{\beta(1 + s/v) + \frac{1}{4}\alpha s/v/D\}.$$

Equate the flows between Departments I and II to obtain:

$$[c_I/(2(1 + s/v))] \cdot \{1 + s/v[1 - \alpha(2 + \frac{1}{4}\beta)(1 + s/v)]/D\} = [c_{II}/(2(1 + s/v))] \cdot \{\beta(1 + s/v) + \frac{1}{4}\alpha s/v/D\}.$$

TABLE 1   Growth rates of output values and labor hours for alternative α, s/v, and β

	α = 0.40		α = 0.20		α = 0.10		α = 0.05	
s/v	β = 2	β = 1	β = 2	β = 1	β = 2	β = 1	β = 2	β = 1
1	7.6%	8.4%	3.8%	4.2%	1.9%	2.1%	0.9%	1.1%
2	10.3%	11.4%	5.2%	5.7%	2.6%	2.8%	1.3%	1.4%
4	12.5%	13.9%	6.3%	7.0%	3.1%	3.5%	1.6%	1.7%

SOURCE: AUTHOR CALCULATION

The *growth rate* of the values of outputs as well as employment[11] is then
$\alpha s / v \div D$.

To take an example, if one half of surplus value is used for accumulation so that α is one-half, if the rate of surplus value is unity, and if β as the ratio of flow of circulating constant capital to new value created is two, then the growth rate is 9.5%. But if the rate of surplus value were two, i.e., then the growth rate would rise to 12.9%.

Table 1 provides growth rates in the two departments under the representation of balance between the departments being maintained. I have not introduced any discussion of technological improvements, which would only increase output growth rates of use-values, but not necessarily for the labor force requirements. Since my interest is primarily on Marxist accumulation of capital regarding labor-power requirements, it is perhaps more useful in this presentation. Even with only 10% of surplus value being allocated for accumulation, still the growth rate exceeds the recent high levels of population growth worldwide. Thus, such employment growth could only be sustained over a longer period by the penetration of non-capitalist modes of production with its conversion of populations into wage laborers.

Through another simple algebra, c_{II} / c_I is represented by the relationship in the text. That relationship also obtains for the relative departmental sizes of v and s – since all are proportional – and, therefore, additionally represents the relative sizes of production levels for Department II compared to Department I.

11 Growth rates are the same in the two departments and so it does not matter which is chosen. Taking Department I, the rate of growth is the allocation to accumulation relative to the level of Department I. This is

$$\alpha(s/v)\left[c_I / (2(1+s/v))\right] \cdot (2 + \tfrac{1}{4}\beta)(1+s/v)]/D \div \left\{\left[c_I / (2(1+s/v))\right] \cdot (2 + \tfrac{1}{4}\beta)(1+s/v)\right\}$$

which simplifies to $\alpha s / v \div D$, as provided in the text.

CHAPTER 7

Three Troubling Issues

1   Conundrum: Value under Marxist Accumulation of Capital

In his draft *Grundrisse*, Marx wrote:

> In all forms of society there is one specific kind of production which predominates over the rest, whose relations thus assign rank and influence to the others. It is a general illumination which bathes all the other colors and modifies their particularity. It is particular ether which determines the specific gravity of every being which has materialized within it. (Marx, 1939–41a, pp. 106–107)

For Althusser (1965) this is an important passage used by him to conclude many prior pages of discussion. He was, however, unaware of any difficulty with the concept of accumulation of capital. If Marx's theoretical object was the capitalist mode of production and it required new concepts appropriate to that object in order to "think the determination of the elements of a whole by the structure of the whole" (Althusser, p. 187), what happens when the theoretical object must include pre-capitalist formations?

As described in Chapter 2, Marx began his theoretical work by recognizing that economic categories are socially determined. In the *Grundrisse*, the "economic concept of value does not occur in antiquity", the "concept of value is entirely peculiar to the most modern economy, since it is the most abstract expression of capital itself and of the production resting on it" (Marx 1939–41a, p. 776). He also wrote Engels:

> Value. ... It already presupposes 1. the destruction of natural communism (in India etc.); 2. the destruction of all undeveloped, pre-bourgeois modes of production which are not governed in their totality by exchange. Although it is an abstraction, it is an abstraction which can only be assumed on the basis of a particular economic development of society. (Marx and Engels, 1948, p. 58)

This abstraction is crystalized in the French edition of *Volume I*, and included in the later German editions by Engels: "capitalist production is established everywhere and has taken possession of every branch of industry" (1867, p. 545, fn. 1). It is restated in 1878 in the drafting of schemes of reproduction (discussed in Zarembka, 2019, p. 52). While this could be understood as a necessary abstraction on Marx's part, particularly as we know full well that he knew the world to be much more complex, still, this presumption is nevertheless problematic within the internal logic of his work, and risks destabilizing the concept of value as such. To this possibility, I now turn.

The problem arises from the fact that the separate concept of Marxist accumulation of capital is not consistent with the presumption of a fully capitalist social formation. Although the theoretical relevance thereof is often underappreciated, in the previous chapter I have tried to demonstrate that Marxist accumulation must also include, at least in the longer period, penetration of non-capitalist relations if it is not to rely upon population increase. Population increase can be a partial element of this increase, but it cannot be the essential aspect. If presumption of a fully capitalist world does not resonate with the understanding of capitalist accumulation found in *Capital*, what then is to be the appropriate object of analysis leading to the concept of value – simply the capital–wage-labor relation, or that relation as well as the penetration of non-capitalist relations of production corresponding to needs for the accumulation of capital? The former has been presumed, but if penetration must be included in the object of analysis, is value left unaffected?

After the publication of *Volume I*, first edition, Marx spent many years studying pre-capitalist societies, reading much Russian literature on the topic. An explanation is offered by White:

> Just as Marx was about to publish the first volume of *Das Kapital* he had run into serious problems with the section of his projected work which would deal with the circulation of capital. He had hitherto assumed that capital would spread throughout the world carrying all before it, but he had overlooked the fact that even in his own native Hunsrücken despite the development of capitalism, the older, collective, social and economic system still survived. Capitalism, apparently, did not necessarily erode traditional peasant society, but coexisted with it. Marx removed much of the philosophical underpinnings for his earlier view of capitalist development from the published version of *Das Kapital*, continuing the excisions in the second and French editions, and he embarked on a lengthy empirical investigation of how capital actually began to circulate. He had an excellent example to hand in Russia, which had just embarked on the capitalist road, having abolished serfdom a few years earlier. In 1870 Marx learnt Russian and got down to the serious job of collecting materials on

Russian economic development. (White, 2001a, pp. 12–13, summarizing a major result of his 1996 book)

In the process of this work, as I mentioned on p. 96 above, Marx read Flerovsky's 1869 *Condition of the Working [Peasant] Class in Russia* (Marx, 1948, p. 165 – worker being used in Flerovsky's title where we would say peasant).[1] Flerovsky's work focused on the process of proletarianization through taxation, as Marx was trying to understand the penetration of capital, an ongoing focus to the end of his life (including correspondence with Russians). Flerovsky's theme also appeared in late 19th century Rhodesian gold mines which were in desperate need of waged laborers. British colonial authorities responded to the need for workers with extraordinarily high taxation on peasant land in Nyasaland (now Malawi), thereby forcing young men from peasant families off the land and into waged employment. Working in the mines could aid families in paying land taxes or provide a market for cash crops, the proceeds from which could be used to pay taxes (van Onselen, 1976). Nevertheless, as peasant land continued to go into receivership, remaining family members were driven into waged labor on large capitalist farms producing subsistence crops, ultimately converting nearly all subsistence peasant farmers into value-producing proletarians. Such a process is clearly a case of Marxist accumulation of capital.

But what of the intermediate step, in which some peasants produce cash crops, in turn purchased by those working in the mines? The miners, working waged jobs, produce value. What of the peasants selling cash crops to pay taxes? This process involves coercion – the power of the state to expropriate land for non-payment of taxes – and more directly than typically involved in the "free market". An example in Marx of value failing to be clearly defined around wage-labor appears in the "Results of the Immediate Process of Production":

> The distinctive character of the *formal* subsumption of labour under capital appears at its sharpest if we compare it to situations in which capital is to be found in certain specific, subordinate functions, but where it has not yet emerged as the direct purchaser of labour and as the immediate owner of the process of production, and where in consequence it has not yet succeeded in becoming the dominant force, capable of determining the form of society as a whole. In India, for example, the capital of the *usurer* advances raw materials or tools or even both to the immediate

---

[1] See Offord (1988) for a survey of Flerovsky's book. A 1987 conspectus by Alan Kimball of Marx's reading of the book is discussed at https://pages.uoregon.edu/kimball/Nikolaevskii. RUS.kng.u.Marksa.htm (accessed November 24, 2019).

producer in the form of money. The exorbitant interest which it attracts, the interest which, irrespective of its magnitude, it extorts from the primary producer, is just another name for surplus-value. (Marx, 1933, pp. 1022–1023, emphasis in original)

However, this is a rare remark and not published by Marx himself.[2]

Luxemburg's *Introduction to Political Economy* (1925) – a draft published posthumously (some chapters never found) – uses many of the same sources Marx had studied, and becomes a more natural point for beginning to address this problem. Unlike Marx who begins with the chapter "Commodities", her work explicitly offers political economy in an historical context. Initial chapters are a context she elaborates first, and her work does not arrive at the meaning of a commodity until after chapters on "What is Political Economy?", "Social Labor" (no existent copy), and two chapters on economic history including discussion of primitive communism, feudalism, the medieval city and guilds. A chapter on commodity production then follows, and thereafter one on "Wage-Labor".[3] Regarding the concept of value, Smith's and Ricardo's great discovery, she says, were to see value as the human labor contained in a commodity (p. 257). However, unlike Marx, neither noticed, she says, that human labor only recently "assumes the strange form of exchange-value, and the puzzling form of money at that".[4] This passage comes after a long discussion regarding

---

[2] In a distinct challenge, Weeks (1982) has claimed that without full realization of all production, Marxist theory of value must be rejected. Focusing on underconsumption, he says that "if one postulates that a 'pure' capitalist system is endemically afflicted by the inability to sell all that is produced, then the Marxian concept of value *must* be rejected" (p. 61, emphasis in original). Weeks' argument is addressed in Zarembka (2019, pp. 58–61). Here, I note that, for Weeks, Lenin's analysis of underconsumption regarding the work of Sismondi is "acute" (p. 60).

[3] Luxemburg's chapter on wage-labor addresses the cost of labor power and the concept of surplus value, but it does not mention the concept of *abstract labor*. Her work neglects to mention the concepts of *production of absolute surplus value* and of *relative surplus value*, although both are very clearly discussed indirectly. Other than labor power, value, and surplus value, Luxemburg's *Introduction* is not interested in reprising concepts developed by Marx so much as in utilizing what can be gained from Marx's expositions.

[4] "Only Karl Marx ... made comparisons between present relations and earlier ones at other times. He showed in this way that people had lived for thousands of years without knowing much about money and exchange.... This meaningless invention [money, itself without any particular use] is thus a necessity without which no exchange would be possible, i.e. the entire history of culture since the dissolution of primitive communism". (Luxemburg, 1925, p. 258).

money.[5] For Luxemburg, value is set in an historical context rather than simply within the capitalist mode of production sui generis that is almost always the case for Marx. But she does not take consideration of value further.

2 Sieber's Query of Value in Marx

Sieber (1871) started his chapter on Marx with the question, "what exactly is value?" (2001, p. 17) and meticulously summarized Marx's first chapter of *Volume I* in its first edition. He then undertook his own comparison of Marx to Ricardo, explained how Marx's theory provided to "Ricardo's theory a fuller and more complete form" (p. 30) and that "Marx's method is the deductive method of the whole English school" (p. 30). Marx (1867, p. 26) cited this last sentence from Sieber in his 1873 "Afterword" to the 2nd edition of *Capital* – without objection – and stated his admiration for Sieber's work.[6] Marx had that reaction even as, within that same paragraph, Sieber had explicitly objected to

---

5   Luxemburg had first pointed out that humans lived without trade for a long time. Trade is then described as developing over time, illustrated by the cobbler producing shoes and the baker producing bread and each requiring the product of the other. Thus, they exchange. As exchanging products becomes more complex, the need for some product that is universally required is very useful, so that the desire for this product and the awareness that it can be utilized for trade is met simultaneously. This product is cattle, which can provide all of life's necessities – "they supply meat, milk, hides, plowing service, etc". (p. 244). Cattle, "a product of labour that was desired by everyone and at all time", became money because they were extremely useful. But, subsequently, "the more that cattle were used as mediator in universal exchange, the more the immediate use of cattle as a means of subsistence fell into the background" (p. 246). Thus, a metal (notably useless for sustaining life) begins to replace cattle as money. Money – whether cattle or a dead piece of metal – does take on the form of wealth. But money is not the basis of wealth, labor is. (She also notes, p. 248, that the "old Roman word *pecunia*, meaning money, stems from *pecus*, meaning cattle".)

Money in capitalism is, at least in part for her, a kind of holding mechanism to be used for value creation when workers are to be hired in exchange for it. Karimzadi (2013) discusses the question of the origin of money over the history of thought in political economy. He is somewhat critical of Marx for failing to get to the bottom of the issue, but does credit Marx with an emphasis on the necessity of exchange occurring in an historical context, even if failing to recognize that money is not synonymous with a generally accepted medium of exchange, whether as a commodity such as cattle, gold or silver, or as paper currency mandated by the state. I have reviewed Karimzadi's work in Zarembka (2015b). Baronian (2013) specifically addresses Luxemburg's perspective which in turn I address in Zarembka (2016), pp. 86–87, fn. 17).

6   "N. Sieber … referred to my theory of value, of money and of capital as in its fundamentals a necessary sequel to the teaching of Smith and Ricardo. That which astonishes the Western European in the reading of excellent work, is the author's consistent and firm grasp of the purely theoretical position". Marx (1867, p. 26, "Afterword" to the second German edition).

Marx's "peculiar language and quite laconic manner of expression" which led to an accusation of a "metaphysical approach". Both Smith (2001, p. 59) and White (2001a, p. 13) have been complimentary of Sieber's understanding of Marx's first edition.[7] And Marx would not say of Sieber what he had said of Rodbertus, who "neither examined nor grasped the substance of value any more than Ricardo did" (Marx, 1930, p. 552).

In 1874 Sieber wrote a new article, "Marx's Economic Theory", an article now containing certain reconsiderations about Marx's theoretical approach. Marx read it and made private notes. This article did not dissuade Marx from his overall approval of Sieber. He confirmed his initial opinion when writing in 1881 that, "Mr. Wagner could have familiarized himself with the difference between me and Ricardo both from *Capital* and from *Sieber's work* (if he knew Russian)" (Marx, 1930, p. 534, emphasis in original). In my opinion, those discussing Marx's understanding of value should be checking their interpretations against Sieber's, given Marx's expressed admiration for Sieber.

Sieber's reconsideration of Marx's work on value in 1874 made two points. The first was that Marx should have started from real relations, not abstractions, and he should have started from simple societies not a complex society such as capitalism (Sieber, 1874, p. 164–165). Second, when discussing value, says Sieber, Marx should have not focused only on production but also on

---

[7] According to Sieber (2001), rather than being only a regulator of exchange, labor itself is value, i.e., "the only *social* creator of those proportions in which acts of exchange take place" (p. 31, emphasis in original). And labor in its universal form only exists in exchange economies (a point also made a few pages earlier, pp. 24–25). Also, Marx's concept of *socially necessary* labor time solves a problem raised by those objecting to Ricardo's theory on narrow, individual grounds (pp. 32–33).

Furthermore, according to Sieber (p. 36), the money form is a necessity for commodities to pass to the stage of being "fully a value". Neither Ricardo nor his followers,

paid any attention to the qualitative difference between the labour contained in money and that contained in other products, and did not notice that only labour of the first type was labour of the directly social form.... The money form, [Marx] says, is indispensable for every commodity, because only by manifesting itself in monetary material can each concrete type of labour become social labour. (pp. 41–42, emphasis in original)

Marx himself, shortly after his 1881 re-statement of appreciation for Sieber, confirmed Sieber's reading when writing that "Ricardo did indeed concern himself with labour solely as a *measure of the magnitude of value*, and was therefore unable to find any link between his theory of value and the nature of money" (Marx, 1930, p. 534, emphasis in original). Marx had made the same point already in his *Contribution*. Sieber also says that money is not merely a convenience (as J.S. Mill had argued) and that "a profound and many-sided division of labour is impossible without money" (p. 40). Economists prior to Marx ignored "the form of value" and "the determination of those specific particularities which characterize monetary exchange in economies with the division of labour" (p. 43).

consumption (pp. 177 and 187–189). These two points run together because Sieber has a long discussion (pp. 166–177) of the basic physiological needs of the human body, including the increased energy required for increased work, obviously applicable for simple societies prior to consideration of complex ones. But, more to the point, Sieber has a long discussion about the value form. The universal relative form and the universal equivalent form "represents two opposite but equally necessary poles of one and the same social form of commodities" (p. 184). Since Marx "leads the reader into the world of abstruce abstractions from the most complex economic forms" (p. 186), readers, being misled by the fetishism of commodities, become confused into thinking of they are seeing reality of value, rather than the appearance.

Upon reading this 1874 article, Marx does not dispute Sieber's considerations regarding value.

3 Prejudices of Marx and Engels

Engels seemed supportive of the U.S. side of the Mexican-American war when he wrote in January 1848, "In *America* we have witnessed the conquest of Mexico and have rejoiced at it" (Marx and Engels, *c.w.*, Vol. 6, p. 527). A year later, in the *Neue Rheinische Zeitung* with Marx as editor-in-chief, Engels made a sarcastic reference to "lazy Mexicans" and referred to the war "waged wholly and solely in the interest of civilization"; he pointed to its importance for U.S. economic development, asking what independence and justice matter "compared to such facts of world-historic significance?" (Vol. 8, pp. 365–366). "Lazy Mexicans"? A U.S. victory, "in the interests of civilization"? While Engels and Marx adjusted their understanding of that war by the time of the U.S. Civil War, becoming aware of the slave-owning interests on the U.S. side, still this example is merely the preverbal tip-of-the-iceberg, when considering some expressed opinions of the two. In the French edition of the "General Law", Section 3, the reader may have noticed Marx's curious reference to "one Yankee [being replaced] by three Chinese", seemingly implying a worker in the North being three times as productive as a Chinese. Did Marx know nothing about the Chinese workers building the transcontinental railroad in the United States?

Diane Paul (1981) tries to understand disturbing expressions of race and cultures available in publications of Marx and Engels or in private correspondence. Paul opens her article by noting that Marx, writing privately to Engels about a book he was reading, used language she had not expected: "the common Negro type is only a degeneration of a much higher one" (p. 115). As a geneticist, she contextualizes this remark within Lamarckian biology of the time, in order to confront the language, without trying to explain it away. Then she moves on to other problems. After surveying issues regarding Blacks, Irish, Jewish, and Slavs, she concludes:

> There is a widespread, and I believe unfortunate, tendency to transform Marx and Engels into progressives on every issue of twentieth-century concern. It was Marx who wrote:
> "With the same right with which France has taken Flanders, Lorraine and Alsace, and, sooner or later, will take Belgium, with that same right Germany takes Silesia: with the right of civilization against barbarism, of progress against stability ... this right is worth more than all treaties, for it is the right of historical development."
> Yet the anti-colonialist image of Marx and Engels is hardly affected by this and other contrary evidence. They were not consistent anti-colonialists, and they were not progressive about race either; they were simply no better or worse than most of their contemporaries.
> More than fifty years ago, Georg Lukacs wrote in *History and Class Consciousness* that all philosophies, including Marxism, reflect certain assumptions of the age in which they were born. The important question today is to what extent Marxist categories are informed by the nineteenth-cultural prejudices of Marx and Engels. (p. 138)

It is not comfortable reading. Marx and Engels made generalizations, pure and simple.

Let us go to Paul's last sentence asking "to what extent Marxist categories are informed by the nineteenth-cultural prejudices of Marx and Engels". Would Marx's concepts of value and of labor power be undermined? Could the concepts of value and labor power be actually connected somehow to prejudices, she is asking? A remarkable Marxist who fully accepted those theoretical concepts, Eleanor Marx, avowed in the context of Jewish worker struggles in London's sweatshops and the beginning of the Dreyfus affair, "I am a Jewess" (H.R. Rosenthal, *Morning Freiheit*, "Eleanor Marx: 'I am a Jewess'", 1987, at www.marxists.org/subject/jewish/marx-daughter.htm, accessed October 21, 2019). She never would have accepted that the theoretically concepts of her father were contaminated by prejudices.

When we address prejudices in others or ourselves, we often try to account for it. Even with only partial answers, we have the potential of effecting change through knowledge. In the particular cases of Marx and Engels, an understanding might be offered that their prejudices seem related to whether a people had or had not shown historically, as far as they were concerned, a capacity for revolution. If so, they fell into inconsistencies, such as comments about Slavs in general, while also praising Poles. Or consider the Haitian revolution before Marx was born and slave resistance and rebellion during the U.S. Civil War (let alone African revolutions after World War II), the Mexican revolution in the early twentieth century, the Irish War of Independence after the First World War, the Chinese revolutions, the Russian revolutions, and southern Slavs some decades later, etc. Further illustrations are unneeded, as the point is made.

For those who haven't been aware, Marx and Engels had prejudices that need to be acknowledged by those who support their work, not excused away. And it also leads more deeply to the cultural aspects, the race and gender issues, that were present in Europe and continue in manifold ways.

As to the question of nationalities, a limited consideration is offered here in Chapter 10 when focusing on Luxemburg's views versus Lenin's reaction.

CHAPTER 8

The Composition of Capital Clarified Theoretically, Empirically

The composition of capital relates prior labor time invested in means of production (dead labor time) – constant capital – to laborers working those means (living labor time). It is a technically challenging concept and evolving one for Marx. In the 1875 French edition of *Volume I*, it became for the first time the opening presentation for the chapter on "The General Law of Capitalist Accumulation". The formulation is also new. Conceptual clarity is important for Marxist accumulation of capital, for discussing potential crises, and for any consideration of the cogency and application of a profit-rate tendency.

Marx's new, more exact definitions of compositions of capital appearing at the beginning of the *Volume I* chapter (included by Engels in his editions), read:

> The composition of capital is to be understood in a two-fold sense. On the side of value, it is determined by the proportion in which it is divided into constant capital or value of the means of production, and variable capital or value of labour power, the sum total of wages. On the side of material, as it functions in the process of production, all capital is divided into means of production and living labour power. This latter composition is determined by the relation between the mass of the means of production employed, on the one hand, and the mass of labour necessary for their employment on the other. I call the former the *value-composition*, the latter the *technical composition* of capital. Between the two there is a strict correlation. To express this, I call the value composition of capital, in so far as it is determined by its technical composition and mirrors the changes of the latter, the *organic composition* of capital. Wherever I refer to the composition of capital, without further qualification, its organic composition is always understood. (Marx, 1867, p. 574, emphasis in original)[1]

---

[1] Marx adds after this paragraph that his focus will be on a country average, not a particular branch of production:
    The many individual capitals invested in a particular branch of production have, one with another, more or less different compositions. The average of their individual compositions

By distinguishing the organic from the value composition, the qualifier, *in so far as*, is significant. Specifically, Marx's "organic composition" refers *only* to changes in the composition *due to technological* changes. Many have passed over Marx's qualification when using "organic composition" and simply state C/v as the organic composition of capital, when actually it is the value composition.[2]

Consider a sentence within Engels' edited version in *Volume III*: "The value-composition of capital, inasmuch as it is determined by, and reflects, its technical composition, is called the *organic* composition of capital" (1994, pp. 145–146). In actuality, this sentence was *not* Marx's definition at the time of his drafting of *Volume III*, but added by Engels, its source being the French edition of *Volume I*. Engels' addition into *Volume III* implied clarity within *Volume III* about the compositions of capital than was not actually the case for Marx.[3]

Stages in the development of Marx's thought were laid out in the article by Orzech and Groll (1989). They noted ambiguities in Marx's *Volume III* draft and in the 1st and 2nd German editions of *Volume I*. The French version corrected what had been ambiguous about the organic versus the value composition, "corrected what had escaped him in 1867 and 1872: it brought together production, distribution, and exchange in their interplay" (pp. 72–73, a conclusion to their longer discussion, pp. 68–69). While, in drafting *Volume III*, Marx had written that "the technical composition of capital … is the real basis of its organic composition" (Marx, 1894, p. 145), the clear articulation among the technical composition, the value composition, and the organic composition alternatives was only made explicit in 1875.[4]

---

gives us the composition of the total capital in this branch of production. Lastly, the average of these averages, in all branches of production, gives us the composition of the total social capital of a country, and with this alone are we, in the last resort, concerned in the following investigation. (pp. 574–575)

2 Wolff (2001, p. 31) and Venida (2007, p. 63) are examples of such a labeling of , while Cámara Izquierdo (2007, p. 551) correctly refers to the value composition. All three attempt consideration of a technical composition but with units of measurement seeming to differ in the numerator and denominator.

3 Engels' own footnote to the sentence (in Marx, 1894, p. 146, fn. 20) is ambiguous but the fact of the sentence's absence in Marx can be confirmed in MEGA², II/4.2, p. 218 (translated in Marx, 2015, p. 253). When reviewing Engels' edition of *Volume III* with Marx's actual drafts in MEGA² (most of which he finds acceptable), Moseley (2015, pp. 16–18) cites the definition of organic composition introduced in Part II, but he misses that Engels added this particular sentence to what Marx actually wrote in 1864–65.

4 Moseley's (2018, p. 129) survey of Marx's history on the rate of profit tendency missed mentioning that this clarity was only arrived in 1875 on the occasion of the French edition.

The texts in *Volume III* were drafted before the 1st edition of *Volume I*, with various levels of completeness (Moseley, 2015, p. 3) and not reconsidered by Marx thereafter. Its chapter, "Different Composition of Capitals in Different Branches of Production and Resulting Differences in the Rates of Profit", presented the organic composition in a static analysis, analysis at a point in time and across industries, as can be learned from the titling. Marx had been defining the organic composition in a context that does not carry without reconsideration into a temporal analysis such as a profit-rate tendency. The denominator of the composition is focused on *employment* of wage-laborers, not the capitalist's *expense* for wage-laborers: Variable capital, Marx writes, "represents a definite quantity of labour-power set in motion, and therefore a definite quantity of materialized labour.... The variable capital thus serves here (as is always the case when the wage is given) as an index of the amount of labour set in motion by a definite total capital". (Marx 1894, p. 144) To be absolutely clear regarding the abstraction from the level of wages, he adds: "a change in the magnitude of the value of variable capital [in prior discussion] might eventually indicate nothing but a higher or lower price of the same mass of labour. But here, where the rate of surplus-value and the working-day are taken as constant, and the wages for a definite working period are given, this is out of question". (p. 146)

In a static context, when the focus for variable capital is the employment of wage-labor, changes in wage levels need not be relevant. Abstraction from the level of payment to labor, however, is no longer appropriate in a temporal context when the portion of the working day paid for labor power may well change. In other words, variable capital is no longer an appropriate index of employment, and so the definition of organic composition in the static context is no longer appropriate. In the first section below, I argue that the concept *materialized composition of capital* is more appropriate in a temporal context and yet is also equally appropriate for the static context discussed. It is therefore the theoretical framework for the remainder of this chapter.

1   Materialized Composition of Capital and the Rate of Profit

Consider the *value* composition of capital. It has been read by many as constant capital c divided by variable capital v.[5] This is fair enough, although

---

5 Orzech and Groll (1989, p. 68) claim that the value composition, as distinct from the organic composition, is used "to express the influence of economic, i.e., market, factors on the composition of capital". Mohun (1991a, p. 404) argues that "divergencies appear between the

constant capital can be understood to be either the flow of constant capital used up – the consumption of constant capital – or the stock of constant capital C with which workers are working, either one of which would be measured in terms of labor hours. Marx is unclear between the two possibilities, even if a *mass* of means of production does suggest a stock concept. Within empirical examples Marx provides elsewhere, Marx is also unclear, but Engels in his editing of *Volume III* for publication explicitly indicates that the stock of constant capital C was meant, not the flow. Circulating constant capital also needs to be addressed.

Apart from the issue of stock or flow in referring to constant capital, two issues with using variable capital v as the denominator in the expression the value composition of capital arise. The first issue is that for the economy as a whole in a temporal context variable capital v *would change without any change in the technical composition* when workers receive more or less, while producing with the same technology. Marx was aware of the issue in his *Volume III* draft (p. 146 and some of the following discussion). The awareness was also in *Theories of Surplus Value*: "If there is any change in the value of variable capital independent of the *organic composition*, it can only occur because of a fall or a rise in the price of means of subsistence" (Marx, 1910, p. 385, emphasis in original). This earlier awareness must have been a factor that led to the greater precision by Marx by the time of the French edition: "I call the value composition of capital, in so far as it is determined by its technical composition and mirrors the changes of the latter, the *organic composition* of capital".

There is a second problem. Changes in the composition of capital are usually considered with production of relative surplus value. Holding variable capital v to be unchanging in such a circumstance seems indefensible for the economy as a whole, since the production of relative surplus value concerns cheapening labor power and thus increasing the rate of surplus value for the benefit of capital.[6] In order to permit a focus on changing technology when addressing the economy as a whole, it is more natural and necessary to focus on the relationship between constant capital C to the hours of work of those laborers working the means of production, distinct from the portion of the

---

values of inputs as they result from previous production processes (the OCC), and those same inputs as they are evaluated in terms of the values emerging from current production processes (the VCC)". In practice, Marx himself (for example, Chapter 8 in *Volume III*) and modern economists doing empirical work refer to the value relation.

6   If, on the other hand, the focus were on an individual capital and making contrasts to other capitals, then holding variable capital v unchanging is not problematic and, indeed, is the opening topic on the composition of capital presented in Part II of *Volume II* where Marx refers to v as the "index of a definite quantity of labour-power" (p. 146).

working day that gets paid. If those hours were labeled l, then the focus would shift toward C/l. Since, for Marx, l has the magnitude of $v+s$, $C/(v+s)$ will be the referenced formulation. Following Shaikh (1987, p. 304), I use his labeling for $C/(v+s)$, namely, the *materialized composition of capital*. It is the number of labor hours invested in the means of production relative to the number of labor hours of workers working those means (not simply the paid portion). I believe that this concept of the *materialized* composition well captures Marx's intentions in 1875 – likely also his underlying intentions for static analyzes when drafting Part II, *Volume III*. It reflects past labor having originated in Department I and now applied (in either department) to total living labor, rather than only the *paid* portion of living labor. That the level of variable capital is an additional factor for the general profit rate is obvious, but should not be conflated/integrated within one expression as would use of the value composition C/v, or even in the phrase "organic composition" if care were not used to delimit it. It is only a pity that Marx himself did not use the expression $C/(v+s)$, as it would have avoided a lot of confusion.[7]

We know that Marx was still working on his rate of profit conceptualization after *Volume I* was published because of his considerable notes on the topic for the period 1871 to 1882 (available in the MEGA², II/14). Therein, mathematical formulations are virtually the entirety of pages 19–150. Never, however, does Marx exhibit an interest in $C/(v+s)$, whether to consider it positively or negatively. Rather, the rate of profit s/C simply falls as C/v rises upon *assuming*, as he does, that the rate of surplus value s/v is unchanging $(s/C$ is $s/v \div C/v)$. Marx considers possible reduction in the cost in labor hours in production of constant capital and the possible rise in the rate of surplus value: they are described, among other possibilities, as counters to a falling tendency of the rate of profit. But with his drafted *Volume III* discussion of the rate of profit, the die unfortunately became cast for this topic in Marxist political economy, particularly with the manner in which Engels' presented it (Marx's version did not divide the discussion into chapters). Equally important, on his own Engels added that sentence I have already mentioned, a sentence Marx had not been in a position to write in 1864–65, namely, that the "value-composition of capital, inasmuch as it is determined by, and reflects, its technical composition, is called the *organic* composition of capital" (Marx, 1894, pp. 145–146). Engels could only have added that having read the French edition text of 1875, but its

---

[7] Marx did suggest as much when he wrote that the "organic composition can be taken to mean the following: Different ratios in which it is necessary to expand constant capital in different spheres of production in order to absorb the same amount of labour" (Marx, 1910, p. 387).

inclusion misled readers as to the status of Marx's draft on the composition of capital in *Volume III*. If Marx had developed his mathematics somewhat more to reflect his discussion of compositions of capital in the French edition, then confusions that have resulted from his *Volume III* presentation could have been avoided.

•••

Marx's discussion of the tendency of the rate of profit in *Volume III* began to receive attention when Tugan-Baranovsky published *Studies on the Theory and the History of Business Crises in England*, particularly in the second edition Chapter VII, "Marx's Theory of Crises" (1900 in Russian; 1901 in German translation). It attempted to present Marx's conception (before criticizing it) and can be said to set off a debate that continues to this day:

> Marx highlights the tendential fall in the rate of profit as the driving force of capitalist development.... The increase in value, which makes up capitalists' profit, can thus solely arise from the unpaid living labor used up in the production process, because the means of production only transfer to the product the value of their consumed part. This is why, according to Marx's terminology, in the production process the living labor makes up the variable capital, whereas the means of production, past labor, whose value cannot increase further and so constitutes the constant capital. The nature of any technical improvement, i.e. of any rise in labor productivity, consists of a relative increase in constant capital and a relative fall in variable capital.... Yet, as only variable capital generates surplus-value, it is evident that the relation between the mass of surplus-value and the total (variable and constant) capital must decrease, which is expressed in a fall of the profit rate. (Tugan-Baranowsky, 1901, pp. 83–84)

Tugan's work became quite influential, even as he is mistaken about Marx: Living labor does not "make up" variable capital; the *paid* portion of labor power makes up variable capital. Variable capital does not generate surplus-value; having laborers working beyond their variable capital generates surplus value.

In 1910 Rudolf Hilferding discussed crises in his book *Finance Capital*. He considered upward and downward movements of the rate of profit, but he stayed within the published *Volume III* of Marx. As the profit issue came to greater attention within Marxist political economy, formulations like Hilferding's above became the dominant presentation:

[T]echnical improvements are expressed in a higher organic composition of capital, and this involves a decline in the rate of profit, a deterioration of the conditions for the valorization of capital. The rate of profit declines for two reasons: first, because the variable capital diminishes as a proportion of total capital, so that the same rate of surplus value represents a lower rate of profit; and second, because the larger the amount of fixed capital in relation to circulating capital the longer is the turnover period for capital, and this too involves a decline in the rate of profit.
(Hilferding, 1910, p. 260)

This formulation persists, for example, in Heinrich (2013) even as he is critical as to whether the profit-rate should have been described by Marx as having a tendency to fall.

Given that *Volume III* was prepared before *Volume I*, Groll and Orzech (1989) makes a case that Marx was changing his mind in several respects about the fall in the rate of profit and that the *Volume I* changes for the French edition more accurately reflect Marx's evolving views on the entire matter of the profit rate. Increasing rates of exploitation – rates of surplus value – were becoming, they say, dominant for Marx in analyzing the rate of profit. Reconsideration of Marx's developing theory can help more carefully discerning contributing factors to any tendency of the rate of profit, as well as for advancing analysis of Marxist accumulation of capital.

Focusing on the ratio $C/(v+s)$ for the composition of capital has considerable precedence. It includes Rosdolsky (1956, pp. 208–226), Mage (1963, pp. 68–74, reaffirmed in Mage, 2013), and Okishio (1961, p. 87), as well as other work cited by Van Parijs (1980, p. 3 and fn. 5) who considered it the "modern" variate against the "textbook" variant C/v.[8] Rowthorne and Harris (1985, p. 347) also captured the idea without offering a new phrase. I am adopting Shaikh's phrase calling this ratio the *materialized composition of capital* in order to avoid confusion with the value or the organic compositions (the latter having varying descriptions in Marx's work).[9] Along the lines I described above, Moseley (1991, pp. 3–5) explained the weaknesses of referring to C/v, cited works by Mage (1963) and Cogoy (1973, pp. 60–61 in the 1987 edition), mentioned other dimensions of the problem, and went on to provide data for

---

8   Van Parijs was likely unaware of unpublished work in 1972 by Rowthorn and Wolfstetter (p. 4) reacting to a 1972 article published in the *Journal of Political Economy*, nor of 1974 lecture notes of Wolfstetter.
9   Shaikh actually uses C rather than c, but the intent is the same. Also, when Shaikh refers to $v+s$ he labels the sum as l (presumably suggestive of "labor" or "labor hours").

$C/(v+s)$ for the United States (p. 66).[10] Laibman (1992, pp. 132 and 231) focused on $C/(v+s)$ but retained the phrase "organic composition" for it, in discussing the theory of technical change. Utilizing the phrase *materialized composition of capital* makes clear the needed distinction between $C/(v+s)$ and Marx's attention toward C/v.

If Marx had discussed the rate of profit in consideration of the working day, then the profit rate s/C could have been restated as $s/(v+s) \div C/(v+s)$ and it could have been written

$$\text{Rate of profit} = \left[s/v \div (1+s/v)\right] \div \left[C/(v+s)\right].$$

In the left-bracketed expression, the distributional effect related to the rate of surplus value is exhibited, while, in the right bracket, the technology change effect on the rate of profit is exhibited. The rate of profit falls when $C/(v+s)$ rises, *as long as* there is not a sufficient rise in the rate of surplus value to contravene it. Utilizing the value composition C/v conflates the two effects. Anticipating several empirical results reported below, $C/(v+s)$ will be indicated to be little changing in the United States; if correct, rising C/v results only from rising s/v.

As a final remark about *Volume III*, when Marx takes the rate of exploitation s/v as unchanged at the beginning of his discussion of the profit-rate tendency, he formally was without error but was avoiding the question as to how s/v could remain unchanging as the production of relative surplus value is proceeding, along with any possible changing composition of capital. The purpose of the production of relative surplus value is to increase the rate of exploitation. So, why hold it as unchanging in such discussion? Such a presumption is more defensible in discussion of accumulation of capital in the schemes of reproduction within *Volume II*: there, the composition of capital (without Marx using the phrase) is also unchanging.

2   Luxemburg's Recognition of the Materialized Composition, Considering It to Be Rising

In lecturing her students on *Capital, Volume III*, in 1912–13, Luxemburg discussed the falling rate of profit (Hudis, 2013, pp. xvi, fn. ‡, and 485–500). While

---

10   Shortly thereafter, Moseley (1997), without explanation, reverted to. However, in a private message to this author said that that reversion was a mistake.

her presentation does not have much distinction from Marx's, let alone Tugan's and Hilferding's, she does state that the rate of exploitation must be rising: "the increasing productivity of labor results in a decline in the cost of maintaining the existence of workers". Nevertheless, she still claims that, "*the rate of profit falls*" (Luxemburg 2013b, p. 499, emphasis in original).

When writing *The Accumulation of Capital* shortly afterwards, Luxemburg desired to address Tugan's work. Even though Tugan's profit-rate discussion was not her interest, Luxemburg is led to issue of the composition of capital through her interest in accumulation. She writes:

> According to Marx's compelling demonstration, which forms one of the cornerstones of his theory, the increasing development of the productivity of labor manifests itself in the fact that the composition of capital and the rate of surplus value cannot remain constant as the accumulation proceeds, as is presupposed in the schema. On the contrary, with progressive accumulation, the constant capital, *c*, in both departments will not only increase absolutely, but also relative to $v+s$ (the total newly created value): this is the social expression of the productivity of labor. (Luxemburg, 1913, p. 240)

Luxemburg thus had recognized that the denominator should be $v+s$. And she appears to be the first political economist within Marxism to have done so. However, $C/(v+s)$ should not have been described by her as the "social expression of the productivity of labor" since productivity as such is not represented, but rather only labor hours.

Luxemburg does expect $C/(v+s)$ to be increasing significantly, the reason that she had earlier expected the rate of profit to fall in spite of the rate of exploitation rising. And she goes on in this portion of her work, to reconsider the schemes of reproduction with the composition increasing while the rate of exploitation is also increasing, but less significantly.

3   Marx's and Engels' Estimations for Cotton Spinning[11]

Empirical estimations by Marx and Engels relating to the composition of capital have received little attention. Yet, in *Volume I*, Chapter 9, Marx offers data from a Manchester spinning factory directly relevant to discussion of accumulation

---

11   Sections 3 and 4 of this chapter are drawn from Zarembka (2010).

of capital and schemes of reproduction. For this factory he reports a *consumption* of constant capital of £378 weekly, compared to variable capital of £52 weekly, implying a ratio of 7.3 (Marx, 1867, p. 211).[12] Most of the consumed constant capital is for cotton, namely, £342 out of £378. Marx lists an additional £20 for wear and tear (depreciation) of spindles, £6 for building rental, and £10 for auxiliary materials. He provides £10,000 as having been the outlay for the *fixed* constant capital in this 10,000-spindle factory. Its weekly depreciation of £20 corresponds to £1040 annually and a depreciation rate of 10%. Marx reports surplus value of £80, so that the rate of surplus value is £80/£52 = 1.54.

In text now by Engels (in Marx, 1894, pp. 75–76), drafted when editing Marx's manuscript in the context of discussing the turnover of capital, *Volume III* refers to the same spinning manufacturer's data that is presented in *Volume I*. Engels repeats the data Marx reported in *Volume I*, including the installation cost for machinery consisting of 10,000 spindles at an assumed £1 for each spindle, a total cost of £10,000. Wear and tear is still £20 weekly (£1040 yearly). Building rent is £6 weekly (£312 yearly), along with £10 auxilary materials costs weekly (£520 yearly). Engels offers an estimate of the yearly level of circulating capital (constant and variable) to be one-quarter of the level of £10,000 for the spindle machinery, i.e., £2500. He thus calculates £12,182 in constant capital as follows: £10,000 for the stock of fixed constant capital and £2182 for the circulating constant capital (i.e., the £2500 yearly total circulating capital, variable included, less £318 as the portion of the circulating cost for wages, this £318 obtained by using the same proportion of circulating capital that variable capital represents in Marx's data, while applying it to the total circulating capital of £2500). Note that the £52 weekly wage cost Marx provided implies £2704 yearly so that a £318 annual *outlay* for wages implies a turnover – a recirculation of wages costs – of 8.5 times in the year (£2704/£318 = 8.5).

Referring explicitly to "composition of capital", Engels (p. 76) obtains a remarkably high level of £12,182/£318 = 38.3. The £10,000 in fixed constant capital exceeds the £2182 for circulating constant capital by more than four times. Given Engels' statement of yearly surplus value or profits as £4160 and the high rate

---

12   Wages for a spinner were less than £1 per week, according to Marx's 1865 lecture (Marx, 1865, p. 21), a spinner being a rather skilled occupation, although here it could be averaging the spinner with an assistant. A very comprehensive study of British wages indicates a mere 160 (old) pence, £ 2/3, weekly wages in 1871 for cotton factory operatives (Wood, 1910, p. 587), and would imply 78 operatives earning £52 total on the 10, 000 spindles. Robson (1957, p. 342) suggests about 150 spindles per operative around 1871, implying 67 operatives on 10,000 spindles. Incidentally, Marx (1867, p. 212, fn. 1) indicates that he assumes prices=values for this calculation.

of wage-cost turnover, Engels calculates a rate of surplus value of £4160/£318 = 13.1. "In times of greatest prosperity, such as we have not indeed seen for a long time, such a rate is by no means a rarity", he writes (p. 76). Modern estimates are not remotely close to such a number, because Engels was using the *outlay* on wages, not the flow: If Engels had used the annual *flow* of variable capital, Engels would have obtained a rate of surplus value of 1.54 – i.e., £4160/£2704. And the materialized composition of capital would be 1.77 – i.e., £12,182/ (£2704+£4160).

Engels (in Marx, 1894, p. 76) qualifies the data by writing that April 1871 used by Marx were particularly favorable for capitalist profits as cotton prices were particularly low and yarn prices particularly high.[13] Should the market price of yarn drop to the level in which surplus value is just £52, instead of £80, surplus value would equal variable capital and the rate of surplus value becomes unity, as Marx assumes in *Volume I*, Chapter 24. The annual surplus value now would equal £2,704 instead of £4,160 in Chapter 9. Alternatively, if yarn prices had not dropped, but cotton prices had risen by enough to raise cotton costs from £342 weekly to £370, then surplus value would still drop to £52 weekly. In other words, Engels is suggesting that a rate of surplus value of unity would be more normal.

Marx's Chapter 24 in *Volume I* moves to discussing converting surplus value into capital, using a rate of surplus value of unity. Continuing with the cotton spinning example, Marx suggests a money advance of constant capital equal to £8,000 for "cotton, machinery, &c". (the reference to machinery seems to be to its depreciation) and of variable capital £2000 for wages paid (Marx, 1867, p. 543). He does not label the ratio of money advanced for constant capital to variable capital as a composition of capital, either because composition of capital has not yet been defined or because this constant capital is its *consumption*, not its level, when a composition should refer to the *stock* of constant capital being utilized by workers (a distinction borne out by Engels when, as I indicated, he makes his calculation of composition of capital in *Volume III*). The ratio now is 4.0, less than the 7.3 ratio implied in Chapter 9, but Marx is only being indicative here. £12,000 is the annual production level with surplus value of £2000 equaling the wages.

By focusing upon converting surplus value into capital, Marx's chapter is focused upon expanding the business and there must be investment in *new* machinery. It would be costly. When Marx discusses the conversion of surplus

---

13 This would call into question whether prices=values but we leave the point aside.

value into capital at the beginning (p. 543), he includes costs of wear and tear of the machinery as part of constant capital *consumption*. But is it possible to convert a £2000 level of surplus value for the year into *new* £1600 constant capital, both consumed and fixed, and £400 variable capital? Returning to the more detailed data of Chapter 9, in order to be able to successfully employ the workers represented by £400 expenditure for new variable capital, the purchase of new machinery totaling £1479 would be required (in Chapter 9 an annual flow of £2704 in wages is associated with £10,000 fixed capital for spindles, implying that an additional £400 for variable capital would require £1479 for new spindles). Circulating constant capital costs would be £3401 when variable capital is £400 (in Chapter 9, £2704 for circulating capital was required when variable capital was £318)? £1479 + £3401 = £4880, which means that £400 of new variable capital requires 12.2 times more constant capital, fixed and circulating. With a total surplus value of £2000, that ratio of new constant capital to new variable capital would imply £152 for variable capital and remainder for new constant capital. While Chapter 24 is only illustrative, it doesn't fit well with the data in Chapter 9, as Marx has slid over the required *new investment* in machinery, the new *fixed* constant capital.

In *Volume II*, still for spinning being noted, Marx (1885, pp. 27 and 38ff) has a consumption of constant capital of £372 and variable capital of £50 and remains close to the Chapter 9 data. For his schemes of reproduction, developed after publication of the French edition (Marx's full drafting of it is provided in MEGA², II/13), Marx uses varying levels of 2, 4 or 5 for the ratio of consumed constant capital to variable capital, although it was almost 7 in Chapter 9 of *Volume I*. However, the schemes do not refer to a specific industry.

Why had Marx not paid more attention to the cost of the machinery, the cost of fixed constant capital, a cost he explicitly states in Chapter 9 of *Volume I* in his empirical example of cotton spinning? What sense can we make of Marx's spinning illustration in Chapter 24, *Volume I*, in which the substantial fixed capital costs for new spindles are not included? While constant capital consumption relative to variable capital is less in Chapter 24 than in Chapter 9 (four times instead of seven times), the growth rates are still too high. The larger reason is that Chapter 24, by ignoring turnover of capital, leads a reader to understand a turnover of unity. The significantly higher ratio of consumed constant capital to variable capital in Chapter 9 is "compensated" by the high annual turnover of 8.5 for the circulating capital when compared to the illustration in Chapter 24. Chapter 24 makes a theoretical point on an intended empirical base that could have been more precise. An illustration to include fixed constant capital costs within accumulation was offered by the model at the end of Chapter 6 above.

4 Estimates of the Composition of Capital, Post-World War II

Some post-World War II estimates of the composition of capital can be discussed. These are typically undertaken as part of a project to determine the behavior of the rate of profit, not for comprehending Marxist accumulation of capital. Still, estimates are needed for both, when engaging in empirical work. Major lines of demarcation for such empirical work include the conceptualization of constant capital in its fixed as well as in its circulating component, turnover, the relation of values to prices, and whether unproductive labor needs to be distinguished from productive labor in the overall calculations leading up to the composition of capital. Although turnover of capital is important for accurate discussion, some modern authors ignore it altogether. Webber and Rigby (1986, pp. 37–38) offer a clear exposition of turnover, including how variable-capital payments and circulating constant-capital payments have implied faster turnover rates. Their calculated turnover for Canadian manufacturing is approximately four times annually between 1950 and 1981, trending upward – calculated as the ratio of annual costs of circulating constant capital to inventories of such capital (p. 50).[14]

As a first step toward a composition of capital calculation, recall that it is easy to confuse the consumption of constant capital, which is a flow of used-up constant capital, with its level, which is a stock and reflective of the labor time required for producing means of production. Only if the stock is turned over once a year would the two magnitudes be identical. In order to keep the distinction clear, I distinguish the flow from the level by referring to *the level as the outlay*. For example, an annual flow of circulating constant capital totaling four million dollars, with a turnover of circulating constant capital equal to four, would require an outlay of one million dollars – once each quarter of the year the products are sold and receipts used to renew that circulating capital. The stock of constant capital is denoted as C throughout discussion here, while c is retained as the annual flow of constant capital consumed.

When authors refer to the organic composition of capital in empirical work, they almost always cite C/v, the *value* composition, likely because too little attention has been paid to what Marx wrote when saying that organic composition is distinct from the value by *only* referring to technological impacts. The value composition, C/v, without qualification confounds two

---

14 Webber and Rigby's calculation of constant capital relative to the outlay on variable capital represents a similar form of calculation to Engels' calculation of 38 for the composition of capital in cotton spinning, as examined in the previous section.

factors – technological requirements and the portion of the working day returned to workers. If technology remains unchanged, the value composition rises as wages fall; likewise, if laborers become cheaper as technology advances in producing commodities they consume (such as textiles). When the empirical question is reformulated in terms of the ratio of labor time invested in constant capital to the labor time of the workers working the constant capital, i.e., the *materialized composition*, $C/(v+s)$, clarity is improved. The value composition is $C/v = (1+s/v) \cdot C/(v+s)$, greater in magnitude than the materialized composition.

Constant capital, as we have stated, includes two components, fixed capital representing the stock of equipment and buildings required for the production process, and circulating capital representing the needs for raw materials, energy requirements and maintenance/depreciation requirements of fixed capital. Fixed capital can last for decades, maintenance being undertaken and included in the consumption of constant capital. Circulating constant capital can turn over much more quickly than one year, meaning that the outlay on it would be much less than the annual needed flow of circulating constant capital. Table 2 reports the manner by which three authors I discuss below differ in incorporating fixed and circulating capital in the calculation of constant capital.

Wolff's work was important in moving the calculations for the United States forward. While his calculations ended for 1976 and can be considered to be superceded by others, his calculations of materialized compositions of capital (although not using the phrase) can be summarized. Wolff (1988, p. 306) reports $C/(v+s)$, when only fixed capital is included, as 1.54 for 1947 and 1.83 for 1976. If circulating constant capital were included, then *turnover* of circulating constant capital must be acknowledged since the invested outlay is distinct from the total annual costs, i.e., the *outlay* on circulating capital is much less. Wolff's circulating constant capital *flows* are 1.13 and 0.99 for those years, respectively. Moseley (1991, p. 74) used some own data for the entire economy and some from Wolff to calculate turnover rates rising from 3.27 in 1947 to 4.32 in 1976,[15] so then the *outlays* on the circulating constant capital would be 0.35 for 1947 and 0.23 for 1976. The drop in turnover times implies an economizing on costs for circulating constant capital. When added to the fixed capital

---

15   Compared to his use of inter-industry flows for estimating such costs, Wolff notes that, only if turnover were one year would his estimates for circulating constant capital be "identical" with Moseley's; as such, Wolff (1988, p. 305) therefore defers to Moseley's. For some elaboration on Wolff's work in this respect, see Zarembka (2010, p. 168, fn. 6).

TABLE 2   Methodologies used for estimates of constant capital

	Constant capital	Fixed capital	Circulating capital
Wolff	= fixed + circulating	"total capital stock owned by each input-output sector"	"intermediate inputs in the input-output tables"
Moseley	= fixed + circulating	"net stock of fixed non-residential private capital" – "net stock of unproductive fixed capital" + "net stock of fixed capital of government enterprises"	"value of total business inventories (current cost)"
Shaikh and Tonak	= fixed only (adjusted for utilization)	"fixed nonresidential gross private capital"	(absent – see text)

Sources: Wolff (1986, p. 105, fn. 6, and 1987, pp. 186–188 utilizing Bureau of Labor Statistics, Bulletin 2034, *Capital Stock Estimates for Input-Output Industries: Methods and Data*, 1979); Moseley (1991, pp. 175–176 utilizing Department of Commerce, *Fixed Reproducible Tangible Wealth in the United States, 1929–85*, 1987); Shaikh and Tonak (1994, p. 125, same data source as Moseley)

figures Wolff provides, the materialized composition would be 1.89 for 1947 and 2.06 for 1976, i.e., a narrowing of the change.[16]

In Table 3, two subsequent estimates for the U.S. productive sectors (unproductive sectors being excluded under definitions offered) are offered, whether or not the authors formally distinguished $C/(v+s)$ from C/v as long as I could undertake the calculation. While Shaikh and Tonak (1994, pp. 120–121) have a separate calculation of the flow (not the outlay) of circulating capital relative to variable capital, it is not included in their values as their calculations

---

16   The numbers for the value composition could be similarly obtained as 5.89 for 1947 and 6.94 for 1976 (Wolff, 1986, p. 95; 1987, p. 133, Table 6.6, line 4, in order to calculate required for; and 1988, p. 306).

TABLE 3 Estimates of C/v and of materialized composition of capital, $C/(v+s)$: Productive sectors in the United States

Author	C/v	u	s/v	C/(v+s)	C/(v+s) updated by revised capacity adjustment[a]		Mohun's correction of s/v for S&T	
					revised u	$C/(v+s)$ revised	s/v corrected	C/v thus revised[b]
S&T, gross stock, no circ. capital, with capacity adj.		incl.						
1948	3.27	0.75	1.70	1.21	0.924	1.49		
1956	4.24	0.84	1.84	1.49	0.869	1.54		
1964	4.73	0.93	2.12	1.52	1.002	1.64	1.99	5.02
1973	5.01	0.96	1.94	1.70	1.005	1.78	1.90	5.46
1976	5.27	0.83	2.11	1.70	0.880	1.80	2.03	5.81
1983	6.11	0.84	2.22	1.90	0.843	1.91	2.20	7.00
1989	6.20	0.89	2.44	1.80	0.968	1.96	2.57	7.47
Moseley, net stock, with circ. capital, no capacity adj.		excl.			$C/(v+s)$ with revised u			
1948	3.60		1.35	1.53	1.41			
1956	3.96		1.44	1.63	1.42			
1964	3.92		1.73	1.44	1.44			
1973	4.39		1.59	1.65	1.66			
1976	5.15		1.66	1.94	1.71			
1983	5.76		1.93	1.97	1.66			
1989	5.03		2.28	1.53	1.48			
1994	4.61		2.33	1.38	1.40			

Notes: While S&T do not include circulating constant capital, Moseley includes it as the outlay. Variable capital is the annual flow for both, and depreciation costs are not included.
a Shaikh and Tonak had adjusted for the capacity utlization levels of equipment u to obtain operating fixed constant capital. Shaikh (2016, Appendix 6.8.II.7) later proposes a new measure of capacity utilization and is applied here, although it is measured for the corporate sector, rather than the productive private sector.
b $C/(v+s)$ is unaffected by a changed calculation of s/v.
Sources: Moseley (1991, p. 74 for turnover, 1997, pp. 25 and 33 for data to calculate $C/(v+s)$ – note that Moseley (1997) calculated C/v while in (1991) had calculated $C/(v+s)$. Shaikh and Tonak (1994, pp. 125–127 and commentary on 200–202). Mohun (2005, p. 812, Fig. 4) with data supplied by him to this author and Shaikh and Tonak's C/v reported above multiplied by their v and divided by Mohun's revision of v.

are for fixed capital only. If their circulating capital flows (which moves from 2.35 in 1948 to 2.89 in 1989) were divided by a measure of turnover (which they do not provide), we could get an a measure of outlay on circulating capital to be added to their measure of fixed capital. As mentioned, Moseley (1991) provided estimates of the ratio of the outlay on circulating constant capital to fixed capital over the relevant time period and are reported in Table 4. These data suggest an economizing process on the outlay on circulating constant capital and again suggest somewhat more stability in the compositions of capital. Mohun (2005) has offered some correction and updating of Shaikh and Tonak's work and his results suggest a faster rise in s/v between 1967 and 1989 (the only overlapping years of data). Without updating measures of capital stock, Mohun's work would imply only little change in $C/(v+s)$, but suggests a change in the calculation of the value composition, C/v, moving from 5.02 to 7.47, i.e., rising at 49% for the 1964–1989 time period.

Shaikh and Tonak's work, explicitly referring (p. 122) to the phrase "materialized composition of capital" and based upon the same national accounts as Moseley, shows a trend upward.[17] Shaikh and Tonak adjust for capacity utilization levels u which lowers the calculation of C for almost all the years. Moseley's work, also based upon national accounts but without considering utilization, is reported in Table 3, and does not exhibit a trend for $C/(v+s)$. Shaikh and Tonak excluded circulating constant capital altogether, unlike Moseley. On the other hand, they utilize gross stock while Moseley utilizes net stock data.

Shaikh and Tonak adjusted for a measure of capacity utilization and their results are reported with that adjustment. However, Shaikh (2016, Appendix 6.8.II.7) offers a new measure of capacity utilization, presumably believed to be more accurate. In Table 3, I have reproduced his new measures of capacity utilization and updated calculations of $C/(v+s)$ to reflect the replacement. The result is in bold. Also, since Moseley did not adjust his calculations for capacity utilization, I have added that to his figures and they are also presented in bold. As updated, Shaikh and Tonak's $C/(v+s)$ shows an upward trend, while Moseley's does not.

The empirical conclusion of Shaikh and Tonak's work for the U.S. economy, compared to Moseley's, seems contradictory but may be explained by the absence

---

17 Curiously, Shaikh and Tonak (1994) discussed the book by Wolff (1987), but not Wolff's (1988) follow-up article. Discussion of the latter would have given them an opportunity to explain the differing estimates for the materialized compositions of capital provided by Wolff in his 1988 article. Shaikh and Tonak did cite earlier work of Moseley (1986) in which Moseley had used the same methodology as for his estimates reported in the table, but a lack of a trend was not yet apparent in those estimates by Moseley as that article had gone only up to 1977.

in Shaikh and Tonak of the circulating constant capital which had been experiencing an economizing trend. With the inclusion of circulating capital, the materialized composition of capital seems stable or rising at a slower rate. A rising rate of surplus value, on the other hand, seems supported and suggests a resulting rise in the value composition of capital. If the U.S. economy is represented well enough by Moseley's work, the materialized composition peaked around the mid-1970s, at least through the end of the 20th century.

Moseley reports fixed capital compared to circulating capital and Table 4 displays two calculations, one based upon current dollars and the other adjusted for price changes (with prices for fixed capital growing more rapidly than for circulating constant capital). Note the increasing relative importance of fixed capital for this period in the United States. Note also that if the outlay on circulating constant capital costs is multiplied by the turnover to obtain the flow, fixed capital costs are, in fact, similar in magnitude to annual circulating constant capital costs, i.e., $C \sim c$. Table 4 also indicates the relation of the outlay on circulating constant capital costs to the flow of $v+s$, again citing data from Moseley.

None of our cited authors include depreciation within their calculations of circulating constant capital costs. If depreciation were roughly 10%, as in Marx's own example, its annual flow would be 0.1 C, so that with $C/(v+s)$ = 2, the required flow for depreciation would be 0.2 ($v+s$). A turnover of four

TABLE 4   Cost ratios

	Fixed capital relative to outlay on circulating constant capital		Outlay on circulating constant capital relative to the flow of $v+s$
	(1) Current dollars	(2) 1972 dollars	(3) Current dollars
1947	2.07	3.14	0.49
1958	3.06	3.47	0.41
1967	3.08	3.28	0.36
1976	3.51	3.91	0.43
1981	3.72	4.37	
1985	4.15	4.89	
1987	4.18	4.88	

Source: Derived from Moseley (1991, pp. 51 and 163–164, noting that his "FC" for 1976 in Table A.3 has a typo and should be 1662, not 662)

would thus imply an outlay of $0.05(v+s)$ with depreciation. In other words, the last column ratio in Table 3 would be increased somewhat to account for depreciation.

5   Updated Estimation for the United States[18]

Wishing to analyze the changing rate of profit in the United States and stimulated by Shaikh and Tonak (1994), Paitaridis and Tsoulfidis (2012) reported calculations of the changing *value* composition of capital C/v for the productive sectors of the economy, C being net fixed capital stock over the period from 1964 to 2007. This composition C/v exhibited a substantial upward movement, nearly doubling over their period (p. 222, Figure 5). They claimed that this "value composition of capital shows the degree of mechanization and the state of technology in an economy, while the rate of surplus value shows the distribution of income" (p. 223). However, the substantial rise in C/v that Paitaridis and Tsoulfidis reported can, as already discussed, be separated between the technical factor and the distributional factor using the materialized composition of capital $C/(v+s)$. That is, $C/v = (1+s/v) \cdot C/(v+s)$, and the value composition may, or may not, or only partially, show the state of technology. With their s/v almost doubling between 1964 and 2007 (p. 222, Figure 4), much less is thus happening regarding the relation of the worker hours invested in constant capital to the hours being worked by the associated workers (leaving out of consideration whether dollar values reflect labor hours as is the case throughout this chapter).

Zarembka (2015a) followed closely Paitaridis and Tsoulfidis's empirical work, using as well the U.S. Bureau of Economic Analysis (BEA) database. My Table 1 reported calculations of $C/(v+s)$ from 1948 to 2011.[19] As in their work, I included the distinction between productive and unproductive labor, while incorporating a few modifications from their choices that should only have a minor effect on the numerical results (see p. 108, fn. 6). A significant addition to Paitaridis and Tsoulfidis's work was to include an adjustment for the level of capacity utilization, rather arbitrarily taking 90 percent as representing full capacity. Shaikh and Tonak (1994) had also used a capacity utilization adjustment,

---

18 A caveat: In this chapter, no consideration for any international transfer of value is included, as, for example, by Cope (2012, particularly Chapter III.3). His analysis finds a vast transfer of value from non-OECD countries to OECD countries to the point that workers in the latter receive more value than they produce.

19 I was able to use the fixed-capital data revision of August 15, 2012 and the value-added revision of April 26, 2012, so that the database reflects updates of those.

as already presented in the previous section, given that workers would not be employed for idle capacity and the composition should reflect the work hours associated with facilities being actually utilized. My capital stock is measured as net, as in Paitaridis and Tsoulfidis, not gross, as in Shaikh and Tonak. Circulating constant capital was not included by them, or by myself, or in Shaikh and Tonak (1994), the intellectual basis of Paitaridis and Tsoulfidis's work. In order to focus on the productive sectors of the economy – the sectors that produce value and surplus value – data on unproductive sectors were subtracted out in a similar manner as Paitaridis and Tsoulfidis had, as well as Shaikh and Tonak had.

From 1956 to 2011 the *materialized composition* of capital calculated for the productive economy is stable at around 1.6 (Zarembka, 2015a, p. 109, Table 1, last line). The only significant movement upward is from 1948 to 1956, reflective of the immediate post war period. The direct conclusion drawn is that the *entire movement of the value composition C/v since 1956 is due to a rise in the rate of surplus value, the distributional concept.* While circulating constant capital costs have been excluded in these calculations, when included, these costs would suggest one-quarter higher levels for constant capital, so that the materialized composition of capital $C/(v+s)$ would be estimated as approximately stable around two after 1956, or perhaps somewhat trending downward since these costs have been somewhat economized.

Paitaridis and Tsoulfidis were ultimately concerned with the growth of unproductive labor and the rate of profit having a long-term falling trend. Since the rate of surplus value in the productive sector is rising substantially, they were able to address a source of a falling profit rate in the rising burden of the unproductive activities. This is appropriate. But they went further and concluded that, "the rising trend of the value composition of capital, when seen from the early 1980s, signifies the capital-bias technological change" (Paitaridis and Tsoulfidis, p. 223). Rather than suggesting an increasing burden of changing technological requirements for the productive sectors, in actuality, changing technology has not been an increasing burden.

Tsoulfidis (2017) updated the work he had undertaken with Paitaridis and did then calculate measures of the materialized composition of capital. He reported a mildly upward movement in materialized composition for the United States for 1964 to 2007, the annual rate being 0.37% (Figure 1, as well as Table 1). He also reported the value composition of capital growing at a 1.19% rate for the period. In spite of the evidence of a mild growth in the materialized composition, Tsoulfidis concludes that, "the rising path of the VCC [value composition of capital] is mainly due to the rising technical composition effect and less to the distributional effect" (p. 310, the distributional effect being due to changing s/v). He makes this claim by referring to the first derivative of the effect of materialized composition against the first derivative of the rate of surplus value, in the formula for the value composition, $C/v = (1+s/v) \cdot C/(v+s)$. Yet, taking such derivatives do not change the empirical facts that materialized composition of capital is only growing by 0.37% against the 1.19% growth for the value composition, driven by the increasing rate of surplus value.

5.1 Introduction by Shaikh of a Revised Methodology for Capital Stock Measurement

Anwar Shaikh had long promoted the falling tendency of the profit rate, claiming it to be an outcome of classical political economy, including Marx. His position was stated in Shaikh (1978b), restated in his 1987 conception of the materialized composition of capital discussed above, and summarized in Shaikh (1992, pp. 174–180). He claimed to prove with mathematics that the long-run trend of the rate of profit must be downward since the materialized composition of capital moves upward: "the rising capitalization of production implies a greater amount of fixed capital tied up per unit of output ... which in turn implies a rising materialized composition $C/(v+s)$" (1992, p. 177, and citing the 1987 article). Its movement upward has more impact long-term than a movement upward in the rate of surplus value. His 1994 book with Tonak followed with the evidence cited in Table 3 above, including calculating $C/(v+s)$ as rising. A consistent perspective on the importance of the long-run decline in the profit rate would, however, be on shaky grounds within Marxism if the materialized composition does not have a strong tendency to rise, given the commonly recognized rising rate of surplus value.

Shaikh's (2016), *Capitalism: Competition, Conflict, and Crises*, covers many topics, but absent except at a distance for background discussion only (such as pp. 237–243) incorporation of basic Marxist concepts or any mention of the materialized composition of capital estimated earlier with Tonak. A major aspect of his new work is reconstruction of U.S. capital stock measurement, a reconstruction that involves his reconsidering the government's BEA data utilized before, and would have implications for calculations of the materialized composition since it can still be calculated. Detailed empirical results are offered in his Appendix Table 6.8 providing a spreadsheet of data covering years up to 2011 – not in the publication but on-line at http://realecon.org/data (accessed November 4, 2018). That spreadsheet includes Shaikh's estimates for the corporate sector of net and gross capital stocks and of value added, along with a new adjustment for capacity utilization.

Shaikh does also report BEA's measure of net corporate capital stock and of value added, with the former to be contested by him. BEA's value added is close to his calculation. Including Shaikh's new measure of capacity utilization, the ratio would correspond to his prior calculation with Tonak for the materialized composition, if now for the corporate sector. For 1948 this ratio is 1.43 and reaches 1.71 for 2011, implying a growth rate of 0.28% annually. This rate is very close to the growth rate of 0.27% that can be calculated from my work for the same period, albeit for U.S. productive sectors, rather than corporate (the composition moving from 1.39 to 1.65 for the period, Zarembka, 2015a, Table 1).

If we turn to Shaikh's new measure of *net* stock, calculations and results are reported in the last column of Table 5 below, which also includes other measures to be discussed. The growth rate is much higher at 1.08%, the level moving from 0.74 in 1948 to 1.46 in 2011. Utilizing Shaikh's measure of *gross* stocks, however, the materialized composition for 1948 is 1.30 and rises to 2.85 for 2011, a growth rate still higher at 1.25%. Choosing his gross stock rather than his net will be discussed below. The BEA measurement is only net. Net stock is the "neoclassical treatment of capital", argues Shaikh, and thus his preference is the gross stock measure, adding that businesses consider gross stock in their practices (p. 243).

Before turning to his measurement of capital stock, I examine Shaikh's argument against net stock. In his Appendix 6.3, "Gross and Net Capital Stocks", he offers an example of a $2000 single piece of capital stock used in production for four years before being retired, with depreciation of $700 in the first year, $505 in the second, $431 in the third, and $365 in the final fourth year (totaling the $2000 investment, and not linear depreciation). Gross stock remains at $2000, while net stock falls from $2000 to $1300, $796, and finally $365 in the fourth year, even with the value of production unchanging. Net capital to the value of production declines greatly, he reports (p. 802). Shaikh then claims a bias upward in calculating the profit rate when using net capital in the measurement, and leads to his charge that using net stock is neoclassical. However, consider four such pieces of equipment, instead of one, each exactly the same except each represents equipment lagged one year behind the preceding in terms of age. At the end of fourth year, the oldest equipment is replaced using its depreciation fund of $2000; and so on.

    Year 1 (four pieces of equipment):
      Gross = 2000 + 2000 + 2000 + 2000 = $8,000
      Net = 2000 (newest) + 1300 + 796 + 365= $4461 (Shaikh's numbers)
    Year 2 (prior oldest machine replaced with new, others move one year older):
      Gross = $8000
      Net = $4461 (i.e., ditto)
    Year 3 and 4: ditto

TABLE 5   Measures of materialized compositions of capital, with Shaikh's data

	1948	1973	2011	'48-'73 post-war boom	'73-'11	'83-'07 boom	'48-'11
BEA net, Shaikh's utilization							
Kbea/VAbea	1.55	1.49	1.82				
uK (Corp utilization)	0.924	1.005	0.942				
Kbea*uK/VAbea	1.43	1.50	1.71	0.18	0.35	0.44	0.28
Shaikh's net or gross and u							
Knet/VA	0.80	1.19	1.55				
Knet*uK/VA	0.74	1.20	1.46	1.95	0.52	0.64	1.08
Kgross/VA	1.41	1.90	3.02				
Kgross*uK/VA	1.30	1.91	2.85	1.54	1.06	1.04	1.25
Shaikh's net / BEA's net	0.52	0.82	0.87				
Shaikh's gross / his net	1.76	1.59	1.95				
Using FRB mfg. util.,	82.5%	87.6%	73.6%				
Kbea*uFRB.mfg/90/VAbea	1.42	1.45	1.49	0.08	0.06	0.16	0.07
Knet*uFRB.mfg/90/VA	0.73	1.16	1.27	1.85	0.23	0.36	0.87
Kgross*uFRB.mfg/90/VA	1.29	1.85	2.47	1.44	0.77	0.75	1.04

Sources: Shaikh (2016): http://realecon.org/data, Appendix 6.8.11.5 and .7, accessed November 4, 2018; FRB Manufacturing Capacity Utilization: https://fred.stlouisfed.org/series/CUMFNS, accessed November 21, 2018

The ratios of gross to net are seen as *unvarying* over time at a 1.79 magnitude (i.e., $8000/$4461). Even if growth were to be presumed, the invariance in the relation of gross to net stock would remain, although the unvarying ratio would be lower – for example, 1.70 for a 10% growth rate.[20] It would be fluctuations in economic conditions that cause these ratios to be other than stable. Thus, I feel that Shaikh's presentation is misleading.

---

20   If we were to take that example of a 10% growth each year, the ratio of total gross investment to total net investment gives remains stable:

In any case, let us turn to his new measurement of capital stock. Shaikh (2016, Appendix 6.5, Sections I and II) criticizes first the perpetual inventory method (PIM) for estimating stocks and also indicates the importance of initial stock levels of earlier years for levels calculated for later years (the period for him is inclusive of the Great Depression and World War II). Instead, he offers a generalized PIM (his GPIM) as a replacement, focusing on the starting value of capital stock, alternative depreciation and retirement rates, and, most importantly, the effects of scrapping levels affected by economic conditions in the interwar period. The impact on these factors, he says, dies out by 1977 at the latest while significant earlier (pp. 845–851). I will break results in two periods, 1948–1973 and 1973–2011. Using BEA's data reported by Shaikh, along his new utilization measure, the materialized composition for the earlier period grows at 0.18% while for the latter period grows at 0.35%. Using Shaikh's net stock data, instead, the growth rate rises to a very high level of 1.95% for the 1948–1973 period, but much less at 0.52% for 1973–2011 (being only somewhat greater than for the BEA data). Therefore, ignoring economic conditions of the earlier inter-war period when assessing capital stocks up to the early 1970s does have a large consequence. Deciding to use Shaikh's gross stock data, instead of his net, does, however, have more significance for the later period of 1973 to 2011 as this measures grows at 1.06%. These data are reported in Table 5.

New equipment		1 year old	2 years old	3 years old	Total	Ratio
1st year						
	2000	1818.2	1652.9	1502.6	6973.7	
	2000	1181.8	657.9	274.2	4113.9	1.695
2nd year						
	2200	2000.0	1818.2	1652.9	7671.1	
	2200	1300.0	723.6	301.7	4525.3	1.695
3rd year						
	2420	2200.0	2000.0	1818.2	8438.2	
	2420	1430.0	796.0	331.8	4977.8	1.695
4th year						
	2662	2420.0	2200.0	2000.0	9282.0	
	2662	1573.0	875.6	365.0	5475.6	1.695

The decade from after the early 1970s was a period of relative slowdown in capitalist expansion in the United States so that depreciated capital stocks becomes relatively more important, and a gap between gross and net would thereby expect to widen. Therefore, this is not a surprise. Yet, for the 1983–2007 sub-period return to growth (labeled "neoliberal recovery" by Shaikh, p. 730), the gap in the growth rate calculations remains (see Table 5) and remains need of explanation (a personal communication with Shaikh did not so provide).[21] One consideration to be examined further would be the importance of sectoral changes that I will discuss here after considering measurement of quality changes in capital stock measurement. In any case, there may be an independent motivation to focus on *net* stock since it may actually reflect declining performance/higher maintenance costs for older equipment that gross stock calculations do not attempt to include. But the puzzle remains.

Moving on, in Sections III and IV of Appendix 6.5, Shaikh discusses the implications of the BEA adjusting for the quality of capital stock. This quality adjustment problem needs attention, particularly given his negative assessment of BEA methodology. Then, in Section V, he considers adjusting chain-weighted aggregates and his Appendix 6.6 offers an alternative measure of capacity utilization. Regarding adjusting for chain-weighted aggregates, I do not have anything to offer. As to capacity utilization, his alternative to the FRB capacity utilization figures displays widely different measures for many years, illustrated in his Figure 6.4 at the end of Chapter 6. However, I do not understand Shaikh's proposed capacity utilization index well enough to judge whether it is preferable, although I do understand his objection that the FRB index may involve a subjective element. In Table 5 both capacity utilization indices are reported, as well as the resulting calculations of the materialized composition.

5.2 *Quality Adjustment in Capital Stock Measurement*

Consider first the BEA methodology. It calculates real stocks for past investments, inclusive of a measure of quality adjustment, then subtracts depreciation, and then reflates the result for the current costs of those measures of real stock investments:

---

21 With BEA's methodology being considered neoclassical by Shaikh and productivity of capital stock stationary thereby, using BEA's data to measure the materialized composition of capital would suggest that "constancy would be merely definitional", Shaikh says (p. 814). But, why would the calculated quality change be at the level such that productivity of capital will not be changing when the profit share is stable? Why couldn't they be moving in opposite directions and compensate for each other? Why were the Shaikh and Tonak measures, nevertheless, increasing?

> ...Nominal investment in the asset in year z is converted to constant-price investment by dividing the nominal value by the appropriate *constant-quality price index* for the asset (i.e., the asset's price in year z divided by its price in the reference year). The constant-price values are treated as if they were quantity (or volume) measures.
>
> We obtain the depreciated value of this investment in constant prices by multiplying its un-depreciated value by the point on the age-price profile for the relevant age of the investment (k-z). This will give us the depreciated values that are shown on table 3. These values are converted back into current prices by reflating, i.e., multiplying the constant-price value by the value for the given year of the price index for the investment. (Arnold J. Katz, "A Primer on the Measurement of Net Stocks, Depreciation, Capital Services, and Their Integration", https://www.bea.gov/research/papers/2015/primer-measurement-net-stocks-depreciation-capital-services-and-their, 6/12/2015, p. 10, accessed December 9, 2018, emphasis added.)

In other words, the BEA is dealing with quality adjustment of capital stocks even when the phrase is "current costs" and, indeed, Shaikh (p. 815) reports the BEA methodology, while noting its "quality-adjusted" investment price index. So, quality adjustment as such is not the issue.

Now consider an example Shaikh offers to motivate his alternative perspective. After mentioning a simple price fall for identical (same-quality) desktop computers, he introduces the problem of a quality change,

> In our preceding example, the price of older desktops falls from $2,000 in period 1 to $1,000 in period 2. Suppose that in period 2 there is also a new type of desktop, twice as powerful as the older model,[22] available at a price of $2,000. If we define the quality of older desktops as 1 and that of newer ones as 2, then from the point of view of the user benefits we have the following result: in period 1, an older desktop representing one unit of quality has a price of $2,000 per desktop, which works out to $2,000 per unit quality; on the other hand, in period 2 a single older desktop representing one quality unit sells for $1,000, while a single newer one representing two units of quality sells for $2,000 – so that the price per

---

22   Regarding the meaning of computing power, Shaikh explains: "computing power is treated here as an absolute measure (e.g., the number of calculations per second on some standard task)" (p. 812, fn. 5).

unit quality is $1,000 in each case.[23] In period 1, the price per machine and the price per unit quality is $2,000 since each old machine also represents one unit of quality; whereas in period 2 the price of an average machine is $1,500 (one old at $1,000 and one new at $2,000) while the price of an average unit of quality is $1,000 (Triplett, 1990, pp. 223–224; 2004, p. 19). The two methods of measuring average price therefore give different estimates of how prices have changed from one period to another: prices per machine fall by 25%, while prices per unit quality fall by 50%.

The current cost of the capital is not affected by quality adjustment because we can calculate it directly from market prices: it is $4,000 in period 1, representing two older types of machines each selling for $2,000; and $3,000 in period 2, representing one older type selling for $1,000 and one newer type selling for $2,000…. [I]nsofar as a quality-adjusted price index falls more rapidly (or rises less rapidly) than an observed price index, the corresponding index of real (quality-adjusted) capital stock will rise more rapidly. (p. 812)

For Shaikh this illustrates the problems with quality adjustments in capital stock measurements and thus for calculating real capital stocks.

Shaikh's spreadsheet calculations for his measures of capital stock, however, implicitly utilize the *BEA price indices that are also inclusive of BEA's attempt at constant quality*. That is, his Appendix Table 6.8.11.5 (http://realecon.org/data, accessed November 4, 2018) utilizes a price-index based upon BEA data to measure current cost capital stock, net or gross,[24] still explaining that quality adjustment should not be included.

---

23 Shaikh explains that for this illustration, "it is assumed that equal amounts of 'quality' sell at equal prices" (p. 812, fn. 6).
24 Shaikh's price deflator references BEA data and, in his notation is pKN = (KNCcorpbea/KNRcorpbea)*100 (Shaikh's descriptive typo corrected – Appendix Table 6.8.11.1, http://realecon.org/data,accessed November 4, 2018, the typo being the omission of "bea" in the description while being correctly included in the Excel operator – confirmed by Shaikh.) The price deflator used by Shaikh to calculate capital stock is indirectly inclusive of both inflation and quality-adjustment because the reported BEA data do not come another way. Consequently, his capital stock measurements are also affected in his,
    KNCcorp = IGC + (1-dcorpnew)*(pKN/pKN(-1))*KNCcorp(-1), and
    KGCcorp = IGC + (1-ρcorpnew)*(pKN/pKN(-1))*KGCcorp(-1).
where KNCcorp and KGCcorp are net and gross corporate capital stock measures, IGC is current-cost gross investment, dcorpnew is the BEA 1993 depreciation rate for net stock,

...ever since the quality adjustments were applied to capital stock measures, the quality-adjusted real output/real capital ratio has ceased to be an index of the trend technological change. This is because the official purpose of quality adjustments is to make the quantity of "real" capital proportion to "real" profit, the latter being is the essential quality of capital. In practice ... quality adjustment tends to make the real output/real capital ratio stationary. (Shaikh, 2016, p. 244)

He prefers instead the classical rate of profit (his label), saying that it is the "ratio of current profits to current capital value, [and] is a real rate". It is "inflation adjusted", he says, whether for gross or net capital stock. "The key is that capital goods must be measured in current prices". (p. 810) How can he obtain *inflation-adjusted* capital stock using BEA data on prices that are measured inclusive of both inflation and quality adjustments? In other words, despite intentions, his 2016 work has not escaped the use of BEA data?[25]

The solution offered by Shaikh for the measurement of the rate of technical change refers to Sraffa's concept of maximum profit, where movements of this maximum can be treated as a measure of technical change, and the empirical aggregate output–capital ratio measured in terms of market prices would be a good proxy (p. 814). This calculation seems identical to taking an adjustment of measured capital stock by its utilization (as calculated in Table 5). The change in empirical aggregate output–capital ratio is Shaikh's measurement, with the result reported in the first row Rn of his Table 16.1 (p. 730). This simply corresponds to the inverse of materialized composition of capital. We seem to have come in a full circle, with certain qualifications discussed above.

5.3 *Paitaridis and Tsoulfidis' Implementation of Shaikh's Methodology*

Tsoulfidis and Paitaridis (2019, p. 632, fn. 8) adopt Shaikh's methodology of Appendix 6.5, albeit with a focus on productive sectors (recall that Shaikh estimated the corporate sector as a whole). Where their earlier growth-accounting

---

and ρcorpnew is the BEA 1993 retirement rate for gross stock (also Appendix Table 6.8.II.3).

Note also that accuracy of his GPIM calculations compared to BEA figures would questionable as his includes a portion of BEA methodology.

25   It may be worth noting that Shaikh is not conceding that a calculation of real capital cannot be made, but rather that an alternative methodology is required. He is not among those Cambridge economists who claim that "real capital" as a measure of means of production fails in its very conception since means of production are themselves produced – the famous Cambridge (U.K.) opposition to the neoclassical conception of "real capital".

COMPOSITION OF CAPITAL CLARIFIED THEORETICALLY, EMPIRICALLY   161

results were on the basis of *net* capital stock, they repeat it "using a longer time span and data we constructed for the *gross capital* stock of the total economy" (p. 632, emphasis added). They present estimates for 1964 to 2016 (acknowledging the sector classification system change from SIC to NAICS) and conclude that the distribution effect contributes to the value composition growth by increasing 0.75% annually, while the materialized composition (using gross stocks) increases at a rate of 1.00% (p. 633, Table 2). If we use their data from 1964 but only up to 2007 to ensure comparability with the prior work I cited, their calculation of the *materialized* composition of gross capital grows at a rate of 1.08% (from 1.93 to 3.06 over those 43 years since 1964, p. 631, Figure 1). This is significantly higher than Tsoulfidis' earlier calculation in 2017 for the same time period, when he utilized net capital. The previous calculation had been 0.37% growth for 1964–2007, probably partly due to the inter-war effect not yet having been worn out by 1964 under Shaikh's procedure they are now implementing.

Those two figures of 1.08% and 0.37% would be almost identical to the results of using Shaikh's data if the FRM capacity index at the bottom of Table 5 were utilized for the time period (they become 1.10% and 0.37%, respectively). The calculations of the materialized composition were unaffected by the choice between estimating for productive sectors versus for corporate sectors.

5.4   Sector Estimates

Table 6 reports calculations for the productive economy similarly to those undertaken in Zarembka (2015a). Data earlier than 1997 are omitted only when the classification system for a sector changed significantly for 1997 and beyond. Current cost accounting of fixed assets is used, in common with most practices, although the BEA does also offer historical cost accounting.[26] Near the

---

26   Given the presence of U.S. inflation, historical costs are much less than current costs and would imply a much lower materialized composition of capital. More important, an elementary example, offered on-line, helps understand the problem with utilizing historical cost accounting in the presence of inflation:
Company A purchased a plant for $100, 000 on 1st January 2006 that had a useful life of 10 years.
Company B purchased a similar plant for $200, 000 on 31st December 2010.
Depreciation is charged on a straight-line basis.
At the end of the reporting period at 31st December 2010, the balance sheet of Company B would show a fixed asset of $200, 000 while A's financial statement would show an asset of $50, 000 (net of depreciation).
The scenario above presents an accounting anomaly. Even though the plant presented in A's financial statements is capable of producing economic benefits worth 50% of Company B's asset, it is carried at a historical cost equivalent of just 25% of its value.

TABLE 6   Sector estimates of materialized composition of capital in U.S., $C/(v+s)$

	1948	1973	1977	1987	1997	2007	2017
Private	2.23	2.31	2.51	2.52	2.33	2.67	2.60
Private excl. Real estate	1.23	1.33	1.47	1.49	1.37	1.49	1.52
Agriculture, forestry, fishing, and hunting					2.83	3.23	3.89
Farms	0.96	1.71	3.06	3.79	3.19	3.66	4.45
Mining					5.20	4.68	7.98
Utilities					5.42	6.61	7.78
Construction	0.30	0.34	0.44	0.33	0.36	0.36	0.42
Manufacturing	0.74	1.00	1.14	1.37	1.41	1.58	1.79
Transportation and warehousing	4.71	3.34	3.72	3.36	2.75	2.47	2.30
Real estate and rental and leasing					8.23	9.73	8.70
Real estate	13.32	9.99	10.98	9.85	9.02	10.49	9.31
Educ. services, health care, social assistance	1.77	1.73	1.66	1.42	1.23	1.39	1.25
Const., Mfg., Trans.	1.32	1.18	1.35	1.44	1.40	1.41	1.58
adj. by capacity util.	1.21	1.15	1.24	1.29	1.29	1.24	1.31
plus Farming	1.16	1.21	1.36	1.41	1.37	1.33	1.42
also plus Edu. and Health	1.19	1.26	1.39	1.41	1.34	1.34	1.37

Source: Estimates in this table are based on the North American Industry Classification System (NAICS) and using https://apps.bea.gov/iTable/iTable.cfm?ReqID=10&step=2, accessed November 25, 2018; as well as https://fred.stlouisfed.org/series/CUMFNS, annual, accessed November 25, 2018. Sectors continuously reported in the table were little changed upon replacement by the BEA of the SIC classification system by NAICS system for 1997 and thereafter. Other sectors are reported only from 1997. The stocks are mid-year from end of preceding year + end current year, divided by two. Sectors not shown – wholesale and retail trade, information, finance and insurance, professional etc., management, administrative, arts, accommodations, and other – are mostly unproductive and usually have classification incompatibilities.

Moreover, the depreciation charged in A's statements (i.e. $10,000 p. a.) does not reflect the opportunity cost of the plant's use (i.e. $20, 000 p. a.). As a result, over the course of the asset's life, an amount of $100, 000 would be charged as depreciation in A's financial statements even though the cost of maintaining the productive capacity of its asset would have notably increased. If Company A were to distribute all profits as dividends, it will not have the resources sufficient to replace its existing plant at the end of its useful life. Therefore, the use of historical cost may result in reporting profits bottom of the table the sectors, Construction, Manufacturing and Transportation, are aggregated. Below it, farming is added in a separate row, and then education and health services. I report 1948, but want to focus on the period from 1973 onward – in order to acknowledge Shaikh's concerns for the effect of the inter-war period for calculations up to the 1970s. The *aggregates* in the last rows show limited historical change, albeit a somewhat an upward movement.

Nevertheless, there are very significant sector differences in the levels of compositions of capital, and sometimes changes within an individual sector are significant over time. The mining sector includes petroleum extraction, and recently fracking. A drop in world oil prices in 2016 dropped the value added of the sector even if the labor hours in the sector has not been reduced to the same degree (if at all – capacity utilization is not available). With value added in the denominator falling thereafter, the materialized composition as calculated for period since 1997 rises. This is a clear illustration of the consequences of having used the price system throughout an investigation of the materialized composition of capital. Farming and manufacturing have upward trends, but transportation and educational services have downward trends. Therefore, aggregating them and considering the trend of the aggregate depends upon the relative weights of the sectors.

The considerable differences in compositions of capital across sectors and within sectors illustrate that aggregate analysis has its limitations and deeper understanding of an economy requires study of the changing characters of the individual sectors and subsectors, even when only addressing those sectors considered to be productive of surplus value.

---

that are not sustainable in the long term (http://accounting-simplified.com/financial/concepts-and-principles/historical-cost.html, accessedMarch 21, 2018).

A more complete analysis is offered elsewhere (India is the example, but the concern is not the country chosen but rather accounting in the presence of inflation): "Historical Cost Accounting (HCA): Meaning, Benefits and Limitations" (www.accountingnotes.net/historical-cost-accounting/historical-cost-accounting-hca-meaning-benefits-and-limitations/5454, accessed March 21, 2018). Basically, by considering business firms as on-going enterprises, historical-cost accounting fails to be accurate in circumstances of inflation.

There are a few who prefer historical-cost accounting, such as Michael Roberts who regularly updates his blog for his profit-rate calculations (https://thenextrecession.wordpress.com/2017/11/18/us-rate-of-profit-update). He uses the same data source as I do, but does not separate productive from unproductive labor.

6 Limitations of Current Discussion

In Chapter 6 above, I have argued that the Marxist accumulation of capital as a concept has been imprecisely used by Marxists. A basic message of this chapter is to note a similar imprecision in the use of the composition of capital and to suggest much more attention to $C/(v+s)$, whether it be called the materialized composition of capital, or something else. If a theory of crisis is to be sustained out of a profit-rate framework, it is a necessary.

Even going this far, however, is only one step in a larger consideration for this topic within Marxist political economy. The production of relative surplus value is a concept describing the cheapening of the cost of labor power for capitalists via technological improvements in producing good consumed by workers. Those new means of production must themselves be produced by workers using the required means of production – the new constant capital for consumption goods needed to sustain workers. Marx had separated out the devaluation of constant capital (as a counter tendency to his falling tendency of the profit rate) from the devaluation of variable capital. But can they be separated? An internal combustion engines is included in certain means of worker consumption, while also in the production of many means of production. Computational hardware is included the worker consumption such as in mobile phones and in controlling production of means of production. Fossil fuels are used in worker transportation consumption and in fertilizer constant capital in agriculture. The problem of *joint-production* has to be introduced.

As to productive versus unproductive labor, while Marx acknowledged the distinction, there was no consideration in his draft *Volume III* discussion of a tendency of the profit rate whether to include or exclude unproductive labor; he only addressed any tendency within the context of productive labor. If unproductive labor were introduced (as done in empirical work reported above), the profit rate of productive labor as commonly measured, i.e., the surplus values generated in those sectors relative to invested constant capital in those sectors, can be rising at the same time as the profit rate on the economy as whole can be moving downward ... or not. As such, consideration must move toward understanding the motivation/encouragement for rise of unproductive labor.

CHAPTER 9

Luxemburg's *Accumulation of Capital* and Consideration of the Evidence

> In accordance with Marx's whole worldview, his magnus opus is no Bible containing ultimate truths that are valid for all time, pronounced by the highest and final authority; instead, it is an inexhaustible stimulus for further intellectual work, further research, and the struggle for truth.
> Luxemburg (1918, p. 453)

Marx is not a political economist of production, but of the class relations in production and distribution and of the exploitation of the working class by the capitalist class. *Capital* is not about things, nor about relations among owners of means of production, but rather about a social relationship between classes. It is written from the standpoint of the class doing the material production and yet exploited in production, the laborers, not from the standpoint of the class dominating the capitalist mode of production. While this mode of production has a calling card imprinted with its mesmerizing, seductive, cold-blue charmer: development of the productive forces, the motivation of capital is the accumulation of capital, of value and surplus value, not the enjoyment of use values: "the industrial capitalist becomes more or less unable to fulfill his function as soon as he wants the accumulation of pleasures instead of the pleasure of accumulation" (Marx, 1905a, pp. 282–283).

With the capitalist mode of production generating overwhelming attention to production, it impels its economists to focus on production. "Real political economy *à la* Smith", says Marx (1905a, p. 270), is correct insofar as

(1) capital (and hence the capitalist, its personification) is treated only as an agent for the development of productive forces and of production; (2) it expresses the standpoint of emerging capitalist society, to which what matters is exchange-value, not use-value; wealth, not enjoyment.

The political economy of Ricardo is "in the interests of the *industrial bourgeoisie,* only *because,* and *in so far as,* their interests coincide with that of production or the productive development of human labor" (1905b, p. 118, emphasis in original; also, Marx, 1939–41a, pp. 96–97). Ricardo's focus on the promotion of production made him the quintessential classical political economist, and

Marx certainly considered him the highest representative of classical political economy: Ricardo is the "economist of production *par excellence*" (1939–41a, p. 97, emphasis in original).

Marx (1905b, Chapter 17) is quite critical of Ricardo for denying overproduction and more than forty pages are devoted to argumentation regarding the problems of overproduction. The conception of Ricardo, adopted from Say, that overproduction is impossible is based upon seeing products being exchanged against products, says Marx, rather than understanding capitalist production as concerned with the expansion of surplus value (pp. 493–495). Crises are thus "reasoned out of existence here by forgetting or denying the first elements of capitalist production: the existence of the product as a commodity, the duplication of the commodity in commodity and money, the consequent separation which takes place in the exchange of commodities and finally the relation of money or commodities to wage-labor". Adds Marx, a *sell* may simply be driven by a need to *pay*: "The immediate purpose of capitalist production is not 'the possession of other goods', but the appropriation of value, of money, of abstract wealth" (pp. 502–503). The assertion by Ricardo that there may be a glut of a particular commodity, but not a general glut, was based upon James Mill's "metaphysical equilibrium of purchases and sales" (pp. 503–504; see also 529–530).

What Ricardo failed to understand is that the law of capital is "to exploit the maximum amount of labor with the given amount of capital, without any consideration for the actual limits of the market or the needs backed by the ability to pay; and this is carried out through continuous expansion of reproduction and accumulation, and therefore constant reconversion of revenue into capital, while on the other hand, the mass of producers remains tied to the average level of needs, and must remain tied to it according to the nature of capitalist production" (Marx, 1905b, pp. 534–535). Ricardo, in the light of Marx's critique, is revealed to lack an understanding of the specific character of capitalist production and circulation.

When offering an assessment of the distinction between Ricardo and Sismondi regarding overproduction, Marx wrote in the *Grundrisse* that the "whole dispute as to whether *overproduction* is possible and necessary in capitalist production revolves around the point whether the process of the realization of capital within production directly posits its realization in circulation.... The attempts made from the orthodox economic standpoint to deny that there is *general overproduction* at any given moment are indeed childish". (Marx, 1939–41a, pp. 410–411, emphasis in original, paragraphing neglected) Sismondi is not among the orthodox. A half decade later, Marx noted that "bourgeois production is compelled by its own immanent laws, on the one hand, to develop the productive forces as if production did not take place on a narrow restricted social foundation, while, on the other hand, it can develop these forces only within these narrow limits, is the deepest and most hidden cause of crises...". This cause "is grasped rather crudely but none the less correctly by Sismondi, for example, as a contradiction between production for the sake of production and distribution which makes absolute development of productivity impossible" (Marx, 1910, p. 84).

It is to Sismondi, not Ricardo, to whom Marx points as having an idea of the "fundamental contradiction" and "deepest" cause of crises. Sismondi, with his awareness of the contradiction between the poverty of the workers and the wealth of the capitalists, was "epoch-making in political economy because he had an inkling of this contradiction" (p. 259).[1] Unfortunately, in the *Communist Manifesto*, Sismondi had been mentioned and characterized as head of a school of petty-bourgeois socialism, and that was enough for Lenin to take him on in 1897, unaware of Marx's later evaluations. Luxemburg, however, was more balanced in her assessment.

This background is helpful for evaluating Luxemburg's *Accumulation of Capital*, the subsequent criticisms, and its message.

1 The Issue Luxemburg Addressed[2]

No Marxist has written more about accumulation of capital than Luxemburg, devoting a long book to it, and then a pamphlet summarizing her position and replying to critics (published two years after her murder). She wrote more

---

[1] There are other references in Marx to Sismondi suggesting limits to Marx's appreciation. In *Volume II*, regarding Smith's neglect of constant capital in the value of a product, Marx comments that Sismondi made no contribution to solving that problem (1885, p. 395). (Marx noted the same deficiency in Ricardo a couple of pages earlier; Lenin, 1897, p. 154, only cited Marx's criticism of Sismondi, not of Ricardo.) In *Theories of Surplus Value, Part II*, within a passage that raises a number of other questions, Marx has a contrast of Sismondi to Ricardo. Ricardo, in his time, "wants production for the sake of production and this with good reason [since it] means nothing but the development of human productive forces, in other words the development of the richness of human nature as an end in itself. To oppose the welfare of the individual to this end, as Sismondi does, is to assert that the development of the species must be arrested..." (Marx, 1905b, pp. 117–118).

While Grossman (1924, p. 59) had favorably cited Marx's appreciation of Sismondi, by 1934 Grossman would say of Sismondi, "since the outbreak of the present world crisis this underconsumption theory, which Lenin justly attacked as non-Marxist, has become the official doctrine of numerous socialist parties and trade unions in Europe and America" (1934, p. 70).

[2] This section and the next is a more concise version of Zarembka (2000, pp. 212–222).

clearly and coherently on the subject than even Marx, of course having him as a stepping-stone. Luxemburg had taught Marxist economic theory for many years at the party school in Berlin, was known as an enthusiastic and popular teacher, and had been preparing an *Introduction to Political Economy*. Undoubtedly during this period and before, she not only read and re-read Marx many times, but had to convey the subject matter to students ... and students do ask questions and push a teacher forward. In the process of preparing her *Introduction to Political Economy* (Luxemburg, 1925), she had uncovered an unexpected difficulty with Marx's work and undertook four months of intensive work of research and writing trying to come to the bottom of the issue. Her *Accumulation of Capital* in its beginning chapters reads as if she already had all of it in her head or on paper for students before tackling the subject in her book. It concludes in fifth chapter: "The rise and fall of bourgeois political economy, not only in a temporal sense, but also in terms of its content, can be traced between the *Tableau économique* and the production schema in the second volume of *Capital*" (1913, p. 67). She does not merely assert this claim, but the preceding pages are devoted to helping the reader understanding how and why it is so important. I myself have never read an analysis of these pages by her critics, and, yet, her subsequent chapters depend upon this starting point.

Luxemburg carefully examines Marx's predecessors Quesnay, Smith, and Ricardo to remind us of their errors and how Marx overcame them. Quesnay was the first to consider the total reproduction but did not get it correct as he could not conceive that agriculture was not any more special than manufacturing in providing a surplus value. Smith and all the classical economists made the error of thinking that the value of each product was only composed of variable capital and surplus without consideration of constant capital – a theoretical category that Marx was to introduce.[3] Nevertheless, Smith's awareness of

---

3 Ricardo followed an important error by Smith when excluding constant capital from a product's value, says Marx (1905b, pp. 470–473, 485–489). This was a major point of Lenin's Sismondi work and Luxemburg also spent a chapter on Smith's error; even Tugan (1901, p. 67) in the second edition (but not the first) of his well-known book mentioned it. Later, Dunayevskaya thought recognition of this error to be of decisive importance for Marxism, *i.e.*, Marx proved that "the constant portion of capital [did] not 'dissolve' itself into wages, but it became the very instrumentality through which the capitalist gained the mastery over the living worker"; this is "the great divide *not alone* between bourgeois economics and Marxism, *but also* between petty-bourgeois criticism, or utopian socialism, and scientific socialism" (1957, p. 130, emphasis in original). Surprisingly, Moseley (1998, p. 184, n. 12) claims that none of the participants in the debate on Marx's reproduction schemes pointed to Smith's error (he mentions Tugan-Baranovsky, Hilferding, Luxemburg, and Lenin). On the other hand, Steedman (1982, pp. 126–139), leaving aside Smith, argues that Ricardo did not, in fact, make the error repeatedly asserted by Marx.

workers producing means of production and his offering the distinction between fixed and circulating capital were important. Furthermore, Smith was sometimes aware that he was not taking adequate account of constant capital, leading to a limited flexibility in understanding. Ricardo, while the most clear and rigorous, did not have the intellectual flexibility in seeing some contradictions that Smith had discussed.

Luxemburg also realizes that classical political economy did not understand the distinction between concrete labor and abstract labor and that it took Marx to understand its importance (pp. 35–37). She turns to Marx's conception of simple reproduction, pointing to the importance of his schemes of reproduction: "Marx repeatedly underscores the fact that he considers the replacement of constant capital from the total social product to be the most difficult, and most important, problem of reproduction" (p. 117, citing passages from *Volume I* and *Volume II*). That is, accumulation cannot take place without basic reproduction of the economic structure also occurring and so she summarizes and elaborates Marx's exposition of simple reproduction. However, Luxemburg also felt that the "other problem of accumulation – i.e. realization of the surplus value for the purpose of capitalization – is thus pushed into the background, such that in the end Marx hardly takes it up at all" (p. 117).

After surveying the simplicity of the mathematics of the schemes, either for simple or extended reproduction, it being too easy to write them down, she argued the necessity to uncover exactly what Marx did accomplish and the consequences when addressing the issue of realization. When completed, she felt forced to conclude that the "realization of surplus value outside of the two existing classes of society appears as necessary as it is impossible" and that in *Volume II* "no solution to the problem is given" (p. 114) – a deficiency in Marx, she goes on to say, only partly due to *Volume II* having never been completed. She thought she had succeeded in understanding the problem: "When I was writing my *Accumulation* I was disheartened from time to time by a particular thought: all supporters of Marx's doctrine who take an interest in theory would make the pronouncement that the points I was trying so exhaustively to demonstrate and substantiate were actually self-evident already. Nobody would voice a different opinion; my solution of the problem would be the only one possible or conceivable" (Luxemburg, 1921, p. 347). This was not to be the reaction.

Attacks on Luxemburg's were widespread, and appeared periodically after her death when she could no longer respond. The most well known was by Nikolai Bukharin, who among other issues thought that, "she has an absolutely atrocious conception of capitalist accumulation". Lenin wrote in 1922 that Luxemburg had been wrong on accumulation of capital, along with many other things (Lenin, 1924). There were later critiques including those by Grossmann, Sweezy, Rosdolsky, Mattick, and Dunayevskaya. Rosdolsky would even claim that her theory reflected lack of sufficient understanding of Hegel, as if it were required.[4] Some of the earlier critics are addressed below, while a more elaborated exposition is provided in Zarembka (2002b). Here I turn lastly to an article by Shaikh (1978a), representative of many critics, that seemed to have settled her work in his mind ... to such an extent that when he arrives at his 2016 book, *Capitalism – Competition, Conflict, Crises*, none of her economic works merits even the slightest recognition. She has disappeared.

The difficulty Luxemburg found is related to, but does not directly concern, the definition of accumulation, the topic of Chapter 6 above. It certainly does concern the question as to whether realization of surplus value in new constant capital and new variable capital can continuously occur in a fully capitalist economy. I now address this.

2 Luxemburg's Critique of Marx on Accumulation and Her Response to Bauer's Criticism

> Realization of the surplus value outside of the two existing classes of society appears as necessary as it is impossible. The accumulation of capital is caught in a vicious circle. In the second volume of *Capital*, at any rate, no solution to the problem is given.
>
> Luxemburg (1913, p. 114)

Expanded reproduction occurs in human societies outside of capitalism. But it takes a very specific form in capitalism, as it is not for increased consumption but arises out of capitalism having a drive for production of value and, indeed, *ever more* value and surplus value. Capitalist society is characterized by the "growth of capital through the progressive capitalization of surplus value or, to

---

[4] Rosa Luxemburg's work in political economy gets unfair treatment to this day. A recent incident is the new translation by George Shriver of her response to critics, within her *Collected Works* edited by Peter Hudis and Paul Le Blanc (the edition of Luxemburg, 1921, published in 2015). The translation appears within a hundred pages, but at a critical point a rather long footnote is added (p. 363) reporting how she "has often been criticized" for not understanding Marx's level of abstraction and citing a 2009 critical book. Why was this footnote necessary? Shouldn't a translation in a *Collected Works* be neutral, rather than becoming a vehicle for opposition? Luxemburg herself would say that this is another, albeit small, example of "experts" being used against her.

use Marx's term, *the accumulation of capital*" (Luxemburg, 1913, p. 16, emphasis in original). For this purpose, it is essential, first, that the capitalist secure

> ...precisely those material means of production – raw materials, machinery, etc. – that he requires for the kind of production he has chosen and planned, in order to give the constant part of capital its productive form. Secondly, however, it must also be possible to carry out the transformation of the portion of capital that has been designated as variable capital, and for this, there are two prerequisites. Above all, there must be sufficient additional labor power available on the labor market in order to set the additional capital in motion, and furthermore, since workers cannot live on money, sufficient additional means of subsistence must be available on the commodity market for the newly employed workers to acquire in exchange for the variable part of capital they have received from the capitalist. If all these preconditions are given, then the capitalist can set his capitalized surplus value in motion in order to generate new surplus value as capital-in-process. However, his task is still not complete.... *So that the accumulation can actually occur in practice, an absolutely essential requirement is that the additional mass of commodities produced by the new capital win a place on the market for itself, so that it can be realized.* (pp. 17–18, emphasis added)

Before dealing with the last sentence which I have emphasized as being essential to her work, it does appear that Luxemburg is applying a definition of accumulation found in the Marx's *Volume I* chapter "Conversion of Surplus Value into Capital" and summarized in the first section of "The General Law of Capitalist Accumulation", consistent with my Marxist accumulation of capital in Chapter 6 above: An increase in the employed labor force under capitalist relations, in addition to required constant capital, is needed for accumulation to occur. This is reinforced in Luxemburg's later argument that the "progressive increase in variable capital that accompanies accumulation must therefore express itself in the employment of a growing workforce" (p. 259), followed up by her subsequent argument that it is "only from noncapitalist strata and countries that capitalist production can continuously draw this additional labor power for capitalist production" (p. 260–261), discussion of the industrial reserve army being inadequate for the question posed.

Marx wrote *Capital* theoretically characterizing an economy only capitalist without other social classes than capitalists and workers (and landlords, in some places). Marx was quite aware, says Luxemburg, of the existence of other classes. His delimitation of the theoretical project to be theory of a purely capitalist structure (which she reviews on pp. 236–238) was only a theoretical posture to understand capitalism. However, according to Luxemburg, this delimitation got Marx into trouble analyzing the accumulation of capital and she proceeds by logical deduction. With the economy assumed to be capitalist and nothing but capitalist, consider that the

> will to accumulate and the technical preconditions for accumulation are not sufficient in a capitalist commodity economy. For accumulation to actually occur – i.e. for production to be expanded – another condition must be fulfilled: the expansion of effective demand for commodities (i.e. demand backed by the ability to pay). What is the source for the constantly increasing demand underlying the progressive expansion of production in the Marxian schema? (pp. 87–88, and for following quotations)

There are only the two basic classes, capitalists and workers. Capitalists, on the one hand, sell to workers basic subsistence, but oppose anything further: The capitalist class "allocates to the working class a precisely determined part of the total social production that corresponds to the value of variable capital". Not "a brass farthing more". Capitalists also sell to themselves subsistence and luxury goods. But there are only so many luxury goods capitalists can increasingly consume, and, furthermore, the drive within capitalism is quite distinctly for accumulation, not merely luxury consumption: "The foundation of accumulation is precisely the non-consumption of surplus value by the capitalists". So the capitalists only other outlet is marketing means of production.

Whatever the short-term possibilities for marketing more and more means of production, with no other outlet (civil servants, military, academics, clergy, etc., being hangers-on to capitalists), the system must reach an impasse: "The production of more means of consumption merely in order to maintain more workers, and the production of more means of production merely in order to employ these additional workers, is an absurdity from the capitalist standpoint" (p. 88). Thus,

> Marx's analysis was compromised by the fact that, in his attempt to resolve the problem, he mistakenly formulated the question in terms of "sources of money". In reality, however, the question is one of actual demand, i.e. of the use to which the commodities will be put, and not one of sources of money to pay for them. (p. 106)

In other words, the problem cannot be resolved since surplus value "must first be realized, transformed in money" (p. 91). Use value is important.

In my view, the first section of Luxemburg's *Accumulation* is decisive. Without it, the remainder would not matter. Without it, it would not matter that she later argues that the "decisive moment here is that the surplus value can be realized by neither by workers – nor capitalists, but by social strata or societies that do not engage in capitalist production" (p. 253). Too many want to reject her argument because of disagreement with the conclusion, her theoretical basis for imperialism. It is similar to rejection of Keynes' *General Theory* when he concludes with an important role for government, without paying attention to the fact that his theory itself is not about government, but rather free-market capitalism, manifested in classical political economy.

Of course, *The Accumulation of Capital* is much more complicated and in places even difficult. Actually this is part of the problem in confronting Luxemburg's work and most rely on the judgment of others and avoid carefully and directly analyzing what she says, going beyond scattered quotes to drill to the essence. The first third of the book leads up to and undertakes a careful analysis of Marx's schemes of simple and extended reproduction in *Capital, Volume II*, Part III. Recall that Marx was in new theoretical territory with the two-department schemes. Luxemburg does not only reproduce the arithmetical examples of Marx, she connects the examples to the concrete products being produced, arguing that it is one thing to assert that a certain numerical value belongs in a department called Department I and a separate question if the number actually refers to a concrete product assignable to that department or to the other department. The reason this is tricky is that Marx is describing an *interrelationship* of one department and another department in circumstances where *both* departments require means of production, produced in what is labeled Department I. And *both* departments require consumption goods[5] produced in what is labeled Department II. We need to keep in mind this complexity as we progress.

So, what did Luxemburg observe as she analyzed the extended reproduction schemes in *Volume II*, an analysis taking up four chapters in her book? What was it for which Marx offered "no solution"? Holding to his unchanging rates of surplus value and unchanging compositions of capital in *Volume II*, thereby abstracting from the production of relative surplus value, the core of the problem Luxemburg finds can be discovered. The problem can be investigated without the complications of what changes in the rate of surplus value or changes in the composition of capital would do.

---

5 Consumption goods include subsistence needs of the workers employed in the two departments as well as the subsistence and luxury consumption of capitalists in the two departments. Sometimes a Marxist economist will add a third department to distinguish the consumption needs of the capitalists; for our purposes nothing would be gained.

Luxemburg does not report problems with Marx's arithmetical examples as such, but she inquires, "whether accumulation does not proceed unimpeded *ad infinitum* merely because an endless series of mathematical equations can be written down on paper" (p. 77). She analyzes both of the numerical examples Marx provides – the first of which has a higher composition in Department I than in Department II, the second of which has them both the same (in both examples, compositions of capital in each department remain unchanged as accumulation occurs). She concludes by saying that accumulation in the consumption-goods Department II is dominated by accumulation by the means-of-production Department I (p. 83).[6] By working through the arithmetical example provided in Marx, Luxemburg also shows that, under extended reproduction, the *increase* of constant capital in the consumption-goods Department II must exactly equal the *increase* in the means-of-production Department I of its variable capital and surplus consumption (pp. 78–83). While the mathematics of such reproduction schemes has been subject to some discussion, Bukharin (1924, p. 159) obtained this same result under a different formulation. The catch is the following:

> For accumulation to actually occur – i.e. for production to be expanded – another condition must be fulfilled: the expansion of effective demand for commodities (i.e. demand back by the ability to pay). What is the source of the constantly increasing demand underlying the progressive expansion of production in the Marxian schema? (Luxemburg, 1913, p. 87)

Luxemburg (pp. 87–91) proceeds to eliminate one-by-one each possibility for increasing demand within a closed capitalist system, noting in the process that a consideration of foreign trade would only beg the question. Since surplus value does not simply transmigrate in the material form of the new means of

---

[6] Joan Robinson (1951, p. 19) in her introduction to the first English translation points out that the "arithmetic is perfectly neutral between the two departments". Rosdolsky (1968, p. 448) labels this simple didactic phrase of Robinson's as having "proved" neutrality and goes on to report that Robinson also proved "that the impulse to accumulation could come equally well from either Department". Actually, Robinson is much less impressed by her own observation than is Rosdolsky. She immediately continues by saying that "behind all this rigmarole lies the real problem which she [Luxemburg] is trying to formulate. Where does the demand come from which keeps accumulation going?" (p. 19).
    While it is formally correct that the arithmetic is neutral between the two departments, a defense for the priority of Department I over Department II within capitalism can be made along the lines that means of production is basic to capital's control.

production and the new variable capital required for accumulation, capitalists must realize their surplus value, and obtain money. And, in order that "this realized surplus value can also be used for expansion of production, i.e. for accumulation, there must be the prospect of an even bigger market, which must likewise lie outside of departments I and II" (p. 92). Luxemburg believes that Marx was vaguely aware of a difficulty, exhibited through his discussion of hoarding of money. This was analyzed by Luxemburg mainly in her chapter "Marx's Attempts to Solve the Problem", and in the first part of her next chapter. The problem is not resolved by Marx. Nor can Luxemburg find a solution internal to the logic; "no solution" persists.

If one has gotten to this point in her argument, the remainder follows even if there is still a lot to discuss and analyze. Note that I have not had to introduce any question, one way or another, about technological change in the process of offering an understanding of her basic point.

Section II of Luxemburg's *Accumulation* deals with attempts by other economists to understand capitalist accumulation, starting with the critic of capitalist society, Sismondi, whom Lenin (1897) had extensively analyzed. Within this section she also addresses Danielson, the editor of the first and second Russian editions of *Capital, Volume I,* and of the first Russian editions of *Volumes II* and *III*. Although Marx had considerable correspondence with Danielson, unquestionably suggestive that Marx respected him, Luxemburg likely was unaware of that. In any case, I would contest Luxemburg when she refers to Danielson's "eulogies to small-scale enterprises", when she relatedly cites Engels' saying in 1875 that communal ownership in Russia had already "long past its period of florescence", and when cites Lenin's negative ascription of Russian "populism" to Sismondi (pp. 206–208 and fn. 231), Danielson being characterized as a "populist".

Section III of *The Accumulation of Capital* represents her solution to the problem. Accumulation of capital compels a reaching beyond the existing space of capitalism, whether through creation of a home market or imperialist expansion. Most Marxists would not oppose much of what is written here, other than contesting whether creation of a home market or imperialist expansion would be a necessary consequence due to an impossibility of realizing progressively increasing surplus value with only the two existing classes in capitalist society. In other words, they may say, penetration may and does happen, and it does aid capitalist accumulation when it does happen, but it is not *required* by the logic of capital. This distinction between what can happen and what must happen is of enormous importance and requires us to examine the arguments of critics of Luxemburg, particularly insofar as they discuss, or do not discuss, the first third of *Accumulation,* the cutting edge of her work.

Before turning to criticism she received, we should note that Luxemburg considers Marx's schemes of extended reproduction a deviation from his overall theory: "If the schema of expanded reproduction is examined from the standpoint of Marx's theory [in its totality], then it will be found that it is in contradiction with the latter from several points of view" (p. 240). Thus, "the schema contradicts the conception of the capitalist total process and its trajectory laid out by Marx in the third volume of *Capital*" with its "restricted capacity for expansion of social consumption under capitalist relations of distribution" (p. 246). She includes a long passage from that volume to support her position.

Luxemburg's work can be related to a 1902 piece by Karl Kautsky. He had extensively reviewed Tugan-Baranowsky's (1901) book, a review over four issues of *Die Neue Zeit*. Within the third of its five sections (this one being "Explanation of Crisis on Account of Underconsumption"), Kautsky writes:

> The capitalists and the workers exploited by them provide a market, which admittedly grows continuously with the increase in the wealth of the former and the number of the latter, but not as quickly as the accumulation of capital and the productivity of labor. This market is, therefore, insufficient for the means of consumption produced by capitalist large-scale industry. This industry must seek additional markets outside its area, in the not yet capitalistically producing trades and nations. It does find supplementary markets and they also expand more and more, but not rapidly enough, because they do not nearly have the elasticity and expansion capacity of the capitalist production process. (Kautsky, 1902, p. 80, as translated by Gaido and Scattolini, 2019, p. 202)

While Kautsky's reading is close to Luxemburg's conclusion, it was not backed up by the type of extensive analytical work she was to do. And Kautsky's statement cannot be taken too seriously, even when confirmed from an earlier, 1884 article of his.[7] That is, neither the first (1887) nor late editions (1919[8]) of Kautsky's widely known and translated *The Economic Doctrines of Karl Marx* gives attention to a necessity for penetration non-capitalist areas. When Kautsky (1887, p. 207) summarizes the conversion of surplus value into capital,

---

7   Howard and King (1989, pp. 83 and 107) confirm Kautsky's conception from an earlier, 1884 unsigned article "Tongking" in *Die Neue Zeit* (indexed under Kautsky's name). As a minor glitch, they date the later Kautsky article as 1901, but the relevant number for *Die Neue Zeit*, i.e. 20, bears the dating for 1901–02 and the relevant passages appear in 1902.

8   The German 17th and 18th editions are both dated 1919; the 1936 English translation fails to provide the edition upon which that translation is based but appears to be a late one.

for example, he only says in answer to the question where additional workers are to come from: "The working class itself produces the additional workers who are necessary for extension of production, for reproduction on an extended scale". Luxemburg (1913, p. 229, fn. 267) comments on Kautsky's review in a long footnote, noting that he "does not engage with the fundamental problem", that he is only concerned with the problem from its connection to crises and does not try to connect it to Marx's schemes of reproduction. She is evidently more favorably impressed with Boudin (1907) when Boudin reviewed a later work of Tugan-Baranovsky.

Rosa Luxemburg's critics – and Kautsky himself – chose to ignore Kautsky's opinion of 1902. His statement against Tugan-Baranovsky was simply forgotten and it was to be she who was to be read as the heretic. Luxemburg quickly learned that she had been wrong to initially think that her *Accumulation* would be easily accepted. Instead, criticisms with clout occurred. First, at least two major issues are at stake: criticism of Marx's *Capital* within Marxism, and the character of the dynamics of capitalism. Second, being one of the clearest of anti-imperialists as well as a proponent of an eventual breakdown of capitalism, many critics read into Luxemburg's theory an instrumentality to these views rather than understanding the theory on its own merits, despite that fact that imperialism does not even come up (except for one footnote reference to another's work, Boudin's) until after she has completed her entire theoretical exegesis and she starts her Chapter 27, "The Struggle against the Natural Economy". And crises and breakdown are ruled out of the discussion near the beginning of her first chapter when noting that, "to present the problem of capitalist reproduction in its pure form, it must instead be considered quite apart from this periodic cycle and crises" (Luxemburg, 1913, p. 11). Only at the end of her book, in the very last paragraph, do we read the implication of her analysis regarding breakdown. Because the logic of capitalism requires a non-capitalist milieu, as capitalism "tends to become the universal form, it is smashed to smithereens by its intrinsic inability to a universal form of production" (p. 341).

2.1   Bauer's Critique and Luxemburg's Reply

After *Accumulation* was published, several critiques immediately followed, including those by Otto Bauer, Gustav Eckstein and Anton Pannekoek. Lenin intended but never completed a critique,[9] although his marginal notes on her

---

9 Immediately after publication of her book, Lenin privately wrote the editor of the *Bremer Buerger-Zeitung*: "I am very pleased to see that on the main point you come to the same conclusion as I did in the polemic with Tugan-Baranovsky and *Volkstuemler* 14 years ago, namely, that the realization of surplus-value is possible also in a *'purely* capitalist' society [cf. Lenin,

book are preserved (Lenin, 1933, English translation by James Lawler, in the Appendix to Zarembka, 2001).[10] Luxemburg's own assessment of the character of the early response to her work was offered as follows, but only published after her murder:

> The 'review' of *Accumulation* [by Eckstein] which appeared in *Vorwaerts* on February 16, 1913, was striking in tone and content even to the less involved reader; and all the more astonishing because the criticized book is purely theoretical and strictly objective, nor was it aimed against any living Marxist. But that was not good enough.
>
> Against those who had published a favorable review of my book a highhanded official campaign was initiated, and the central newspaper [*Vorwärts*] pursued this campaign with notable warmth.
>
> There was an unparalleled, and in its way rather comical, sequel: With regard to my purely theoretical work about a complicated issue involving

---

1899a, P.Z.]. I have not yet seen Rosa Luxemburg's book, but *theoretically* you are quite correct on this point" (Lenin, 1913a, p. 332, emphasis in original). By March 1913 he could write Kamenev, "I have read Rosa's new book *Die Akkumulation des Kapitals*. She has got into a shocking muddle. She has distorted Marx. I am very glad that Pannekoek and Eckstein and O. Bauer have all with one accord condemned her, and I intend to write about Rosa for No. 4 of *Prosveshcheniye*" (1913b, p. 94). While Lenin never completed a critique, the editor's note to Lenin (1913b, p. 579) suggests the level of preparation.

In 1915 Lenin noted Luxemburg's book with its "incorrect interpretation" of Marx and also mentioned her critics, Bauer, Eckstein and Pannekoek (Lenin, 1915, p. 90).

10   The marginal notes typically mark what Luxemburg says, but sometimes indicate Lenin's reaction. There are about a dozen notes for the first two chapters of Luxemburg, the most significant perhaps being no more important than her using the same citations from Adam Smith that Lenin himself used in his *Development of Capital in Russia*. *There are no marginal notes to any of the entire remainder of her Section One*. Without critiquing that section, Lenin would not be confronting her argumentation, an absence speaking more than the marginal notes that do follow. There are fifteen notes on Luxemburg's Section Two, "Historical Exposition of the Problem". For example, Lenin has a "N.B." next to her statement that "it is a howler if Bulgakov, Ilyin [Lenin] and Tugan Baranovsky imagine [capitalism] as an economic system in which production is an end in itself and human consumption merely incidental" (Lawler in Zarembka, 2001, Appendix, p. 229, citing p. 320). There are more notes to her third and last section, the bulk of Lenin's marginal notes being to the first two chapters there. The most important of these are perhaps for her quotations regarding Marx's delimitation to a purely capitalist economy. Lenin notes those citations from Marx as being "against Rosa L." (p. 230).

I should note that Rosdolsky (1968, pp. 480–483) concludes that Lenin's misreading on Marx of crises back in 1899 conditions his subsequent rejection of Luxemburg's *Accumulation* and his use of two Austro-Marxists against Luxemburg. Rosdolsky says that Lenin's greatest deficiency is in thinking that the schemes of reproduction are themselves sufficient to understand the issue of realization.

abstract scientific analysis, the entire Editorial Board of a political daily paper came forward – although two members, at the most, might have read the book – and as an official body handed down a collective judgment against it. In the process they denied that men like Franz Mehring and S. Karski [Julian Marchlewski] possessed any expertise on the questions of political economy. Only those who had torn my book apart were to be designed as 'experts'.

Such a fate has befallen no other party publication as far as I know, and over the decades Social Democratic publishers have certainly not produced all gold and pearls. ... (Luxemburg, 1921, pp. 347–348; according to Froelich, 1939, p. 159, Mehring and Marchlewski were the only theorists who greeted her book favorably, indeed, they do so with "great enthusiasm".)

She also reminded the reader that Kautsky's (1902) own earlier critique of Tugan-Baranovsky had been in line with her book. Even as she lets pass Kautsky's use of the word "underconsumption" and his only seeing the problem of crises, not deeper problems, still she notes that Kautsky had already refuted the attacks against her and had shown that, "even when properly used, these schemas [of Tugan] do not prove Tugan-Baranovsky's thesis but, on the contrary, prove the theory of crises as caused by 'underconsumption'" (p. 379).

Pannekoek's and Eckstein's critiques at the time were not well developed and have not survived as interesting ones – a later intervention by Pannekoek in 1934 is considered below. Bauer's, however, became an important reference point for some and was reportedly even reproduced in some Soviet editions of Luxemburg's works such as the 1934 edition, "evidently to serve as a kind of antidote" (Rosdolsky, 1968, p. 502, fn. 137, citing the Polish economist Kowalik). When Sweezy (1942, p. 212) pointed to Bauer's critique he must have felt it definitive since he merely stated that "Bauer's scheme was satisfactory for the purpose for which it was devised, namely, to demonstrate the possibility of realizing surplus value within a closed system". That's it: Bauer had proved the point against Luxemburg, no further explanation or analysis by Sweezy is required. Since Sweezy indicates having read Luxemburg's *Anti-Critique* and should have been alerted, through her, to difficulties in Bauer's model, it can only be concluded that Sweezy did not analyze Bauer's model in the depth Luxemburg herself had.

Bauer (1913) recognized that accumulation of capital includes increases in both means of production and labor power, but also wanted to include the idea that the composition of capital is rising. He starts with reproduction schemes appearing in the last part of Marx's *Volume II* of *Capital* (as do many debating these points), but unlike Marx's schemes has c/v rising. He assumes that labor power v is growing at 5% annually (unrealistically high, for which no explanation is provided, but we can re-interpret the theoretical exercise as two year or five-year periods) and assumes that constant capital c grows twice as fast (leading to the rising value composition of capital, c/v). The rate of surplus value s/v remains constant at 100% (which of course implies that real wages are increasing at the rate of technological change in the production of goods consumed by workers – assuming work hours per worker constant). Bauer then purports to show that such a capitalist economy can grow in a balanced manner under these assumptions without restoring to issues of the penetration of new markets.

The bulk of Luxemburg's (1921) reply to critics is devoted to Bauer, but she also restates her overall position in more succinct manner (pp. 349–361), skips over the mathematics, and makes a few comments on Eckstein, Pannekoek and other unnamed critics. Basically, she finds that her critics are simply following Tugan-Baranowsky (1901) that "(1) capitalist production builds a market for itself through its own expansion, so that the [problem of finding] a sales outlet should pose no difficulties for accumulation (apart from lack of proper proportion); (2) the proof that this is so is provided by mathematical models such as those used by Marx, i.e. exercises in addition and subtraction on uncomplaining paper" (pp. 377–378). She recalls that, in 1902 "when attacking Tugan-Baranovsky, Kautsky refuted the same assertions which the 'experts' now use to oppose my *Accumulation*" (p. 379).

Perhaps the most revealing portion of Luxemburg's response to Bauer specifically is her criticism for his blithely "transferring" 4666 units of value from Department II to Department I in order to get his arithmetic to work out. She shows (pp. 389–395) that this is the very epitome of the realization problem that is at the heart of her book: such *a "transfer" must consist of material objects, not numbers or symbols on a scheme*. Indeed, here it is pertinent to note that Lenin had had a prescient comment about schemes (if only he had applied this to Bauer's case): "schemes alone cannot prove anything: they can only *illustrate* a process, *if its separate elements have been theoretically explained*" (1899a, p. 62, emphasis in original). Froelich understood the issue involved:

> [W]hen Bauer went on to extend the Marxist model in order to adapt it to the real and essential conditions of the capitalist system of economic competition, he discovered that it was indeed impossible for capitalists to realize the whole of their surplus-value within the framework of

a purely capitalist society. He thus confirmed Luxemburg's theory. But only up to a point, for he tried to solve the problem by simply transferring the unrealizable commodity surplus in the consumer-goods sector to the production-goods sector.... At the critical point Bauer had overlooked the fact that the accumulation process did not only involve values but also tangible objects belonging to definite categories, both of which had to be properly arranged. (Froelich, 1939, p. 160)

Rosdolsky (1968, pp. 497–499), later, not only agrees with Luxemburg on the issue, his rebuttal is complementary to and perhaps even clearer than Luxemburg's. Rosdolsky (largely unsympathetic to the basic point of Luxemburg's *Accumulation*) had noted the importance of a passage in *Capital, Volume II*, describing how value categories not only are important, but also material objects, the use-values involved (Rosdolsky, p. 454). Values must be found "in a particular useful form – in the form of machines, raw materials, means of subsistence – and all this in the proportions determined by the technical requirements of production" (p. 455). Therefore, when Rosdolsky confronts Bauer he is in a position to get to the heart of the problem: "why did Marx himself not resort to the mode of capital transfer recommended by Otto Bauer, instead of drawing up schemes with such complicated quantitative relations in the two Departments? The answer is simple enough, at least in words: because he wanted to use these schemes to show how the antinomy of use-value and exchange-level can be, and is, resolved at a social level" (p. 499).

Two decades after Rosdolsky, Howard and King (1989, p. 121) state that "Luxemburg dismisses Bauer's treatment of disproportions between the two departments as involving 'sheer swindles', and deny that the capitalists in department II could conceivably purchase the 4666 units of means of production which are needed to maintain equilibrium growth". Then they flatly say, "this is simply wrong" (and going on to tell how she could have been better spending her time!). They do not explain *why* she is "simply wrong". She, on the other hand, had spent seven pages (pp. 389–395) explaining her position. And they ignore Rosdolsky.

In sum, for Luxemburg, realization of surplus value through increasing production within Department I as a market for itself takes no account of consumption. Realization through consumption via increasing real wages of workers is antithetical to the interest of capital (although it may be a result from labor struggle). Realization through increasing luxury consumption of capitalists is no "Moses and the prophets" of capitalism (although it will surely occur as a secondary consequence of any expanded reproduction).

3   Criticisms of Luxemburg's *Accumulation* after her Death: Bukharin to Shaikh[11]

> Even writers sympathetic to Rosa Luxemburg's revolutionary leftism have been highly critical of her economic analysis. Almost no one has been convinced by her attempt to demonstrate that accumulation is impossible in a closed capitalist system.
> Her theory was wrong.
>   Howard and King (1989, pp. 112 and 317)

Five years after her 1919 murder, Bukharin (1924) published a detailed analysis of Luxemburg's position, the same year as his aligning with Stalin in the post-Lenin struggles. Bukharin's work has marks of theoretical hatchet work and helped bury much, although not all, interest in Luxemburg's *Accumulation*. Rosdolsky (1968, p. 450, fn. 6) says that "Bukharin saw his task as that of breaking the still very strong influence of 'Luxemburgism' within the German Communist Party (KPD), and any means seemed justified". An interpretation by Paul Mattick (1974, p. 92) went beyond the German situation, saying that it was part of the Bolshevik struggle at that time "to clean the tradition linked to her out of the communist parties". As editor of *Pravda*, Bukharin surely knew Lenin's unpublished 1922 manuscript that Luxemburg "was mistaken on the theory of the accumulation of capital" among many other "mistakes" and perhaps he caused Lenin's manuscript to be published in *Pravda* in April 1924, entitled "Notes of a Publicist". I have discussed Bukharin in Zarembka (2002b, pp. 11–14) and so will only offer some limited remarks here, before turning to a few other critics.

Bukharin's criticisms often attack the words Luxemburg uses to express herself. After eight pages of such style of argumentation against her, Bukharin already concludes, "we hope we have thoroughly exhausted the fundamental arguments of Comrade Rosa Luxemburg as far as they are developed in the *Accumulation of Capital*" (p. 169). Virtually the only portion of her *Anti-Critique* of interest to him is her summary (in thirteen pages) of her explanation in *Accumulation*. Clearly, Bukharin wants to get the job done without too much work on his part.[12] Bukharin offers a long quotation from Luxemburg from her

---

11   This section, with some addition, is a much concised version of Zarembka (2002, pp. 10–35), while the following section draws from pp. 36–37.
12   Bukharin's last page citation to Luxemburg's *Anti-Critique* is to a page only halfway through the second of her six chapters, i.e. to her p. 76 in Bukharin (1924).

Anti-Critique (Luxemburg, 1921, pp. 357–358; Bukharin's citation of her is on his pp. 171–172) as she tries to understand the difficulty of realization under extended reproduction within the context of Marx's theoretical delimitation to a purely capitalist society. He proceeds to pick one phrasing and wipes her off the map: "she has an absolutely atrocious conception of capitalist accumulation. For she *identifies* the accumulation of the total social capital with the accumulation of money capital! ... She is of the opinion that the aim of the capitalists is in *money* as an end in itself". (Bukharin, 1924, p. 179, emphasis in original) And in the middle of the next chapter to again justify his reading, Bukharin quotes and italicizes Luxemburg's observation: "To accumulate capital does not mean to produce higher and higher mountains of commodities, but to convert more and more commodities into money capital" (p. 371), but without referring to her very next sentence: "Between the accumulation of surplus value, there always lies a decisive leap, the *salto mortale* of commodity production, as Marx calls it: selling for money". In other words, he simply ignores her saying that money is something between two other things.[13] Instead he once again refers to her defining "accumulation as *accumulation of money capital!*" (p. 194, emphasis in original).[14] Actually, Luxemburg (1913) says at the

---

13   I am at a loss how Bukharin could so distort her position by skipping over the full sentence reproduced here. He even plays with the words *salto mortale* in his own text, getting into the reader's subconscious that he Bukharin has read her: the reader can take his word for the fact that, yes, she really does *define* accumulation as the amassing of money capital.

14   This citation is actually in his section entitled "Definition of Accumulation" and Bukharin continues:
   Under no circumstances should the accumulation of capital be confused with the purely functional role of the latter (the money phase of capital circulation). Still less, as we have seen above, should one confuse the accumulation of capital with the accumulation of its *detached* functional form, i.e. with the accumulation of money capital in the real sense of the word, of interest-bearing capital ("moneyed capital in the English sense"). The fact that the movement of the total social capital is *accompanied* by an accumulation of money capital (as Marx correctly stresses), in no way means that the accumulation of capital is *equivalent* with the latter. (p. 194, emphasis in original)
   Note that even Luxemburg's biographer was sucked into this distortion by Bukharin:
   After Rosa's death Bukharin published a criticism of her theory of accumulation. As we have already mentioned, he succeeded in fact in uncovering several weaknesses in her presentation. In various places in her book she made the obviously wrong claim that capital accumulation was the amassing of money capital; this was what mattered to the capitalists. In reality, the building up of money capital is only a link in the accumulation process.... Bukharin was right in criticizing this. (Froelich, 1939, p. 161)
   Froelich, however, does not state any other weakness by which Bukharin succeeded in his criticism of Luxemburg.

very beginning of her Chapter 8 that complete abstraction from the circulation of money in the analysis of simple reproduction "was completely justified. There, production was exclusively for consumption.... Here, in accumulation, the money-form fulfills an essential role". (p. 93). A "role" is not a definition.

That Bukharin's critique had an effect cannot be doubted. As an example of Luxemburg's standing in Stalin's Soviet Union, one of its leading political economists, Leontiev (1935, pp. 222–223, cited in Zarembka, 2002, p. 14) has a lie or distortion in virtually every sentence about her work: Contrary to his claims, she was an opponent of Kautsky; imperialism is not a "policy" subject to possible change; much of her book was devoted to the internal contradictions of a purely capitalist environment; she was no "semi-Menshevik"; she did not have a theory of "automatic collapse of capitalism"; etc.

In his principal work Henryk Grossmann (1929), at the Frankfort School since 1925 and a "close sympathizer" of the German Communist Party (Kuhn, 2000, p. 151), displays no more sympathy for her work than does Bukharin, even as an earlier Grossman (1924) had had an appreciative reading of Luxemburg's reading of Sismondi.[15] In 1929 he observes (p. 125) that Marxism had been dominated by the idea of a breakdown of capitalism up until Tugan-Baranovsky's work attempted to show that capitalism is a sustainable system within Marx's own schemes. Luxemburg, "instead of testing Marx's reproduction scheme within the framework of his total system and especially of the theory of accumulation, instead of asking what role it plays methodologically in the structure of his theory, instead of analyzing the schemes of accumulation down to its ultimate conclusion, [Luxemburg] was unconsciously influenced" by Tugan and by Hilferding (p. 125), influenced because they had created the interpretation of Marx Grossmann contests but she accepts. Given Luxemburg's entire Section 1 analyzing Marx's schemes of accumulation and also devoting a chapter on Tugan with an explicit, biting criticism, this position is a cavalier one to take. The argument would not be strange if, instead, it were taken against Lenin who, as noted in Chapter 6, was not very critical of Tugan's basic point.

After his 1913 reaction to Luxemburg's *Accumulation,* Pannekoek (1934) returned to the issue twenty-one years later. He used an arithmetical example similar to the "second illustration" of extended accumulation in Marx (1885, p. 548ff) except that the organic composition is 4:1 in both sectors, rather than

---

15 Grossman's reading in 1924 seems to be without knowledge of Lenin's (1897) quite critical work of Sismondi. Grossman (1934) later changed his opinion and came close to Lenin's evaluation of Sismondi. (For both the 1924 and 1934 publications, the spelling of the author's name is Grossman, but for the 1929 book it is Grossmann.)

the 5:1 in Marx, an easier illustration to follow, and is elaborated in Zarembka (2000, pp. 156–159). Pannekoek then concludes that Luxemburg was "mistaken" as:

> [A]ll the products are sold within capitalism itself.... Nor is it pointless: to produce, to sell products to each other, to consume, to produce more is the whole essence of capitalism.... There is no unsolved problem here which Marx overlooked. (pp. 64–65)

Looking at mathematical schemes is enough and there is no awareness that he ever understood Luxemburg's critique of Marx, including depending decisively upon recognizing uses-values and upon the class character of capitalism.[16]

Paul Mattick (1935, 1974, pp. 88ff, and 1978) undertook extensive discussion of Luxemburg. In the first work he cites Lenin as being correct about her theory (p. 36, 38), while in his later, more developed, work, he sustained a dismissal of Luxemburg not so much in his own words but using the words of others (minus the polemics), and only providing in 1978 a few quotations from her first section of *Accumulation* and none at all from her Second (pp. 117–119).[17] Mattick does exhibit awareness that, for Luxemburg, the problem is not directly one of production of surplus value, but rather of its realization, and that crises are "crises of overproduction, characterized by quantities of unsold goods". He adds, though, that such overproduction "had nothing to do with Marx's theory of accumulation" (1974, p. 90) and reformulates and repeats Bukharin without his own critical attention. Bauer's critique seems to interest him more, but he misses the technical issue of Bauer's inappropriate transfer

---

16   Pannekoek does go on to agree with Luxemburg regarding the misplaced emphasis on population growth in Bauer's 1913 critique, an issue not taken up here, but I do note him concluding that "making population growth the regulator of accumulation was so contrary to the spirit of Marxian teaching that the sub-title of her anti-critique 'What the Epigones have done to Marxian Theory' was this time quite suitable" (p. 66).
    In a less well-known work, Evenitsky (1963) tries to summarize Marx's reproduction schemes and claims that if Luxemburg had known of Lenin's (1937) unpublished first work she might have been saved from writing "a lot of nonsense" (p. 170, fn. 22). However, Evenitsky is as weak as Pannekoek in confusing how to relate a mathematical model to the underlying economic problem. Evenitsky, nevertheless and to his credit, is able to see a connection between focus on the theoretical concept of a rising organic composition of capital and the Soviet practice of emphasis on Department I over Department II (pp. 170–175).

17   The Russian edition of Luxemburg's *The Accumulation of Capital* apparently did not even bother to translate the second section, judging from Dunayevskaya (1982) in which her citations to the Russian edition move from pagination at the end of the first part immediately to the beginning of the third part.

of units of value from Department II to Department I discussed above. Mattick (1978) supports a falling-rate-of-profit theory of crises and re-iterates Grossmann's focus on an increasing shortage of surplus value as capitalism develops, claiming this against Luxemburg. I would react that possibilities of crises due to a falling rate of profit do not affect Luxemburg's own argument.

Sweezy (1942) and Rosdolsky (1968) have been significant critics. Taking accumulation to mean employing additional workers and adding to constant capital, Sweezy states that when additional variable capital, resulting from accumulation, "is spent by workers it realizes a part of the surplus value which has the physical form of consumption goods. Since Luxemburg did not understand this, it seemed to her that consumption could not increase within the framework of capitalism". (p. 181) However, Sweezy made a basic conceptual mistake, as there is no such thing in Marx as increased consumption by workers as any realization of surplus value. Rather, increased consumption would either be from more workers employed, thus producing additional surplus value, or from increased variable capital v for each worker (setting aside technological change in production). If workers get more variable capital, more v, they get more; period.[18] Any increased wages is not a gift from the capitalist class out of its surplus value but would be an outcome of the hostile struggle between capital and wage-labor (see, for example, Lapides, 1998). As Luxemburg (1921, p. 356) says, "from the standpoint of the capitalists as a class in its entirety ... the workers are not buyers of their commodities, not 'regular customers' like other people, but only labor-power, the maintenance of which is merely a sad necessity ... reduced at any given time to the lowest socially acceptable amount".

Rosdolsky's critique goes a bit beyond Sweezy. After favorably noting Grossmann's claims, he adds that if "in the abstract model of a pure capitalist society, it is possible for surplus-value to be realized and for capital to accumulate – within certain limits – then there is no theoretical need to have recourse to external factors, such as foreign trade, the existence of a third person, or state intervention. In this sense, Marx's model completely stood the test" (1968, pp. 492–493; also, pp. 63–72 for elaborated discussion). Did not Luxemburg

---

18 Luxemburg (1921, pp. 399–401) found the same conceptual error in Bauer. Says Luxemburg, "if the means of subsistence are sold to the working class, that does not mean *socially* that capital has realized its surplus value. It only means that variable capital in both money form and commodity form (money wages and wages in kind) has been forked over in precisely the same amount [as is later spent by the workers, R.L.], and thus capital retrieves in money form what it paid out at a previous time" (p. 401, emphasis in original). Sweezy missed, ignored, or misunderstood the relevant remarks of Luxemburg on Bauer in his own reading of her *Anti-Critique*.

spend pages upon pages showing in Section I of *Accumulation* that Marx's model does not pass this test and that Marx himself was somewhat aware of difficulties? Luxemburg did stay with a theoretical abstraction of a purely capitalist economy – until its weakness regarding accumulation of capital could no longer be avoided. I repeat again that Luxemburg turns to a serious analysis of the role of a non-capitalist environment, but only *after* discovering the weakness in Marx's presentation.

Ernest Mandel (1978) provided the introduction of a new edition of Marx's *Volume II* and included rather extensive remarks on Luxemburg's *Accumulation* in his Section 10. It has the merit of attempting a clear understanding of her basic position, and avoiding an overall negative assessment. Among other observations, however, he says that Luxemburg was considering only total capital and neglected competition and individual capitals, and, at that level, there is no reason that realization could not still obtain. In my understanding, such a redirection of the issue is misplaced: Surely, individual capitalists can demand for themselves ever more luxuries, but this is limited and not Marx's presentation of the drive for accumulation of capital, a drive for more value and surplus value. Yes, individual capitalists can demand more and more means of production, but those means of production are not purchased just to sit idle (which would be a costly stupidity), but ultimately must be for some purpose. Mandel goes on to favorably cite Bauer but without consideration of Luxemburg's reply to Bauer demanding attention to use-values.

Howard and King (1989) say that her work is in part a continuation of the struggle beginning around 1898 over Eduard Bernstein's revisionism.[19] After summarizing other parts of her position, they come to "her chief error" (p. 109), her error in thinking that capitalists cannot be sufficient mutual customers for each other's products to avoid a realization problem.

> Over and over again it has been urged against her that capitalists can, do and must constitute each other's customers [sufficient to avoid a realization problem, P.Z.], and that demand for that part of the social product which is destined for accumulation comes from capitalists intent upon increasing their employment of constant and variable capital.... The

---

19 Howard and King (p. 78) describe her as "young, aggressive and very ambitious". Is there something special about being a woman? Neither Bernstein nor Kautsky nor Lenin is so described, nor do others get personality typing. Luxemburg's criticism of Bernstein is a "diatribe" (p. 80). After summarizing Bauer's answer to Luxemburg's *Accumulation,* they claim (p. 120) that her work is "an easy target". Luxemburg's *Anti-Critique* is "distinctly ill-tempered". On the other hand, Bukharin's (1924) style of rebutting her is unchallenged (p. 114).

capitalist is motivated by profit, not by concern for the growth of consumption, and if endlessly increasing the production of machines which produce machines for the production of machines appears profitable, there is no reason why it should ever cease. (pp. 112–113)

Even Lenin by 1899 did not go this far. Production cannot be flat-out divorced from consumption.

Another author should be mentioned. Dunayevskaya's writings sustain a Hegelian humanist interpretation of Marx, even arguing that none of the post-Marx Marxists, Engels being no exception, understood the importance of Hegel for Marx. Luxemburg must have offended Dunayevskaya's deep Hegelian approach (see 1982, pp. 63, 115–116, 156, and 176). While respecting Luxemburg's political work, including women's issues, she devoted a full chapter to *The Accumulation of Capital* with rarely offering a supportive comment. Dunayevskaya has her followers who do not exhibit any more support for Luxemburg's *Accumulation*. Thus, Hudis (2014, end of Section III) reconsiders Luxemburg and reaches the same conclusion that her *Accumulation* can be passed over, because she "foreclosed" the place of a subjective force that "can transcend the realities of capital accumulation from within". He then goes exactly where Dunayevskaya goes: the organic composition of capital and the falling rate of profit.

If Shaikh's (2016) recent book on crises gave Luxemburg the slightest attention, his earlier commentary may be less interesting. Absent that, I turn to Shaikh's (1978a, p. 226) article, which claimed that Luxemburg concerns lay within the underconsumption problem. However, Luxemburg (1921, p. 378) had denied that she was an underconsumptionist and had quoted Marx to clarify:

> It is sheer tautology to say that crises are caused by the scarcity of effective consumption, or of effective consumers.... But if one were to attempt to give this tautology the semblance of a profounder justification by saying that the working-class receives too small a portion of its own product and the evil would be remedied as soon as it receives a larger share of it and its wages increase in consequence, one could only remark that crises are always prepared by precisely a period in which wages rise generally and the working-class actually gets a larger share of that part of the annual product which is intended for consumption. (Marx, 1885, pp. 414–415)

In further argumentation against Luxemburg, Shaikh said that "[i]f investment grows by 10% then output grows by 10%. If therefore capitalist consumption also grows by 10%, each year's output will find waiting for it the effective demand to buy it". Marx had shown that "balance growth" is quite possible (p. 227). In other words, Shaikh was reproducing his particular version of Bauer discussed above and had failed to understand the importance of use-value when Bauer silently transferred 4666 units of value from one department to the other to have the arithmetic works out. And he failed to answer Luxemburg's question:

> Where will we then find the consumers for this mass of commodities that has grown much larger? ... If the capitalists as a class are always the only buyers of this total social stockpile, or mass of commodities – aside from the part that they must from time to time hand over to the working class ... – if they are forever buying their own commodities from each other with their own money, ... it would be impossible on the whole for accumulation to take place for the capitalists as a class. (Luxemburg, 1921, p. 358)

4   Luxemburg Gets Assists from Robinson and Kowalik

Joan Robinson (1951) wrote the introduction to the first English translation of Luxemburg's *The Accumulation of Capital*. She was one of the most important leaders of the Cambridge (U.K.) critique of neoclassical economics and of its capital theory particularly. She took Marx seriously, even if she was not a Marxist and few Marxists would be satisfied with her rendering of Marx's economics. Robinson tried to understand Luxemburg, mostly out of respect but perhaps also as a preparation (conscious or not) for her own work in capital theory, including a book in 1956 of the same main title as Luxemburg's (Robinson, 1956). In trying to understand Luxemburg, Robinson cuts into remarks to the effect that capitalists can endlessly buy and sell more and more means of production to and from each other, and gets right to the point. First she makes a critical remark about Luxemburg missing the savings and investment problem highlighted in Keynesian economics: Luxemburg "does not admit the savings and investment problem, for she takes it for granted that each individual act of saving out of surplus is accompanied by a corresponding amount of real investment, and that every piece of investment is financed by saving out of surplus of the same capitalist who makes it" (p. 20). But then Robinson goes on to explain and appreciate the basic problem Luxemburg raises:

> What she appears to be concerned with is rather the inducement to invest. What motive has the capitalists for enlarging their stock of real capi-

tal [means of production, P.Z.]? How do they know that there will be demand for the increased output of goods which the new capital will produce [actually, labor produces. P.Z.], so that they can 'capitalize' their surplus [value, P.Z.] in a profitable form? ...

Needless to say, our author does not formulate the problem of inducement to invest in modem terminology, and the ambiguities and contradictions in her exposition have left ample scope for her critics to represent her theory as irredeemable nonsense. But the most natural way to read it is also the clearest. Investment can take place in an ever-accumulating stock of capital only if the capitalists are assured of an ever-expanding market for the goods which the capital can produce. On this reading, the statement of the problem leads straightforwardly to the solution propounded in the third Section of this book.

... [T]he numerical examples [in Marx's schemes], as she shows, fail to help. And this is in the nature of the case, for (in modem jargon) the examples deal with *ex post* quantities, while she is looking for *ex ante* prospects of increased demand for commodities. If accumulation does take place, demand will absorb output, as the model shows, but what is it that makes accumulation take place? (Robinson, 1951, pp. 20–21)

Robinson sees clearly the major problem that Luxemburg found with Marx.

In a sympathetic discussion, Kowalik also has a reading of Luxemburg that deserves notice, particularly since his doctoral dissertation was on her work and he continued to write about her work subsequently (Kowalik, 1966, 1971, and 2009). His article for *The New Palgrave* dictionary presents a quick and fair survey (1987, pp. 248–249 and 251–252), while also commenting that "Luxemburg promised much more than she was able to deliver.... [S]he did not succeed in transforming the schemes of reproduction into a form which would suit her purpose". (p. 249) The comment may imply that she could only have succeeded if she had successfully mathematized into new schemes her conclusions. In any case, it does lead Kowalik to be able to interpret her as attempting to solve the problem that conditions of production and realization are distinct, that "pure capitalism provides by itself too weak a basis for rapid economic growth". He goes on to say that it was Michał Kalecki who was "the most successful in taking up problems posed by Rosa Luxemburg and solving them correctly" (p. 250), although this is an assertion I cannot accept as Kalecki failed to deal with the underlying problems of surplus-value production (he did not even show interest in value theory), nor with capitalist penetration of non-capitalist production.[20]

---

20   In the same dictionary as Kowalik's article, a related entry by Desai (1987) has the remark that "the most searching critical analysis of Marx's scheme came from Rosa Luxemburg"

5   Historical Accumulation and Fraction of Surplus Value Required

I would like to conclude discussion of Luxemburg's work with brief empirical work referring to the United States and to Germany, and then go on a little exercise at the world level.

The United States became the leading industrial power by the 20th century. While the decade of 1860 to 1870 included Civil War and then conversion of slaves into share croppers, tenant farmers, or wage laborers, the period thereafter included massive immigration into the country. In 1870, the U.S. census population was 38.6 million and by 1920 was 106.0 million, a 2.0% annual rate of increase, net immigration of course included (www.census.gov/population/www/censusdata/files/table-4.pdf). Now, Weinberg (2002, p. 185) reports that the number of wage laborers increased from 5,600,000 in 1870 to 23,300,000 in 1920, representing a growth rate of 2.9% annually. These figures do not include "clerical" workers which moved from 260,000 to 3,715,000. If included, the growth rate would be somewhat higher at 3.1%. If reduction in hours in the workweek were included, the increase in produced value would be somewhat lower.

For Germany, measured over a twenty-five year period, growth rates of the wage-laborers were similar. According to Guttsman (1981, p. 86), wage-laborers measured by "manual workers in industry, commerce, transport" increased from 4,134,000 in 1882 to 8,385,000 in 1907, an annual growth rate of 2.9% over those 25 years.

(p. 340), but he does not offer as clear a statement of Luxemburg's thought as does Kowalik's entry. Another dictionary of Marxist thought has an entry on reproduction schemes saying that, for Luxemburg, the schemes show demand deficiency, but that "by generalizing Marx's simple numerical examples it is easy to see that the growing demand originates inside the two Departments themselves" (Giussani, 1983, p. 474). This claim is indistinguishable from Bauer's or Pannekoek's.

Kuehne's (1972) earlier survey of dynamics in the Marxian system includes a number of comments on Luxemburg's *Accumulation*, although none referring to her *Anti-Critique*. Most are scattered comments, and the more important centers upon the relative weight of Department I over Department II (pp. 89–90 and 104–109; see also Zarembka, 2002b, 42–45) rather than upon issues of realization. Luxemburg "undoubtedly erred in the very heart of her growth theory, for she assumed ... that capitalism could not keep growing on the strength of its own resources" (p. 108). Rather than *assuming* such a point, Luxemburg's effort was to *prove* the insufficiency of an internal market to sustain capitalism. After claiming that she was proved wrong by Bauer, Bukharin, and Sweezy, Kuehne adds that "the great post-war boom of 'late capitalism' ... clearly demonstrated that industrial countries, and not semi-feudal states or under-developed 'third persons', are the best customers of industrial countries" (p. 108).

Even with a fast developing capitalist economy, represented by U.S. or German history, only something like *fifteen percent of surplus value would be needed to sustain the employment rise*, insofar as suggested in Chapter 6 by Table 1 (interpolating between 10% and 20% depending upon the rate of surplus value). We are therefore compelled to ask as to the destination of a major portion of surplus, the portion neither used for capitalist consumption nor accumulation of capital. This is the very large portion of surplus value upon which Marx did not focus. *Has the accumulation of capital been overplayed as a role in the dynamics of the capitalist mode of production?*

According to United Nations figures, in 1850, of the total world population of 1262 million, 64.1% was in Asia, 21.9% in Europe, 8.8% in Africa, 3.0% in Latin America and the Caribbean, 2.1% in Northern America, and 0.2% in Oceania.[21] In that year of 1850, only Europe with its 276 million persons had a significant working class of wage-laborers. By 1900 the world is estimated to have had 1650 million persons, representing an annual growth rate of 0.54% since 1850. Then, we had 0.85% annually between 1900 and 1950 to arrive at 2521 million, and yet another 1.78% annually between 1950 and 1999 to reach six billion. Currently, we have passed 7.7 billion persons which means that the *increase* since 1999 is equal to the *total* world population in 1900. People born in the early 1950s and perhaps now retired live in a world with three times more people, who collectually rape the planet, mostly without even being caused to think much about solutions! For comparison, Marx was writing at a time of considerably lower *levels* of world population, albeit with 1% growth rates in the United Kingdom (including net migration).[22]

If, for a loose estimate, the world in 1850 had 3% of its population as working class – i.e., 38 million – and in 1900 had 10% its population of 1650 million as working class, that growth rate of the working class would be 3.0% annually, in other words, similar to the United States or Germany that I mentioned above. This could represent accumulation of capital if all of the working class were producing value and surplus value (unproductive wage-labor not involved, an issue not seeming to be as substantial a phenomenon until the 20th century).

---

21   "The World at Six Billion", Population Division, Department of Economic and Social Affairs, United Nations Secretariat, (ESA/P/WP.154), 12 October 1999, p. 6, Table 2, at https://search.archives.un.org/uploads/r/united-nations-archives/4/b/8/4b8e1e4538ee528ec43c72fcbdd3bddb9718410f3e414240617f97ac98d388e2/S-1092-0117-01-00002.pdf.

22   In Marx's time, based upon census data, the population of the United Kingdom grew from 27,368,800 in 1851 to 34,934,500 in 1881 (https://en.wikipedia.org/wiki/Demography_of_the_United_Kingdom#cite_note-20,accessed July 22, 2018), implying 1.0% population growth rate.

Still, such a 3% growth rate would seem to correspond to merely 10–15% of surplus value being utilized by capitalists for accumulation of constant and variable capital (Table 1 in Chapter 6). *A balance of surplus value at an 85–90% level not used for accumulation of capital would remain a very large portion of surplus value upon which Marx did not focus.*

PART 3

Considering Nationalism and State Machiavellianism

∴

CHAPTER 10

Luxemburg's "The National Question and Antonomy" and Lenin's Criticism

by Narihiko Ito

The historical mission of the bourgeoisie is the creation of a modern "national" state; but the historical task of the proletariat is the abolition of this state as a political form of capitalism, in which they themselves, as a conscious class, come into existence to establish the socialist system.
    Luxemburg (1908–09, p. 1670)

Only such a self-government will make it possible to unite various nationalities to jointly take care of the local economic and social interests, and on the other hand, to take into consideration in a natural way the different proportion of the nationalities in each country and each commune.
    Luxemburg (1908–09, p. 279)

The appearance of nationalism exhibits much diversity,[1] but there is no theoretical viewpoint to observe nationalism in totality. This could be a reason why nationalism could be called as an "Aporia" – a problem which is impossible to solve – even in the study of history and in social science. But if we call nationalism an "Aporia" of humanity, does it not mean that we cannot solve the struggle caused by nationalism? If we scientists give up on considering nationalism by calling it an "Aporia", how can we contribute to create a world with peace and justice?

Those who theoretically and comprehensively studied nationalism were the colonialists and the Marxists. Colonialists studied it from the viewpoint of imperialism ruling colonies with the objective of effectively invading and dominating the colonies. Its purpose was not to solve the national question. On the other hand, Marxists studied it from the standpoint of internationalism: "Let's

---

1 [This chapter is an extract, with permission, from Ito (2010), citations checked and corrected as needed, and the text considerably edited for improved English. The original includes contextual background for Luxemburg's coming to write "The National Question and Autonomy". I thank my brother-in-law Jacek Banas for some Polish translating. P.Z.]

unite workers in the world!" To create socialism internationally it is necessary to solve the national question. It is thus useful to consider the national question in the legacy of Marxist study. Among Marxists, I would like to read Luxemburg's main work on nationalism, "The National Question and Autonomy"[2] and to consider the essence and solution of the national question.

1 The Features of Luxemburg's Theory on the National Question

The first feature of Luxemburg's work is the absolute negation of "the right of nations to self-determination". She criticized article 9 in the program of the

---

2 "The National Question and Autonomy" ("Kwestja narodowosciowa i autonomja" 1908–1909) was printed in the magazine "Przeglad Socjaldemokratyczny" (*Social democratic Review*, theoretical organ of the Social Democratic Party of Poland (SDKP) which had been established 1893 by Rosa Luxemburg, Leon Jogiches, Julian Marchlewski, etc.; in 1901, the SDKP developed into the SDKPiL by joining with the Lithuanian Social Democratic party). Her work on the national question and autonomy was published over 2 years as follows:
  Chapter 1. The Right of Nations to Self-Determination (Prawo narodow do stanowienia o sobie), August 1908, No. 6.
  Chapter 2. The Nation-State and the Proletariat (Panstwa narodowe a proletariat), September 1908, No. 7.
  Chapter 3. Federation, Centralization and Particularism (Federacja, centralizacja i partykularyzm), October-November 1908. No. 8–9.
  Chapter 4. Centralization and Autonomy (Centralizacja i samorzad), December 1908, No. 10.
  Chapter 5. The Nationality and Autonomy (Narodowosc i autonomja), June 1909, No. 12.
  Chapter 6. The Autonomy of the former Polish Kingdom (Autonomja Krolewstwa Polskiego), September 1909, No. 14–15.
  These articles were printed separately and never published as a book in Poland. After World War II, the first chapter was printed in the Volume 2 of the Rosa Luxemburg's *Selected Works* (Rosa Luxemburg, Wybor Pism, T. 1–2, 1959). In Germany, the first chapter was translated into German: Rosa Luxemburg, "Internationalismus und Klassenkampf. Herausgegeben und eingeleitet von Jürgen Hentze", Sammlung Luchterhand 41, 1971. In France, a part of the first chapter was summarized in the book by Georges Haupt, Michael Löwy, Claudie Weill, *Les marxistes et la question nationale 1848–1914*, (Francois Maspero, 1974).
  In English, American socialist Horace B. Davis translated up to Chapter 5, in *The National Question, selected writing by Rosa Luxemburg*, edited and with an introduction by Horace B. Davis. New York: Monthly Review Press, 1987.
  In Japan, the whole was translated from Polish into Japanese and published in 1984 as a book. In China, the first chapter was translated into Chinese (Volume 2 of Rosa Luxemburg's "Selected Works", 1990). In Spain, *La Cuestion Nacional* (Traduccion y prologo de Maria Jose Aubet, El viejo topo 1998) was published, with the translation based on Horace B. Davis' English edition; therefore, it lacks Chapter 6.

Russian Social Democratic Labor Party "which admits the right of national self-determination to all nations constituting the state [but] does not give practical guideline for the day-to-day politics of the proletariat, nor any practical solution of national problems". It is "not a political and problematic guideline to the nationality question, but only a means of avoiding that question" (Luxemburg, 1908–09, pp. 109–110).

She asks: "The 'nation' should have the 'right' to self-determination. But what is that 'nation' and who has authority and the 'right' to speak for the 'nation' and express its will?" She further asks: "Does there exist even one political party which would not claim that it alone, among all others, truly expresses the will of the 'nation', whereas all other parties give only perverted and false expressions of the national will? All the bourgeois, liberal parties consider themselves the incarnation of the will of the people and claim the exclusive monopoly to represent the 'nation'". She then indicates the actual reality of the "nation" from the Polish example when "the party of the Black Hundreds, the National Democracy, had a claim to be the will of the people, and in the name of 'the self-determination of the nation' incited 'national' workers to assassinate socialist workers". (p. 141–142).

She also says (pp. 135 and 138–140) that "such a concept of the 'nation' is one of those categories of bourgeois ideology.... In a class society, 'the nation' as a homogeneous sociopolitical entity does not exist". Indeed, "the nation" is an abstract and vague concept. But surely the national question exists, so what is the essence of the "national question"? "For Social Democracy, the national question is, like all other social and political questions, primarily *a question of class interests*" (emphasis in original), she says. "'The right of nations to self-determination' stops being a cliché only in a social regime where the 'right to work' has stopped being an empty phrase". In other words, "'the right of nations to self-determination' is only a metaphysical formulation of an idea which in bourgeois society is completely nonexistent and can be realized only on the basis of a socialist regime". Therefore, the historical task of the social democracy is "called upon to realize not the right of nations to self-determination but only the right of the working class, which is exploited and oppressed, of the proletariat, to self-determination". Here expressed is her fundamental idea that unless the right to self-determination of the working class cannot be realized, the right of nations to self-determination is meaningless.

From such a fundamental viewpoint she opposed consistently the restoration of the Polish independent state. Why did she oppose so strongly the restoration of the Polish state? We have to think of two reasons at least. The first is her strong distrust in the modern nation-state in general. For her, the modern nation-state was an imperialist state that domestically oppresses and exploits the working class and ethnic minorities, and internationally invades and dominates the minor nations and weak states. She described the reality of the modern "nation-state" as following:

> The substance and essence of the modern state consists not in freedom and independence of the 'nation', but only the class dominance of the bourgeoisie, protectionist policy, indirect taxation, militarisms, war, and conquest. The bourgeoisie uses the obvious technique of trying to cover it up by offering the purely negative happiness of 'independence and national freedom'. (p. 170)
>
> The struggle to stay in the world market, to play international politics, and to have overseas territories is both a necessity and a condition of development for capitalist world power. The form that best serves the interests of exploitation in the contemporary world is not the 'national' state, as Kautsky thinks, but a state bent on conquest. (p. 131)

As an example of such a "state bent on conquest", Luxemburg pointed out the British and German states which are "based on national oppression in Europe" and indicated the United States of America as "a state which keeps in its bosom like a gaping wound the oppression of the Negro people, and seeks to conquest the Asiatic peoples" (p. 131). At the same time, she indicated that the Polish people are seeking independence as an oppressed nation, yet there is a possibility that they would oppress other nations after the establishment of the Polish state:

> We do not have to go far for an example, Polish bourgeois nationalism is directed as much against the Ruthenians as against the Lithuanians. The very nationality which had to endure the bitter policy of extermination by the partitioning powers – Prussia and Russia – now refuses the right of independent existence to other nationalities. (p. 164)

Such were her observations on "the right of the national self-determination" and independent nation state. At the same time, they represented a historically accumulated observation regarding the Polish labor movement, summarized in Ito (2010, pp. 7–13 and 15–37).

The great difficulty before Luxemburg was not Polish nationalists, such as Dashinski and Mendelson who were not in Poland, but Marx and Engels who supported consistently the Polish independent national movement. She began to address this already in 1895/96 (which the reader may consult in Ito, pp. 15 ff).

2 The Polish Question and Marx and Engels

Marx and Engels, already before the Cracow uprising of January 1846, had expressed remarks on the Polish question. I pick up some of their subsequent statements here.

1. Meeting in London on November 29, 1847, to mark the 17th anniversary of the Polish insurrection of 1830.

After the rout of the November insurrection of 1830, many Polish democrats emigrated to Western Europe. The famous historian Joachim Lelewel (1786–1861) had been a leader of the November insurrection and emigrated to Brussels in 1845; Marx and Engels met with him. In January, 1846, in Cracow, the Polish national government was declared, but there was no uprising in other districts. General Ludwik Mieroslawski (1814–1878) who organized the Cracow insurrection was arrested in Poznan and the insurrection was lost. The Cracow Free Republic was then integrated into the Austrian Empire. But after that insurrection, the reconstruction of Poland was put in as the basic foreign policy of the Western labor movement, especially in Britain, Germany, and France.[3]

In November 1847, Lelewel established in Brussels "La association democratique" and Marx was elected Vice President. On November 29, 1847, the "Society of Fraternal Democrats" in London organized a meeting to mark the 17th anniversary of the Polish insurrection of 1830 and Marx and Engels joined the meeting and made official speeches for the first time. According to the report of "The Northern Star", Marx was introduced as following:

> Dr. *Marx*, the delegate from Brussels, then came forward, and was greeted with every demonstration of welcome, and delivered an energetic oration in the German language.... The middle classes, the *Free Traders*, had held a congress, but fraternity was one-sided one, and the moment they found that such congress was likely to benefit workingmen, that moment their fraternity would cease, and their congress be dissolved. The Democrats of Belgium felt that the Chartists of England were the real Democrats, and that the moment they carried the six points of their Charter, the road to liberty would be opened to the whole world. "Effect this grand object, then, you working men of England", said the speaker, "and you will be hailed as the saviours of the whole human race". (Marx and Engels, *c.w. Vol. 6*, p. 619)

---

3 Rjasanoff (1916, p. 178). I learned many things on this subject from Rjasanoff's work.

After a few more speakers, then Engels was reported:

> Citizen *Engels* (from Paris) ... Fellow Citizens, the commemoration of the Polish Revolution is not only an advantage to Poland, but to the whole world, as it causes the principles of democracy to be spread far and wide. He, as German, had great interest in Polish success, as it would much hasten liberty in Germany, and freedom was resolved to be obtained sooner or later. And he firmly believed that no one nation could become free without benefitting all others. He had resided for some time in England, and was proud to boast himself a Chartist in "name and all". Who were now their chief oppressors? Not the aristocracy, but the wealth takers and scrapers, the middle classes. Hence, it was the duty of the working classes of all nations to unite and establish freedom for all. (Marx and Engels, *c.w.*, *Vol. 6*, p. 620–621)

2. From the *Communist Manifesto* (February 1848):

> In Poland they support the party that insists on an agrarian revolution as the prime condition for national emancipation, that party which fomented the insurrection of Cracow in 1846. (Marx and Engels, 1848, p. 518)

3. Marx, speech at the Polish Meeting in London, January 22, 1867:

> There is only one alternative left for Europe. Asiatic barbarism under Muscovite leadership will burst over her head like a lawine, or she must restore Poland, thus placing between herself and Asia 20 millions of heroes, and gaining breathing time for the accomplishment of her social regeneration. (Marx and Engels, *c.w.*, *Vol. 20*, p. 201)

4. Marx gave the "Instructions" to the Delegates of the Provisional General Council of the First International. The ninth was on the Polish question (February 20, 1867). He said as follows:
   (a) Why do we the workmen of Europe take up this question? ...
   (b) In the present changed state of central Europe, and especially German, it is more than ever necessary to have a democratic Poland. Without it, Germany will become the outwork of the Holy Alliance, with it, the cooperator with republican France. The working-class movement will continuously be interrupted, checked, and retarded, until this great Europe question will be set at rest:

(c) It is especially the duty of German working class to take the initiative in this matter, because Germany is one of the partitioners of Poland. (Marx and Engels, *c.w.*, Vol. 20, p. 193)

5. Marx and Engels. They sent a message to the meeting in Geneva held to commemorate the 50th Anniversary of the Polish Revolution of 1830, November 27, 1880. The following is one paragraph from it.

> The cry "Long live Poland!" which resounded throughout Western Europe was not merely an expression of sympathy and admiration for the patriotic fighters who were crushed with brutal force – with this cry men hailed the people whose revolts ended so unhappily for itself but always halted the advance of the counter-revolution, the people whose best sons never ceased to fight the struggle of resistance by everywhere going into battle under the banner of the popular revolutions. On the other hand, the partition of Poland consolidated the Holy Alliance, which served as a disguise for the Tsar's hegemony over all the governments of Europe. Thus, the cry "Long live Poland!" has really meant: Death to the Holy Alliance, death to the military despotism of Russia, Prussia, and Austria, death to Mongol rule over modern society. (Marx and Engels, *c.w.*, Vol. 24, p. 343–344)

Marx and Engels wrote and spoke many times on the Polish question. Their expressions shifted according to the situation. Around 1848, they emphasized "revolution" of the Polish movement from the standpoint of class solidarity. After 1863, their support to Polish nationalism, rather than to the solidarity of the class struggle, came to the fore. There were two elements. One was the sympathy to the Polish people deprived of the national independence and democracy. The other side was the Polish role as a seawall to protect Western democracy from Russian barbarism. They looked at the Polish national movement as an important buffer zone between East and West Europe.

3 Luxemburg's "The National Question and Autonomy"

3.1 *Negation of the Right of National Self-determination*

"The National Question and Autonomy" consisted of six chapters. First, it is necessary to notice the fact that Luxemburg often called this article in her letters an "article regarding the Polish autonomy". However, because her article is titled "The National Question and Autonomy", it is often read as her general opinion on the "National Question". Still, the purpose was not her general explanation of the "National Question", but a special purpose with a polemical character: She clearly wished to put the "Polish autonomy" as a decisive solution against Polish Socialist Party's (PPS) argument for the restoration of the independent Polish state and to end the fatal antagonism when the Polish socialist movement in 1893 was divided into the PPS and the Social-Democratic Party of Poland and Lithuania (SDKPiL).

Why did Luxemburg have the first chapter as "The Right of Nations to Self-Determination"? Because "The Right" was, according to her and SDKPiL, an ideology by which the big nationality composing the "Nation-State" oppressed, integrated, and assimilated the small nationalities and the PPS was a party aimed at reconstructing the Polish independent state based upon this ideology. The SDKPiL was against the ideology of the "Nation-State" and criticized PPS policy for being based on "The Right". The Russian Social Democratic Labor Party (RSDLP) also admitted "The Right of Nations to Self-Determination" in its program. Thus, when the SDKPiL unified with the RSDLP, the RSDLP was requested to eliminate article 9 from its program. Since Luxemburg and Lenin were at the time in a very friendly relationship, her purpose of writing and publishing "The National Question and Autonomy" was not to criticize Lenin, but to explain her and the SDKPiL's standpoint as comrades fighting together against the Czarist rule. She put "The Right of Nations to Self-Determination" as a first chapter to point out the theoretical error of the RSDLP. She explained – by showing many materials such as the Bruen thesis of the Austrian Social-Democratic Party and the resolution at the Congress of the Socialist International 1896 in London – how the RSDLP made a mistake by keeping article 9 of "The Right of Nations to Self-Determination" in their program. The central point of her insistence was that "The Right" gives no practical guidelines for the day-to-day politics of the proletariat, not any practical solution of nationality problem. (Luxemburg, 1908–09, p. 109)

What we should notice is that Luxemburg considered always "The Right" from the viewpoint of the "practical guidelines for the day to day politics of the proletariat". According to this viewpoint, a "'right of nation' which is valid for all countries and all times is nothing more than a metaphysical cliché of the type of 'rights of man' and 'rights of the citizen'" (Luxemburg, 1908–09, p. 110–111).

Young Marx pointed out in works such as "Contribution to the Critique of Hegel's *Philosophy of Right*: Introduction" and "On the Jewish Question" that the legal guarantee of *equality before the law* and *rights of man* can only be the *political liberation* of the people and "nothing more than a metaphysical cliché", without the social condition to support and practically to assure the rights. And he went on the same path in the "Manifesto of the Communist

Party". Luxemburg was not against the idea of the *right of the nation*. She was against the illusion of this slogan which cannot solve the national question, but, on the contrary, reproduces the class society by establishment of the *nation-state*. Therefore, she wrote:

> Social Democracy is the class party of the proletariats. Its historical task is to express the class interests of the proletariat and also the revolutionary interests of the development of capitalist society toward realizing socialism. Thus, Social Democracy is called upon to realize not the right of nations to self-determination but only the right of the working class, which is exploited and oppressed, of the proletariat, to self-determination. (Luxemburg, 1908–09, p. 140)

Notice that she did not see the relation between the *right of nations* and the *right of the working class to self-determination* as an absolute antagonism. She writes that, "the position of socialists with respect to the nationality problem depends primarily on the concrete circumstances of each case, which differ significantly among countries, and also change in the course of time in each country" (Luxemburg, 1908–09, p. 112). Therefore, it is possible theoretically to have coincidence of the *right of nations* with the *right of the working class*. But as a precondition for it, the problem of the class must be solved. Chapter 2 entitled "Nation-State and the Proletariat" treats this problem.

3.2 Abolition of the Nation-State

Luxemburg points out that Karl Kautsky enumerates, in his article published over ten years earlier on the struggle of nationalities and the Social-Democratic program in Austria, that there are "three factors, which, according to him, make up the 'roots of the modern national idea', as found in the rise of the modern state in all of Europe. These factors are, first, the desire of the bourgeoisie to assure for itself an internal or domestic market for its own commodity production; second, the desire for political freedom – democracy; and finally, expansion of the national literature and culture to populace". (Luxemburg, 1908–09, p. 159)

In relation to his first factor, i.e., *the desire of the bourgeoisie to assure for itself an internal or domestic market for its own commodity production*, she insists against Kautsky that the bourgeoisie needs not only that but also "many other conditions for its proper development: a strong military, as a guarantee of the inviolability of this 'fatherland', as well as a tool to clear a path for itself in the world market; furthermore, it needs a suitable customs policy, suitable forms of administration in regard to communication, jurisdiction, school system, and financial policy. In a word, capitalism demands for its proper development not only markets, but also the whole apparatus of a modern capitalistic state". So, she says,

> the specific form of national aspirations, the true class interest of the bourgeoisie, is *state independence*. The nation-state is also simultaneously that indispensable historical form in which the bourgeoisie passes over from national defensive to an offensive position, from protection and concentration of its own nationality to political conquest and domination over other nationalities. Without exception, all of today's "nation-states" fit this description, annexing neighbors or colonies, and completely oppressing the conquered nationalities. (Luxemburg, 1908–09, pp. 162–163, emphasis in original)

And she looks at the Polish case where "we do not have to go far for an example, Polish bourgeois nationalism is directed as much against the Ruthenians as against the Lithuanians. The very nationality that had to endure the bitter policy of extermination by the partitioning powers – Prussia and Russia – now refuses the right of independent existence to other nationalities". (Luxemburg, 1908–09, p. 164)

Based on such analysis, she insists upon her core argument of Chapter 2: "The historical mission of the bourgeoisie is the creation of a modern 'national' state; but the historical task of the proletariat is the abolition of the state as a political form of capitalism, in which they themselves, as a conscious class, come into existence to establish the socialist system" (Luxemburg, 1908–09, p. 167).

What about the relation between the national question and the proletariat aiming for the abolition of the nation-state and establishment of socialism? This problem connects strongly with the national autonomy of the proletariat, i.e., Luxemburg's central theme. After she insists that "the *nation-state*, as an apparatus of the domination and conquest of foreign nationalities while indispensable for the bourgeoisie, has no meaning for the class interests of the proletariat", she explains the method to resolve the national question after the abolition of the states:

> Therefore, of these "three roots of the modern national idea" which Kautsky enumerated, for the proletariat as a class only the last two are important: democratic organization, and education of the populace. Vital for the working class as condition of its political and spiritual maturity, are the freedom in using its own national language, and the unchecked

and unwrapped development of national culture (learning, literature, the arts) and normal education of the masses, unimpaired by the pressures of the nationalists – so far as these can be "normal" in the bourgeois system. It is indispensable for the working class to have the same equal national rights as other nationalities in the state enjoy. Political discrimination against a particular nationality is the strongest tool in the hands of the bourgeoisie, which is eager to mask class conflicts and mystify its own proletariat. (Luxemburg, 1908–09, p. 169, emphasis in original)

3.3 Centralization or Local Autonomy

In her first chapter Luxemburg rejected the establishment of the *nation-state* by denying "the right of nation to self-determination" and, in Chapter 2, by insisting on the abolition of the *nation-state* from the standpoint of "the right of proletariat to self-determination". Thus, she imagined Polish autonomy beyond the modern nation-state. Her Chapter 3, "Federation, Centralization, and Particularism", and Chapter 4, "Centralization and Autonomy", have a role in introducing Chapter 5, "The National Question and Autonomy", and Chapter 6, "Autonomy of the Polish Kingdom". I will therefore consider here Chapter 3 and Chapter 4 together.

Among the three aspects in the title of Chapter 3, she rejects federation and particularism but supports centralization. It may look strange that she would support centralization against the other two since she is against the nation-state in principle and insists on Polish autonomy. So, why does she support centralization? According to her conception, she thought federation and particularism are reactionary before the historical development of the capitalism and that only centralization accommodates the development of the capitalism. Hence she wrote: "As capitalism develops, centralization increasingly pierces all obstacles and leads to a series of uniform institutions, not only within in each major state, but in the entire capitalistic world, by means of international legislation" (Luxemburg, 1908–09, p. 189–190). She saw this centralization as a necessary result of – in current terms – the globalization of capitalism's development. She thought that this centralization will make a basis of the socialism in the future. She writes:

> This central tendency of capitalistic development is one of the main bases of the future socialist system, because through the highest concentration of production and exchange, the ground is prepared for a socialized economy conducted on a worldwide scale according to uniform plan. On the other hand, only through consolidating and centralizing both the

state power and the working class as militant force does it eventually become possible for the proletariat to grasp the state power in order to introduce the dictatorship of the proletariat, a socialist revolution.

...

Therefore, the modern socialist movement, legitimate child of capitalistic development, possesses the same eminently centralistic characteristic as the bourgeois society and state. Consequently, Social Democracy is, in all countries, a determined opponent of particularism as well as of federalism....

Luxemburg, 1908–09, p. 190

Did Luxemburg really think that centralization is the necessary tendency of the capitalistic development and that capitalistic centralization will change at its highest point to the socialist movement which also includes the centralistic tendency? If she really thought that of socialism, what does her criticism mean against Lenin's "Organizational Problem of the Russian Social Democracy"? Her answer to this question is Chapter 4, "Centralization and Autonomy" which begins, "We have noted the general centralizing tendency of capitalism in the bourgeois state. But local autonomy also grows simultaneously out of the objective development and out of the needs of bourgeois society". (Luxemburg, 1908–09, p. 214)

Why does capitalistic development that includes necessarily the centralizing tendency also need local autonomy which seems to be against the centralizing tendency? Let us listen to Luxemburg's explanation: While the "centralism of the modern states is of necessity connected with a bureaucratic system", however,

Capitalist production and exchange are characterized by the highest sensitivity and elasticity, by the capacity, and even the inclination for constant change in connection with thousands of social influences which cause constant fluctuations and undulations in market conditions, and in the conditions of production themselves. As a result of these fluctuations, the bourgeois economy requires subtle, perceptive administration of public services such as the centralized bureaucracy, with its rigidity and routine, is not able to afford. Hence, already as a corrective to the centralism of the modern state, there develops, in bourgeois society, along with legislation by representative assemblies, a natural tendency toward local autonomy, giving the possibility of a better adjustment of the state apparatus to social needs. For local autonomy takes into account the manifold variety of local conditions and also bring about a direct influence and cooperation of society through its public functions. (Luxemburg, 1908–09, p. 215)

The local autonomy appears "as a corrective to the centralism of the modern state"; yet, at the same time, she did not overlook that local autonomy "originates in all modern states very early, above all in the form of transferring the material burden of a series of social functions to the population itself". Therefore, modern autonomy "in all these forms is by no means the abolition of state centralism but only its supplementation; together they constitute the characteristic form of the bourgeois state" (Luxemburg, 1908–09, pp. 215 and 217–218).

While, on the one hand, Luxemburg looks at the relation between the centralization and the local autonomy, on the other hand, she notices the contradiction and conflict between them.[4] The more capitalism enters into the period of imperialism, the more it needs a strong authority. "On the other hand, autonomy itself puts up barriers to legislative centralization, because without certain legislative competences, even narrowly outlined and purely local, no self-government is possible". Therefore, the "power of issuing within a certain sphere, of its own initiative, laws binding for the population, and not merely supervising the execution of laws issued by the central legislative body, constitutes precisely the soul and core of self-government in the modern democratic sense…" (Luxemburg, 1908–09, pp. 248). And she points out the role of the social democracy:

> Social Democracy defends the view that a commune, district, or province is a social body called upon to take care – in a local sphere – of a number of social matters and not only financial ones. The practical conclusion of those two theories is that the bourgeois parties insist that electoral rights to self-government bodies should be limited by a property qualification, while Social Democracy calls for a universal and equal electoral right for the whole population. (Luxemburg, 1908–09, p. 249)

Luxemburg concludes Chapter 4 by stating that "precisely from the same foundations from which, in all capitalistic states, grows local self-government, there also grows in certain conditions national autonomy, with local legislation as an independent manifestation of modern social development, which has as little in common with medieval particularism as the present-day city council has

---

4 Rosa Luxemburg uses here the two terms, *Samorzad lokalny (local autonomy)* and *Samorzad miejscowy (provincial autonomy)* in almost the same meaning.

with a parliament of the ancient Hanseatic republic" (Luxemburg, 1908–09, p. 250).

3.4 Conditions of "National Autonomy"
Luxemburg ends Chapter 4 by indicating that "there also grows in certain conditions national autonomy". The role of Chapter 5 is to consider what these "certain conditions" are.

From the end of the 19th century, especially in her dissertation *The Industrial Development of Poland* Luxemburg insisted that the capitalistic development of Poland needed the integration with the Russian market and thereby negated the possibility of the independence of Poland. Therefore, she emphasized the "National Autonomy" of Poland instead of the national independence of Poland. She explained the "certain conditions" of the "National Autonomy" as follows:

> Capitalism annihilated Polish national independence but at the same time created modern Polish national culture. This national culture is a product indispensable within the framework of bourgeois Poland; its existence and development are a historical necessity, connected with the capitalistic development itself. The development of capitalism, which chained Poland to Russia by socio-economic ties, undermined Russian absolutism, united and revolutionized the Russian and Polish proletariat as a class called upon to overthrow absolutism, and in this way created, under the Tsars, the indispensable preconditions for achieving political freedom. But within the framework and against the background of this general tendency toward the democratization of the state, capitalism at the same time knit more closely the socioeconomic and cultural-national life of the Polish kingdom, thus preparing the objective conditions for realization of Polish national autonomy. (Luxemburg, 1908–09, pp. 255–256)

Luxemburg insists here that the capitalistic development in Poland united Poland and Russia in socioeconomic ties and created solidarity between the Polish and Russian proletariat to undermine the Russian absolutism. At the same time, this general tendency toward the democratization of the state knit more closely the socioeconomic and cultural national life of the Polish Kingdom and prepared the objective conditions for the realization of Polish national autonomy.

National autonomy, however, is not possible everywhere under the social and cultural national lives. So, what are "the objective conditions for realization of Polish national autonomy"? She insists further that where "inside a modern state there exist distinct nationality districts constituting at the same time territories with certain economic and social distinctions, the same requirements of the bourgeois economy make self-government on the highest, country-wide level, indispensable. On this level, local self-government is also transformed, as a result of a new factor – national-cultural distinctness – into a special type of democratic institution applicable only in quite specific conditions". (Luxemburg, 1908–09, p. 256)

What we must notice here is that according to the requirements of the bourgeois economy, the local self-government is indispensable, yet at the same time, Luxemburg emphasizes that the local government is not always democratic, thus it must be transformed into "a special type of democratic institution applicable only in quite specific conditions". She further writes:

> The national autonomy of the Kingdom of Poland is primarily necessary for the Polish bourgeoisie to strengthen its class rule and to develop its institutions in order to exploit and oppress with no restrictions whatsoever. In the same way as the modern state-political parliamentary institutions, and, as their corollary, the institutions of local self-government are on a certain level an indispensable tool of bourgeois rule and a close harmonization of all state and social functions with the interests of the bourgeoisie, in a narrower sense, national autonomy is an indispensable tool of the strict application of the social functions in a certain territory to the special bourgeois interests of that territory. (Luxemburg, 1908–09, p. 258)

Furthermore, while she considers the "national autonomy" as the "most mature political form of bourgeois rule in Poland", she points out that "precisely for this reason, autonomy is an indispensable class need of the Polish proletariat" (Luxemburg, 1908–09, pp. 258–259). This observation is her special dialectical logic. "National autonomy has the same aims as are contained in the political program of the Polish proletariat: the overthrow of absolutism and the achievement of political freedom in the country at large; this is but a part of the program resulting both from the progressive trends of capitalist development and from the class interests of the proletariat" (Luxemburg, 1908–09, p. 259).

According to Luxemburg the national autonomy in Poland will be established after the overthrow of the Czarist absolutism and birth of the Russian Democratic Republic, but socioeconomically it will still be within the capitalistic system. This kind of the "national autonomy" is more favorable for the "self-determination of proletariat" compared to PPS's "independent" Poland that will be established by avoiding the struggles against Czarist absolutism.

But why will it be possible only in the Polish Kingdom? She answers this question by saying that "local autonomy in the sense of self-government of a certain nationality territory is only possible when the respective nationality possesses its own bourgeois development, urban life, intelligentsia, its own literary and scholarly life. The Congress Kingdom demonstrates all these conditions". (Luxemburg, 1908–09, p. 265)

From this point of view, Luxemburg considers the possibility of the national autonomy among Jew, Lithuanian, Byelorussian, Caucasus, etc. After her conclusion that there are no conditions for their national autonomy other than in Poland, she writes:

> Just as in Lithuania, the only method for settling the national question in the Caucasus, in the democratic spirit, securing to all nationalities freedom of cultural existence without any among them dominating the remaining ones, and at the same time meeting the recognized need for modern development, is to disregard ethnographic boundaries, and to introduce broad local self-government – communal, urban, district, and provincial – without a definite nationality character, that is, giving no privileges to any nationality. Only such a self-government will make it possible to unite various nationalities to jointly take care of the local economic and social interests, and on the other hand, to take into consideration in a natural way the different proportions of the nationalities in each country and each commune. (Luxemburg, 1908–09, p. 279)

Her solution to the national question was "broad local self-government without a definite nationality character giving no privileges to any nationality" and "only such a self-government will make it possible to unite various nationalities to jointly take care of the local economic and social interests".

3.5 The Domain of "Polish Autonomy"[5]

At the beginning of Chapter 6, "Autonomy of Polish Kingdom", Luxemburg summarizes her views. She writes on the nations and area outside of the Polish

---

5 [As noted by Ito in the second footnote to this chapter, this portion of Luxemburg's work is unavailable in English translation and most other languages, but was translated into Japanese. I believe Ito translated into English from the Japanese since his texts citing the Polish texts are not close enough to the Polish to suggest Ito's reading of the original Luxemburg (1909). Within this section only, as a consequence, I have removed quotation marks of texts

Kingdom and says national autonomy is not a political form which can be applied only to all national groups, nor a purely free ideal which will be aimed by the socialist under any condition. As the case of Lithuania shows, the application of autonomy would go against the freedom and democracy. Regarding the territory of the Polish Kingdom, the social, cultural and historical conditions of the country demand that autonomy in the Polish Kingdom be indispensable. Precisely for this reason, autonomy becomes a demand of the program for the Polish revolutionary proletariat. And Luxemburg firmly insists that *national autonomy* in the Polish Kingdom be based on the grounds that the capitalistic development there is higher compared to other nations and areas.

What is the necessity and merit of this argument? Chapter 6 was written to answer these questions. To do so, Luxemburg divides the otherwise inseparable discussion of the whole Polish Republic from a discussion with which the *national autonomy* must especially grapple. She recounts first trade and tariff. Then, traffic and communication. She sees that, if these issues were separated in the name of autonomy, such a policy would be against development and weaken labor's unity and unification. As far as the military is concerned, she insists upon abolishing the standing army and proposes the militia as the armament of all people. Regarding the taxation system, she insists on the abolition of all indirect taxes and explains the policy of the Social-Democratic Party in that the reform of the tax-system by the spirit of the social-democratic program is only possible in relation with reform of militarism, tariff-trade and world policy. The general and fundamental legislation of the tax-system must belong to the domain of the central parliament and derive from the nature of the capitalistic development as well as from the fundamental position of the Social-Democracy.

She further insists that public education, civil law, and criminal procedure code as well as legislation to protect laborers should be united within the Republic (Luxemburg, 1909, p. 351). Also she writes that in the area in which the democracy should in general guarantee such rights as those of coalition, association, assembly as well as freedom of speech and press, there needs to be central legislation. So, she was against the division and decentralization since reference to de-centralism is solely used by the reactionary such as a means of conspiracy in the Republic of Switzerland as well as in the Monarchy of Germany (Luxemburg, 1909, p. 356).

---

citing Luxemburg (1909) and left the relevant portions as paraphrases, rather than in Ito's English original. P.Z.].

If the fundamental part of the people's life would be decided by the central government and the Parliament of the Republic, where is the basis of the *national autonomy*?

What Luxemburg indicates as a task of the *domestic autonomy* is creation and development of public education and other fields such as agriculture, forestry, mining, traffic on the sea and land, and public health. First, she insists on public education belonging naturally to a competence within autonomy. The long experiences of all cultural states prove that public education cannot well exist if it were not organized by the organization of autonomy under the positive participation of the interested inhabitants. Second, the problem of public education is indivisibly connected as a thread of national life, that is, with the original language and spiritual culture of the each nation (Luxemburg, 1909, p. 356).

The situation for education of Polish people under Russian domination since 1815, which Luxemburg shows as a reason and background for her insistence, was cruel. Each fact which she exhibits overlaps with the facts elsewhere such as the Japanese domination of the people of Ainu, Taiwan, and Korea. The feudalistic rule of the Polish aristocracy and Russian colonial rule deprived Polish people of public education and pushed them into spiritual poverty. Therefore, she writes that as far as public education is concerned, in the country the legislation and administration of autonomy – after removal of the characterized works by managers of the Czar – will stay total *tabula rasa* upon which must be constructed a whole new building of the public education system from the ground to top – with the direct participation of the mass of the people. Whole re-building of the public education system means not only that general education and the elementary, middle and higher school especially must respond to the social request, but also include all institutes of the spiritual culture which were neglected by the administration of the absolutism, that is, institutions for scientific study and experiment, supporting funds for scientific study, school for arts and museum, etc. (Luxemburg, 1909, pp. 370–371) Incidentally, it might be added, in 1900 Luxemburg wrote an article "For Defense of Nationality" ("W obronie narodwosci") to protest strongly against the abolition of the Polish lectures in the schools in Posen under the Prussian rule.

In "The National Question and Autonomy" Luxemburg criticized the destruction of national culture under the Russian rule. She would close this long series of articles published from August 1908 until September 1909 via a letter to Jogiches:

> If we add to the above mentioned areas and concerning legislation for public health including hospitals and every kind of medical institutions,

we arrive at the legislation and administration of autonomy, that is, the original culture, the culture of economic, social and spiritual activities. This culture has the most local and national character and connects directly with the interests of all the local inhabitants.

To arrange the vast interests of these material and spiritual culture as much as possible from the standpoint of revolution and social progress, and also from the standpoint of the working mass of people is the original task of administration. The working class of the Kingdom of Poland must make solidarity with the proletariat in the whole country to consciously point out this task.

> Luxemburg, 1971, p. 24

3.6 Is "The National Question and Autonomy" an Unfinished Work?

There is a conception that Luxemburg's series of articles "The National Question and Autonomy" is an unfinished work. This originates from Warski's 1929 article in the Polish magazine *Z Pola Walki* (From Battle Field) in which he said:

> Only by reading quickly the last chapter of her articles ("The National Question and Autonomy") can we see that she did not finish her work. She did not want to answer this point. She would not explain its reason. But anyway it looks to me that she wanted to take this problem completely out from her memory. However, when we read from her letters the history of the demand for autonomy in Lithuania, her article "What We Want" and other articles in the *Przeglad Socjaldemokratyczny* (Social-Democratic Review), she arrived at a result that it lacks some element for solving completely the national question for the nations under the Czarist Empire. (Warski, 1929)

Feliks Tych, editor of Luxemburg's letters to Jogiches, introduced Warski's article in his own footnote to her letter dated May 25, 1909 (Luxemburg, 1971, p. 24). But the explanation regarding the unfinished part of "The National Question and Autonomy" is only based on Warski's conjecture, while Luxemburg herself did not so state and did not later add to the article. This does not mean that "The National Question and Autonomy" is a completed work.

Luxemburg wrote to Jogiches in her letter dated August 10, 1909:

> My plan of work on autonomy is the following: Till now I argued the area belonging to the central authority, now I argue the area of autonomy. The latter was essential because otherwise after highlighting the authority of

the central parliament, an impression must be avoided that nothing was left for the Sejmu (local parliament) and that our *autonomy* was a lie. (Luxemburg, 1971, p. 45)

I suppose she wrote the last part of Chapter 6 (of "The National Question and Autonomy") with such an anxiety. Nevertheless, her explanation on the question why *national autonomy* has a possibility only in Poland is not enough. Further, if the national question could be solved in another district composed of many nationalities, the following question will arises: why must only Poland persist in *national autonomy*? Nevertheless, I understand that "The National Question and Autonomy" is not an article that argued the national question in general, but explained the national question in Poland from the viewpoint of the *Autonomy in Poland*.

4 Criticism and an Evaluation of "The National Question and Autonomy"

4.1 *Lenin's Criticism*

Lenin was the first person who violently criticized Luxemburg's "The National Question and Autonomy". Yet Lenin wrote his criticism after October 1913, four years after the publication of her work in 1909.

The relationship between Lenin and Luxemburg was very good when she had published her article. However, many problems arose between them after 1910, such as: (1) her party, the SDKPiL, tried mediating the split and antagonism between Bolsheviks and Mensheviks; (2) the relationship between the German Social-Democratic Party and Lenin's Bolsheviks became worst because of the antagonism about the management of the Bolshevik's funds (see Laschitza, 1996, pp. 404–409);[6] (3) as a result of Lenin's intervention into internal antagonisms within the SDKPiL so that after 1912 relations between them became poor; and (4) especially after the disclosure that Lenin met Pilsudski, Luxemburg's political enemy as a leader of PPS, leading to the relationship between them becoming still worse.

An article in which Lenin criticized her "The National Question and Autonomy" was titled "Critical Remarks on the National Question" (written in October–December 1913). He might have read the Russian translation of her

---

6 Also, Dietrich Geyer, "Kautsky's Russisches Dossier. Deutsche Sozialdemokraten als Treuhander des russischen Parteivermogens 1910–1915", Internationales Institut für Sozialgeschichte, Amsterdam: Campus Verlag, 1981.

work in a village near by Cracow.⁷ I would guess that Lenin read her work after their relationship became poor.

A main subject of the "Critical Remarks" was cultural-national autonomy, insisted upon by the Jewish Party Bund. But at the end of this article Lenin criticized Luxemburg's article. Lenin wrote that "Rosa Luxemburg admits – and being a Marxist she is of course bound to admit – that all the major and important economic and political questions of capitalist society must be dealt with exclusively by the central parliament of the whole country concerned, not by the autonomous Diet of the individual regions". He stands here on the same ground as Luxemburg. Then he criticizes her: "One cannot help smiling ... when reading how our magnificent Rosa Luxemburg tries to prove, with a very serious air and 'pure Marxist' phrases, that the demand for autonomy is applicable *only* to Poland and *only* by way of exception!" (Lenin, 1913–14, pp. 46–47, emphasis in original)

Lenin had clearly misread her text; perhaps he read an inexact Russian translation. She did not wish to prove that the demand of autonomy can be applied only in Poland as an exception. Rather, she separated the general *regional autonomy* and the *national autonomy* and tried to prove that *national autonomy* can be applied only in Poland. As I already mentioned in the previous section, this separation has no persuasiveness. Nevertheless, she persisted upon this theory because she had to compete with the argument of PPS for the recovery of the independent Poland State. The basis of her argument that *national autonomy* can be applied only in Poland was as follows:

> [L]ocal autonomy in the sense of the self-government of a certain nationality territory is only possible where the respective nationality possesses its own bourgeois development, urban life, intelligentsia, its own literary and scholarly life. The Congress Kingdom demonstrates all these conditions. Its population is nationally homogeneous because the Polish element has a decisive preponderance over other nationalities in the country's whole area, with the exception of the Suwałki gubernia in which the Lithuanians prevail. (Luxemburg, 1908–09, p. 265)

Luxemburg insists that in the area of the Polish population the development of capitalism and culture is advantageous compared with another area and nationality, and the Polish population is uniform and overwhelmingly a majority

---

7   Lenin, "Note on the National problem (II)", 1912, in Krakow. [This is Ito's citation, p. 51, fn. 133, that I have not located. The "village nearby Krakow" mentioned in the text is most likely Poronin where Lenin lived from May 1913; if so, 1912 should be 1913, P.Z.].

except for two prefectures. "Thus, in all the gubernias except two, and in the country as a whole, the Polish element constitutes more than 70 percent of the population; it is, moreover, the decisive element in sociocultural development of the country" (Luxemburg, 1908–09, p. 266).

If we look at another side of her explanation, less than 30% of the population in Poland was not Polish. They belong to another nationality. Must they then live outside of the Polish national autonomy? No, they should live equally in Poland (as I noted above when citing her concerning broad self-government in connection with Caucasus). Therefore, I wonder why she must apply the national autonomy only to Poland. My guess is that the reason she persisted on *national autonomy* in Poland was that she must oppose the recovery of independent Poland argued by the PPS. In any case, Lenin disregarded the difference between the *national autonomy* and *general autonomy* that Luxemburg made, and denied *autonomy in general*, because he believed that *autonomy* fundamentally opposes the *self-determination of the nation*.

Lenin wrote his second long article "The Right of Nations to Self-Determination" (February–May 1914) to criticize again Luxemburg's "The National Question and Autonomy", Lenin writing now a very emotional sentiment. It is not a polemic, but almost abusive. Relation between her party (SDKPiL) and his party (RSDLP) was at its worse and Lenin attacked Luxemburg extremely. Hence, this article by Lenin is at the lowest level among his works, and theoretical difference between them is very clear.

4.2 Nation-State vs. Autonomy

Lenin's theory of nationalism completely depends on Karl Kautsky's theory. In the first section "What Is Meant by the Self-Determination of Nations" of his article, he expresses irritation that Luxemburg did not accept Kautsky's theory, and he intimidated her: "A precise formulation of this question, which no Marxist can avoid, would at once destroy nine-tenths of Rosa Luxemburg's arguments" (Lenin, 1913–14, p. 396).

Lenin's argument in this article, in my view, is summarized in the following sentence: "Consequently, if we want to grasp the meaning of self-determination of nations, not by juggling it with a legal definition, or 'inventing' abstract definitions, but by examining the historico-economic conditions of the national movement, we must inevitably reach the conclusion that the self-determination of nations means the political separation of these nations from alien national bodies, and the formation of an independent national state". (Lenin, 1913–14, p. 397)

If I would state their antagonism in short, it would be *nation-state* (but there is no *pure national state*, therefore the *nation-state* in the ideological meaning) versus *autonomy*. But we should not forget that her article "The National Question and Autonomy" does not deal the *national question* in general but the national question in Poland only from the standpoint of *autonomy*. Luxemburg opposed the PPS which, under Russian rule, insisted upon the recovery of the Polish State dominated earlier by Polish aristocracy (Szlachta). At the same time, she tried to make solidarity with the Russian labor party to fight together with them against the Russian rule. Therefore, she insisted upon not *national independence* but *autonomy*.

Lenin belonged to the ruling nationality and could not understand such a difficult position as Luxemburg's and the SDKPiL's. Because he did not understand such a difficult position, he pushed all nationalities under Russian rule by his theory of the *national self-determination* in order to get out psychologically as quickly as possible from his *national yoke* of the ruling nationality. And he made accusations against those who would not accept his national theory. For example, he accused Luxemburg:

> It is here that we come up against the weakest point in Rosa Luxemburg's arguments. With extraordinary zeal, she embellishes her article with a collection of hard words directed against article 9 of our Programme, which she declares to be "sweeping", "a platitude", "a metaphysical phrase", and so on without end. It would be natural to expect an author who so admirably condemns metaphysics (in the Marxist sense, i.e. anti-dialectics) and empty abstractions to set us an example of how to make a concrete historical analysis of the question. The question at issue is the national program of the Marxists of a definite country – Russia, in a definite period – the beginning of the twentieth century. But does Rosa Luxemburg raise the question as to *what historical* period Russia is passing through, or *what are the concrete* features of the national question and the national movement of that *particular* country in that *particular* period?
>
> No, she does not! *She says absolutely nothing about it!* In her work you will not find even the shadow of an analysis of how the national question stands in *Russia* in the present historical period, or of the special features of *Russia* in this particular respect! (Lenin, 1913–14, p. 402, emphasis in original)

The subject of her article, however, is the solution of the Polish question. Therefore, it is very natural that she deals with the Russian national problem only in the context in the Polish question.

It is obvious that the way to deal the Russian problem belongs to Lenin, but he still puts strange questions. "When, in her anxiety not to 'assist' the nationalist bourgeoisie of Poland, Rosa Luxemburg rejects the *right* to secession in the program of the Marxists *in Russia*, she is in fact assisting the Great-Russian Black Hundreds" (Lenin, 1913–14, p. 412, emphasis in original). However, Luxemburg and the Polish Social Democrats of the SDKPiL fought against the Polish nationalists, the Polish Socialist Party (PPS). So, they must reject *the right to secession in the programme of the RSDLP* because they cannot fight together with Russian comrades if the RSDLP holds in their program *the right to secession*. Why then must Luxemburg be accused that they are *assisting the Great-Russian Black Hundreds*? To fight against *Great-Russian Black Hundreds* is the task of Lenin and the Russian socialists, but not task of Luxemburg and the Polish Social Democrats. That is a preposterously unjust charge to make against Luxemburg and the Polish socialists.

In this article, Lenin is arrogant and would not cut out "the right of nations to self-determination" from the program of his party. His argument became no more logical in its last part. For example, he explains the right to secession compared with the right to divorce as follows: "To accuse those who support freedom of self-determination, i.e., freedom to secede, of encouraging separatism, is as foolish and hypocritical as accusing those who advocate freedom of divorce of encouraging the destruction of family ties" (Lenin, 1913–14, p. 422). This is an absurd and unreasonable analogy. Luxemburg did not oppose absolutely "the right of nations to self-determination". Her opposition depends on the case. She had written that in her article: "On the basis of the general assumptions of historical materialism, the position of socialists with respect to nationality problems depends primarily on the concrete circumstances of each case, which differ significantly among countries, and also change in the course of time in each country" (Luxemburg, 1908–09, p. 112). But Lenin denounces Luxemburg for "her inability to see things from a viewpoint any deeper and broader than that of the Cracow anthill" (Lenin, 1913–14, p. 426).

This is a very discriminating attitude toward a Jewish woman born in Poland by Lenin who belongs to a big nation. What was important for her was to fight against the Polish national-chauvinism. It was necessary for her to cut out the *right on nations to self-determination* from the program of the RSDLP. Her policy stands on the Polish concrete situation at that time even from the *viewpoint of the Cracow anthill*.

At the end of his article, Lenin writes: "In 1906 the Polish Marxists joined the Party: *neither* upon joining *nor* afterwards (at the Congress of 1907, the conferences of 1907 and 1908, or the plenum of 1910) *did they introduce* a single proposal to amend the article 9 of the Russian Programme!" (Lenin, 1913–14, p. 446, emphasis in original) This is also a lie. At the time of the unity of two parties, on April 1906, the Bolsheviks cut out one clause in the contract presented by

SDKPiL but without agreement (see Ito, 2010, Section 5.3, pp. 25–29). And her long article "The National Question and Autonomy", which Lenin denounced harshly, had been written to request Lenin to cut out article 9 from the Russian Program.

4.3 Theoretical Differences between Lenin and Luxemburg and Historical Reality

What was Lenin's attitude later after he denounced Luxemburg? He wrote as follows in a 1916 article "Discussion on Self-Determination Summed Up":

> We do not want to haggle over words. If there is a party that says in its programme (or in a resolution binding on all – the form does not matter) that it is against annexation, against the forcible retention of oppressed nations within the frontiers of *its* state, we declare our complete agreement in principle with that party. It would be absurd to insist on the *word* "self-determination". And if there are people in our Party who want to change *words* in this spirit, who want to amend Clause 9 of our Party Programme, we should consider our difference with *such* comrades to be anything but a matter of principle! (Lenin, 1916, p. 329, emphasis in original)

Note the difference in tone from 1914 when he had accused Luxemburg of "her inability to see things from a viewpoint any deeper and broader than that of the Cracow anthill", just because she wanted to take out article 9 from Lenin's Party Program. I wonder, did Lenin really write this article by himself? Further down the article,

> take Poland's *specific* conditions in place of these general arguments: her independence *today* is "impracticable" without wars or revolution. To be in favour of an all-European war merely for the sake of restoring Poland is to be a nationalist of the worst sort, and to place the interests of a small number of Poles above those of the hundreds of millions of people who suffer from war. Such indeed, are the "Fracy" (the Right wing of the P.S.P.) who are socialists only in word, and compared with whom the Polish Social-Democrats are a thousand times right. To raise the question of Poland's independence *today*, with the *existing* alignment of the *neighbouring* imperialist powers, is really to run after a will-o'-the-wisp, plunge into narrow-minded nationalism and forget the necessary premise of an all-European or at least a Russian and a German revolution. (Lenin, 1916, p. 350, emphasis in original)

What Lenin is now writing in 1916 was precisely what Luxemburg and the Polish Social Democrats had insisted in 1903.

Did Luxemburg and Lenin theoretically completely match? Speaking plainly, the theoretical difference between them lay in the point whether they admitted the formation of the State or not. The reason why Lenin persisted to keep article 9 of their Party Program was because Lenin thought that the formation of the State, namely division and independence, is inevitable in order to solve the national question of the oppressed nationalities. For example, Lenin writes in his *theses* "The Socialist Revolution and the Right of Nations to Self-Determination" (January–February 1916):

> Victorious socialism must necessarily establish a full democracy and, consequently, not only introduce full equality of nations but also realize the right of oppressed nations to self-determination, i.e., the right to free political separation. Socialist parties which did not show by all their activity, both now, during the revolution, and after its victory, that they would liberate the enslaved nations and build up relations with them on the basis of a free union – and free union is a false phrase without the right to secede – these parties would be betraying socialism. (Lenin, 1916, p. 143)

But at the same time, he writes: "The aim of socialism is not only to end the division of mankind into tiny states and the isolation of nations in any form, it is not only to bring the nations closer together but to integrate them" (Lenin, 1916, p. 146).

The difference between Lenin and Luxemburg lay in the issue that Lenin insisted upon the *right to free political separation* of oppressed nations as a precondition for *free union*. Luxemburg insisted that what is important is not the *right to self-determination of the states* but rather the *right to self-determination of the people* and strongly rejected the *formation of the nation-state*. Luxemburg put the right of *people* against the s*t*ate because the state always includes a *minority* and constitutes the class society. Her fundamental principle was that the *state and socialism cannot coexist*. On the other hand, what is important is that Lenin and Luxemburg had the same aim, that is, *free union of all the nationalities* albeit through different means.

After the collapse of the Russian Empire, Lenin designed the formation of many small independent states and Luxemburg wanted the Polish autonomy in the vast Russian Republic. However, the collapse of the Russian Empire by the Russian revolution and the collapse of the German and Austrian Empires by the defeat in the World War I liberated at once the nationalities under the rule of these empires which began to move the dynamics of class struggle in each nation. This was a course that Luxemburg as well as Lenin did not foresee. Poland got independence because of the defeat of the three empires which had dominated Poland, against Luxemburg's expectation. Her hope to establish Polish autonomy in the Russian Republic vanished. Pilsudski, Luxemburg's political enemy, formed an independent Republic of Poland and raised war against Lenin's Russia (1919–1921).

Among the nationalities under the rule of the Russian Empire, Poland, Finland, Estonia, Latvia, and Lithuania became independent states. Other nationalities such as Ukraine, Belarus, Caucasus, in 1922 after the end of the Civil War, gathered to build the Union of Soviet Socialist Republics (USSR) together with Russia. Later, in 1924 Uzbekistan and Turkmenistan, in 1929 Tadzikistan, and in 1936 Azerbaydzhan, Armenia, Gruzia, Kazakhstan, and Kirgiztan joined the USSR. In 1940 Estonia, Latvia, Lithuania, and a part of Finland were forced to integrate into USSR. Lenin had written in his article "The Right of Nations to Self-Determination" that "Marxists cannot include the defense of federalism in general in their programme" (Lenin, 1913–14, p. 441, fn. *). History showed another reality against Lenin's theory.

4.4   Luxemburg's Theory on the National Question

Paradoxically speaking, Luxemburg developed her theory on national question after her work "The National Question and Autonomy", written to solve the national question of Poland from the viewpoint of *autonomy*. She did not argue about the national question in general. Her argument on the national question in general was developed later as the arguments on imperialism in works such as *The Accumulation of Capital*, "The Crisis in German Social Democracy", and "The Russian Revolution".

Lenin became irritated when Luxemburg did not accept Kautsky's theory on nationalism that "for the whole of Western European, nay, for the entire civilized world, the national state is *typical* and normal for the capitalist period". He abused her in that article, "The Right of Nations to Self-Determination", when he wrote that a "precise formulation of this question, which no Marxist can avoid, would at once destroy nine-tenths of Luxemburg's arguments" (Lenin, 1913–14, pp. 397 and 396, respectively)

At that time, what Luxemburg put against the *national state* of Kautsky was the *imperial state*. She wrote as follows in her work "The National Question and Autonomy":

> The form that best serves the interests of exploitation in the contemporary world is not the "national" state, as Kautsky thinks, but a state bent

on conquest.... [D]o we look to the British and German states as models, for they are based on national oppression in Europe and the world at large – and to the United States of America, a state which keeps in its bosom like a gaping wound the oppression of the Negro people, and seeks to conquer the Asiatic peoples. (Luxemburg, 1908–09, p. 131)

She wrote this in 1908. Later in her *Accumulation of Capital* she described minutely using many documents and materials how the European states penetrated into the non-capitalist areas to invade and exploit and became the *conquering state*. After the publication of the book, Lenin accused her: "After reading such arguments, one cannot help marveling at the author's ability to misunderstand" (Lenin, 1913–14, p. 398).

This was Lenin's level of argumentation in 1914. Sumio Takanashi, the Japanese scholar, analyzed Lenin's argument as follows:

As far as I read Lenin's *The Right of Nations to Self-Determination* the opinions of Lenin and Rosa Luxemburg clash each other and do not engage, because their standpoints are completely different. Lenin argues the national question from the standpoint of the bourgeois democratic revolution, but Rosa Luxemburg stands on the precondition of imperialism. To speak more critically of Lenin, in June 1914 he had not yet established his understanding of the imperialism. That was a reason why their debate was fruitless.[8]

This is a very sharp remark. He quoted from Luxemburg's work after the outbreak of World War I, "The Junius Pamphlet: The Crisis in German Social Democracy", and he also point out that the "invasion of the big powers of imperialism into the Balkan countries changed the slogan for the national unity and the building up of the independent state". Indeed, wrote Luxemburg:

Imperialism, with all its brutal policy of force, with the incessant chain of social catastrophe that it itself provokes, is, to be sure, a historic necessary for the ruling classes of the present world. Yet nothing could be more detrimental than that the proletarians should derive, from the present war, the slightest hope or illusion of the possibility of an idyllic and peaceful development of capitalism. (Luxemburg, 1915, pp. 337–338)

---

8 Sumio Takanashi, "The National Question and Lenin," BOC Publishing House, 1987, p. 47. [This is Ito's citation, p. 68, fn. 154–155, I have not located; likewise for the following citation, P.Z.].

Luxemburg had watched the rise of imperialism since the end of the 19th century, and after the publication of her work "The National Question and Autonomy", she analyzed in many facets imperialism in *Accumulation of Capital*, "The Crisis in German Social Democracy", and "The Russian Revolution" which I have already mentioned, as well as in "Fragment on War, National Question and Revolution" and "Fragment on the History of the 1st and 2nd International and for the Problems of the Postwar" (Luxemburg, 1996, p. 580). In these works, she describes imperialism and nationalism as the front and the back. For instance, German imperialism organized German nationalism to build the war system including German social democracy. But in this chapter I have focused on her "The National Question and Autonomy".

5 Epilogue

Let's go back to the question at the beginning of this essay. Was, for Luxemburg, the National Question an Aporia – a problem which is impossible to solve?

From her personal history (Ito, 2010, pp. 59–61), we can know that Luxemburg's internationalism was not only her political policy and philosophical ideology. It comes directly from her heart. Hence, she stands always on the side of the oppressed and discriminated. This might be the origin of her national question. For her, the nationalities are always a real existence, and support and help each other, not an *illusion connected with powerful state*. The nationalists, however, connect always with *states*. They wish to expand their *states* not only in their illusion, but also in the world. Invasion, national struggle, and war take away the illusion of nationalism. Nationalists cover up their class contradiction in their society and put it onto the other nation. As a result, strong states oppress weak states. The typical examples are invasions into Afghanistan by Soviet Union in the 1980s and by the United States of America, and also invasion into Iraq, by the Bush administration. Therefore, the solution of the national questions depends on the international democracy. We use often the phrase *democratic state*. But the *democratic state* originally cannot exist. As Luxemburg insisted, the state and democracy cannot coexist. The solution of the national question is not *Aporia*. It will be solved only by the people's power, mutual support, and help of the many people beyond the national border and the nation-states.

It depends on the people of the 21st century how and when they will be able to abolish the state from the Earth.

CHAPTER 11

Marxism, Machiavellianism, and Conspiracy Theory

Adam Smith's *Wealth of Nations* contains a rather long passage that speaks to the behavior of capitalists regarding wages for workers. Capitalist masters are in "combinations", secret ones, against workers:

> We rarely hear, it has been said, of the combinations of masters, though frequently of those of workmen. But whoever imagines, upon this account, that masters rarely combine, is as ignorant of the world as of the subject. Masters are always and everywhere in a sort of tacit, but constant and uniform combination, not to raise the wages of labour above their actual rate.... We seldom, indeed, hear of this combination, because it is the usual, and one may say, the natural state of things which nobody ever hears of. Masters too sometimes enter into particular combinations to sink the wages of labour even below this rate. These are always conducted with the utmost silence and secrecy, till the moment of execution, and when the workmen yield, as they sometimes do, without resistance, though severely felt by them, [the combinations of masters] are never heard of by other people.... (Smith, 1776, pp. 66f)

Smith is discussing the relationship of capitalists to their workers, not either classes' relation to the state. He is describing a *conspiracy* by capitalists around wages.

While Smith was not discussing the role of a state in engaging in conspiracies, in 1852, Marx would. But let's go back a few years.

Around the same time that Marx and Engels were writing *The Communist Manifesto*, Abraham Lincoln in the U.S. House of Representatives as newly elected Representative was raising questions directed at President James Polk as to how the Mexican-American war was initiated, given a U.S. boundary treaty with Mexico. Indeed, he was submitting resolutions for House consideration as to the spot that the claimed military incident had occurred. Lincoln was asking whether President Polk had provoked the war by falsely claiming territory above the Rio Grande as being U.S., not Mexican, in spite of treaty stating otherwise. He was asking if the President was perhaps lying and engaging in a conspiracy for a war of conquest.

Although Lincoln, and Whigs generally, raised the issue of a Presidential lie being the basis of the war, and although that controversy was out in the open,

Marx and Engels initially failed to see the issue of a possible lie or that slave-owning interests could be behind the U.S. expansionary interests. Indeed, I noted in Chapter 7 that they seemed supportive of the U.S. side. Their failure to see a conspiracy, however, did not long last, as they were educated by events elsewhere. And, by the time of the U.S. Civil War, both Marx and Engels became aware of the slave-owning interests involved. Perhaps they also learned that they should earlier have been paying more attention to Lincoln in the U.S. House of Representatives. Perhaps they even gave some thought to a "detail" – the "spot" where the earlier war had started. Political knowledge is acquired by experience and the decade and half since Polk's war undoubtedly educated both to realities that were not transparent.

Insufficient attention in Marxist thought has been provided to the distinction between the concealed, secret, and indeed conspiratorial, compared to acts that are open; but this neglect cannot be laid too much on Marx himself. His 1852 analysis in *Cologne Communist Trial* exposed the arrest and imprisonment of German communist leaders achieved through the conspiratorial networks of the Prussian secret police. The resulting beheading of the German workers' movement destroyed resistance in that country for more than a decade. More personally, Prussian intelligence bought and paid for Marx and Engels' satirical 1852 pamphlet *The Great Men of Exile* that attacked rival émigré groups in England; they were shocked when learning that their erstwhile collaborator on the pamphlet, a Hungarian named Bangya, was an agent of Prussia's extensive secret apparatus (Fernbach, 1973, pp. 7–8). Marx's account of the rise to power of Louis Bonaparte will be examined in Section 2 here. All are examples of the advancing education of Marx and Engels into political realities, realities not to be ignored. The sections that follow explore the complexities of conspiracies.

1 Conspiracies and Marxist Theory of the Nation State

> "The insult of truth"
> Hervey Allen, *Anthony Adverse*, p. 1212

Care is warranted when considering any charge of a conspiracy. While the allies in World War I were not totally innocent about the Lusitania sinking, the U-boot was surely German. Although President Roosevelt has been charged with allowing the destruction of Pearl Harbor to occur knowing in advance the attack plans, the attacking planes were Japanese. Contrasted to responsibilities by the attacker, levels of responsibility on the side of those attacked were more in the order of a manipulation. Still, incidents can be manufactured by governments for Machiavellian acts, wishing to gain thereby. Citizens may be quite willing to accept that governments *other than their own* could engage in such acts, *pace,* the Mukden (or Manchurian) 1931 incident initiating the Japanese war in Asia, or the Gleiwitz (Germany) 1939 incident initiating the Nazi war in Europe. Truth seems harder to accept when such possibilities of a conspiracy refer to one's own government, particularly around the time of occurrence and with heavy propaganda. It becomes an "insult of truth" in the face of inculcated nationalism.

Any sustainable assertion of a conspiracy in a specific instance requires careful attention to evidence. If witches were not conspiring in Salem, but President Nixon with others were conspiring regarding Watergate, neither informs us about the murders of the two Kennedys, Malcolm X, or King, U.S.'s September 11th, London bombing in 2005, etc. We must examine evidence, unafraid of answers. Some may raise a concern as to whether accurate knowledge of such conspiracies is of importance, given the problem of their concealed nature, their lack of transparency. Does accurate rendering of the USS *Maine* in 1898, or Mukden in 1931 or Gleiwitz in 1939 matter? Does it matter who caused the death of Kennedy? Yet it must, since in each of the cases, the allegations as to the perpetrators (collective or individual) were very major foci for subsequent state practices.

After elucidation in Section 2 of Marx's understanding of the French state under Louis Bonaparte, in Section 3, important 19th and 20th century episodes are surveyed showing a wide variety that cannot be reduced to one label. Then the Kennedy assassination of 1963 is discussed in Section 4, while Section 5 addresses the King assassination in 1968 and subsequent civil trial. Finally, we consider the evidence concerning the U.S.'s September 11th (Chile had its own September 11th in 1973).

These turning-point events are presented here to motivate/reinforce serious, objective discussion within Marxist thought of possible conspiratorial acts of a capitalist state, acts that interface with recognizable, publicly-known facts.

2   Marx on Louis Bonaparte's Conspiratorial Coup

The fundamental Marxist notion that the capitalist state is a masked form of bourgeois rule, i.e., a covert meeting of minds to monopolize the means of production and power, is itself an accusation of conspiracy on the grandest of historical scales. This is the primary message of Marx's 1852 classic *The Eighteenth Brumaire of Louis Bonaparte*, which followed upon his prior *The Class Struggles in France: 1848–1850* (C.W., Vol. 11, and Vol. 10, respectively). Together they discuss the means by which the actors conspired (with the critical assistance of the military) to retain their stranglehold on French society during the bloody aftermath of the Revolutions of 1848. Perhaps an advance warning of the potential for bourgeois democracy to slide into fascist dictatorship, *The Eighteenth Brumaire* is much more, as it stands as a primer on the conspiratorial and secret devices regularly employed in times of crisis by the bourgeoisie to maintain sway over civil society, even to the extent (in the French case) of foisting a Swiss-naturalized parvenu named Louis Bonaparte into power, contradicting a constitutional requirement and with a person who had been a former English special constable (*C.W.*, Vol. 11, p. 119).

Page after page of *Brumaire* concerns undercover machinations among various political contenders for power in France. Unlike earlier work of Marx, these pages instead replaced an earlier conviction in "*The German Ideology* to *The Class Struggles in France*, that the nature of society and its relationship to politics were becoming increasingly visible" (Seigel, 1978, p. 203). *Brumaire* went below the surface, the most prominent motif from the start being the conscious intent of Bonaparte, along with his military allies and lumpenproletarian enforcers, to bring about, by whatever covert means required, the replacement of democratic rule in France with a proto-fascist dictatorship dedicated above all to preserving bourgeois relations of production.

The persuasiveness of Marx's account was hardly the conventional view of the period.[1] Marx's chronology of parliamentary seizure relies on a sophisticated and then-unrivaled appreciation of complex social class forces at work in France and points to the dark, conspiratorial figure of Bonaparte as an overwhelming presence concomitant with the cowardice of various factions among the republican bourgeoisie. Marx's essay with its 1850 predecessor can teach us that episodes of "bourgeois terrorism" periodically remove the mask of benign legitimacy that veils capitalist rule in more "normal" times.

The events are covered in more detail in MacGregor and Zarembka (2010). Back in June 1848 the Parisian proletariat, then leaderless, responded to incendiary provocations by mounting a "gigantic insurrection" against the French Provisional Government. General Cavaignac, head of the republican Provisional Government and fresh from savage Algerian campaigns that helped cement French colonialism in northern Africa, put down the workers' insurrection

---

1 "*The Eighteenth Brumaire*, which proves that Marx was the only historian and politician of 1848 who understood and disclosed the real nature of the causes and results of the coup d'état of December 2, 1851, was completely ignored. In spite of the actuality of the work not a single bourgeois newspaper even mentioned it". (Lafargue, 1890).

with the usual bourgeois methods; more than 3000 captured insurgents were brutally murdered by Cavaignac's troops and an additional 15,000 workers deported (*c.w.*, Vol. 10, p. 68 and Vol. 11, pp. 118–119). Says Marx, "bourgeois rule, freed from all fetters, was bound to turn immediately into *bourgeois terrorism*" (*c.w.*, Vol. 10, p. 69, emphasis in original). Thereafter, Louis Bonaparte won election by universal male suffrage on December 10, 1848, almost six months after Cavaignac's slaughter, most of the votes coming from the French peasantry.

With his presidential term slated to end in May 1852, Bonaparte, after a series of manufactured crises, dissolved the Republic on December 2, 1851, and bombarded Paris with incendiary rockets two days later. Preparation for the December 1851 coup had begun two and a half years earlier that would lead to the elimination of the Party of Order as an alternative. Bonaparte's surprise assault had been, in fact, foretold. "If ever an event has, well in advance of its coming, cast its shadow before it, it was Bonaparte's coup d'état. As early as January 29, 1849, barely a month after his election, he had made a proposal about it to Changarnier". (*c.w.*, Vol. 11, p. 176) Rumors of a coup d'état had multiplied during 1851, and murder plots, parliamentary chaos, mass arrests, and suspected communist conspiracies turned the bourgeoisie against its own creation, the democratic republic, and pushed it into the welcoming arms of Bonaparte who demanded, "*Rather an end with terror than terror without end!*" (p. 176, emphasis in original).

Bonaparte deftly maneuvered France toward the brink. The ruthless takeover was sudden and bloody, surprising the royalists and republicans and burying democracy in France for a generation. Conspiracy theorist *avant la lettre*, Marx portrays the heinous outcome. Louis Bonaparte

> robs the Bank of France of twenty-five million francs, buys General Magnan with a million, the soldiers with fifteen francs apiece and liquor, comes together with his accomplices secretly like a thief in the night, has the houses of the most dangerous parliamentary leaders broken into, and Cavaignac, Lamoricière, Le Flô, Changarnier, Charras, Thiers, Baze, etc., dragged from their beds, the key points of Paris and the parliamentary building occupied by troops, and cheapjack placards posted early in the morning on all the walls, proclaiming the dissolution of the National Assembly and the Council of State, the restoration of universal suffrage, and the placing of the Seine Department in a state of siege. In like manner, he inserted a little later in the *Moniteur* a false document which asserted that influential parliamentarians had grouped themselves around him and formed a state *consulta*. (*c.w.*, Vol. 11, p. 180 emphasis in original)

3 Were Wars Initiated by Provocations, Prevarications, or False-Flags? Some Background

I now want to review several major war-initiating events in order to exhibit their diversities and to highlight the ever-present need for critical thinking. Social theory must be prepared to analyze major events critically, for example, the assassination of John F. Kennedy. They must be analyzed in a manner that is not dismissive before analysis that the state could be involved, while also recognizing that no two events are the same. These events may have causes that are not transparent and open to easily obtainable knowledge, yet, the objective must be to deepen the theory and analysis of the state, and likewise to crack the ideological weapon that the phrase "conspiracy theory" has been attempting to impose upon us.

3.1 "Spotty Lincoln" and the Mexican-American War

The U.S. President from 1845 to 1849 was James K. Polk, a Jacksonian Democrat, slave owner, former Speaker of the House of Representatives and then Governor of Tennessee. In his candidacy for President he promised to annex the Republic of Texas, which had declared its independence from Mexico in 1836 with a constitution permitting ownership of slaves (not permitted by Mexican law). It was annexed to the United States as a slave-state on December 29, 1845, completing what the previous President Tyler had supported against Mexican opposition. Next, Polk conspired to declare war on Mexico in order to expand the United States, hoping that Sam Houston, former President of independent Texas, would aid the endeavor. When Houston declined and thus Polk experienced an initial failure (Price 1967), Polk had the U.S. Army enter in April 1846 territory north of the Rio Grande that was Mexican under an earlier treaty, claiming the territory as United States, and that Mexicans had started an incident in which U.S. soldiers were killed. In the North it was often referred to as "Polk's War".

The war was ongoing when Abraham Lincoln was elected a Whig House member and in office from March 1847 to March 1849. He was to become known as "Spotty Lincoln" for when that session of Congress first met on December 7, 1847,[2] Lincoln began offering resolutions – three from December 22 to January 22 – demanding the exact spot on the map where Polk was making his claim that the Mexicans had entered in April 1946 on Texas territory that the U.S.

---

[2] Only in 1933 did sessions of Congress start in January (that particular Congress would be only fourteen months in length). In other words, although Lincoln was in office from March, Congress didn't meet until December.

now claimed.[3] Although the war was basically already won by the U.S. (the war-ending Treaty of Guadalupe Hidalgo would be signed on February 2, 1948), nevertheless, Lincoln was asking for evidence from a President concerning a war-initiating incident, a President expounding the U.S. "Manifest Destiny" toward Latin America generally and Mexico specifically. The extension of slavery may also have been partly behind Lincoln's asking of Polk for the "spot",[4] not least because of Polk's interest in acquiring Mexican land west of Texas. In any case, Lincoln's questioning was directed against the war as such and was the Whig position. The questioning, unpopular in his Illinois district, likely undermined his being the Whig nominee for the next Congress, and contributed to his defeat in the 1858 Senate race. He did not disavow his earlier position.

3.2   *The Explosion of the USS Maine and the Spanish-American War*
The Spanish did not blow up the USS *Maine* in Havana harbor, but the media, as if it had, led the way forward to war under the slogan, "Remember the Maine!" In his request to Congress for war, although under considerable pressure even before the explosion, President McKinley did not directly claim Spanish responsibility (Gleijeses, 2003), and the Senate passed a war resolution, albeit adopting an amendment with a 42–35 vote that the U.S. would not annex Cuba. The House concurred 311 to 6. An unexpectedly easy military victory resulted in Spain's loss of Cuba and the U.S. acquiring Puerto Rico, the Philippines and Guam from Spain. It was followed, however, by significant resistance to the United States in Cuba and the Philippines.

At the time, there were those who questioned whether the explosion was caused by a Spanish mine, or similar device, instead caused internally by an explosion onboard (the Spanish position, many in Europe, and much of U.S. business community). The Sampson Board of Inquiry before war concluded the cause as external, but did not assign responsibility. Since it did not express doubt of Spanish responsibility either, its conclusion was one of convenience to warmongers. Even if it were an externally caused explosion, there are other possibilities than a Spanish mine: McMorrow is convinced that the Spanish were not in a position to gain by blowing up the USS *Maine*, which would be like a "virtual suicide" ("What Destroyed the USS Maine – An Opinion" at www.spanamwar.com/Mainem01.htm, accessed July 24, 2018), and concludes that Cuban rebels were the most likely as they had the most to gain from getting the U.S. directly involved. If so, why did not the Spanish so claim?

---

3   More detail about Lincoln's resolution are contained in Fisher (2009).
4   Although highlighting Lincoln's questioning, Tarpley (2006, pp. 336–339) neglects to mention the relationship to the slave question.

3.3 Assassination of Archduke Ferdinand

Gavrilo Princip was the uncontested assassin of Austro-Hungarian Archduke Franz Ferdinand, and a member of Black Hand. Black Hand was a conspiratorial organization and other Black Hand members were involved in the June 28, 1914 assassination, which eventually led to World War I. Black Hand's interest could be studied and even claimed to be implementing Austro-Hungarian interests to pursue a provocation to be blamed on Serbia, i.e., a charge of a false-flag.

In 2014, *Scientific American*, on the hundredth anniversary of the assassination, published an article seemingly outside its raison d'être: "Gavrilo Princip, Conspiracy Theories and the Fragility of Cause and Effect" (available at https://blogs.scientificamerican.com/the-curious-wavefunction/gavrilo-princip-conspiracy-theories-and-the-fragility-of-cause-and-effect). The article wishes to undermine "conspiracy theorists", saying they are not "scientific". Yet, this article does not even hint at what Black Hand might be about and Princip's role (an agent of Austro-Hungary? double-agent for Serbia? something else?). Thus, the article has no substance against consideration of a conspiracy. Its purpose was to attack "conspiracy theories" as such.

3.4 Mukden or Manchurian Incident

The Mukden or Manchurian Incident of September 18, 1931 (also called the September 18 Incident) initiated the Japanese murderous intervention in China. This incident was used by the Japanese government as the raison for its subsequent attack on China, even if the Japanese military seems to have initiated the operation independent of the government in Tokyo. The incident itself was a sabotage of a Japanese owned railway line in Mukden, Manchuria, in territory that included Japanese troops, a bombing blamed on locals but done by Japanese. So, yes, it can be labeled a *false-flag*. Nevertheless, the explosion on the rail line was so minor that no one was injured and even a train could pass on the tracks shortly thereafter! A better description might be a "ruse of war". With either phrasing, nothing of real significance happened and simple propaganda was the actuality.

3.5 Reichstag Burning and the Gleiwitz Incident

The Reichstag fire of 1933 is frequently cited as a *false-flag*, meaning that the Nazis initiated the fire of the parliament building but blamed the arson on communists with many arrests and focusing, later, on a single individual, a Dutch Communist Marinus van der Lubbe. The over-arching purpose would be to obtain total control of the German government, i.e. a dictatorship, abrogating civil liberties as the first step (signed, indeed, the next day by President

Hindenburg). At issue is evidence as to what caused the burning to occur at all. William Shirer (1960, p. 192) thought that it is "beyond reasonable doubt" that the Nazi planned the arson. A book by Benjamin Hett (2014) addressed prior analyzes and also concluded the Nazis engineered the burning. A review article of that book by Richard Evans claimed, however, Hett's conclusion to be a minority position and otherwise dismissed the conclusion (*London Review of Books*, www.lrb.co.uk/v36/n09/richard-j-evans/the-conspiracists, accessed October 29, 2019). Against Hett's survey of the evidence, Evans' review asserted that the alleged culprit repeatedly confessed, that the underground passage Nazis could be thought to have used was far too difficult for their alleged role, that the Soviet regime (including, later, East Germany) had a good motivation for diverting attention away from a claim for it being caused by a Communist, and that Goering dining at the time with Hitler seemed to be quite taken by surprise. Evans also said the issue of the lack of accelerants needed to enflame the Reichstag in a short period of time had been side-stepped by Hett. In other words, for Evans, it was a Nazi good fortune that the fire happened at all.

Significant new evidence came out in 2019 from a buried archive in a Hanover court of testimony. In a 1955 affidavit, an SA man, namely, Hans-Martin Lennings, stated that he had taken van der Lubbe to the Reichstag *after* the fire had already started. The new evidence was reported in several German outlets, including, with much added detail, the *Elbe-Jeetzel-Zeitung*, July 25, 2019 (www.ejz.de/blick-in-die-welt/politik/dokument-in-hannover-belegt-sa-mann-will-beim-reichstagsbrand-1933-geholfen-haben_241_111748996-122-.html, accessed October 29, 2019), also mentioning other evidence against van der Lubbe having been the perpetrator. On July 26 the *Hannoveriche-Allegemeine* and the *Frankfurter Rundschau* also included Hett's reaction that he wished having had this evidence for his book (www.fr.de/politik/sa-mann-will-reichstagsbrand-beteiligt-gewesen-sein-12861189.html, accessed October 29, 2019), the conclusion of which he maintains.

After the Reichstag fire, the Gleiwitz incident starting the war in Europe became particularly well known as a result of Shirer's book, *The Rise and Fall of the Third Reich*. While Hitler did not explicitly mention Gleiwitz in his declaration of war against Poland on September 1, 1939, he did cite three border incidents occurring the night before, and Gleiwitz was considered the key one. On that September 1, the *New York Times* reported Gleiwitz and Nazi claims under a title "Border Clashes Increase", including the following in its five-paragraph report:

> Berlin, Friday, Sept. 1 – An increasing number of border incidents involving shooting and mutual Polish-German casualties are reported by the

German press and radio. The most serious is reported from Gleiwitz, a German city on the line where the southwestern portion of Poland meets the Reich.

At 8 P.M., according to the semi-official news agency, a group of Polish insurrectionists forced an entrance into the Gleiwitz radio station, overpowering the watchmen and beating and generally mishandling the attendants. The Gleiwitz station was relaying a Breslau station's program, which was broken off by the Poles. (https://archive.nytimes.com/www.nytimes.com/learning/general/onthisday/big/0901.html#article)

The *Times* article did not suggest that the German news reports were inaccurate, and generally news coverage focused on the invasion of Poland by the Germans, and the resulting acts of other state actors.

There was an exception to lack of critical coverage that appeared September 9, 1939, in a Perth, Australia, weekly, *Mirror* (p. 5; it ceased existence in 1956). Written from London by "L.F.", he or she reports knowing Gleiwitz well, including the location of the radio station too far from the border, and was sure the Germans had set it up (https://trove.nla.gov.au/newspaper/article/75868006?searchTerm=GLEIWITZ&searchLimits=sortby=dateDesc, accessed October 4, 2019). It would be a false-flag event, but the article did not claim any proof.

Proof was offered at the Nuremburg trial via an affidavit from a German prisoner of war who claimed that he, Alfred Naujocks, was in charge of the operation. Shirer (1960, pp. 518–520) describes the confession that reported that German soldiers dressed as Polish soldiers invaded the German radio station at Gleiwitz in Germany on the border with Poland. One person was killed. The affidavit was used at Nuremburg. Dated November 20, 1945 and thus one day before the Nuremburg trial's opening statement by Robert H. Jackson, it was this affidavit that Shirer relied upon. Left open is the possibility that Naujocks, to serve his own interest as a prisoner, was fabricating his involvement and perhaps even the whole story. Indeed, Naujocks was not prosecuted. Shirer himself reported no trace of him by the time he published his 1960 book, although in fact there were previous reports of his early and subsequent life (see Altenhöner, 2015). In 1960, Naujocks himself reported his life story in a book entitled *The Man Who Started the War* (written by Gunter Peis, seemingly listening to Naujocks), which of course included Gleiwitz (presented in a chapter of thirteen pages). Does this book represent a confirmation: it is only one person's statement?

Altenhöner does not doubt the existence of such an incident, and mentions the name of the victim. The *Mirror* article had provided good reason to discount the possibility that Poles were responsible as the radio station was, in fact, seven miles from the heavily guarded Polish border (a distance that can be confirmed) and the station was only 150 yards from barracks with about a thousand soldiers (according to the article). It is beyond belief that Polish forces would attempt such an act as alleged. Gleiwitz does therefore seems be confirmed as a *false-flag* in the usual sense that Nazis did set up an event in a manner to give the appearance of Poles attacking a radio station in Gleiwitz.

3.6   The Second Gulf of Tonkin Incident before Escalation in Vietnam

Given so many sources now establishing that the Gulf of Tonkin Resolution of the U.S. Congress was based upon a *prevarication* about what had happened in the Gulf of Tonkin in 1964 – or rather what did not happen, the evidence need not be reviewed. For those unfamiliar, an overview article is available, "30-year Anniversary: Tonkin Gulf Lie Launched Vietnam War" (*FAIR*, July 27, 1994, at http://fair.org/media-beat-column/30-year-anniversary-tonkin-gulf-lie-launched-vietnam-war, accessed October 29, 2019). At the time, only two members of the U.S. Congress voted against the infamous Resolution authorizing the expansion of U.S. war on Vietnam, Senators Ernest Gruening of Alaska and Wayne Morse of Oregon, and only highlights the continuing and desperate need for critical thought.

4   "Conspiracy Theory" Becomes a Weapon of the State after the Assassination of John F. Kennedy

> The CIA's campaign to popularize the term "conspiracy theory" and make conspiracy belief a target of ridicule and hostility must be credited, unfortunately, with being one of the most successful propaganda initiatives of all time.
>
> deHaven-Smith (2013, p. 25)

The forces behind the John F. Kennedy assassination has been convincingly presented by the Catholic scholar/activist James W. Douglass (2008), with some of the evidence popularly known due to Oliver Stone's film *JFK*. Douglass had attended the entire 1999 Memphis jury trial and its conviction of government forces for participation in the assassination of Martin Luther King, Jr. (discussed below). He was undoubtedly strengthened by what he witnessed.

When Kennedy was assassinated, "conspiracy theory" was not a pejorative. So reading press reports in the first years regarding those who doubted the Warren Commission did not include comments against "conspiracy theorists". That developed later. Something happened to put those two words into political use; by deHaven-Smith's (2013) reckoning, it was the CIA's recognition of the increasing efficacy of critiques of the Warren Commission and the need to counter it. And it surely became very useful as propaganda for any number of later instances, useful even for cases for which it would not be needed so as to lump everything together, i.e., cases in which the government tells a truth and cases when not.

Bertrand Russell (1964) was one of the opponents of the Warren Commission even before the report was concluded and his critique retains much relevance. In Kennedy's case we also have the remarkable subsequent fact to deal with that the alleged assassin was himself killed, in a Dallas police station no less, after having said he did not kill anyone, "I am a patsy". Given Oswald's murder, the alleged killer of Kennedy would not be entitled to proper defense in a fair trial. In this case, there was only the related Garrison trial in New Orleans.

Douglass' book deals with both the motivation for assassinating Kennedy, i.e., his Presidential acts, as well as the personality of Kennedy himself that matters. Motivation goes well beyond the issue of Vietnam. Kennedy's personality matters in order to address such issues as to whether Kennedy would actually have withdrawn from Vietnam as he had told advisers and had begun to undertake before assassination. Earlier he had faced down a setup in the Bay of Pigs.

The plot itself is elaborated by Douglass, part of which included the little know attempt against Kennedy set for execution in Chicago on November 2, 1963, along the same lines as Dallas three weeks later ... foiled by canceling the President's trip. Kennedy would have been assassinated in the Chicago Loop by marksmen with high-powered rifles, a patsy having been setup, but the Secret Service operated in this case as intended. Curtains were tightly drawn around knowledge of the trip's cancelation so as not to impact execution of the same plot in the same manner shortly thereafter in Dallas. (Douglass, 2008, pp. 200–201 and 213–218)

Kennedy had made many enemies, too many powerful enemies, first and foremost what Eisenhower had called the military-industrial complex. After the Bay of Pigs, he fired the CIA Director Allen Dulles, Deputy Director Richard Bissell, Jr., and Deputy Director General Charles Cabell, providing a very important initial message of what President Kennedy was capable. Other steps confronting the military-industrial complex included Kennedy's handling of the U.S. Steel, the Cuban missile crisis, secret moves at softening of relations with Cuba, calling for world peace in his American University speech of June 10, 1963 (a genuine peace, "not a Pax Americana enforced on the world by American weapons of war"), the nuclear test ban treaty, a telling rapprochement with Sukarno of Indonesia, and of course a beginning of withdrawal from Vietnam. Could his enemies afford to wait for the next election, or was this growing list enough when they had the right kind of man in Kennedy's Vice-President and successor?

The mechanics of the assassination are important but the motivation for it is even more important. Still, the mechanics are addressed in Douglass (2008, Chapter 6). There is an extremely rich literature on that subject.

5 Dismissing a Jury Trial Conviction of State Conspiracy in the Assassination of Martin Luther King, Jr.

Lee Harvey Oswald never had any trial, let alone with a jury exposed to responsible representations for the defense. Once an accused is dead, the press is not even obligated to refer to "the alleged" or "the accused". Easier and simpler is it when the alleged is dead without the legal right to a sound defensive.

Sometimes, however, a light is shown by an unanticipated occurrence showing that conspiracy really does happen and a guilty verdict actually rendered. Such is the case with jury trial for conspiracy of the U.S. government and others to assassinate Martin Luther King, Jr. in 1968. The history of it is complicated, but can be started with Ralph Abernathy, King's successor at the Southern Christian Leadership Conference, and attorney William F. Pepper, a friend of King. In 1978, they interviewed the man who had originally confessed to the murder, namely, James Earl Ray. Because of his guilty plea, Ray had not had a jury trial but did avoid a possible death sentence. Shortly after being sentenced in 1969 and arriving in the penitentiary, he recanted and filed for a trial. Ray was never to achieve that trial before he died in 1998. A seriously engaged, albeit mock, trial in London, England, aired on TV in 1993, had found Ray not guilty and exposed aspects of a cover-up, with Pepper the attorney for the defense. The U.S. media did not cover it.

In 1997, the King family joined the struggle for a trial of James Earl Ray and hired Pepper as lead attorney for a jury trial of possible conspiracy in order to establish the truth of the matter. Given Ray's death soon thereafter, another avenue for justice was needed and was found, namely, to prosecute as an accomplice to the murder the owner of the bar across from the hotel King stayed at, i.e., Loyd Jowers, who had already confessed to being an accomplice, without naming co-conspirators. The King family asked only for an award of $100 for partial compensation of burial costs. The civil case became *King et al. v. Jowers et al.*, filed in October 1998. It was tried by jury that began on November 15, 1999.

At the trial, overwhelming evidence of conspiracy by Loyd Jowers and local and national governmental agencies was presented, laid out in the book by Pepper (2003, pp. 107–131). Co-conspirators included the Memphis Police Department (MPD), U.S. Army Security Agency (ASA), the U.S. Army 111th and 902nd Military Intelligence Groups (MIG), and the Green Beret Alpha 184 unit. These conspirators did *not* include James Earl Ray. The plot itself was not arranged by Jowers. It included making King vulnerable to being shot by a hitman and removal of King's security. A cover-up was also presented at the trial:

> A large number of witnesses testified to the extensive range of activities which caused the truth in this case to remain hidden and justice denied for nearly 32 years. Incredibly, the chronicle of events and actions included murder, solicitation of murder, attempted bribery, suppression of evidence, alteration of the crime scene, and the control, manipulation, and use of the media for propaganda purposes. (Pepper, p. 131)

The jury unanimously found the defendants guilty. The judge awarded the liability at 30 percent to Loyd Jowers and 70 percent to all other co-conspirators. (Incidentally, being in ill health, this momentous case was this judge's last one.) To Pepper's bewilderment, Clinton's Justice Department manipulated a subsequent investigation to condemn the trial (Pepper, pp. 218–261). The King family's efforts were finally given some attention in 2018 by the *Washington Post* in an article "Who killed Martin Luther King Jr.? His family believes James Earl Ray was framed", although with a titling that downplays the role of the jury trial and focuses on personal opinions (*Washington Post,* March 30, 2018, available at https://www.washingtonpost.com/news/retropolis/wp/2018/03/30/who-killed-martin-luther-king-jr-his-family-believes-james-earl-ray-was-framed/?utm_term=.be00cd57b59f).

What motivated the desire to kill Martin Luther King, Jr.? Could it be King's joining of the civil rights and anti-poverty movements to the movement against the Vietnam war in his speech at the Riverside Church exactly one year before his assassination?

Robert F. Kennedy, candidate for President, was killed two months and a day later. After fifty years, doubt about this assassination appeared in the same newspaper by the same reporter in an article entitled, "Who killed Bobby Kennedy? His son RFK Jr. doesn't believe it was Sirhan" (*Washington Post,* May 26, 2018, available at https://www.washingtonpost.com/news/retropolis/wp/2018/05/26/who-killed-bobby-kennedy-his-son-rfk-jr-doesnt-believe-it-was-sirhan-sirhan/?noredirect=on&utm_term=.801a78da3470). Without saying who was responsible, the story focused on a second person behind Kennedy as the assassin, rather than Sirhan who was in front of Kennedy and not close. Further, the number of bullets fired exceeded the number in Sirhan's gun and the fatal bullets were fired into the back of Kennedy's head according to the coroner's report. Shortly after this story, one of Kennedy's daughters was also to indicate support for a new investigation (*Boston Globe*, May 31, 2018, "RFK's children divided over calls for a fresh investigation of his assassination", available at https://www.bostonglobe.com/metro/2018/05/31/rfk-children-divided-over-calls-for-fresh-investigation-his-assassination/B5ubwQd9GFDttwNx-JOAn6N/story.html).

6 Utilization of the "Conspiracy Theory" Weapon: the World Trade Center and the Pentagon in 2001

> Never before has it been as imperative to struggle for a true rendering of the 9/11 reality, and never before have the incentives been greater to prevent such a rendering.
> Falk (2007, p. 127)

We all know the importance of September 11, 2001, for motivating a vast array of new U.S. policies, including wars and domestic surveillance and control. After the fall of the Soviet Union, the U.S. military-industrial complex would need to have and to define a new "enemy" if it were to maintain its overwhelming domination, including at least seven hundred military bases outside the United States and over much of the world[5] and extraordinary financial flows. A new "enemy" must be widespread and be defined. For the beginning of the 21st century the enemy became Muslim terrorists. Did not the dramatic event on September 11, 2001 on the scale of Pearl Harbor achieve a new raison d'être fronting the U.S. military-industrial complex and the national security state? And President Obama in Cairo in 2009 assured us all as to the facts of the matter:

> I'm aware that there's still some who would question or even justify the events of 9/11. But let us be clear: Al Qaeda killed nearly 3,000 people on that day. The victims were innocent men, women and children from

---

5 Johnson (2004) reports seven hundred openly stated and one thousand more probable. A later count of bases of seven hundred is provided in Vine (2015) but does not seem to take account of secret bases.

America and many other nations who had done nothing to harm anybody. And yet al Qaeda chose to ruthlessly murder these people, claimed credit for the attack, and even now states their determination to kill on a massive scale. They have affiliates in many countries and are trying to expand their reach. These are not opinions to be debated; these are facts to be dealt with.

> Transcript of speech in Cairo, June 4, 2009 (https://obamawhitehouse.archives.gov/the-press-office/remarks-president-cairo-university-6-04-09, accessed December 17, 2019).

"These are facts to be dealt with".

6.1 Alleged Muslim Hijackers

The *9/11 Commission Report* was published in 2004, nearly three years after the terrorist event. Within it, there is no attempt whatsoever to provide any *evidence* that the alleged nineteen hijackers were on the planes and correctly identified, not even flight manifests. These "facts" were presented without any need for evidence. The Commission had plenty of time. It is an insult to criminal processes and lay readers. This problem goes deeper. The FBI's initial list of alleged hijackers after September 11th was changed within days, without explanation. A security video from the Portland, Maine airport was provided for two of the alleged with date/time stamp, but no video from the relevant Logan airport in Boston. A security video but without a date/time stamp was provided for the alleged being in the Dulles airport; only later would a mother state her daughter, a victim on American 77, to be in the same video,[6] although being in an airport is not evidence of being on a specific flight, let alone hijacking it. To this day, I have not seen a reasonable explanation, rather than an excuse, for the U.S. government's failure to simply provide all four flight manifests.

---

6 The security video for Dulles airport was released just a day before the report of the 9/11 Commission and then became an exhibit at the Moussaoui trial that ended in May, 2006 (this huge file is at www.vaed.uscourts.gov/notablecases/moussaoui/exhibits/prosecution/NT00211.html, while a less sharp, smaller version is available at www.youtube.com/watch?v=uLEqjpHVPhM&t=132s). It can be complemented with attention to Mari-Rae Sopper who died on American Airlines flight 77, but went through security immediately before the named Khalid Al-Mihdhar (available at www.youtube.com/watch?v=ohhHaFyyXIg). Her mother Marion Kminek confirmed her daughter's identity ("Lasting Mark in Altered Lives", *Northwest Herald*, September 10, 2006, p. 1). Around the same time, Kminek was published in the *Santa Barbara Independent* expressing some of her own outstanding questions of that day: "A Grieving Mother Wonders What Really Happened on 9/11", September 7, 2006, at www.independent.com/2006/09/07/unanswered-questions. (All videos accessed December 22, 2019).

International press reports had many alleged hijackers reporting themselves alive after September 11th when identifications were made public. Kolar (2008, p. 12, fn. 11, 12, and 13) notes multiple reports of alleged American 77 hijacker Khalid al-Mihdhar being alive after September 11th (from BBC, from an FDIC report, and from CNN). The Commission, like a kangaroo, jumped over these reports as if such evidence did not need to be addressed. Kolar examined published photos of the alleged hijacking pilot Ziad Jarrah (for United 93 ending in Pennsylvania) that exhibit different people claimed to be the same alleged, including a May 2000 visa, a October 2000 holiday photo (appearing in McDermott, 2005, among photos after p. 140), and a May 2001 Florida driver's license – Kolar's seven-picture collage is on his p. 1 and discussed on pp. 24–26. He noted a "Ziad Jarrah" having lived in New York City at the same time as the real Jarrah was in Lebanon. There is evidence of doubles for others as well (Kolar, p. 21).

Philip Zelikow was the Executive Director of the *9/11 Commission Report* (Commission, 2004), arguably the most important person involved with it. In 2007, I had an occasion to confront him personally about the alleged hijackers. After querying him and listening to his answer, I stated to him that he had not attempted to prove his claims (the *Report* did not even attempt to do so). A video of the interchange "Philip Zelikow's Parallel Universe" can be viewed at www.youtube.com/watch?v=4XQWBQKsqBU (accessed October 4, 2019). A detailed examination concerning lack of identifying the alleged hijackers and related matters is contained in Davidsson (2013).

6.2 Falling Skyscrapers

Do skyscrapers fall at all, due to fire? We are supposed to have had *three* in New York City in the single day of September 11, 2001, but none anywhere before or after. Two of the collapses on September 11th have been widely shown, but a third is rarely shown – for World Trade Center 7 (WTC 7). The third was not even hit by a plane, had relatively light damage and small fires, and was separated from WTC 1 by WTC 6 (having heavy damage, as did WTC 3, 4, and 5). Its collapse can be seen, for example, at https://commons.m.wikimedia.org/wiki/File:WTC_Building_7_Collapse_001.gif (accessed December 16, 2019). Evidentiary research led by Professor J. Leroy Hulsey, University of Alaska, Fairbanks (http://ine.uaf.edu/wtc7, accessed June 30, 2020), funded at more than $300,000, concludes that WTC 7 did not collapse due to fire, although having been so claimed by the government's investigative agency.

If skyscrapers do fall, why would these three go virtually straight down, very close to the physics of free fall, without human intervention to initiate the collapses and ensure such symmetry? We have testimonials from an excess of a hundred fire-fighters as to explosions being heard (MacQueen, 2006) and the Board of Fire Commissioners of the Franklin Square and Munson Fire District in New York City contests the alleged claims for the collapses of WTC 1, 2 and 7, after having been convinced that the collapses were caused by "pre-planted explosives and/or incendiaries" (www.ae911truth.org/news/540-new-york-area-fire-commissioners-make-history-call-for-new-9-11-investigation, assessed December 25, 2019). Why were dust samples not tested by governmental authorities for explosive materials, particularly after independent researchers outside of the U.S. government confirmed the existence of nano-thermite in the dust?

6.3   The Pentagon

The most important operational structure of the American military is left undefended fifty minutes after the first plane hits the World Trade Center, about one hour and twenty minutes after the first warning. Is it at all credible that the alleged pilot Hani Hanjour is capable of maneuvering a Boeing 757 in a spiral manner at high speed into the Pentagon, approaching exceedingly close to the ground? Security cameras were all around the Pentagon. These videos and images were confiscated very quickly after the incident and not released. Why? How is the absence of identifiable debris of American Airlines 77 to be explained, an absence correlating to the statement of Pentagon survivor April Gallop who crawled through the hole in the building and saw no plane debris ("After 9/11, Woman who was at Pentagon remains Skeptical", *Washington Post*, September 9, 2011)?

There is independent research work of credible eyewitnesses – those truly in a position to observe, not merely so claiming – of the flight path of the plane going toward the Pentagon approaching in a manner inconsistent with the official story of flight 77 (Citizens Investigation Team at www.citizeninvestigationteam.com/evidence, accessed October 4, 2019).

6.4   Calls from Planes?

United 93 had the most reported calls from inside the planes, but American 11 and 77 as well as United 175 also had them. Immediately after September 11th, there were many news reports of cell phones having been used for these calls. Later, many reports came in that such cell calls from planes were impossible at anything but low altitudes. One pilot, after a flight I was on, even told me that he or other pilots might forget to turn off their private cell phones when entering a cockpit and only received voice-message alarms from their cell phones after descending down to 1000 to 2000 feet at the end of their flights. I affirm my own inability to use cell phones above such an altitude, albeit without nearly the experience.

By the time of the 2006 Zacarias Moussaoui trial, the government was claiming that all United 93 calls were airphone calls except the last two. This government claim is in direct contradiction of the wife of passenger Tom Burnett who, in her book, explicitly states that she knew that he was using his cell phone because she was looking at her own phone's caller ID and recognized her husband's ID (Burnett, 2006, p. 61). She also says she received four calls from Tom, while the government acknowledges only three, for which times and durations differ from her report. A book about flight 93 by the New York Times reporter Jere Longman (2002) discussed four, not three, calls (in order: a cell on p. 107, an airphone, p. 110, a cell, p. 111, and without type indicated, p. 118). One can wonder about the truth regarding the reported calls when such direct contradictions to the government's statements appear. Of course, phone company reports could be produced, but no one has. In any case, there are witnesses claiming that the United 93 flight was shot down, rather than having been taken over at all. These issues matter, not least because flight 93 had movies made about "heroes". (Details regarding the alleged calls are discussed in Zarembka, 2008, pp. 305–310, and more extensively in Davidsson, 2013, Part III.)

6.5   *Insider Trading*

In the month after September 11th, there was much discussion in the financial press regarding possible insider trading occurring in the days preceding the event, specifically regarding put options on American and United stocks. The put-option levels were quite high. But suddenly all discussion stopped until a brief, unsatisfactory mention in the report by the Commission (2004). It seems that those reporting the data had thought it would lead to proof of Osama bin Laden's alleged role. Did the word get around in October 2001 that no such proof would surface so that media interest fell like a lead balloon?

In 2006, a professor at the University of Illinois Urbana-Champaign, Allen Poteshman, published a scientific study leading to the empirical conclusion that insider trading was, indeed, highly probable directly before September 11th in put options for American and United (Poteshman, 2006). Furthermore, his research was published in the *Journal of Business*, an outlet no one can accuse of being "anti-American". In my own evaluation, being an economist who has worked with similar methodology to that used by Poteshman, it is even more striking that this research conclusion has not been challenged by other scholars. Important results have almost always led to disputes, but not this time. Another study was published subsequently, with a similar conclusion when examining the evidence from the S&P500, and a third, extensive study on many companies has also been published. I have analyzed the entire issue in Zarembka (2012).

6.6 September 11th and Conspiracy Theory

What has been introduced above in questioning the official version of what happened on September 11th has been labeled and will continue to be labeled as "conspiracy theory". Those who introduce such questions are sometimes placed in the category of the Salem witch trials, not of sound mind and perhaps mentally unstable. Yet, evidence is evidence, and the substantial role of the CIA in creating "conspiracy theory" as a propaganda concept – indeed, as a weapon – has been presented in deHaven-Smith (2013, Chapter 4).

6.7 Conclusion

One might think that Marxists would consider the full range of possible explanations for the cause(s) of the September 11th event and not leave it unaddressed, not avoid responding to books like that by Kay (2011) where those interested in the evidence about U.S.'s September 11th are considered "cranks" offering baseless beliefs and "often reacting to male midlife crises" (females being ignored).

Having offered my concerns, I leave the reader with Marx's scholarly statement: "There is no royal road to science, and only those who do not dread the fatiguing climb of its steep paths have a chance of gaining its luminous summits" (Marx, 1867, "Preface" to the French edition of *Capital, Volume I*).

References

Note: Except for letters and Marx's speech represented by Value, Price and Profit, *the original date of publication for the original language edition is listed after the author, followed by the cited source, in English if available. For letters, the date is mentioned, and the source cited, although knowing they were not public knowledge at the time of writing and made public at various times later. Since Marx's* Capital, Volume 1, *had many editions starting in 1867, usually the 1974 Lawrence and Wishart edition is cited, the translation undertaken by those who knew Marx well and reflects historical considerations addressed here; when that edition is inadequate it is so stated.*

Allisson, F. (2015), *Value and Prices in Russian Economic Thought: A Journey inside the Russian Synthesis, 1890–1920*, New York: Routledge.

Altenhöner, F. (2015), "'I Am the Man Who Started the War': Alfred Naujocks and His Postwar Stories about His 'Adventures'", in *A Nazi Past: Recasting German Identity in Postwar Europe*, D.A. Messenger and K. Paehler, eds., Lexington: University Press of Kentucky, pp. 203–224.

Althusser, L. (1965), "The Object of *Capital*", in L. Althusser and E. Balibar, *Reading Capital*, new and abridged edition, translated by B. Brewster, London: New Left Books, London, 1970, pp. 71–198.

Althusser, L. (1969a), "Preface to *Capital* Volume One", in *Lenin and Philosophy and Other Essays*, translated by B. Brewster. London: New Left Books, 1971 and 1977 2nd ed., pp. 69–101.

Althusser, L. (1969b), "Lenin before Hegel", in *Lenin and Philosophy and Other Essays*, translated by B. Brewster, London: New Left Books, 1971 and 1977, 2nd ed., pp. 103–120.

Althusser, L. (1974), "Elements of Self-Criticism", in *Essays in Self-Criticism*, translated by G. Lock, London: New Left Books, 1976, pp. 101–161.

Althusser, L. (2006), *Philosophy of the Encounter: Later Writings, 1978–87*, F. Matheron and O. Corpet, eds., translated by G.M. Goshgarian, New York: Verso.

Anderson, K. (1983), "The 'Unknown' Marx's *Capital*, Volume 1: The French Edition of 1872–75, 100 Years Later", *Review of Radical Political Economics*, Vol. 15, No. 4, pp. 71–80.

Anderson, K. (2010), *Marx at the Margins: On Nationalism, Ethnicity, and Non-Western Societies*, Chicago: University of Chicago Press.

Arthur, C. J. (1996), "Engels as Interpreter of Marx's Economics", in *Engels Today*, C.J. Arthur, ed., Houndmills, U.K.: Macmillan, pp. 173–209.

Baronian, L. (2013), *Marx and Living Labour*, London and New York: Routledge.

Bauer, O. (1913), "The Accumulation of Capital", translated by J.E. King, *History of Political Economy*, Vol. 18, No. 1, 1996, 87–110.
Bergman, J. (1983), *Vera Zasulich: A Biography*, Stanford: Stanford University Press.
Biernacki, R. (1995), *The Fabrication of Labor: Germany and Britain, 1640–1914*, Berkeley, University of California Press.
Bonefeld, W., ed., (2008), *Subverting the Present, Imagining the Future*, Brooklyn, New York: Autonomedia.
Boudin, L. (1907), "Mathematische Formeln gegen Karl Marx", *Die Neue Zeit*, 25, pp. 524–535, 557–567 and 603–610.
Bronner, S.E. (1978), *The Letters of Rosa Luxemburg*, Boulder, Colorado: Westview Press.
Bukharin, N.I. (1920), *Economics of the Transformation Period, with Lenin's Critical Remarks*. New York: Bergman, 1971.
Bukharin, N.I. (1924), *Imperialism and the Accumulation of Capital*, New York and London: Monthly Review Press, 1972.
Burnett, D. with A. Giombetti (2006), *Living Life Beyond Ourselves: Fighting Back*, Longwood, Florida: Advantage Books.
Cámara Izquierdo, S. (2007), "The Dynamics of the Profit Rate in Spain (1954–2001)", *Review of Radical Political Economics*, Vol. 39, No. 4, pp. 543–561.
Carchedi, G. (2010), *Behind the Crisis: Marx's Dialectics of Value and Knowledge*, Leiden: Brill.
Clark, J.B. (1899), *The Distribution of Wealth*, New York: Macmillan.
Cleaver, H. (1979), *Reading Capital Politically*, 2nd ed., San Francisco: AK Press, 2000.
Commission (2004), *The 9/11 Commission Report: Final Report of the National Commission on Terrorist Attacks upon the United States*, Authorized Edition, New York: W.W. Norton.
Cogoy, M. (1973), "The Falling Rate of Profit and the Theory of Accumulation: A Reply to Paul Sweezy", *Bulletin of the Conference of Socialist Economists*, Winter 1973, pp. 52–67; in 1987, published in *International Journal of Political Economy*, Vol. 17, No. 2, pp. 54–74.
Cope, Z. (2012), *Divided world divided class: Global political economy and the stratification of labour under capitalism*, Montreal: Kersplebedeb.
Correa y Zafrilla, P. (1985), "La primera traducción castellana de El Capital", *Cuadernos Hispanoamericanos*, No. 420, pp. 201–210.
Das, R.J. (2012), "Reconceptualizing Capitalism: Forms of Subsumption of Labor, Class Struggle, and Uneven Development", *Review of Radical Political Economics*, Vol. 44, No. 2, pp. 178–200.
Davidsson, E. (2013), *Hijacking America's Mind on 9/11: Counterfeiting Evidence*. New York: Algora Publishing.
De Angelis, M. (2001), "Marx and Primitive Accumulation: The Continuous Character of Capital's 'Enclosures'", *The Commoner*, No. 2, at www.commoner.org.uk, revised in W. Bonefeld, 2008, pp. 27–49.

deHaven-Smith, L. (2013), *Conspiracy Theory in America*. Austin: University of Texas Press.

Desai, M. (1987), "Simple and Extended Reproduction", *The New Palgrave: Marxian Economics*, London and Basingstoke: Macmillan, pp. 338–341.

Desai, M. (1989), editor, *Lenin's Economic Writings*. Atlantic Highlands, New Jersey: Humanities Press International.

Douglass, J.W. (2008) *JFK and the Unspeakable: Why He Died and Why It Matters*. Maryknoll, New York: Orbis Books.

Dunayevskaya, R. (1957), *Marxism and Freedom*. Amherst, New York: Humanities Press, 2000.

Dunayevskaya, R. (1982), *Rosa Luxemburg, Women's Liberation, and Marx's Philosophy of Revolution*, 2nd ed., Urbana and Chicago: University of Illinois Press, 1991.

Dussel, E. (2001), "The Four Drafts of *Capital*: Towards a New Interpretation of the Dialectical Thought of Marx", *Rethinking Marxism*, Vol. 13, No. 1, pp. 10–26.

Engels, F. (1891), "Introduction" [for new edition of *Wage-Labour and Capital* by Karl Marx], in Marx and Engels, MEGA, Vol. 32, Berlin: Akademie. 2010, pp. 21–28.

Ettinger, E. (1986), *Rosa Luxemburg: A Life*, Boston: Beacon.

Evenitsky, A. (1963), "Marx's Model of Expanded Reproduction", *Science and Society*, Vol. 27, No. 2, pp. 159–175.

Falk, R. (2007), "Global Ambitions and Geopolitical Wars: The Domestic Challenge", in *9/11 and American Empire: Intellectuals Speak Out*, D.R. Griffin and P.D. Scott, eds., Northampton, Massachusetts: Olive Branch Press, pp. 117–127.

Favilli, P. (1996), *The History of Italian Marxism: From its Origins to the Great War*, English edition, Brill, 2016.

Fernbach, D. (1973), "Introduction" to Karl Marx, *Surveys from Exile. Political Writings*, Vol. II, Harmondsworth, Middlesex: Penguin Books.

Fine, B. (1991), "Accumulation" in *A Dictionary of Marxist Thought*, 2nd ed. Oxford: Blackwell, pp. 2–4.

Fine, B. and A. Saad-Filho, eds. (2012), *The Elgar Companion to Marxist Economics*, Cheltenham, U.K.: Elgar.

Fisher, L. (2009), "The Mexican War and Lincoln's 'Spot Resolutions'", *The Law Library of Congress*, available at https://www.loc.gov/law/help/usconlaw/pdf/Mexican.war.pdf.

Foley, D. (1983), "Labour power", in *A Dictionary of Marxist Thought*, 2nd revised ed., T. Bottomore, ed., Oxford and Cambridge, Massachusetts: Backwell, 1991, pp. 296–297.

Frank, A.G. (1977), "On So-Called Primitive Accumulation", *Dialectical Anthropology*, Vol. 2, No. 2, pp. 87–106.

Frank, A.G. (1978), *World Accumulation, 1492–1789*, New York: Monthly Review.

Froelich, P. (1939), *Rosa Luxemburg: Her Life and Work*, newly translated from the third 1967 edition, by Johanna Hoomweg, New York and London: Monthly Review Press, 1972.

Giussani, P. (1983), "Reproduction Schema", *A Dictionary of Marxist Thought*, T. Bottomore, ed., Oxford and Cambridge, Mass.: Blackwell, 2nd revised ed., 1991, pp. 471–474.

Gleijeses, P. (2003), "1898: The Opposition to the Spanish-American War", *Journal of Latin American Studies*, Vol. 35, No. 4, pp. 681–719.

Göçmen, D. (2007), "Rosa Luxemburg, the Legacy of Classical German Philosophy and the Fundamental Methodological Questions of Social and Political Theory", *Critique: Journal of Socialist Theory*, Vol. 35, No. 3, pp. 375–390.

Graßmann, T. (2018), "Did Marx Relinquish His Concept of Capital's Historical Dynamic? A Comment on Fred Moseley", in *Marx's Capital: An Unfinishable Project?*, M. van der Linden and G. Hubmann, eds., Leiden: Brill, pp. 144–156.

Groll, S. and Z.B. Orzech (1989), "From Marx to Okishio Theorem: A Genealogy", *History of Political Economy*, Vol. 21, No. 2, pp. 253–272.

Grossman, H. (1924), "Simonde de Sismondi et ses theories economiques (Une nouvelle interpretation de sa pensee)", Bibliotheca Universitatis Liberae Polonae, Warsaw, Fasc. 11, 77 pp.

Grossman, H. (1934), "Jean Charles Leonard Simonde de Sismondi", in *Encyclopedia of the Social Sciences*, E.R.A. Seligman and A. Johnson, eds., New York: Macmillan, pp. 69–71.

Grossmann, H. (1929), *The Law of Accumulation and Breakdown of the Capitalist System: Being also a Theory of Crisis*, translated and abridged by J. Banaji, with a foreword and introduction by T. Kennedy, Pluto Press, 1992. Further material translated into English by K. Lapides, "Henryk Grossmann on Marx's Wage Theory and the 'Increasing Misery' Controversy", *History of Political Economy*, Vol. 26, No. 2, pp. 239–266.

Guttsman, W.L. (1981), *The German Social Democratic Party, 1875–1933: From Ghetto to Government*, London: George Allen & Unwin.

Hall, S. (2003), "Marx's Notes on Method", *Cultural Studies*, Vol. 17, No. 2, pp. 113–149.

Heinrich, M. (2013), "Crisis Theory, the Law of the Tendency of the Profit Rate to Fall, and Marx's Studies in the 1870s", *Monthly Review*, Vol. 64, No. 11, pp. 15–31.

Heller, H. (2019), *A Marxist History of Capitalism*, New York: Routledge.

Hett, B. (2014), *Burning the Reichstag: An Investigation into the Third Reich's Enduring Mystery*, Oxford: Oxford University Press.

Hilferding, R. (1910), *Finance Capital: A Study of the Latest Phase of Capitalist Development*, edited with an Introduction by T. Bottomore, translated by M. Watnick and S. Gordon. London: Routledge & Kegan Paul, 1981.

Holmes, R. (2014), *Eleanor Marx: A Life*, London: Bloomsbury Publishing.

REFERENCES 251

Howard, M.C. and King, J.E. (1989), *A History of Marxian Economics, Volume 1, 1883–1929*, Houndmills and London: Macmillan.

Hudis, P. (2012), *Marx's Concept of the Alternative to Capitalism*. Leiden: Brill.

Hudis, P. (2013), "Introduction", *The Complete Works of Rosa Luxemburg: Volume 1: Economic Writings 1*, P. Hudis, ed., translated by D. Fernbach, J. Fracchia and G. Shriver, London and New York: Verso.

Hudis, P. (2014), "The Dialectic of the Spatial Determination of Capital: Rosa Luxemburg's *Accumulation of Capital* Reconsidered", *Logos Journal*, available at: http://logosjournal.com/2014/hudis.

Hunt, E.K. (2002), *History of Economic Thought*, 2nd ed., Berkeley: University of California Press.

Ito, N. (2010), "Is the National Question an Aporia for Humanity? How to Read Rosa Luxemburg's 'The National Question and Autonomy'", *The National Question and the Question of Crisis, Research in Political Economy, Volume 26*, P. Zarembka, ed., Bingley, U.K.: Emerald Group, pp. 3–68.

Johnson, C. (2004), "America's Empire of Bases", *Global Policy Forum*, available at www.globalpolicy.org/component/content/article/153/26119.html.

Karimzadi, S. (2013), *Money and its Origins*, London and New York: Routledge.

Kates, S. (2010), "Influencing Keynes: The Intellectual Origins of the *General Theory*", *History of Economic Ideas*, Vol. XVIII, No. 3.

Kautsky, K. (1887), *The Economic Doctrines of Karl Marx*, translated [from an unspecified German edition seemingly as late or later than the 17th and 18th editions of 1919] by H.J. Stenning, New York: Macmillan, 1936, reprint edition, Westport, Connecticut: Hyperion Press, 1979.

Kautsky, K. (1902), "Krisentheorien", *Die Neue Zeit*, Vol. 20, 37–47, 76–81, 110–118, 133–143. The last three sections as "Theories of Crises" are translated by D. Gaido and D. Scattolini, in *Class History and Class Practices in the Periphery of Capitalism, Research in Political Economy, Volume 34*, P. Zarembka, ed., Bingley, U.K.: Emerald Group, 2019, pp. 199–224.

Kay, J. (2011), *Among the Truthers*, Toronto: HarperCollins.

Kindersley, R. (1962), *The First Russian Revisionists: A Study of "Legal Marxism" in Russia*, Oxford: Clarendon Press.

Kliman, A.J. (2000), "Marx's Concept of Intrinsic Value", *Historical Materialism*, Vol. 6, No. 1, pp. 89–113.

Kolar, J. (2008), "What We Now Know about the Alleged 9–11 Hijackers", in *The Hidden History of 9–11*, 2nd ed., P. Zarembka, ed., New York: Seven Stories Press, 3–44 and 293–304.

Kowalik, T. (1966), "R. Luxemburg's Theory of Accumulation and Imperialism (An Attempted Interpretation)". in *Problems of Economic Dynamics: Essays in Honor of Michal Kalecki*, Warsaw: Polish Scientific Publishers, 203–219.

Kowalik, T. (1971), *Rosa Luxemburg: Theory of Accumulation and Imperialism*, translated and edited by J. Toporowski and H. Szymborska, Basingstoke: Palgrave Macmillan, 2014.

Kowalik, T. (1987), "Rosa Luxemburg", *The New Palgrave: Marxian Economics*, London and Basingstoke: Macmillan, pp. 247–253.

Kowalik, T. (2009), "Luxemburg's and Kalecki's Theories and Visions of Capitalist Dynamics", in R. Bellofiore, ed., *Rosa Luxemburg and the Critique of Political Economy*, Oxon, U.K.: Routledge, pp. 102–116.

Kristjanson-Gural, D. (2005), "Exchange, Demand and the Market-Price of Production: Reconciling Traditional and Monetary Approaches to Value and Price", in *The Capitalist State and Its Economy; Democracy in Socialism, Research in Political Economy, Volume 22*, P. Zarembka, ed., Amsterdam: JAI/Elsevier Science, pp. 137–169.

Krupskaya, N. (1933), "How Lenin Studied Marx", Labor Monthly pamphlet No. 2, available at http://marxists.org/archive/krupskaya/works/howleninstudiedmarx.htm.

Kuczynski, T. (2017), Karl Marx, *Das Kapital*, Erster Band, new edition.

Kuehne, K. (1972), *Economics and Marxism, Volume 2, The Dynamics of the Marxian System*, translated by R. Shaw, New York: Macmillan, 1979.

Kuhn, R. (2000), "Henryk Grossman, a Marxist Activist and Theorist: On the 50th Anniversary of his Death", in *Value, Capitalist Dynamics and Money, Research in Political Economy, Volume 18*, P. Zarembka, ed., Stamford, CT and Amsterdam: JAI/Elsevier, pp. 111–170.

Lafargue, P. (1890), "Reminiscences of Marx (September 1890)", in *Marx and Engels through the Eyes of Their Contemporaries*, Moscow: Progress Publishers, 1972.

Laibman, D. (1992), *Value, Technical Change and Crisis*, Armonk, New York: M.E. Sharpe.

Laibman, D. (1998), "Accumulation, Technical Change, and Prisoners' Dilemma: A Rejoinder to Frank Thompson", *Review of Radical Political Economics*, Vol. 30, No. 2, pp. 87–101.

Lapides, K. (1998), *Marx's Wage Theory in Historical Perspective: Its Origins, Development and Interpretation*. Westport, Connecticut, and London: Praeger.

Laschitza, A. (1996), *Im Lebensrausch trotz alledem: Rosa Luxemburg, Eine Biographie*, Berlin: Aufbau-Verlag.

Laschitza, A., G. Adler, and P. Hudis, eds. (2011), *The Letters of Rosa Luxemburg*, translated by G. Shriver, Verso.

Lefebvre, J.-P. (1983), "Introduction" to K. Marx, *Le Capital*, Paris: Presses Universitaires de France, 1993 edition.

Lenin, Vladimir (1894), "What the 'Friends of the People' Are and How They Fight the Social-Democrats", *Collected Works, Volume 1*, London: Lawrence & Wishart, 1960, pp. 131–332.

Lenin, V.I. (1895), "The Economic Content of Narodism and the Criticism of it in Mr. Struve's Book", in *Collected Works, Volume 1*. Moscow: Progress Publishers, 1960, pp. 333–507.

Lenin, V.I. (1897), *A Characterization of Economic Romanticism (Sismondi and Our Native Sismondists)*, in *Collected Works, Volume 2*, Progress Publishers, Moscow, 1960, pp. 129–265.

Lenin, V.I. (1899a), "A Note on the Question of Market Theory (Apropos the Polemic of Messrs. Tugan-Baranovsky and Bulgakov)", *Collected Works, Volume 4*, Moscow: Progress Publishers, 1960, 55–64.

Lenin, V.I. (1899b), *The Development of Capitalism in Russia*, Moscow: Progress Publishers, 1956.

Lenin, V.I. (1899c), "Reply to Mr. P. Nezhdanov", *Collected Works, Volume 4*, Moscow: Progress Publishers, 1960, pp. 160–165.

Lenin, V.I. (1909), *Materialism and Empirio-Criticism*, *Collected Works, Volume 14*, Moscow: Foreign Languages Publishing House, 1962.

Lenin, V.I. (1913a), "To the Editor of Bremer Buerger-Zeitung", *Collected Works, Volume 43*, Moscow: Progress Publishers, 1969, pp. 332–333.

Lenin, V.I. (1913b), "Letter to 'L.B. Kamenev'", *Collected Works, Volume 35*, Moscow: Progress Publishers, 1966, pp. 93–94.

Lenin, V.I. (1913–14), "Critical Remarks on the National Question" and "The Right of Nations to Self-Determination", *Collected Works, Volume 20*. Moscow: Progress Publishers, 1964, pp. 17–51 and 393–454.

Lenin, V.I. (1914), "Conspectus of Hegel's book The Science of Logic", *Collected Works, Volume 38*, Moscow: Progress, 1972, pp. 85–241.

Lenin, V.I. (1915), "Karl Marx: A Brief Biographical Sketch with an Exposition of Marxism", *Collected Works, Volume 21*, Moscow: Progress Publishers, 1964, pp. 43–91.

Lenin, V.I. (1916), "The Socialist Revolution and the Right of Nations to Self-Determination" and "The Discussion on Self-Determination Summed Up", *Collected Works, Volume 22*, Moscow: Progress Publishers, 1964, pp. 143–156 and 320–360.

Lenin, V.I. (1917), *Imperialism, The Highest Stage of Capitalism*, *Collected Works, Volume 22*, Moscow: Progress Publishers, 1964, pp. 185–304.

Lenin, V.I. (1918), "How to Organize Competition?", *Collected Works, Volume 26*, Moscow: Progress Publishers, pp. 404–415.

Lenin, V.I. (1924, written 1922), "Notes of a Publicist", *Collected Works, Volume 33*, Moscow: Progress Publishers, 1966, pp. 204–211.

Lenin, V.I. (1933, written 1913), "Marginal Notes of V.I. Lenin on Rosa Luxemburg's *Accumulation of Capital*", *Leninskii Sbornik, Volume 22* [in Russian], Reprint of the 1933 Moscow edition, Nendeln, Liechtenstein: Krauss Reprint Ltd., pp. 337–390; English translation by J. Lawler as Appendix to Zarembka (2000).

Lenin, V.I. (1937, written 1893), "On the So-called Market Question", *Collected Works, Volume 1*, Moscow: Progress Publishers, 1960, pp. 75–125, reprinted in Desai (1989).

Leontiev, A. (1935), *Political Economy – A Beginner's Course*, translated by S.D. Kogan, Moscow and Leningrad: Cooperative Publishing Society of Foreign Workers in the USSR.

Longman, J. (2002), *Among the Heroes*. New York: HarperCollins.

Luxemburg, R. (1899), "Hohle Nüsse" ["Empty Nuts"], *Leipziger Volkszeitung*, 27 July.

Luxemburg, R. (1901), "Aus dem Nachlaß unserer Meister" ["From the estate of our masters"], *Vorwärts* (Berlin), Nr. 217, 17 September [*Gesammelte Werke*, Band 1/2, Berlin 1970, S. 130–141].

Luxemburg, R. (1908–09), "The National Question and Autonomy", in *The National Question: Selected Writings by Rosa Luxemburg*, translated by H.B. Davis, New York: Monthly Review Press, 1976, pp. 101–287.

Luxemburg, R. (1909), "Autonomja Krolewstwa Polskiego", *Przeglad Socjaldemokratyczny*, No. 14–15.

Luxemburg, R. (1913), *The Accumulation of Capital: A Contribution to the Economic Theory of Imperialism*, in *The Complete Works of Rosa Luxemburg, Volume II: Economic Writings 2*, P. Hudis and P. Le Blanc, eds., translated by N. Gray, London and Brooklyn, Verso, 2015, pp. 1–342.

Luxemburg, R. (1915), "The Junius Pamphlet: The Crisis in German Social Democracy", in *The Rosa Luxemburg Reader*, P. Hudis and K.B. Anderson, eds., New York: Monthly Review Press, 2004, pp. 312–341.

Luxemburg, R. (1918), "The Second and Third Volumes of *Capital*", in *The Complete Works of Rosa Luxemburg, Volume II: Economic Writings 2*, P. Hudis and P. Le Blanc, eds., translated by E. Fitzgerald, London and Brooklyn, Verso, 2015, pp. 453–461.

Luxemburg, R. (1921, written 1915), *The Accumulation of Capital, Or, What the Epigones have made out of Marx's Theory – An Anti-Critique*, in *The Complete Works of Rosa Luxemburg, Volume II: Economic Writings 2*, P. Hudis and P. Le Blanc, eds., translated by G. Shriver, London and Brooklyn, Verso, 2015, pp. 343–449.

Luxemburg, R. (1925, mostly written in 1909–10), *Introduction to Political Economy*, in *The Complete Works of Rosa Luxemburg: Volume I: Economic Writings 1*, P. Hudis, ed., translated by D. Fernbach, J. Fracchia and G. Shriver, London and New York: Verso, pp. 89–300.

Luxemburg, R. (1971), *Listy do Leona Jogichesa-Tyszki: (1908–1914)*, Volume 3, Książka i Wiedza, English translation here by N. Ito.

Luxemburg, R. (1996, written 1918) "Fragment on the History of the First and Second International and for the Problems of the Postwar", in A. Laschitza (1996, p. 580).

REFERENCES

Luxemburg, R. (2013a), *The Complete Works of Rosa Luxemburg: Volume 1: Economic Writings 1*, P. Hudis, ed., translated by D. Fernbach, J. Fracchia and G. Shriver, London and New York: Verso.

Luxemburg, R. (2013b, written about 1911), "Practical Economics: Volume 2 of Marx's *Capital*", in *The Complete Works of Rosa Luxemburg: Volume 1: Economic Writings 1*, P. Hudis, ed., translated by D. Fernbach, J. Fracchia and G. Shriver, London and New York: Verso, pp. 421–460.

MacGregor, D., and P. Zarembka (2010), "Marxism, Conspiracy, and 9-11", *Socialism and Democracy*, Vol. 24, No. 2, pp. 139–163.

MacQueen, G. (2006), "118 Witnesses: The Firefighter's Testimony to Explosions in the Twin Towers", *Journal of 9/11 Studies*, Vol. 2, available at www.journalof911studies.com/articles/Article_5_118Witnesses_World TradeCenter.pdf.

Mage, S. (1963), *The Law of the Falling Tendency of the Rate of Profit*, Ph.D. dissertation, New York: Columbia University.

Mage, S. (2013), "Response to Heinrich – In Defense of Marx's Law", *Monthly Review*, at https://monthlyreview.org/commentary/critique-heinrich-marx-abandon-logical-structure, accessed Aug. 10, 2019.

Mandel, E. (1978), "Introduction", to K. Marx, *Capital, Volume II*, translated by D. Fernbach, Harmondsworth: Penguin, pp. 11–79.

Marx, K. (1847), *The Poverty of Philosophy*, in K. Marx and F. Engels, *Collected Works*, Volume 6, New York: International Publishers, 1975, pp. 105–212.

Marx, K. (1859), *A Contribution to the Critique of Political Economy*, in in K. Marx and F. Engels, *Collected Works*, *Volume 29*, New York: International Publishers, 1975, pp. 257–417.

Marx, K. (1865), *Value, Price and Profit,* edited by Eleanor Marx Aveling, Moscow: Progress Publishers, 1947; also, as abridged from original publication by P. Zarembka, in *Value, Capitalist Dynamics and Money, Research in Political Economy, Volume 18*, P. Zarembka, ed., Amsterdam: JAI/Elsevier, pp. 3–39.

Marx, K. (1867), *Capital: A Critical Analysis of Capitalist Production, Volume I*, translated by Samuel Moore and Edward Aveling from the third German edition and edited by Frederick Engels in 1887, Moscow: Progress Publishers, 1954, and London: Lawrence and Wishart, 1974, 767 pages. Translated also by Ben Fowkes, New York: Penguin Books, 1976. Pagination here refer to the Lawrence and Wishart edition, except when Fowkes is indicated. For translation of the "Appendix" to the 1st ed., see Marx (1978).

Marx, K. (1872–1875), *Le capital*, traduction de M.J. Roy, entièrement revisée par l'auteur, Paris: Maurice LaChatre, available in MEGA² II/7, 1989, on-line at http://telota.bbaw.de/mega/ or https://thecharnelhous.org/wp-content/uploads/2016/02/megac2b2-ii-7-karl-marx-le-capital-paris-1872e280931875-text.pdf.

Marx, K. (1885), *Capital: A Critical Analysis of Capitalist Production, Volume II*, edited by Frederick Engels, Moscow: Progress Publishers, and London: Lawrence and Wishart, 1956, 551 pages, 1974.

Marx, K. (1894), *Capital: A Critical Analysis of Capitalist Production, Volume III*, edited by Frederick Engels, Moscow: Progress Publishers, and London: Lawrence and Wishart, 1959, 948 pages, 1974.

Marx, K. (1905a), *Theories of Surplus Value: Part I*, Moscow: Progress Publishers, 1963.

Marx, K. (1905b), *Theories of Surplus Value: Part II*, Moscow: Progress Publishers, 1968.

Marx, K. (1910), *Theories of Surplus Value: Part III*, Moscow: Progress Publishers, 1971.

Marx, K. (1930), "Marginal Notes on Adolph Wagner's *Lehrbuch der Politischen Oekonomie*", in K. Marx and F. Engels, *Collected Works, Volume 24*. New York: International Publishers, 1989, pp. 531–559.

Marx, K. (1932), *The Economic and Philosophic Manuscripts of 1844*, translated by Martin Milligan and edited with an introduction by D. J. Stroik, New York: International Publishers, 1964.

Marx, K. (1933), "Results of the Immediate Process of Production", Appendix to *Capital, Volume I*, translated by R. Livingstone, New York: Penguin, 1976, pp. 948–1084.

Marx, K. (1939–41a), *Grundrisse*, translated by Martin Nicolaus, New York and Toronto: Vintage Books, 1973.

Marx, K. (1939–41b), *Grundrisse*, in K. Marx and F. Engels, *Collected Works, Volumes 28 and 29*, New York: International Publishers, 1986.

Marx, K. (1978), "The Value-Form", translation of the "Appendix" to the *Capital, Volume I*, 1st ed., by M. Roth and W. Suchting, *Capital & Class*, Volume 4, Spring, pp. 134–150.

Marx, K. (2015), *Marx's Economic Manuscript of 1864–65*, translated by B. Fowkes and edited by F. Moseley, Leiden: Brill Academic.

Marx, K. and F. Engels (1848) *Manifesto of the Communist Party*, in *Collected Works, Volume 6*, New York: International Publishers, 1948, pp. 467–519.

Marx, K. and F. Engels (1948), *Letters on "Capital"*, translated by A. Drummond, London: New Park Publications, 1983.

Marx, K. and F. Engels (c.w.), *Collected Works*, New York: International Publishers, various volume numbers and years.

Marx, K. and F. Engels (MEGA²), *Karl Marx/Friedrich Engels Gesamtausgabe*, zweite abteilung, various publishers, volume numbers and years.

Mattick, P. (1935), "Luxemburg versus Lenin, Part I", in *Modern Monthly*, Vol. 9, No. 5, pp. 300–308; entire article printed in his *Anti-Bolshevik Communism*, White Plains, NY: Sharpe, 1978, pp. 19–48 and cited here.

Mattick, P. (1974), *Economic Crisis and Crisis Theory*, translated by P. Mattick, Jr., White Plains, NY: Sharpe, 1981.

Mattick, P. (1978), "Rosa Luxemburg in Retrospect", *Root and Branch,* Number 6.
McCracken, H.L. (1933), *Value Theory and Business Cycles,* Binghamton, New York: Falcon Press.
McDermott, T. (2005), *Perfect Soldiers: The Hijackers: Who They, Were and Why They Did It,* New York: HarperCollins.
Milios, J. (1999), "Preindustrial Capitalist Forms: Lenin's Contribution to a Marxist Theory of Economic Development", *Rethinking Marxism,* Vol. 11, No. 4, pp. 38–56.
Milios, J., D. Dimoulis, and G. Economakis (2002), *Karl Marx and the Classics: An Essay on Value, Crises and the Capitalist Mode of Production,* Hampshire, England and Burlington, VT: Ashgate.
Mironov, Boris (1990), "The Russian Peasant Commune after the Reforms of the 1860s", in B. Eklof and S. Frank, eds., *The World of the Russian Peasant: Post-Emancipation Culture and Society.* Boston, Massachusetts: Unwin Hyman, pp. 7–43.
Mohun, S. (1991a), "Organic composition of capital", in *A dictionary of Marxist Thought,* T. Bottomore, ed., 2nd ed., Cambridge, MA: Blackwell, pp. 403–404.
Mohun, S. (1991b), "Value", in *A Dictionary of Marxist Thought,* 2nd ed., T. Bottomore, ed., Oxford and Cambridge, Massachusetts: Backwell, pp. 564–568.
Mohun, S. (2005), "On Measuring the Wealth of Nations: the US Economy, 1964–2001", *Cambridge Journal of Economics,* Vol. 29, pp. 799–815.
Moseley, F. (1986), "Estimates of the Rate of Surplus-Value in the Postwar United States Economy", *Review of Radical Political Economics,* Vol. 18, Nos. 1&2, pp. 168–189.
Moseley, F. (1991), *The Falling Rate of Profit in the Postwar United States Economy,* New York: St. Martin's Press.
Moseley, F. (1997), "The Rate of Surplus Value and the Future of Capitalism", *Review of Radical Political Economics,* Vol. 29, No. 4, Fall, pp. 23–41.
Moseley, F. (1998), "Marx's Reproduction Schemes and Smith's Dogma", in *The Circulation of Capital: Essays on Volume Two of Marx's* Capital, C.J. Arthur and G. Reuten, eds., London and New York: Macmillan, pp. 159–185.
Moseley, F. (2015), "Introduction", to Marx (2015).
Moseley, F. (2018), "The Development of Marx's Theory of the Falling Rate of Profit in the Four Drafts of *Capital*", in *Marx's* Capital: *An Unfinishable Project?,* M. van der Linden and G. Hubmann, eds., Leiden, Brill, pp. 95–143.
Nelson, M. K. (2020), *The Three-Cornered War: The Union, the Confederacy, and Native Peoples in the Fight for the West,* New York: Scribner.
Oakley, A. (1984), *Marx's Critique of Political Economy: Intellectual Sources and Evolution, Volume I: 1844 to 1861,* London, Boston, Melbourne and Henley: Routledge & Kegan Paul.
Oakley, A. (1985), *Marx's Critique of Political Economy: Intellectual Sources and Evolution, Volume II: 1861 to 1863,* London, Boston, Melbourne and Henley: Routledge & Kegan Paul.

Offord, D. (1988), "The Contribution of V.V. Bervi-Flerovsky to Russian Populism", *Slavonic and East European Review*, Vol. 6, No. 2, pp. 236–251.

Oishi, T. (2001), *The Unknown Marx: Reconstructing a Unified Perspective*, London and Sterling, Virginia: Pluto.

Okishio, N., (1961), "Technical Change and the Rate of Profit", *Kobe University Economic Review*, Vol. 7, pp. 85–99.

Orzech, Z.B., and S. Groll (1989), "Stages in the development of a Marxian concept: The composition of capital", *History of Political Economy*, Vol. 21, No. 1, pp. 57–76.

Paitaridis, D., and L. Tsoulfidis (2012), "The growth of unproductive activities, the rate of profit, and the phase-change of the U.S. economy", *Review of Radical Political Economics*, Vol. 44, No. 2, pp. 213–233.

Pannekoek, A. (1934), "The Theory of the Collapse of Capitalism", translated by A. Buick, *Capital & Class*, Vol. 1, No. 1, Spring 1977, pp. 59–81.

Patriquin, L. (2004), "The Agrarian Origins of the Industrial Revolution in England", *Review of Radical Political Economics*, Vol. 36, No. 2, pp. 196–216.

Paul, D. (1981), "'In the Interests of Civilization': Marxist Views of Race and Culture in the Nineteenth Century", *Journal of the History of Ideas*, Vol. 42, No. 1, pp. 115–138.

Pepper, W.F. (2003), *An Act of State: The Execution of Martin Luther King*, London and New York: Verso, 2008.

Perelman, M. (2000), *The Invention of Capitalism: Classical Political Economy and the Secret History of Primitive Accumulation*. Durham (North Carolina) and London: Duke University Press.

Plekhanov, G.V. (1885), *Our Differences*, 2nd ed., 1905, in *Selected Philosophical Works, Volume I*, Moscow: Progress Publishers, 1960, pp. 107–352.

Plekhanov, G.V. (1891), "For the Sixtieth Anniversary of Hegel's Death", in *Selected Philosophical Works, Volume I*, Moscow: Progress Publishers, pp. 401–426.

Plekhanov, G.V. (1896), "Essays on the History of Materialism", in *Selected Philosophical Works, Volume II*, Moscow: Progress Publishers, 1976, pp. 31–182.

Plekhanov, G.V. (1908), "Fundamental Problems of Marxism", in *Selected Philosophical Works, Volume III*, Moscow: Progress Publishers, 1976, pp. 117–183.

Postone, M. (1993), *Time, Labor and Social Domination: A Reinterpretation of Marx's Critical Theory*, Cambridge, U.K. and New York: Cambridge University Press.

Poteshman, A.M. (2006), "Unusual Option Market Activity and the Terrorist Attacks of September 11, 2001", *Journal of Business*, Vol. 79, No. 4, 1703–1726.

Pradella, L. (2015), *Globalisation and the Critique of Political Economy: New Insights from Marx's Writings*, London: Routledge.

Price, G.W. (1967), *The Origins of the War with Mexico: The Polk-Stockton Intrigue*, Austin, Texas: University of Texas.

Ramos, M.A. (1998–99), "Value and Price of Production: New Evidence on Marx's Transformation Procedure", *International Journal of Political Economy*, Vol. 28, No. 4, pp. 55–81.

Ranganayakamma (1999), *An Introduction to Marx's "Capital" (in 3 volumes), Volume 1*, Hyderabad: Sweet Home Publications.

Resis, A. (1970), "Das Kapital Comes to Russia", *Slavic Review*, Vol. 29, No. 2, pp. 219–237.

Reuten, G. (2019), "Marx's Conceptualization of Value in *Capital*", in *The Oxford Handbook of Karl Marx*, M. Vidal, T. Smith, T. Rotta, and P. Prew, eds., New York, NY: Oxford University Press.

Ricardo, D. (1821), *On the Principles of Political Economy and Taxation*, edited by P. Sraffa with the collaboration of M.H. Dobb, Cambridge: Cambridge University Press, 1951.

Rjasanoff, N. (1916), "Karl Marx und Friedrich Engels über die Polenfrage", in *Archiv für die Geschichte des Sozialismus und der Arbeiterbewegung*, VI, Jg.

Robinson, J. (1951), "Introduction" to the first English edition of R. Luxemburg, *The Accumulation of Capital*, translated by A. Schwarzschild, New York: Monthly Review Press, and London: Routledge and Kegal Paul, 1951, pp. 13–28.

Robinson, J. (1956), *The Accumulation of Capital*, London: Macmillan.

Robson, R. (1957), *The Cotton Industry of Britain*, London: Macmillan.

Rosdolsky, R. (1956), "Zur neuren Kritik des Marxschen Gesetzes der fallenden Profitrate", *Kyklos*, Vol. 9, pp. 208–226.

Rosdolsky, R. (1968), *The Making of Marx's "Capital", in Two Volumes*, translated by P. Burgess, 2nd (unabridged) paperback ed., London: Pluto Press, 1989.

Roth, R. (2018), "Editing the Legacy: Friedrich Engels and Marx's *Capital*", in *Marx's Capital: An Unfinishable Project?*, M. van der Linden and G. Hubmann, eds., Leiden: Brill, pp. 31–47.

Rowthorne, B. and D. Harris (1985), "The Organic Composition of Capital and Capitalist Development", in *Rethinking Marxism: Struggles for Marxist Theory: Essays for Harry Magdoff and Paul Sweezy*, S. Resnick and R. Wolff, eds., New York: Autonomedia.

Rubin, I.I. (1927), "Abstract Labour and Value in Marx's System", translated by K. Gilbert, *Capital & Class*, Volume 2, No. 2, Summer 1978, pp. 109–139.

Rubin, I.I. (1928), *Essays on Marx's Theory of Value*, translated by M. Samardžija and F. Perlman from the 1928 Russian 3rd ed., Detroit: Black and Red, 1972.

Russell, B. (1964), "16 Questions on the JFK Assassination", cited in *The Hidden History of 9–11*, 2nd ed., P. Zarembka, ed., New York: Seven Stories Press, 2008, pp. 349–352.

Seigel, J. (1978), *Marx's Fate: The Shape of a Life*. Princeton, NJ: Princeton University Press.

Shaikh, A. (1978a), "An Introduction to the History of Crisis Theories", in *U.S. Capitalism in Crisis*, New York: U.R.P.E., pp. 219–241.

Shaikh, A. (1978b), "Political Economy and Capitalism: Notes on Dobb's Theory of Crisis", *Cambridge Journal of Economics*, Vol. 2, No. 2, pp. 233–251.

Shaikh, A. (1987), "Organic Composition of Capital", in *The New Palgrave: Marxian Economics*, J. Eatwell, M. Milgate, and P. Newman, eds., London: Macmillan, pp. 304–309.

Shaikh, A. (1992), "The Falling Rate of Profit as the Cause of Long Waves: Theory and Empirical Evidence", in *New Findings in Long-Wave Research*, A. Kleinknecht A., E. Mandel, and I. Wallerstein (eds), London: Palgrave Macmillan.

Shaikh, A. (2016), *Capitalism: Competition, Conflict, Crises*, Oxford.

Shaikh, A. and E. Tonak (1994), *Measuring the Wealth of Nations. The Political Economy of National Accounts*, Cambridge: Cambridge University Press.

Shanin, T., ed. (1983), *Late Marx and the Russian Road: Marx and "the Peripheries of Capitalism"*, New York: Monthly Review Press.

Shirer, W.L. (1960), *The Rise and Fall of the Third Reich*, New York: Simon and Schuster.

Sieber, N.I. (1871), *David Ricardo's Theory of Value and of Capital* [in Russian], Kiev: University Press.

Sieber, N.I. (1874), "Marx's Economic Theory", translated by J.D. White, in *Revitalizing Marxist Theory for Today's Capitalism, Research in Political Economy, Volume 27*, P. Zarembka and R. Desai, eds., Emerald Group, Bingley, U.K., 2011, pp. 155–190.

Sieber, N.I. (2001), "Marx's Theory of Value and Money", Chapter IV of Sieber (1871), translated by R. Mananova and J.D. White, in *Marx's* Capital *and Capitalism; Markets in a Socialist Alternative, Research in Political Economy, Volume 19*, P. Zarembka, ed., Amsterdam, London, and New York: JAI/Elsevier Science, pp. 17–45.

Sinha, A. (1996), "A Critique of Part One of *Capital* Volume One: The Value Controversy Revisited", in *Recent Developments in Marxist Theory, Research in Political Economy, Volume 15*, P. Zarembka and A. Sinha, eds., Greenwich, Connecticut: JAI Press, pp. 195–222.

Sinha, A., (2010), *Theories of Value from Adam Smith to Piero Sraffa*, New Delhi: Routledge.

Sismondi, J.-C.-L. Simonde de (1819), *New Principles of Political Economy: Of Wealth in its Relation to Population*, translated and annotated by R. Hyse, New Brunswick and London: Transaction Publishers, 1991.

Smith, A. (1776), *An Inquiry into the Nature and Causes of the Wealth of Nations,* New York: The Modern Library, 1937.

Smith, D.N. (2001), "The Spectral Reality of Value: Sieber, Marx, and Commodity Fetishism", in *Marx's* Capital *and Capitalism; Markets in a Socialist Alternative, Research in Political Economy, Volume 19*, P. Zarembka, ed., JAI/Elsevier Science, New York, pp. 47–66.

Steedman, I. (1982), "Marx on Ricardo", in I. Bradley and M. Howard, eds., *Classical and Marxian Political Economy: Essays in Honor of Ronald L. Meek*. London and Basingstoke: Macmillan, pp. 113–156.

Swanson, P.A. (1986), "The Labor Theory of Value and Fixed Capital", *Review of Radical Political Economics*, Vol. 18, No. 3, pp. 44–64.

Sweezy, P. (1942), *The Theory of Capitalist Development*, New York: Monthly Review, 1968.

Tarpley, W.G. (2006), *9/11 Synthetic Terror: Made in USA*, 3rd ed., Joshua Tree, California: Progressive Press.

Thompson, F. (1998), "The Composition of Capital and the Rate of Profit: A Reply to Laibman", *Review of Radical Political Economics*, Vol. 30, No. 1, pp. 90–107.

Tsoulfidis, L. (2017), "Growth Accounting of the Value Composition of Capital and the Rate of Profit in the U.S. Economy: A Note Stimulated by Zarembka's Findings", *Review of Radical Political Economics*, Vol. 49, No. 2, pp. 303–312.

Tsoulfidis, L. and D. Paitaridis (2019), "Capital Intensity, Unproductive Activities and the Great Recession in the US Economy", *Cambridge Journal of Economics*, Vol. 43, No. 3, pp. 623–647.

Tugan-Baranowsky, M.I. (1901), *Studien zur Theorie und Geschichte der Handelskrisen in England*, 2nd ed., Jena: Gustav Fischer. Chapters 1 and 7 translated by A. Ramos-Martinez, in P. Zarembka, ed., *Value, Capitalist Dynamics and Money, Research in Political Economy, Volume 18*. Stamford (Connecticut) and Amsterdam (Holland): JAI/Elsevier Science, 2000, pp. 43–110.

Turchetto, M. (2000), "The Historicity of Marx's Categories", *Science & Society*, Vol. 64, No. 3, pp. 365–374.

van der Linden, M. and G. Hubmann (2018), "Introduction", in *Marx's Capital: An Unfinishable Project?*, M. van der Linden and G. Hubmann, eds., Leiden: Brill, pp. 1–30.

van Onselen, C. (1976), *Chibaro: African mine labour in Southern Rhodesia, 1900–1933*. London: Pluto.

Van Parijs, P. (1980), "The Falling-Rate-of-Profit Theory of Crisis: A Rational Reconstruction by Way of Obituary", *Review of Radical Political Economics*, Vol. 12, No. 1, pp. 1–16.

Venida, V.S. (2007), "Marxian Categories Empirically Estimated: The Philippines, 1961–1994", *Review of Radical Political Economics*, Vol. 39, No. 1, pp. 58–79.

Vine, D. (2015), "Shut Bases There, Save Money Here", *New York Times*, July 27, p. A19.

Walicki, A. (1979), *A History of Russian Thought: From the Enlightenment to Marxism*, Standard, California: Stanford University Press.

Warski, A. (1929), "Documents on the 4th Congress of the SDKPiL and the 2nd Congress of the RSDLP", in *Z Pola Walki* (From Battle Field).

Watters, F.M. (1968), "The Peasant and the Village Commune", in *The Peasant in Nineteenth-Century Russia*, Wayne S. Vucinich, ed., Stanford, California: Stanford University Press, pp. 133–157.

Webber, M.J. and D.L. Rigby (1986), "The Rate of Profit in Canadian Manufacturing, 1950–81", *Review of Radical Political Economics*, Vol. 18, Nos. 1&2, pp. 33–55.

Weeks, J. (1982), "A Note on Underconsumptionist Theory and the Labor Theory of Value", *Science & Society*, Vol. 46, No. 1, pp. 60–76.

Weeks, J. (1990), "Abstract Labor and Commodity Production", in *Research in Political Economy, Volume 12*, P. Zarembka, ed., JAI Press, Greenwich, Connecticut, and London, pp. 3–19.

Weinberg, M. (2002), *A Short History of American Capitalism*, available online at www.newhistory.org.

White, J.D. (1996), *Karl Marx and the Intellectual Origins of Dialectical Materialism*, Houndmills, U.K.: Macmillan and New York: St. Martin's.

White, J.D. (2001a), "Nikolai Sieber and Karl Marx", in *Marx's Capital and Capitalism; Markets in a Socialist Alternative, Research in Political Economy, Volume 19*, P. Zarembka, ed., JAI/Elsevier Science, New York, pp. 3–16.

White, J.D. (2001b), *Lenin: The Practice and Theory of Revolution*. Houndmills, U.K. and New York: Palgrave.

White, J.D. (2011), "Nikolai Sieber: An Introduction to a Political Economist Approved by Marx", in *Revitalizing Marxist Theory for Today's Capitalism, Research in Political Economy, Volume 27*, P. Zarembka and R. Desai, eds., Bingley, U.K.: Emerald Group, pp. 151–154.

White, J.D. (2019a), *Marx and Russia: The Fate of a Doctrine*, London: Bloomsbury Academic.

White, J.D. (2019b), "The Development of Capitalism in Russia in the Works of Marx, Danielson, Vorontsov, and Lenin", in *Class History and Class Practices in the Periphery of Capitalism, Research in Political Economy, Volume 34*, P. Zarembka, ed., Bingley, U.K.: Emerald Group, pp. 3–31.

Wolff, E.N. (1986), "The Productivity Slowdown and the Fall in the U.S. Rate of Profit, 1947–76", *Review of Radical Political Economics*, Vol. 18, Nos. 1 & 2, pp. 87–109.

Wolff, E.N. (1987), *Growth, Accumulation, and Unproductive Activity: An Analysis of the Postwar U.S. Economy*, Cambridge, Cambridge University Press.

Wolff, E.N. (1988), "The Rate of Surplus Value, the Organic Composition of Capital and the General Rate of Profit in the U.S. Economy, 1947–1967: Reply", *American Economic Review*, Vol. 78, No. 1, March, pp. 304–306.

Wolff, E.N. (2001), "The Recent Rise of Profits in the United States", *Review of Radical Political Economics*, Vol. 33, No. 3, pp. 315–324.

Wood, G.H. (1910), "The Statistics of Wages in the Nineteenth Century. Part XIX – The Cotton Industry. Section V. Changes in the Average Wage of all Employed, with some Account of the Forces Operating to Accelerate or Retard the Progress of the Industry", *Journal of the Royal Statistical Society*, Vol. 73, Part IV, pp. 585–633.

Zarembka, P. (1976), "Characterizations of Technology in Capital Theory" and "Reply" to Discussion of R.M. Solow, in *Essays in Modern Capital Theory*. Amsterdam, M. Brown, K. Sato and P. Zarembka, eds., New York, and Oxford: North-Holland, pp. 123–138 and 141–143.

Zarembka, P. (2000), "Accumulation of Capital, Its Definition: A Century after Lenin and Luxemburg", in *Value, Capitalist Dynamics and Money, Research in Political Economy, Volume 18*, P. Zarembka, ed., New York: JAI/Elsevier Science, pp. 183–241

Zarembka, P. (2001), "The Declining Importance of Hegel for Marx: J.D. White's Provocative Work", *Historical Materialism*, Vol. 8, No. 1, Summer, pp. 355–365.

Zarembka, P. (2002a), "Primitive Accumulation in Marxism, Historical or Trans-historical Separation from Means of Production?", *The Commoner, A Web Journal for Other Values* ("Debate: on Primitive Accumulation", available at http://citeseerx.ist.psu.edu/viewdoc/download?doi=10.1.1.455.5465&rep=rep1&type=pdf). Revised in W. Bonefeld (2008, pp. 67–75).

Zarembka, P. (2002b), "Rosa Luxemburg's *Accumulation of Capital*: Critics Try to Bury the Message", in J. Lehmann, ed., *Bringing Capitalism Back for Critique by Social Theory, Current Perspectives in Social Theory, Volume 21*, New York: JAI/Elsevier Press, pp. 3–45.

Zarembka, P. (2003), "Lenin as Economist of Production: A Ricardian Step Backwards", *Science & Society*, pp. 276–302.

Zarembka, P. (2008), "Initiation of the 9–11 Operation, with Evidence of Insider Trading Beforehand", in *The Hidden History of 9–11*, 2nd ed., P. Zarembka, ed., New York: Seven Stories Press, 47–74 and 305–314.

Zarembka, P. (2010), "Low Surplus Value Historically required for Accumulation, seen in a Model derived from Marx", *The National Question and the Question of Crisis, Research in Political Economy, Volume 26*, P. Zarembka, ed., Bingley: Emerald Group, pp. 145–172.

Zarembka, P. (2012), "Evidence of Insider Trading before September 11th Re-examined", in *The 9/11 Toronto Report: International Hearings on the Events of September 11, 2001*, James Gourley, ed., International Center for 9/11 Studies, pp. 129–149 and 405–408 for endnotes. [The original 2011 text, available at https://web.archive.org/web/20160522131946/http://ithp.org/articles/septemberinsidertrading.html, was significantly edited for this publication without consulting the author.].

Zarembka, P. (2014), "Marxist Political Economy without Hegel: Contrasting Marx and Luxemburg with Plekhanov and Lenin", in *The Legacy of Rosa Luxemburg, Oskar*

Lange and Michał Kalecki: Essays in Honour of Tadeusz Kowalik, Houndmills, England, and New York: Palgrave Macmillan, pp. 58–77.

Zarembka, P. (2015a), "Materialized composition of capital and its stability in the United States: Findings stimulated by Paitaridis and Tsoulfidis (2012)", *Review of Radical Political Economics*, Vol. 47, No. 1, pp. 106–111.

Zarembka, P. (2015b), Review of S. Karimzadi, "Money and its origins", *Review of Keynesian Economics*, Vol. 33, No. 3, pp. 438–441.

Zarembka, P. (2016), "Value: Marx's Evolution and Luxemburg's Legacy", in *Rosa Luxemburg: A Permanent Challenge for Political Economy*, J. Dellheim and F.O. Wolf, eds., London: Palgrave Macmillan, pp. 55–89.

Zarembka, P. (2019), "Late Marx and the Conception of 'Accumulation of Capital'", in *Confronting Capitalism in the 21st Century*, M. Silver, ed., Cham, Switzerland: Palgrave Macmillan, pp. 47–65.

Index

abstractions   15, 28, 30, 32, 124, 129, 135, 170
accumulation   58–59, 65–67, 69–73, 75–79, 86–87, 98–119, 121–23, 141, 165–66, 169–72, 174–75, 177–78, 180, 182–90
accumulation of capital   1–4, 100–103, 107–10, 112, 114–20, 124–25, 167–73, 175–76, 182–83, 187–89, 192–93, 223–25
   defining (*see also* Marxist accumulation of capital)   102, 116, 119, 170–71, 183
   Marx   103, 107–8, 112, 115–16
      ambiguity in   3, 89, 108, 111, 114, 116–17, 190
      Smith and Ricardo   107
   Tugan, importance of   104
   Kautsky on   103, 107, 176–77
   Lenin's emphasis   103, 106
alienation   1, 29, 40
Allen, Hervey   227
Allisson, François   17
Altenhöner, F.   235
Althusser, Louis   9, 21, 23, 27, 38, 87–88, 124
Anderson, Kevin   12, 54–55, 60–61, 89
Anthony Adverse   227
"Aporia"   197, 225
Arkhipov, Vice Admiral Vasily A.   5
Arthur, Chris   40, 54–55
autonomy   197–98, 203–4, 207, 209, 211, 213–19, 221, 223, 225
Aveling, Edward   54, 89–90

Baronian, Laurent   27, 32, 128
Barton, John   77–78
Bauer, Otto   170, 177–81, 185–87, 189, 191
Bergman, Jay   18
Bernstein, Eduard   48, 187
Biernacki, Richard   34
Boccardo, Gerolamo   85
Bogdanov, Alexander A.   22
Böhm-Bawerk, Eugen von   42–43
Bolshevik Revolution   3
Bolsheviks   182, 216, 220
Bonefeld, Werner   99–101
Bortkiewicz, Ladislaus   41
Boudin, Louis   177
Bronner, Stephen E.   23

Bulgakov, Sergei   105, 169, 174, 178, 182–85, 187, 191

Cámara Izquierdo, Sergio   134
capital   1–4, 9–21, 27–28, 30–33, 35–43, 47–49, 51–65, 67–83, 86–89, 91–98, 100–126, 128–29, 133–46, 148–55, 159–83, 185–93
   its meaning for Marx   107–8
Capital, Volume I   1–2, 10–13, 17–19, 23, 27–28, 30, 33–34, 36, 39, 41–44, 47–49, 51, 53–54, 62, 85–86, 88–89, 92, 94–98, 100, 107–9, 113–14, 116–17, 121, 124–25, 128, 133–35, 137, 139, 141–44, 169, 171, 175, 245
   Afterword to 2nd German edition   11, 13–14, 16, 21, 53, 128
   division of   47–48, 52–54, 85–86, 90–91, 97–98
   English edition
      edited by Engels   54
      modern   90, 98
   French edition
      edited by Marx   53, 62, 90–91
      modern   54, 90
   German editions   48, 54–55, 90
   Luxemburg's critique, importance of   177
   Part VIII, primitive accumulation (*see also* primitive accumulation)   62, 85, 87, 89, 100
   various editions
      "1882" by Marx   48
      Dutch   91
      English   47, 54, 64, 86, 89–90
         1st by Engels   54, 83, 90–91, 93
      French   1–3, 10–13, 15–16, 19–20, 28, 47–65, 67–71, 73, 81–83, 85–86, 88–92, 97–98, 100–101, 111–12, 114–16, 124–25, 130, 133–34, 136, 138–39, 144, 229, 245
         importance of   54
         translation by Roy   47, 54
      German   1–2, 10–16, 19–20, 45, 47–64, 71, 73, 77, 85–86, 89–93, 97, 101, 104, 111–12, 116, 124, 128, 134, 176, 198, 202, 227, 235

Capital, Volume I (cont.)
    Lenin citing 1st edition in
        Development of Capitalism in
        Russia 20
    new by Kuczynski 97
    German and French 11, 28
    instructions for American 52
    Italian 85
    Polish 97
    Russian 12–13, 16, 18–21, 45, 53, 92–93, 216–17
        2nd edition 19, 53, 90–93, 97, 175
        Danielson's Preface 91–95
    Spanish 85, 91
Capital, Volume II 10–11, 23, 44, 47–48, 95–97, 103–4, 109, 111, 113–14, 117, 119, 136, 140, 144, 166–68, 173, 175, 179, 181, 187
Capital, Volume III 43, 48, 95–97, 98, 104, 116–17, 119, 134–40, 142–43, 164, 175
capitalism 1–2, 5, 15–16, 20, 29–32, 37, 87–88, 98, 105, 128–29, 170, 172, 174–75, 177–78, 184–86, 207–10
capitalist class 37, 61, 88, 107, 110–11, 165, 172, 186
capitalist mode of production 27, 31, 43, 45, 59, 63, 68–71, 88, 100–101, 117, 165
capitalist production 57, 60, 68, 70, 79–81, 110–11, 166, 171, 173, 180
capitalist relations 35, 99, 171, 176
capitalists 1–2, 33–36, 38–39, 78, 102–3, 105–6, 108–10, 112, 118–19, 164–65, 171–73, 175–76, 180–81, 186–87, 189–90, 226
capital stock 149, 152, 154, 156–59
    adjustment for quality 158–59
    gross 148–49, 153–54, 156–57, 160–61
    net 151, 160–61
capital stock measurement 153–54, 157, 159–60
Carchedi, Guglielmo 14
centralization of capital 58–59, 70–72, 76, 198, 207–9
Chinese worker 81, 130
circulating capital 77–78, 139, 142, 144–47, 149–50, 169
Civil War, U. S. 1, 130, 132, 191, 223, 227
Clark, John B. 107
classes 44, 110–11, 165, 169–71, 175, 186, 189, 205–6, 210
Class Struggles in France 228–29

Cleaver, Harry 30–31
Cogoy, Martin 139
Cologne Communist Trial 227
commodities 30–36, 39–45, 67, 70, 102, 127–30, 166, 171–72, 183, 186, 189–90
commune, Russian 17, 86–87, 175, 197, 209, 212
Communist Manifesto 19, 89, 96, 167, 202, 205, 226
composition of capital 57–59, 65, 67, 79, 111, 114, 118, 121, 133–45, 149, 152, 163–64, 173–74, 179
    estimates
        in cotton spinning by Marx and Engels 141–44
        in post-World War II, U. S. 145–51, 144–63
    materialized 3, 120–21, 135, 137, 139–40, 143, 146–57, 160–64
    recognized by Luxemburg 141
    organic 3, 40, 59, 114, 133–37, 139–40, 145, 184, 188
        alternatives to 134
        definition of 134–35
        static versus temporal 135
    technical 58, 65, 67, 69, 72, 133–34
    value 67, 72, 115, 121–22, 133–37, 140, 145–47, 149–53
        changing 67, 151, 161
concentration of capital 58, 69–71, 108, 114, 117, 206–7
corollary to accumulation 69–70
conspiracy 4, 213, 226–30, 233, 238–39
    Archduke Ferdinand, assassination 233
    Bonaparte, Marx on 227–30
    capitalist, Adam Smith on 226
    false-flag 231
    Gleiwitz incident 228, 233–36
    Golf of Tonkin resolution 236
    Kennedy
        John F., assassination 228, 231, 236–38
        Oswald 238
        Robert F., assassination 239–40
    King, assassination 4, 228, 238–39
        jury conviction 4, 236, 238–39
        Ray, James Earl 238
    Manchurian incident 228, 233
    Polk's war, Lincoln on 226–27, 231–32

INDEX

Reichstag fire 233–36
  Naujocks 235
  theories 230, 233, 236
"conspiracy theory", as weapon 236–37, 240
  September 11th 245
conspirators 227–28, 233, 239
constant and variable capital 59, 65, 67–68, 104, 111, 114, 121, 135, 138, 141–42
constant capital 67, 75, 77, 102–4, 110, 112–18, 120, 133, 135–38, 141–48, 151–52, 164, 167–69, 171
  additional 118, 120–21
  consumption of 119, 122, 136, 141–46
  estimates of 147, 149
  labor time embodied in 43
  new 120–21, 144, 164, 170
  replacement of 106, 169
  stock of 119, 136, 142–43, 145
  turnover of circulating 121, 145–46
consumption 15, 34–35, 43–44, 50, 103–5, 113, 172–73, 176, 181, 184, 186–88
  luxury 121–22, 172–73, 181, 188, 192
Contribution to the Critique of Political Economy 20, 27, 29–31, 41, 97, 99, 108, 129, 167
cooperation 68, 209
Correa y Zafrilla, Pablo 85
crises 79–80, 104–5, 116, 119, 138, 164, 166–67, 170, 176–79, 185–86, 188
  19th-century Russian agrarian 86
  manufactured by Bonaparte 230
  potential 133
  present world, Grossmann 167
  theories 164
Crisis in German Social Democracy 223–25
Cuban missile crisis 237
current cost accounting 161
Czar 204, 211–12, 214–15

Danielson, Nikolai 47, 53, 90–92, 95–96, 175
Davidsson, Elias 242, 244
Davis, Horace B. 198
De Angelis, Massimo 99–100
deHaven-Smith, Lance 236–37, 245
demand 76, 78, 80, 82, 112, 114–16, 172, 174, 187, 189–90, 213, 217
department of production 38, 121–23, 137, 141, 173–75, 180–81, 185, 189, 191

267

depreciation 142–43, 150–51, 154, 156, 158, 161–62
Desai, Meghnad J. 190
dialectical materialism 9, 20–22, 96
dialectics 10, 14, 18, 21–22, 219
Diefenbach, Hans 23
Dietzgen, Joseph 10
dispossessions/enclosures 98–99
Dobb, Maurice 32
Domela-Nieuwenhuis, Ferdinand 45
Douglass, James B. 236–38
Dreyfus affair 131
Dühring, E. E., review of Marx 10–11
Dulles, Allen 237
Dunayevskaya, Raya 10–11, 40, 89, 168, 170, 185, 188
Dussel, Enrique 41

Eckstein, Gustav 177–78, 180
Economic and Philosophical Manuscripts of 1844 27, 29, 108
economic concepts, eternalized 28, 124
economists 19, 28, 31–32, 37, 39, 77, 80, 113, 165–66
Eighteenth Brumaire of Louis Bonaparte 228–29
Emancipation of Labor, emigre group in Geneva 19, 96
employment 2, 51, 55, 58, 60, 114, 133, 135, 187, 192
Engels, Frederick 1, 3–4, 10–12, 16–17, 19, 21–22, 27, 37–41, 44, 47–65, 67–71, 73, 77–78, 81, 83–101, 114–17, 124, 130–34, 136–37, 141–43, 175, 188, 200–203, 226–27
  on Lavoisier's theoretical revolution and Marx's 1, 37–38
  on Marx's completion of theory by 1859 107–8
  on Marx's research on Russia 95–96
Engels, Frederick, *Anti-Dühring* and *Feuerbach and the End of Classical German Philosophy* 21
England 61, 66, 74, 76, 82, 88, 90–91, 96, 138, 201–2
Ettinger, Elżbieta 20
Evans, Richard 234
Evenitsky, Alfred 185

Falk, Richard 240
Favilli, Paolo 85
Fernbach, David 21, 227
fetishism, of commodities 9, 45, 55, 100, 130
First International 202
Fisher, Louis 232
fixed capital 77–78, 119–22, 139, 142, 144, 146–47, 149–50, 153
Flerovsky, Beri-Vassily V. 96, 126
Foley, Duncan K. 35
Foner, Philip 89
François, Allisson 92
Frank, Andre Gunter 88
Froelich, Paul 179–81, 183

Gaido, Daniel 176
General Law of Capitalist Accumulation 55–57, 64–86, 89–91, 98, 101, 111, 114–16, 118–19, 121, 130, 133, 171
Giussani, Paolo 191
Gleijeses, Piero 232
Göçmen, Dogan 23
Gotha Program 9
Graßmann, Timm 60, 82
Groll, Shalom 134–35, 139
Grossman, Henryk (*see also* Grossmann) 167, 184
Grossmann, Henryk (*see also* Grossman) 170, 184, 186
growth rates 123, 144, 154–56, 191–93
Gruening, Ernest 236
Grundrisse 10, 27, 29, 32–33, 109, 124, 166
Guttsman, Wilhelm L. 191

Hall, Stuart 10
Harris, Donald 139
Haupt, Georges 198
Hegel, Frederick 2, 9–23, 32, 96, 101, 170
 importance of 21, 23, 29, 188
Hegelian
 language in Marx 10–11, 13–17, 19–21, 30, 40
 Lenin on 22
 Luxemburg on 23
 Plekhanov on 20–21
 universality, particularity, individuality 10, 12, 14
Heinrich, Michael 139
Heller, Peter 117

Hilferding, Rudolf 105, 114, 120, 138–39, 141, 168, 184
Hilferding, Rudolf, *Finance Capital* 138
Holmes, Rachel 90
Hook, Sidney 10
Howard, Michael C. and J. E. King 176, 181–82, 187
Hubmann, Gerald 49
Hudis, Peter 11, 140, 170, 188

Ilyin, Vladimir (*see* Lenin, Vladimir) 105, 178
Ilyinishna, Anna 19
imperialism 173, 177, 184, 209, 223–25
Ito, Narihiko 4, 197–98, 200, 202, 204, 208–25
Itoh, Makoto 40

Jogiches, Leon "Leo" 19–20, 198, 214–15
Johnson, Chalmers 240
Jones, Richard 78, 103, 115
Jowers, Loyd 238–39

Kalecki, Michal 23, 190
Kamenev, Lev 178
Kant, Immanuel 10
Karimzadi, Shahzavar 128
Karski, S. 179
Kates, Steven 43
Katz, Arnold J. 158
Kautsky, Karl 21, 96, 103, 105, 176–77, 179–80, 184, 187, 200, 205–6, 218, 223
Kay, Jonathan 245
Keynes, John M. 42–43
Keynes, John M., *General Theory*, rejection of, related to rejection of Luxemburg 173
Keynesian economics 33, 189
Kimball, Alan 126
Kindersley, Richard 105
Kliman, Andrew 40
Kolar, Jay 242
Kovalevsky, Maksim M. 18, 95
Kowalik, Tadeusz 23, 179, 189–91
Kristjanson-Gural, David 46
Krupskaya, Nadezhda K. 19
Krzywicki, Ludwik 85
Kuczynski, Thomas 97
Kuehne, Karl 191
Kugelmann, Louis 39, 44
Kuhn, Rich 184

labor
  abstract   29–31, 45, 127, 169, 183
  abstract universal   30
  living labor   32, 40, 43–44, 117, 137–38
  productive   30, 102–3, 145, 164
  unproductive   37, 102, 145, 151–52, 163–64
labor power   1–3, 16–17, 32–39, 42–43, 58–59, 65, 67–68, 86–87, 103, 110–15, 131, 135–36, 179–80
  cost and use-value of   35–36, 127, 164
  distinguishing   37
  Marx's discovery of   37
  value of   42
labor theory of value, classical, interpretation by Hunt   37
labor time   31–35, 39, 41–42, 107, 145–46
  socially necessary   39, 42, 129
Lafargue, Paul   229
Laibman, David   102, 140
Lamarckian biology   130
Lapavitsas, Costas   40
Lapides, Kenneth   186
Laschitza, Annelies   19–20, 216
Lavrov, Pyotr   95, 116
Lawler, James   178
law of population   77
Le Blanc, Paul   170
Lefebvre, Henri   50, 54, 90, 98
Lelewel, Joachim   201
Lenin, Vladimir   4, 9, 19–22, 87, 96, 103–7, 167–68, 170, 175, 177–78, 180, 182, 184–85, 187–88, 204, 208, 216–24
  on Luxemburg's *Accumulation of Capital*   178, 217
  on Luxemburg's *National Question and Autonomy*   4, 216–25
Lenin, Vladimir, *Development of Capitalism in Russia*   20, 105, 177–78
Lenin, Vladimir, *Materialism and Empirio-Criticism*   22
Leontiev, A.   184
Lincoln, Abraham   226–27, 231–32
London bombing   2005, 228
Longman, Jere   244
Löwy, Michael   198
Lukacs, George   131
Lusitania, sinking of   227
Luxemburg, Rosa   4, 9, 19–20, 23, 43–44, 87, 100–101, 105–6, 111, 118, 120, 127–28, 132, 140–41, 165, 167–91, 197–201, 203–25

Luxemburg, Rosa, *The Accumulation of Capital*   4, 167–93
  first English edition   174, 189
Luxemburg, Rosa, *Anti-Critique*   179, 182–83, 185–87, 191
Luxemburg, Rosa, *Crisis in German Social Democracy*   223–25
Luxemburg, Rosa, *Industrial Development of Poland*   210
Luxemburg, Rosa, *Junius Pamphlet*   224
Luxemburg, Rosa, *National Question and Antonomy*   197–225
Luxemburg, Rosa, *The Russian Revolution*   223, 225

MacGregor, David   229
Machiavellianism   4, 226–45
MacQueen, Graeme   243
Mage, Shane H.   139
Malcolm X, assassination   228
Malthus, Thomas   81
Mandel, Ernest   89, 187
Manifest Destiny   232
Marchlewski, Julian   179, 198
Marx, Eleanor   48, 89–90, 93, 131
  on Jewish workers   131
Marx, Jenny   47–48
Marx, Karl   1–5, 9–23, 27–45, 47–62, 64–65, 73, 77–78, 80, 83–104, 106–21, 124–45, 151, 153, 164–76, 178, 180–81, 183–90, 192–93, 201–2, 226–30, 245
  library on Russia   97
  on Sieber   3, 13, 16–17, 128–29
  on Wagner   16, 45, 129
Marx and Engels
  "common Negro type"   130
  prejudices of   3, 130–32
Marxism   4, 9, 19, 21–23, 96, 102, 105, 115–16, 168, 177
Marxist accumulation of capital   3, 117–19, 125–26, 133, 139, 145, 164, 171
  and proletarianization   118, 126
Marxists   3–4, 19, 22–23, 106, 137–38, 164, 167–68, 189, 197–98, 217–20, 223
Mattick, Paul   170, 182, 186
Maurer, Georg   11
McCracken, Harlan L.   42–43
McDermott, Terry   242
MEGA^2 48–49, 52–54, 61–62, 64, 109, 119, 134, 137, 144

Mehring, Franz   179
method, deductive   13, 128
Mexican-American War   1, 130, 226, 231–32
Mikhaylovsky, Nikolay K.   14, 16–17
Milios, John   31, 42
Mill, James   34, 166
Mironov, Boris   87
model of capitalist accumulation, with fixed capital   119–22, 144
Mohun, Simon   148–49
money
    cattle as, Luxemburg   128
    money form   41, 129, 186
Morgan, Lewis   18
Morse, Wayne   236
Moseley, Fred   134–35, 139–40, 146–50, 168
Mukden incident (*see* conspiracy, Manchurian incident)

Nagasaki   5
Narodniks   21, 96, 106
national autonomy   4, 206, 209–14, 216–18
nationalism   4, 197–98, 218, 223, 225
    as inculcated   228
nationalists   207, 221, 225
nationalities   132, 197–98, 200, 204–7, 212, 214, 216–19, 222–23, 225
    conquered   204, 206
national movement   203, 218–19
    Polish independence, Marx and Engels on   200
national question   4, 197–99, 204–6, 212, 215–16, 219, 222–25
national question and autonomy   197–98, 203–4, 207, 214–16, 218–19, 221, 223, 225
national security state   240
national state   197, 200, 206, 218, 223, 227
    independent   218
nations   57, 198–200, 202, 204–5, 207, 212–15, 218, 220, 222–26
    oppressed   200, 221–22
nation-state   198–200, 204–7, 218, 222, 225
Nelson, Megan Kate   1
nuclear weapons   5

Oakley, Allen   33, 109
Offord, Derek   126
Oishi, Takahisa   29
Okishio, Nubuo   139

On the Jewish Question   204
Orzech, Ze'ev B.   134–35, 139
overproduction   60, 105, 166, 185

Paitaridis. Dimitris, and L. Tsoulfidis, on composition of capital   151–52, 160
Pannekoek, Anton   177–80, 184–85, 191
Patriquin, Larry   88
Paul, Diane   130–31
Pearl Harbor   227, 240
peasants   20, 61, 86–87, 96, 103, 126
Pepper, William F.   238–39
Perelman, Michael   98–99
Philippines   232
Plekhanov, Georgi   9, 16, 18–22, 96, 105
Poland   4, 20, 85, 91, 198–204, 206–7, 210–12, 214–23, 234–35
    1830 insurrection   201
    1846 Cracow uprising   201
Polish nationalism   200, 203, 206
Polish nationalists   200, 220
Polish question, Marx and Engels on the   201–3
Polish state   199–200, 204, 219
political economists, classical   27, 98, 107, 165
political economy   2–4, 9–10, 27–29, 31–34, 37, 80–81, 96–97, 106–8, 127–28, 137–39, 164–65, 167–68
    classical   2, 27–28, 31, 108, 153, 169, 173
population increase   81, 118, 125
Postone, Moishe   31
Poverty of Philosophy   27–29
Pradella, Lucia   101
primary accumulation, as *proposed* by Frank   88
primitive accumulation   2, 54, 56–57, 60–62, 85–89, 98–101, 109, 117
    expropriation   61–63, 98
    Marx's delimitation to consideration of Western Europe   12, 16, 61–62, 88, 94
productive forces   27, 104–6, 165–67
Proudhon, Pierre-Joseph   28–29

Quesnay, François   168

Ramos, M. Alejandro   41
Ranganayakamma   40

rate of profit, falling tendency of   117, 133–35, 137, 140–41, 153, 164, 186, 188
realization   117, 166, 169–70, 177–78, 181, 183, 185–87, 190–91
  problem of   180, 187
relative surplus value   33, 39, 109, 111, 118, 121, 127, 136, 140
reproduction   38, 41–42, 69–71, 78, 100, 102–3, 106, 112–14, 118–19, 166, 169, 177
  schemes of (*see* schemes of reproduction)
reserve army, industrial   58–60, 73, 77, 79–83, 118, 171
Resis, Albert   12
Reuten, Geert   30, 40
Ricardo, David   13, 16–18, 28–29, 31, 33–34, 36–39, 78, 93, 102, 104, 106–7, 113, 127–29, 165–69
  error with Adam Smith, Luxemburg on   168
  mistake, Marx on   45
  theory of accumulation, Marx on   118
right of nations to self-determination   198–200, 203–5, 207, 213, 218–20, 222–24
Rjasanoff, N.   201
Roberts, Michael   163
Robinson, Joan   174, 189–90
Robson, R.   142
Rodbertus, Johann K.   129
Rosdolsky, Roman   23, 139, 170, 174, 178–79, 181–82, 186
Roth, Regina   49, 119
Rowthorn, Bob   139
Rubin, Issak I.   22, 30, 40
Russell, Bertrand   237
Russia   1, 3, 11–14, 16–20, 61–62, 86, 88, 94–97, 125–26, 210, 219–20, 222–23
Russian   12–20, 87, 90, 92–96, 126, 129, 132, 138, 214, 219–22
Russian-occupied Poland   19, 23
Russian Social Democratic Labor Party   199, 204, 208, 220–21
Ryazanov, David   18

Saad-Filho, Alfedo   23
Say, Jean Baptiste   105
Sayer, Sean   10
Scattolini, Dario   176

schemes of reproduction   44, 103–5, 113–14, 119–21, 140–41, 144, 169, 173–74, 176–81, 184, 190–91
  expanded/extended   101, 119–20, 169–70, 173–74, 176, 181, 183
Secret of Primitive Accumulation   56, 60
sectors
  productive   118, 147–48, 151–52, 154, 160–61
  unproductive   152
Seigel, Jerrold E.   229
Sekine, Thomas T.   40
self-determination, the right of nations to   4, 198–99, 204–5, 207, 212, 218, 220–24
September 11th
  alleged Muslim hijackers   241–44
    Mari-Rae Sopper, victim   241
  Citizens Investigation Team   243
  Commission Report   241–43
    Zelikow as Executive Director   242
  insider trading   244
    Poteshman   244
  Osama bin Laden   244
  Pentagon   240
  phone calls from planes in question   243–44
    Burnett   244
  WTC falling skyscrapers   242
    Hulsey's Report   242
    statement by Franklin Square and Munson Fire District   243
Shaikh, Anwar M.   120, 137, 139, 148–49, 153–61, 163, 170, 188–89
  with E. Ahmet Tonak   120, 147–149, 151–52, 157
  on Luxemburg's Accumulation of Capital   182
  on materialized composition of capital   139
Shanin, Teodor   12, 17–18
Shirer, William   234–35
Sieber, Nikolai I.   3, 9, 13–19, 21, 39, 96, 103, 128–30
  impact   13, 15, 17, 22, 93
  on Marx's value theory   15, 128–30
Simonde, Jean Charles Leonard   103, 106, 127, 166–68, 175, 184
simple reproduction   56, 86, 108, 110, 112–13, 120, 169, 184

Sinha, Ajit   35, 38, 42
Sismondi, Jean Charles Léonard de
   106, 110
Smith, Adam   28, 30–31, 34, 38, 40, 43–44, 56,
   65, 68, 86, 88, 102–3, 106–7, 113, 127, 165,
   168–69, 178, 226
So-Called Primitive Accumulation   52, 60,
   62, 89–90, 100
social capital   59, 69–77, 79, 134, 183
social relations of production   2, 28, 37–38,
   103, 118
Social Democratic Party of Poland   198, 213
Social Democratic Party of Poland and
   Lithuania (SDKPiL, see also Social
   Democratic Party of Poland)198, 204,
   216, 218–21
Sorge, Victor   47
Soviet Marxist culture   22, 29, 179, 185
Spanish-American war, explosion of USS
   Maine   228, 232
Sraffa, Pierro   160
Steedman, Ian   38, 168
Stolypin reforms   87
Stone, Oliver   236
Struve, Peter   105
subjection/subsumption of labor   51–52, 57,
   64, 108, 126
Sukarno   238
surplus value   1, 42–43, 86–88, 103, 108–11,
   113–15, 118–19, 127, 138, 143–44, 152–53,
   163–70, 172–75, 179–81, 185–87, 192–93
   large portion not needed for
      accumulation   192–93
   rate of   114, 120–23, 136–37, 139–43, 151–53,
      173, 180, 192
Swanson, Paul A.   120
Sweezy, Paul   23, 32, 170, 179, 186, 191

Takanashi, Sumio   224
Tarpley, Webster G.   232
taxation of peasantry, Malawi   126
Theories of Surplus Value   28, 39, 43, 109, 113,
   115, 118, 136, 167
Thompson, Frank   102
Tonak, E. Ahmet (*see* Shaikh, Anwar, with)
Trotsky, Leon   23
Tsoulfidis, Lefteris   151–52, 160–61
Tugan-Baranovsky, Michael (*also* Tugan-
   Baranowsky)   103–5, 138, 141, 168, 177,
   179–80, 184

Kautsky on   105, 176, 180
Luxemburg on   105, 141, 178, 184
Turchetto, Maria   88
turnover of capital   121, 139, 142, 144–46,
   148–51
Tyler, John   231

underconsumption   127, 167, 176,
   179, 188
   as used by Kautsky and Shaikh
      179, 188
United Nations, population data   192
United States   1, 3, 5, 140, 146–48, 150–52, 157,
   191–92, 224–25, 231–32
universal stage, Marx on   12, 16, 18, 94
use value   30, 32, 35, 37, 165, 172
Utina, Natalia   33

value   3, 13–15, 27–46, 67–68, 76, 102–3, 110,
   117, 120, 124–31, 133, 138–39, 141–43,
   151–53, 162–63, 165–68
   form of   10, 12, 22–23, 39–40, 130
   issue when including non-capitalist
      relations   125
value and exchange value   15, 29, 31–34, 36,
   40–42, 45–46, 111, 127, 165
van der Linden. Marcel   49
van Onselen, Charles   126
Van Parijs, Philippe   139
variable capital   60, 67–68, 74–77, 103–7,
   110–11, 113–16, 121–22, 135–39, 141–45,
   147–48, 171, 186–87
   additional   60, 106, 116, 121, 144, 170, 175,
      186
   relative size of   59, 67–69, 72 74, 80, 111,
      115, 138
   temporal context   136
   value of   135–36, 172
Venida, Victor S.   134
Vorontsov, Vasily P.   96

Wada, Haruki   17–18
wage-labor
   productive   112, 118
   unproductive   192
Wagner, Adolph   45
Walicki, Andrzej   16
Walras, Leon   39
Warren Commission   236–37, 241–42, 244
Warski, Adolf   215

Watters, F. M.   86–87
Webber, M. J. and D. L. Rigby   145
Weeks, John, on Marx's concept of value   127
Weinberg, Meyer   191
White, James B.   9–12, 15–20, 23, 29–30, 40, 51, 87, 92, 95–96, 125–26, 129
Wolff, Edward   146
Wolfstetter, Elmar   139

Zarembka, Paul   9–10, 17, 23, 27, 40, 100, 102, 105–7, 119, 125, 127–28, 133, 146, 151–52, 154, 161, 167, 170, 178, 182, 185, 191, 229, 244
Zasulich, Vera   12, 16–19
Zhukovsky, Yuly G.   15–16
Ziber, Nikolay I. (*see* Sieber, Nikolay I.)

www.ingramcontent.com/pod-product-compliance
Lightning Source LLC
Chambersburg PA
CBHW070913030426
42336CB00014BA/2402